Ghosts of the Past in Southern Thailand

Ghosts of the Past in Southern Thailand

Ghosts of the Past in Southern Thailand

Essays on the History and Historiography of Patani

Edited by Patrick Jory

Published by:

NUS Press
National University of Singapore
AS3-01-02, 3 Arts Link
Singapore 117569

Fax: (65) 6774-0652
E-mail: nusbooks@nus.edu.sg
Website: http://nuspress.nus.edu.sg

ISBN 978-9971-69-635-1 (Paper)

First Edition 2013
Reprint 2019
Reprint 2020

National Library Board, Singapore Cataloguing-in-Publication Data

Ghosts of the past in Southern Thailand : essays on the history and historiography of Patani / edited by Patrick Jory. – Singapore : NUS Press, c2013.
 p. cm.
 Includes bibliographical references and index.
 ISBN : 978-9971-69-635-1 (pbk.)

 1. Pattani (Thailand : Province) – History. 2. Malays (Asian people) – Thailand – Pattani (Province) – History. 3. Muslims – Thailand – Pattani (Province) – History. I. Jory, Patrick

DS588.P29
959.3 -- dc23   OCN794702009

The cover shows a representation of the new "monthon" (administrative division) of Patani, including one of the iconic Patani cannons, at a Thai government exhibition from the early 20th century (Photo courtesy of the National Archives of Thailand).

Typeset by: Forum, Kuala Lumpur, Malaysia
Printed by: Markono Print Media Pte Ltd

CONTENTS

List of Illustrations — vii

Acknowledgements — x

Introduction   Ghosts of the Past in Southern Thailand — xiv
Patrick Jory

Part One: **Pluralism and Identity in Patani's History**

Chapter 1   Patani as a Paradigm of Pluralism — 3
Anthony Reid

Chapter 2   Gates, Elephants, Cannon and Drums: Symbols and — 31
Sounds in the Creation of a Patani Identity
Barbara Watson Andaya

Chapter 3   The Patani Region in Chinese Texts of the 6th to the — 53
19th Centuries
Geoff Wade

Part Two: **Patani's Place in Southeast Asian and Middle
Eastern Islamic Networks**

Chapter 4   The Patani 'Ulamâ': Global and Regional Networks — 87
Azyumardi Azra

Chapter 5   The Intellectual Network of Patani and the Haramayn — 110
Numan Hayimasae

Chapter 6   Patani's Creole Ambassadors — 129
Christopher M. Joll

Part Three: **Alternative Histories of Patani's Decline and Fall**

Chapter 7   Siam's Conquest of Patani and the End of *Mandala* — 149
Relations, 1786–1838
Francis R. Bradley

Chapter 8   A Tin Mine in Need of a History: 161
                 19th-Century British Views of the Patani Interior
                 Philip King

Part Four: The Struggle for Control of Patani and Its History

Chapter 9   The Formation of the Islamo-Malay Patanian Nation: 185
                 Ideological Structuring by Nationalist Historians
                 Dennis Walker

Chapter 10   Historical Identity, Nation, and History-Writing: 228
                 The Malay Muslims of Southern Thailand,
                 1940s–1980s
                 Kobkua Suwannathat-Pian

Chapter 11   Locating Traditional, Islamic, and Modern   255
                 Historiography in Patani-*Jawi* Identity
                 Iik Arifin Mansurnoor

Chapter 12   Patani Militant Leaflets and the Uses of History   277
                 Duncan McCargo

Bibliography   298

Contributors   322

Index   326

LIST OF ILLUSTRATIONS

Maps

Map 0.1   Simone de la Loubere's 1691 map of Siam, showing Patani ("Patane") in the south (Source: Simon de la Loubere, *The Kingdom of Siam*, with an introduction by David K. Wyatt [Singapore: Oxford University Press, 1986]).   xii

Map 0.2   Southern Thailand and neighboring countries today (Adapted from *Thai South and Malay North*, edited by Michael J. Montesano and Patrick Jory, 2009).   xiii

Map 8.1   Excerpt from Crawfurd's 1828 "Map of the Kingdoms of Siam and Cochin China," showing the middle part of the Malay peninsula (Source: John Crawfurd, *Journal of an Embassy from the Governor-General of India to the Courts of Siam and Cochin China: Exhibiting a View of the Actual State of those Kingdoms* [London: Colburn, 1828]).   163

Map 8.2   1862 British map of the Malay peninsula showing approximate boundaries and political status of the various peninsular states, including Patani (Source: A.M. Skinner, "Geography of the Malay Peninsula," *Journal of the Straits Branch of the Royal Asiatic Society* [July 1878]: 52–62).   170

Map 8.3   1878 British map of the Malay peninsula following the establishment of the British protectorate over Perak in 1974, showing the region of Raman and the various mountain chains and river systems (Source: A.M. Skinner, "Geography of the Malay Peninsula," *Journal of the Straits Branch of the Royal Asiatic Society* [July 1878]: 52–62).   171

Map 10.1 Map showing the division of the former Sultanate of Patani into seven principalities (*hua muang*) in the early 19th century. — 229

Map 10.2 1915 map showing the new *monthon* (administrative divisions) of southern Siam, including the *monthon* of Pattani (Adapted from Tej 1977). — 230

Figures

Chapter 1

Figure 1.1 The image of Lin Guniang ("Lim Kor Niaw"), sister of the legendary Chinese cannon-builder of Patani, Lin Daoqian ("Lim Toh Khiam"), from the shrine in her honor in Pattani town (also known as the Leng Ju Kiang shrine) (Photo courtesy of Parati Benreem). — 8

Figure 1.2 The remains of the Krue Se mosque, Pattani province, flanked by flags of the King and Queen and the Thai national flag (Photo courtesy of Parati Benreem). — 12

Chapter 2

Figure 2.1 The captured "Phaya Tani" cannon, known among Patani Malays as "Seri Patani," now situated outside the Ministry of Defence building, Bangkok (Photo courtesy of Vachira Saijampa). — 44

Figure 2.2 The Thai government's official seal of Pattani province since 1939 (Source: Wikimedia Commons). — 45

Chapter 3

Figure 3.1 Envoy to Liang China from the country of Lang-ya-xiu in the sixth century CE (Source: *Liang zhi-gong tu* 梁職工圖, as illustrated in Enoki Kazuo, "The Liang chih-kung-t'u," *Memoirs of the Research Department of the Toyo Bunko* 42 [1984]: 75–138). — 59

Figure 3.2 One of the maps from the *Wu-bei-zhi* 武备志 dating probably to the early 15th century (Roman script identifications added by author). — 62

Figure 3.3   Tombstone of a Chinese woman named Chen Shu-qin   77
(Tan Siok-kin in Hokkien), dating to the *ren-zhen* year
of the Wan-li reign (1592), found in Patani (Source:
Wolfgang Franke *et al.*, *Chinese Epigraphic Materials in
Thailand* [Taipei: Shin Wen Fung, 1988]).

Chapter 6

Figure 6.1   Historical location of trans-peninsula trade routes   130
in the Langkasuka/Patani region (Source: Jacq-
Hergoualc'h, 2002, Document 17).

Figure 6.2   Genealogies of Patani's creole ambassadors.   138

Figure 6.3   Site of the former location of the palace in Krue Se in   139
relation to modern-day Pattani and Cabetigo (Source:
Bougas, 1994, p. 116).

Chapter 9

Figure 9.1   From the 1958 edition of Ibrahim Syukri's *Sejarah*   193
Kerajaan Melayu Patani: the Siam-Thai raja, angered by
the Sultan of Patani's refusal of a request to help him
resist a Burmese attack in 1776, begins to plan Patani's
subjugation.

Figure 9.2   Cover of the 1958 *Jawi* edition of Ibrahim Syukri's   194
Sejarah Kerajaan Melayu Patani, published by the
Majlis Ugama Islam Kelantan in Pasir Puteh,
Kelantan.

Chapter 12

Figure 12.1   Militant leaflet in *Jawi* script found in Jo Airong   281
district, Narathiwat province, 2005 (Courtesy of
Duncan McCargo).

ACKNOWLEDGEMENTS

When the Regional Studies Program at Walailak University in Nakhon Si Thammarat, southern Thailand, was established in the early 2000s, it soon began to contribute to efforts to understand the long-running conflict in Thailand's southern border provinces, which erupted into violence again in early 2004. Not only were we located near to where the conflict was occurring, but many of our students were from the region and were directly affected by the violence. Our efforts involved establishing a program of research, producing teaching curricula, networking with local scholars in the south and academics from Malaysia and other countries in Southeast Asia, as well as in Western academia, and organizing a series of conferences on such themes as political change in the region, pluralism on the Malay Peninsula, and Islam and Muslim societies in Southeast Asia. It became clear to us that much of the burgeoning scholarship on the south had largely overlooked the importance of the historical dimension of the conflict, in particular, how different interpretations of Patani's history continue to inform the political stances of the different parties involved.

This book grew out of a conference jointly organized by the Regional Studies Program, Walailak University, the Department of History, Chulalongkorn University, the National Discovery Museum Institute and the Thailand Research Fund (TRF) on the theme of the continuing influence of nationalist histories of Patani. The aim was to create a dialogue between scholars in Thailand — both mainstream Thai academics and local scholars from the southern border provinces — as well as scholars from Malaysia, Indonesia and from further afield in the world of international academia, in order to examine more closely the history and historiography of Patani. The conference was held at Chulalongkorn University, Bangkok, on December 11–12, 2009. Unfortunately, only a small selection of the total number of papers presented at the conference has been able to be included in this volume, but the work of those scholars not included has nevertheless been influential in shaping the major themes of the book.

The conference could not have been possible without the leadership of Chalong Soontravanich, then head of the History Department at Chulalongkorn University. We are also grateful to Cholthira Satyawadhna, Dean of the School of Liberal Arts, Walailak University. My former colleagues at Regional Studies Program worked very hard to make the conference a success, in particular the project leader Davisakd Puaksom, Jirawat Saengthong, Phailada Chaisorn, Abdulrazak Panaemalae, Rheinhard Sirait, Amnuayvit Thitibodin, Thanaphat Detphawuttikun, Atcharawan Buriphakdi and Thaweelak Phonrachom. It was a great pleasure to work with colleagues in history at Chulalongkorn, including Suwimon Rungjaroen, Suthachai Yimprasert, Thanaphon Limaphichat, Phawan Rueangsin and Villa Vilaithong. We received enthusiastic and generous support from the staff at the Siam Discovery Museum, especially Junlada Mijun, Badhama Taganananda, Davisakd Woraritrueangurai, Siriphorn Fueangfuloi, Worakan Wongsuwan and Phatcharalada Junphet. As usual, we had expert administrative assistance from Thasanee Kanwinphruet and Waraphorn Nimnuan.

The conference was generously sponsored by the National Siam Discovery Museum and the Thailand Research Fund. We are particularly grateful for the support given to the project by the then Director of the Thailand Research Fund, Piyawat Bunlong.

My thanks also go to two anonymous readers for their close reading of the manuscript and useful suggestions for improvement. I thank my former colleague, Jirawat Saengthong, for sourcing the cover photograph. Publishing Director of NUS Press Paul Kratoska gave his encouragement to this project at an early stage and has generously guided it to its conclusion. Production Editor Eunice Low rendered invaluable assistance in preparing the manuscript.

Patrick Jory
Brisbane, November 2012

Map 0.1 Simone de la Loubere's 1691 map of Siam, showing Patani ("Patane") in the south.

Map 0.2 Southern Thailand and neighboring countries today.

Ghosts of the Past in Southern Thailand

Patrick Jory

An 18-year-old girl takes a history course at a state university in southern Thailand. Her group assignment is to study a topic of debate in Thai history. As the representative of the group, she takes the stage to give her oral presentation. Speaking Thai in a thick Malay accent, she gives an impassioned address to her class about the tragedy of Patani history and the persecution of the Patani Malays over centuries at the hands of the Thai state. Some of her Thai classmates are embarrassed at the display of emotion, others are offended but feign indifference, many have no idea what she is talking about, the remainder is not listening. The girl is from Narathiwat province, in the heart of the southern border region where, according to official figures, over 5,000 people have been killed since 2004 in what is today Southeast Asian's most violent conflict. Her narrative differs fundamentally from the one which most Thais have been taught, a comforting story of Thai sovereignty over a rebellious and ungrateful Patani "since time immemorial."[1] But for her compatriots her story is familiar: it is the classic Patani nationalist history of the suffering her people have endured over centuries, and of their ongoing resistance and struggle for independence.

That Patani nationalist history can be publically expressed in so open a fashion in the Thai domain says something not only about the reproduction

---

[1] As declared by the "Father of Thai History," Prince Damrong Rachanuphap in the early 20th century; see Davisakd Puaksom, "Of a Lesser Brilliance: Patani Historiography in Contention," in *Thai South and Malay North: Ethnic Interaction on a Plural Peninsula*, ed. Michael J. Montesano and Patrick Jory (Singapore: NUS Press, 2008), pp. 71–90.

of Patani nationalism among the youth of the region today, but also about the nature of the Thai state today. Half a century earlier saw the publication in Kelantan of the classic *Sejarah Kerajaan Melayu Patani*, by Ibrahim Syukri — believed to be the pen-name used by a number of writers associated with Patani separatist circles in Malaya in the 1950s — on which the student's classroom presentation was based. Walker in this volume characterizes the book as a "fast-moving, stripped-down nationalist mathematics, its clarity and muscular speed fuelled by a hatred of Thailand, whose Buddhists it depicted as the age-old "enemy" (*musuh*) of the "Patanian Malay nation." The book, written in Malay in the *Jawi* script, was banned both in Thailand and Malaysia soon after its publication. Yet today the work is freely available in Thailand, in English *and* Thai translation,[2] courtesy of a Thai publisher.[3] Since the outbreak of the violence in southern Thailand in early 2004, Thai-language scholarship on the history of Patani has experienced a boom, much of it portraying the plight of the Muslims of the region in a sympathetic light.[4] Most of these publications were produced by Thai academics within universities, often with government grants. Patani scholars in Thailand,[5]

---

[2] In general, Thai-language publications are subject to much greater censorship than those in English, since the influence of the latter is restricted to a very small readership.

[3] Ibrahim Syukri, *Sejarah Kerajaan Melayu Patani* [*History of the Malay Kingdom of Patani*], trans. Connor Bailey and John N. Miksic (Chiang Mai: Silkworm Books, 2005); Ibrohim Chukri, *Prawatisat anajak melayu patani* [*History of the Malay Kingdom of Patani*] (Chiang Mai: Silkworm, 2006).

[4] Some of the more prominent works include: Chaloemkiat Khunthongphet, *Hayi Sulong Abdunkade: kabot … rue wiraburut haeng si jangwat phak tai* [*Haji Sulong Abdulkadir: Rebel … or Hero of the Four Southern Provinces?*] (Bangkok: Sinlapawathanatham, 2004); Arifin bin Chik, 'Abdullah La'umen and Suhaymi Isma'il, *Patani: prawattisat lae kan mueang nai lok melayu* [*Patani: History and Politics in the Malay World*], 2nd ed. (Hat Yai, Songkhla: The Foundation for the Presentation of Islamic Culture in Southern Thailand, 2009); Chaiwat Satha-Anand, ed., *Phaendin jintanakan* [*Imagined Land*] (Bangkok: Thailand Research Fund, 2008); Prinya Nuanpian, ed., *Nok niyam khwan pen thai. Thai-Patani: muea rao mai at yu ruam lae baeng yaek jak kan dai* [*Outside the Definition of Thainess. Thailand — Patani: When We Can Neither Live Together Nor Separate*] (Songkhla: Sun thale sap sueksa, 2008).

[5] The term "Patani scholars" used here refers to Muslim scholars from the region of the former sultanate who speak the local Patani Malay dialect. Of course, they are also Thai citizens and therefore by definition "Thai scholars" too. Some prominent recent works produced by local scholars in Thai include Arifin bin Chik, Abdullah La'umen and Suhaymi Isma'il, *Patani: prawattisat lae kan mueang* referred to above;

some of whom are now writing in Thai, are producing an increasing number of academic theses and publications. The Thai reading public is thus being increasingly exposed to a historiography sympathetic to Patani, at a time when criticism of Thai nationalist historiography is *de rigueur* in Thai academic discourse.[6]

Despite 50 years of effort by the Thai government to erase their history and assimilate the majority inhabitants of the region as "Thai Muslims,"[7] the memory of the Malay Sultanate of Patani refuses to die. Indeed, in the new multiculturalism that has influenced the Thai state and academia since the 1990s,[8] increasing reference is made even by state organs to the Malay heritage of the Muslims of the southern border provinces. The government-appointed National Reconciliation Council's somewhat paternalistic report into the violence in the south in 2006 even recommended that the Patani Malay dialect be made a "working language."[9] The report also touched on the importance of understanding the region's history:

> … the violence in the three border provinces of the south may be considered an historical problem. People in this region have their own history in relation to Ayutthaya-Bangkok. Since memory and historical

---

Isma'il Benjasmith, "Botbat tan kan sueksa lae kan muang khong chaik wan ahmad al-fatani (2399–2451)" [The Roles of Shaykh Ahmad al-Fatani (1865–1908 AD) in Education and Politics], MA thesis submitted to the Faculty of Islamic Studies, Prince of Songkhla University (P), 2008; and Numan Hayimasae has written an influential thesis in Malay on the religious leader Haji Sulong: *Numan Hayimasae*, "Hj Sulong Abdul Kadir (1895–1954): Perjuangan dan Sumbangan. Beliau Kepada Masyarakat Melayu Patani" [Hj Sulong Abdul Kadir (1895–1954): Struggle and Contribution to the Patani Malays], MSc. diss., Universiti Sains Malaysia, 2002.

[6] See Patrick Jory, "Historiography in Thailand since 1945," in *The Oxford History of Historical Writing*, Vol. 5, ed. Daniel Woolf and Axel Schneider (Oxford: Oxford University Press, 2011), pp. 551–3.

[7] Patrick Jory, "From 'Melayu Patani' to 'Thai Muslim': The Spectre of Ethnic Identity in Southern Thailand," *Southeast Asia Research* 15, 2 (July 2007): 255–79.

[8] On this multiculturalist trend, see Patrick Jory, "Political Decentralisation and the Resurgence of Regional Identities in Thailand," *Australian Journal of Social Issues*, Special Issue: National and Cultural Identities, 34, 4 (November 1999): 337–52; Charles F. Keyes, "Cultural Diversity and National Identity in Thailand," in *Government Policies and Ethnic Relations in Asia and the Pacific*, ed. Michael Brown and Sumit Ganguly (Cambridge, MA: MIT Press, 1997), pp. 197–231.

[9] National Reconciliation Commission, *Raingan khanakammakan itsara phuea khwamsamanachan haengchat ao chana khwamrunraeng duai phalang samanachan* [*Report of the National Reconciliation Commission: Besting Violence Through the Power*

consciousness about 'homeland' of the people in Pattani [*sic*] remains powerful in the present, their history 'is resistant to' and cannot be incorporated into the standard history which is controlled by state power.[10]

Similar sentiments can be heard at the frequent seminars and workshops held in Thailand, supported by government funding, ostensibly aiming at solving the violence.[11] The challenge to Thai political authority over the southern border provinces of the former Patani sultanate is paralleled by a weakening of official Thai control over the region's historiography and the burgeoning of alternative and empowering historical narratives, produced both from within and outside the country.

In Malaysia, a number of scholars with Patani roots, foremost among whom are Mohammad Zamberi 'Abdul Malek, Ahmad Fathi al Fatani, Nik Mahmud Nik Anuar, and Wan Kadir Che Man,[12] have over the last two decades produced notable works, mostly written in Malay, on Patani's history that conform to the conventions of modern academic scholarship, and which make use of sources in a variety of languages. The works are read not only by Malaysians but also among the educated Malay-literate Muslims in Thailand's border provinces, many of whom have studied in Malaysian

---

of Reconciliation] (Bangkok: National Reconciliation Commission, Office of the Cabinet Secretary, 2006), p. 91. English, Patani Malay, and Arabic versions of the report were also published.

[10] Ibid., p. 33; original speech marks.

[11] This should not be viewed as a softening of the Thai state's approach to the problem. Financial support from the government for "peace-building" seminars and the like is dwarfed by the budget for counter-insurgency operations by the Thai security forces in the region. Since the coup of 2006, Thailand's defense expenditure has risen well over 50% as a proportion of the country's GDP; see "Thailand's Hungry Military — An Update," *New Mandala*, at http://asiapacific.anu.edu.au/newmandala/2010/09/30/thailands-hungry-military-an-update/ [accessed January 12, 2011].

[12] For example, Nik Anuar Nik Mahmud, *Sejarah Perjuangan Melayu Patani, 1785–1954* [*History of the Struggle of the Patani Malays 1785–1954*] (Bangi: Penerbit University Kebangsaan Malaysia, 1999); Mohammad Zamberi 'Abdul Malek, *Patani Dalam Tamadun Melayu* (Selangor: Dewan Bahasa dan Pustaka, 1994); Mohammad Zamberi 'Abdul Malek, *Ummat Islam Patani: Sejarah dan Politik* (Selangor: Hizbi, 1993); and Ahmed Fathi al-Fatani, *Pengantar Sejarah Patani* (Kota Bharu: Pustaka Aman Press, 2001). The major English-language work is Wan Kadir Che Man's *Muslim Separatism: The Moros of Southern Philippines and the Malays of Southern Thailand* (Oxford, Singapore and Manila: Oxford University Press and Ateneo de Manila University Press, 1990).

universities. Since they are written in Malay, these works are largely unread by Thai scholars, yet because they do appear in the footnotes of some local Patani scholars writing in Thai, their arguments are now exposed to a Thai readership.

While there has been an outpouring of Western scholarship on "Patani," much of it is in the field of security studies and politics, and is primarily focused on explaining the current insurgency in southern Thailand. Perret *et al.*'s edited volume of 2004, however, has done much to clarify Patani's early history;[13] a collection of essays edited by Montesano and Jory in 2008 on the history of the middle part of the "Malay" peninsula, examines the role of ethnic interaction between Thais, Malays and Chinese in shaping the politics and economy of that region — including Patani;[14] and Tamara Loos's *Subject Siam* (2006) is one of the first Western works to study Siamese-Patani relations within a postcolonial framework.[15]

Heightened interest in the history of Southeast Asian Islam, partly as a result of the Islamic revival of the last three decades, has also brought a greater appreciation of Patani's prominent place in Southeast Asian Islam. The Indonesian scholar of Southeast Asian Islam, Azyumardi Azra, has shown that Patani played a prominent role in the networks of Southeast Asian Muslim scholars during the 17th and 18th centuries, particularly in transmitting the reformist Islam in the Middle East to Southeast Asia.[16] More recently, Francis Bradley's path-breaking doctoral thesis has highlighted the large corpus of works on Islam penned by Patani's greatest scholar, Shaykh Dawud al Fatani, who is, according to Bradley, "arguably the most influential figure in nineteenth-century Southeast Asian Islam." The

---

[13] Daniel Perret, Amara Srisuchat and Sombun Thanasuk, eds., *Études sur l'histoire du sultanat de Patani* (Paris: École Francaise d'Extreme-Orient, 2004). In fact, this and the next cited work contain numerous contributions from Southeast Asian scholars writing in English.

[14] Montesano and Jory, *Thai South and Malay North*.

[15] Tamara Loos, *Subject Siam: Family, Law, and Colonial Modernity in Thailand* (Ithaca, NY: Cornell University Press, 2006).

[16] Azyumardi Azra, *The Origins of Islamic Reformism in Southeast Asia: Networks of Middle Eastern 'Ulama' in the Seventeenth and Eighteenth Centuries* (Honolulu: University of Hawai'i Press, 2004), pp. 122–6. Earlier, Matheson and Hooker highlighted the work of these Patani religious scholars in an important article, Virginia Matheson and H.B. Hooker, "Jawi Literature in Patani: The Maintenance of an Islamic Tradition," *Journal of the Malaysian Branch of the Royal Asiatic Society* 61, 1 (1988): 1–86.

"Patani School" that his work inspired has had a significant influence in the world of Southeast Asian Islam.[17] It helped transform Patani in the second half of the 19th and the early 20th century into "the unparalleled center for Islamic learning on the peninsula," drawing students and scholars from all over Southeast Asia to its famous religious schools.[18] Patani's illustrious history as a source of Islamic scholarship in Malay and a major educational centre for Islam in the Southeast Asian region is a source of local pride and has attracted the interest of contemporary historians.[19]

Patani's historiography has thus entered a very productive phase. Patani scholars, intellectuals and students in Thailand are expressing their history more openly and confidently. There is increasing interaction between historians writing in Thai, Malay and English, who are engaging with sources and scholarship in other languages, including English, Chinese and Arabic. The professionalization of scholarship and increased resourcing of academic institutions in the Southeast Asian region have resulted in the production of works by local scholars of high quality. There is a market for academic works that purport to explain the reasons for the violence of Southeast Asia's most bloody conflict. Yet the production of works about Patani's history is no mere academic enterprise. Duncan McCargo, author of a recent study of the insurgency based on detailed fieldwork in the conflict zone, concludes in his book that "the main device for recruitment [of militants] is the invocation of political myths concerning Patani history and the oppression of Malay identity by the Thai state."[20] While the southern insurgency continues, the history of Patani will continue to be a battleground. The aim of this volume of essays is to draw attention to this burgeoning historical scholarship on Patani and the spirit that animates it. The concern that much of this scholarship has with the question of the region's past relationship to the Thai state is not something of disinterested historical curiosity but is directly related to the present conflict.

---

[17] Francis R. Bradley, "The Social Dynamics of Islamic Revivalism in Southeast Asia: The Rise of the Patani School," PhD diss., University of Wisconsin-Madison, 2010, p. 263.

[18] Ibid., p. 415.

[19] See, for example, Isma'il Benjasmith, *Botbat tan kan sueksa*, and Hasan Madmarn's *The Pondok and Madrasah in Patani* (Bangi: Penerbit Universiti Kebangsaan Malaysia, 1999).

[20] Duncan McCargo, *Tearing Apart the Land: Islam and Legitimacy in Southern Thailand* (Singapore: NUS Press, 2009), p. 180.

The opening chapter by Anthony Reid highlights Patani's history as a pluralistic polity. Reid argues that Patani was a casualty of the imposition of borders drawn up by European colonial powers in Southeast Asia between the 17th and 20th centuries. Its fate was shared by regions in other peripheral parts of Southeast Asia, including the borderlands between northern mainland Southeast Asia, northeastern India and southern China, as well as Aceh and Sulu. Although the conflicts in the latter two regions are often discussed in terms of religion, as Reid points out, Islam was once an expression of their cosmopolitan nature as centers of trade, frequented by people of diverse ethnicities. While Patani nationalism tends to emphasize the "Malayness" of Patani's Muslims, Reid stresses the fact of Patani's pluralism from the earliest times. Apart from the Malays, Patani's population in the 16th and 17th centuries included Chinese, a smaller group of Thais, as well as Javanese, Japanese, Portuguese and Indian Muslims. Patani was a paradigm of this pluralistic cosmopolitanism in the era prior to the rise of nationalism and nation-states. Reid's chapter also includes a contemporary portrait of Patani's pluralism by the Dutch trader Jacob van Neck in 1602, presented here for the first time in English translation.

Despite this history of pluralism as argued by Reid, Andaya shows in her chapter that there are indeed certain core aspects of Patani identity which were visible even before the era of nationalism and the construction of ethnic and national identity. A number of these elements are described in the *Hikayat Patani*, a key source for pre-19th-century Patani history, and a text which until recently was still recited in households in the Patani region. Andaya highlights some of the most potent symbols of Patani identity referred to in the *Hikayat Patani*, including the Pintu Gajah (elephant gate), elephants, the great Patani cannons cast in the 16th and 17th centuries (the most famous of which, the "Phaya Tani," now stands outside the Ministry of Defence in Bangkok — a bitter symbol of Patani's subjugation by the Thai state); drums, and the *nobat* orchestra. Andaya argues that these are not mere symbols but "'sites of memory' in the Patani consciousness."

The Malay-, Thai- and European-language sources loom large in Patani historiography, but comparatively little attention has been given to the Chinese accounts. Geoff Wade's chapter presents a summary of various Chinese source materials referring to Patani, dating from the sixth to the 19th century. The Chinese evidence is particularly important for giving the earliest known reference to a polity in the Patani area in an account dating from the seventh century but referring to the sixth century. The text refers to a "country" (*guo*) it calls "Lang-ya-xiu," which is presumably the "Langkasuka" mentioned in Arabic, Cola, Javanese and Malay sources. The Chinese sources suggest that Langkasuka was a trading state of considerable size, that it was Indianized, a center of Buddhism, and was subject to Sri Vijaya. These sources still refer to "Langkasuka" as late as the 15th century. The name "Da-ni" — presumably the Chinese pronunciation of "Patani" — appears in Chinese records relatively late — at the end of the 16th century. Wade's examination of the Chinese sources also offers tantalizing evidence about one the most vexed questions in the historiography of Patani: the question of Patani's political relationship with Siam.[21] One late 16th-century reference suggests that Patani was "beyond the borders of Siam," while another account dating from 1617 states, "Originally it was subject to Java but now it is under Siam." Thus, the Chinese evidence suggesting both Patani's long prehistory as a Buddhist trading state, as well as Patani's status as subject to Siam, presents problems for the nationalist narrative of Patani's history.

While Wade's chapter explores the Chinese connection with Patani, Azyumardi Azra's chapter shows how Patani, despite its position at the periphery of the "Islamic World" was closely connected to developments in Islam in the Middle East. Relatively little attention has hitherto been given to this golden age of Islamic scholarship produced by Patani scholars based in the Middle East. Azra highlights the importance of the Patani scholars to the reformist "impulse" in Southeast Asian Islam. The Patani *ulama* played a major role in the Islamic scholarly networks of the 18th and 19th centuries, and "proved to be the most important vehicle for the transmission of the renewal spirit of Islam from the Haramayn (Mecca and Medina) to the Malay-Indonesian world." Foremost among these scholars was Shaykh Dâwûd b. `Abd Allâh al-Fatânî, who, having studied in his native Patani and then Aceh, spent the rest of his scholarly life in the Haramayn. Based in Arabia, Shaykh Dawud was the author of a huge corpus of Islamic scholarly works written in Malay, and thus contributed to making Malay the major language of Islamic scholarship in Southeast Asia. He was a key figure in reconciling the tensions between the mystical and legalistic dimensions of Southeast Asian Islam. Besides composing, publishing and distributing scholarly works, this network of Patani *ulama* was also responsible for training large numbers of scholars who went on to found *pondok* (traditional Islamic schools) and become Muftis throughout the Malay peninsula and even as far as Kalimantan and Cambodia. Patani's importance to the development of Southeast Asian Islam partly accounts for the considerable sympathy that exists for Patani among Southeast Asian Muslims today.

---

[21] On the historiographical dispute over Patani's political relationship to Siam, see Davisakd, "Of a Lesser Brilliance: Patani Historiography in Contention."

Patani's relations with the Middle East are also the subject of Numan Hayimasae's chapter. Numan describes the role of the Haramayn (the holy cities of Mecca and Medina) as the prime destination for Islamic education for Patani Malays at least from the 18th century (and probably earlier) up until the middle of the 20th century. Numan argues that the Haramayn experience played a crucial role in the development of Patani's Islamic education system, once one of the most famous in Southeast Asia, and which still draws Muslims from various parts of Southeast Asia to study today. The *pondok* have recently been the subject of controversy, accused of promoting jihadist teachings among their students. For the Patani Malays, attempts by the Thai government to reform Islamic education in the south are seen as a direct attack on Patani's Malay Muslim heritage and identity.[22] Numan describes the extensive network of Patani scholars in the Haramayn, the subjects they studied, the mode of learning (in particular the traditional *halaqah* and the more modern *madrasah* system that gained popularity from the end of the 19th century), their publication activities, and the roles they played in founding Islamic schools in Patani and the northern states on the Malay peninsula.

While the early Patani scholars have often been appropriated by Patani nationalists and acclaimed as "Malays," Chris Joll's chapter argues that such modern ethnic categories should be used only very carefully to describe these scholars. Using terminology drawn from the work of Michael Laffan,[23] Joll terms these scholars "creole ambassadors" for Islam. That is, they were "mobile, multi-lingual members of cosmopolitan coastal trading communities." The narrowly ethnic connotations that the labels "Malay," "Arabic" or "Indian" convey today inadequately describe the diverse backgrounds and outlooks of these scholars. It was precisely their pluralistic backgrounds that enabled them to play a role in helping the expansion of Islam in Southeast Asia, and in mediating the Islam of the Middle East and that of Southeast Asia, in an environment in which Islam "circulated" in different directions around the Indian Ocean.

One of the anomalies in Patani's history is that the flourishing of Islamic scholarship postdates Patani's zenith as a powerful and prosperous trading state by two centuries. Part of the reason for this lag was due to

---

[22] See Joseph Chinyong Liow, *Islam, Education and Reform in Southern Thailand: Tradition and Transformation* (Singapore: Institute of Southeast Asian Studies, 2009).

[23] Michael F. Laffan, *Islamic Nationhood and Colonial Indonesia: The Umma below the Winds* (London: Routledge, 2003).

technological improvements in transportation and communications in the 18th and 19th centuries, which enabled more Patani Muslims to travel to the Middle East where some of them established themselves as accomplished and influential scholars. But Bradley has argued elsewhere that it was also due to the conquest of the Patani sultanate by the Siamese at the end of the 18th century, and the subsequent need to re-establish a "moral order" in the wake of this catastrophe.[24] Bradley's chapter in this volume recounts the Siamese siege and destruction of Patani in 1786, and the massacres and deportations of its inhabitants which followed. He regards this as a cataclysmic event in Patani's history. It occupies a special place in the nationalist historiography of Patani. Indeed, the legacy of this great defeat and the subsequent sufferings and indignities of the Patani people preserved in this historiography may explain the resentment felt toward the Thai state today. Subsequent wars in 1789–1791, 1808, 1831–1832, and 1838, destroyed any notion of Patani's status as an independent state, effectively ending the centuries-old system of *mandala* relations whereby Patani had enjoyed a measure of autonomy from its more powerful Thai overlord. Bradley also highlights the brutality of the Siamese conquest of Patani, and challenges the view of premodern Southeast Asian warfare as being characterized by low casualties due to the need to preserve valuable manpower. He argues that the Siamese wars against Patani in the late 18th and early 19th century should be viewed rather as a deliberate and systematic attempt to destroy a recalcitrant territory by means of depopulation.

The events of 1785–1786 stand out in Patani nationalist historiography as the sultanate's great defeat at the hands of the Thai state. According to King, however, "the image of Siam as a colonial aggressor that broke-up the once great sultanate of Patani is simplistic at best." The sultanate had been in a long period of economic decline since its heyday of the 16th and 17th centuries. The history of Patani's economy is dominated by the role of the port polity, but as King points out, the growth of Raman as a result of the Chinese demand for tin and gold in the 18th century, highlights the economic importance of Patani's interior. By the late 18th century, Raman was attracting settlers from Patani, and its ruler had already developed a considerable degree of independence from the sultanate — well before the Siamese broke up the sultanate into seven "principalities" (*hua muang*) — another key event in Patani nationalist historiography. King describes the British struggle with the Siamese in the 19th century to claim the tin

---

[24] Bradley, "The Social Dynamics of Islamic Revivalism in Southeast Asia," p. 190.

rich region. As part of this struggle, both the British and the Siamese went about manufacturing new histories of the region using arguments based on assumptions about ethnic identity to back their territorial claims.

Competing historical claims over Patani would become more intense with the rise of nationalist historiography in the middle of the 20th century. Dennis Walker's chapter examines the historiography of Patani produced by "Patanians," writing in both Malay and in Thai, in Malaysia and in Thailand, and increasingly via the freer medium of the internet. Walker describes the formation of a "rock hard Islamo-Patanian national identity" that is the product of centuries of conflict with Siam-Thailand to the north, and which has defied attempts by the Thais to assimilate or crush it. Walker argues that history has instilled in considerable numbers of Patanians a belief that the "Buddhist Siamese" to their north are their "traditional enemy." The Middle East has acted as a sanctuary to which Patani Malays have been able to escape the harassment of the Thai state. Intellectual networks that have for centuries bound Patani intellectually to the Middle East have fostered the role of Sunni Islam in sharply distinguishing the Patani Muslims from the Thais. Indeed, the strength of Islam in Patani is directly related to the need for an ideology that would enable Patanians to stand up to the ever-constant threat from the giant to the north. The radical version of Patani's brand of Islamism can and does spin out into *jihad*. Indeed, the illustrious Patani-born scholar of Southeast Asian Islam, Shaykh Dawud al Fatani, in his *fiqh* works of the 19th century, wrote that Muslims had an obligation to resist "idol-worshipping infidels" with *jihad* if they found themselves under attack. This *fatwa* was taught in Patani's *pondok* schools at least up until the 1980s and has not been formally annulled.[25] The secular nationalism of Ibrahim Syukri in the 1950s has been transformed today into one much more oriented to the Middle East and Islam. Walker does note, however, the pluralistic aspects of Patani's identity. It is well-known that Patani achieved political and economic greatness when it was an outwardly-oriented trading state confidently welcoming foreigners — including non-Muslim Westerners and Chinese — from many parts of the world. Patani's historians can likewise hardly deny the Hindu-Buddhist heritage of Langkasuka, the precursor state to Patani — a religious and cultural heritage that is shared by the

---

[25] Thus the tendency of some studies of the violence in the south to dismiss the ideology of *jihad* may be misplaced; see, for example, International Crisis Group, "Southern Thailand: Insurgency, Not Jihad," International Crisis Group, Asia Report No. 98, Brussels, May 18, 2005.

Thais. Patanians today, therefore, maintain a marked ambivalence toward the outside world, what Walker describes as "a multicultural-constructive/jihadist-resistant duality."

Whereas in his chapter Bradley situates Patani's great downfall in the late 18th and early 19th centuries, Kobkua Suwannathat-Pian locates the root cause of the conflict today in the period between 1897 and 1907. During this period, the Thai state removed the rulers of the seven principalities (*hua muang*) into which the sultanate had been divided in the first decades of the 19th century and replaced them with appointments from Bangkok. The seven formerly semi-independent territories were reorganized into three new administrative divisions (*monthon*), Pattani, Yala, and Bang-Nara (later, Narathiwat) ruled directly from Bangkok. While political relations with Bangkok were fundamentally changed, this reorganization did not succeed in destroying the identity of the inhabitants of the region — despite attempts by the Thai government through education reform and assimilationist campaigns. According to Kobkua, this historically-rooted identity has fuelled the separatist campaigns that continue to this day. She argues that the conflict lies in a clash between two different conceptions of the nation-state: one, a Malay-Muslim nation of people who share "the historical experiences based on the ethnic and socio-cultural identity," and the other, a multi-ethnic, multi-cultural and multi-religious Thai nation made up of citizens loyal to the nation. Kobkua describes the way in which history writing has been mobilized to legitimize the political claims of the two sides. One of the results has been the re-emergence of the politically and culturally loaded term, "Patani," almost two centuries after the state itself had been dismembered. Patani's historiographical rebirth was due in particular to the great influence of Ibrahim Syukri's *Sejarah Kerajaan Melayu Patani*. Kobkua notes the novel situation in Thailand today where for the first time "divergent histories" are allowed to contend in the Thai public sphere — a positive development for history writing.

The representation of Patani's identity through works of history is also the subject of Iik Arifin Mansurnoor's chapter. He examines some of the most widely circulated *Jawi*-Malay works in Patani nationalist historiography among Patani Malay Muslims, including the *Hikayat Patani*, Ibrahim Syukri's *Sejarah Kerajaan Melayu Patani*, Nik Anuar's *Sejarah Perjuangan Melayu Patani*, and the lesser known *Tarikh Fatani*, arguing that Patani ethnic identity has been constructed upon a certain historical interpretation circulated by these works. Mansurnoor describes the representation of key events and themes by these well-known historical works, which, he proposes, have a special place in conceptions of a Patani-Jawi national identity today.

Patani's historiography competes with official Thai versions of history not only in university classrooms, seminar rooms, newspapers, and bookshops but also in the midst of the conflict in southern Thailand. McCargo's chapter discusses the references to Patani's history that appear in anonymous leaflets which are widely distributed in the conflict zone, and which often form the topic of conversation in tea shops, mosques, and in the home. The leaflets are issued by various groups, including the militants, the Thai security forces, as well as Muslim and Buddhist groups with varying agendas. McCargo argues that the leaflets represent a form of "decentralized communication," reflecting the nature of the violence in the south and the apparent lack of a clear leadership among the militants — what McCargo describes as "the murkiness and ambiguity at the core of the conflict." Such leaflets are not exclusive to the violence in southern Thailand; similar leaflets with historical references can be found in other conflict zones such as Maluku in Indonesia and Afghanistan. Common themes discussed in leaflets issued by the militants include Patani's renown in former times as a center of Islamic scholarship, the question of Patani's historical independence, the Siamese conquest of Patani and mistreatment of the Patani Malay captives, and the murders of Patani's leaders at the hands of the Thai state. The leaflets do not, however, reflect a single historical "master-narrative," but rather express a diversity of historical views. Some are versions of Malay and Patani nationalism, while others are more Islamic in tone. Given the lack of formal communications by the militants themselves about their ideology or political aims, the leaflets illustrate the role that Patani's history continues to play in the propaganda war waged by the militants.

What lessons can be learned from the state of Patani historiography today? For nationalist historians, highlighting Patani's history can be a double-edged sword. Patani historiography may point to a golden age in which the sultanate enjoyed *de facto* independence and it was one of Southeast Asia's most prosperous entrepôts, frequented by traders from all over the world. Later, scholars from Patani residing in the Middle East produced an outpouring of Islamic scholarship written in Malay that has a significant place in Southeast Asian Islam and Patani became a center of Islamic education for Southeast Asian Muslims. But these achievements were overshadowed by the Siamese-Thai conquest, colonization and subjugation and eventually disappeared from history. Such a rendering of Patani's history can be a counterbalance to the triumphalist Thai nationalist historical narrative which once sought to erase the memory of Patani and which remains influential in Thai classrooms in which Patani Malay students also study. It can give heart to a people who have experienced great suffering in recent times and endure everyday humiliations and condescending treatment at the hands of Thai security forces and government officials. Yet the same history also shows that Patani's roots as a port polity and religious centrer were in the long-lived Hindu-Buddhist kingdom of Langkasuka, and therefore Patani shares at least the same religious roots as the Thais — and indeed of other people of the formerly Indianized regions of Southeast Asia. Patani at its height was an outward-looking, pluralistic polity, comprising peoples of differing ethnicities, languages and religions. And it can hardly be denied that Patani has, for most of the last 500 years, been subject to the gravitational force of the much larger and more powerful Thai state. During certain periods it has enjoyed a considerable measure of independence; at other times, it has been most firmly and often very violently held under the Thai yoke.[26]

Yet Patani nationalist historiography, whose parameters were laid out by "Ibrahim Syukri" in the era of Southeast Asian independence struggles and the formation of nation-states, may have passed its heyday — though it is by no means a spent force. It is becoming hybridized with[27] and may indeed have been overpassed in terms of popular influence by discourses of Patani's past — and possible future — informed by Islam. For the very reason of Patani's small size and political weakness, Islam as a great world religion offers both a measure of dignity and an ideology of resistance that can prove empowering in standing up to the Thai colossus. The Islamic revival and Patani intellectuals' organic links to the Middle East are likely to continue the trend where Patani's history is seen in Islamic terms. This trend has only been accentuated since the US-led "war on terror" and the invasions of fellow-Muslim countries Iraq and Afghanistan by Western nations with which Thailand is closely allied. The more radical versions of this Islamic version of Patani's history employ a jihadist framework in which to understand Patani's struggle.[28] As Walker describes it in his chapter in

---

[26] See the discussion in Davisakd, "Of a Lesser Brilliance," pp. 72–84. One could even locate the origins of this geopolitical problem to the period before the establishment of the state of Patani. The empires of Sri Vijaya and Majapahit, based in south Sumatra and Java respectively, extended their authority northward only as far as the middle part of the peninsula.

[27] For a critical view arguing that radical Malay nationalism has distorted Islam in southern Thailand, see "Bahrun", *Yihad si thao: khrai sang khrai liang fai tai* [*Grey Jihad: Who Started and Who is Stoking the Southern Fire*] (Bangkok: Sarika, 2005).

[28] See, for example, the "Berjihad di Pattani," claimed to be a militant text, in Rohan Gunaratna *et al.*, eds., *Conflict and Terrorism in Southern Thailand* (Singapore: Marshall Cavendish Academic, 2005), pp. 117–45.

this volume, for some it is conceived of as an epic struggle between two warring blocs, the "Anglo-Saxon neo-crusaders/Siam/India/Israel" and "pan-Islamic Patanian/Nusantara/Arab/Palestinian/Iran/Muslim South Asia." Peace-building measures on the part of either the Thais or the West are thus viewed with suspicion. The unreliability of "Perfidious Albion" can be traced back in Patani's history far enough for Patani's Muslims today to distrust the agendas of Western peacemakers. "Islamist" versions of Patani's history are popular among the youth and cyber warriors, suggesting that as internet usage expands and Patani's youth reaches positions of greater influence, such interpretations of Patani's history may exert a more powerful influence.

Wan Kadir Che Man, author of an important academic study of separatism in southern Thailand (and the southern Philippines)[29] and nominal head of an umbrella group of separatist organizations, Bersatu, aptly summed up Patani's predicament in a short paper titled "The Problem of Patani Malays in Thailand: Neither Assimilation nor Separation." The paper has recently been translated and published in Thai. The translated title reads slightly differently from Wan Kadir's English title, but perhaps sums up the dilemma even better than the original: "The Problem of Patani and Thailand: When We Can Neither Live Together Nor Separate from Each Other."[30] The burden of the past could suggest that Thailand and Patani are cursed to be forever bound in an antagonistic relationship.

History does not, however, necessarily have to determine Patani's destiny. The bloody quarrels between the ruling houses of Europe, its religious wars, and the nationalist conflagrations of the 20th century have (for now at least) been consigned to "history" with the formation of the European Union, which has at the same time encouraged a recrystallization of regional and sub-national identities and respect for their right to autonomy within the new European order. Could a more integrated ASEAN (at least economically, if not politically) within a multi-polar, liberalized global economic system, where neither "Buddhist Thailand" nor the "Christian West" figure as largely in determining Patani's fate, provide a similar environment in which Patani's Muslims can find a place of dignity that will allow them to put the ghosts of their history to rest?

---

[29] Wan Kadir, *Muslim Separatism: The Moros of Southern Philippines and the Malays of Southern Thailand*.

[30] Wan Kadir Che Man, "Panha patani lae thai: muea rao at yu ruam lae baeng yaek jak kan dai" [The Problem of Patani Malays in Thailand: Neither Assimilation nor Separation], trans. Prinya Nuanpian, in *Nork niyam khwam pen thai*, ed. Prinya, pp. 19–25.

Such a shared future may require a more shared past. The primordial nationalisms that have haunted the historiographies of the two sides in the conflict for the last half century are showing signs of losing their hold upon Patani's history. The more diverse and interconnected academic environment that is emerging in which scholars and students can access and debate the merits of works and sources written in languages other than their own national languages, particularly in the growing *lingua franca* of English, and who are interacting with one another in conferences, seminar rooms and even undergraduate classrooms, may open the way to a more pluralistic historiography. The essays collected in this volume suggest that the writing of Patani's history may already be moving in this direction.

PART ONE

Pluralism and Identity in Patani's History

CHAPTER 1

Patani as a Paradigm of Pluralism

Anthony Reid

The rise of nationalism and the ideology of sovereign equality among uniform nation-states brought huge advances to Europe in the 19th century and Asia in the 20th. The ideology included, however, alarming implications for precisely those societies that had arisen to mediate goods, people and ideas creatively between the major population centers. Among these implications was the doctrine that has caused most of Asia's insurrections since 1945 — that a more-or-less arbitrary line on the ground could mark the boundary between the absolute sovereignty of one nation-state and that of another. Of course this doctrine, the so-called "Westphalia system" of mutual recognition of competing sovereignties, was introduced by Europeans, as part of their ongoing rivalries projected into Asia. Drawing borders between their respective spheres of sovereignty had become in the 17th century their way to cope with the demons of religious conflict and nationalism.

Only after the Congress of Vienna in 1815 was there a century of sufficient peace between European states for this ideology of sovereign equality to begin to work, and to be extended to Asia as a "system." A series of agreements between Britain and the Netherlands (1824, 1871), Britain and France (1896, 1904), the Netherlands and Portugal (1860) laid the basis for Southeast Asia's modern boundaries. In turn, the Europeans insisted that the Asian states that survived join this pattern of demarcating sovereign borders. As Burney told the Siamese court in 1826, only fixed boundaries between territories would "prevent all chance of mistake or dispute," and enable the British in Lower Burma to have more stable and harmonious relations with the Siamese than the Burmese had had.[1]

---

[1] Henry Burney, *The Burney Papers*, 2 vols. (Farnborough: Gregg International, 1971), I: 85–6.

This doctrine proved relatively congenial to the two historic Asian polities that most successfully rode it into nation-state-dom — Japan, because its borders had been created by geography and consolidated by the Tokugawa, and Siam, which had most of its potential problem areas shorn from it by expanding European imperialism in the late 19th and early 20th centuries. Elsewhere wholly new nationalisms had to be invented to match the imperial borders, which were heavily contested before the imperial and national power centers — Rangoon, Hanoi, Manila, Jakarta — imposed the new idea on their respective spheres.

The most cosmopolitan crossroads of the old order were transformed by this process into embittered "problem" peripheries. All the peoples of the borderlands of Northeast India, southern China and northern Mainland Southeast Asia are in this category (Jim Scott's "Zomia") — notably the Kachin, Wa, Shan and Karen.[2] For our purpose, however, there is particular interest in the maritime centers between British, Dutch and Spanish imperial cores in Southeast Asia — Sulu, Aceh and Patani. Today their "problem" is often expressed in terms of Islam, but they became centers of Islam because they were first centers of cosmopolitan trade. Each of these centers was strategically placed for the long-distance trade: Aceh as the first Southeast Asian landfall of travelers across the Indian Ocean; Sulu as the strategic passage between China and the two archipelagoes of the Philippines and eastern Indonesia; Patani as the new Melaka, a staging port for the China trade and much of the trans-Peninsula traffic. Despite these strategic positions, attractive to predatory Europeans, each retained its autonomy through the dangerous 17th and 18th centuries because it was plural, and impossible for any one power to control.

Patani was paradigmatic of this kind of pre-nationalist cosmopolis, plural in its essence.

Plural Origins

Although the Peninsula has not been a very rich source of literary output before the 19th century, we do have extant and distinct Thai, Malay, and Chinese literary traditions on its origins. One of the oldest in Thai is the Nakhon Si Thammarat chronicle edited by David Wyatt. Its part-mythical account of the origins of the polities that eventually in the 19th century were regarded as either Thai Buddhist or Malay Muslim gives a major role

---

[2] James Scott, *The Art of Not Being Governed: An Anarchist History of Upland Southeast Asia* (New Haven: Yale University Press, 2009).

to Chinese, Khmer, Cham and *Khèk*. The origins of the peninsula dynasties are there traced to a moment of Chinese interaction with the salt-exporting center of Phetburi in the Gulf of Siam at a time evidently pre-dating the rise of Ayutthaya — perhaps the 13th century. The ruler of Phetburi, himself possibly a Khmer with connections to Angkor, provides sandalwood to a visiting Chinese ship, and is rewarded by the Chinese emperor with his daughter (or granddaughter) by a Champa princess, Candradevi. She is sent to Phetburi with 19 ships and 7,400 servants and concubines to serve the king of Phetburi. He then sends out his sons and retainers, some endowed with Chinese consorts and *Khèk* (likely to be Austronesian, and/or possibly Khmer) auxiliaries, to found other polities including the predecessor of Nakhon. The principal son, ancestor-figure of the Nakhon line, in turn sends out *Khèk* in boats to become rajas of the *Khèk* principalities further south, including areas we now know as Trang, Songkhla, Patani, Kedah and Pahang.[3] Terms such as Thai or Malay would have been inappropriate for this period before they were invented, and they do not occur in the chronicle. All we can be sure of for the identity of *Khèk* is that they were "outsiders" to the Buddhist writers of a Thai-language chronicle.

If this might be considered a Thai version of plurality, the Malay versions of Patani's past are similarly plural. The 18th-century compilation labeled *Hikayat Patani* by Teeuw provides no ethnic labels for its characters, but begins its story at the point an inland king from "Kota Mahligai" (perhaps evoking the Yarang ancient site 15 kilometers south of Patani)[4] decides to

---

[3] David Wyatt, *The Crystal Sands: the Chronicles of Nagara Sri Dharrmaraja* (Ithaca, NY: Cornell University Southeast Asia Program, 1975), pp. 102–10. One of the *Khèk* tributaries thus founded is intriguingly listed as Aceh. Wyatt (see p. 104n5) translates *Khèk* throughout this section as Malay which, though politically more correct, means imposing a modern ethnic term backward to a pre-Muslim period when no such term was known. *Khèk* literally means guest or outsider, and has come in modern Thai to be used somewhat disparagingly for Malays, peoples of darker complexion, and Muslims more generally. A later Thai chronicle of Patani is cited by Teeuw and Wyatt but not accessible by me — Phraya Wichiankiri (Chom na Songkhla), "Phongsawadan muang pattani" [Chronicle of Pattani], first published in 1914 though written some 20 years earlier.

[4] These Yarang excavations were displayed in the Songkhla National Museum when I visited in 2004, with a confident claim to its being the site of ancient Langkasuka. However Daniel Perret, "Réflexions sur l'émergence du sultanat de Patani," in *Etudes sur l'histoire du sultanat de Patani*, ed. Daniel Perret, Amara Srisuchat, and Sombun Thanasuk (Paris: EFEO, 2004), pp. 23–4, warns that the absence of Chinese ceramics at the site does not fit with Chinese descriptions of a commercial center at

move his capital to the coast. The succeeding three chapters are all about the arrival of outsiders — Muslims from Sumatra who bring Islam, Chinese who bring trade and technology, and Mon (Pegu) and Lao (Lancang) captives reportedly presented to the Patani king by Ayutthaya to populate his city.[5] Ibrahim Syukri's ethicized rewriting of the 1940s makes the people of Kota Mahligai *Siam-Asli*. They appear to have coexisted in his analysis with the aboriginal Jakun who mingled with people from India and Sri Vijaya (Sumatra) to form the Malay people, later arrivals on the scene.[6]

Besides the Thai and Malay-language traditions of Patani's early centuries, there is also a Chinese-language history, most coherently put together in a 1946 Singapore publication accessible to me only indirectly.[7] Chinese official sources on Patani are dominated by the negative image with which the Ming court regarded all overseas Chinese communities which had evaded its ban on private trade or residence abroad. They were labeled in Ming sources "sea bandits" (*haikou*), or "dwarf bandits" (*wokou* — in reference to Japanese who were [wrongly] accused of dominating the category) both of which have too readily been translated as "pirates." In the 16th century, foreign traders anxious to evade the Ming trade ban, whether Japanese, Southeast Asian or European in origin, needed to work with Chinese traders on the fringes of the imperial system, officially regarded as smugglers, who in turn exaggerated the importance of the foreign element among them to evade and also intimidate local officials.[8] Even court sources

---

Langkasuka, while the absence of signs of occupation after the ninth century seems to rule out a direct ancestry of Patani.

[5] A. Teeuw and D.K. Wyatt, eds., *Hikayat Patani: The Story of Patani* (The Hague: Nijhoff, 1970), pp. 68–81 (Malay) and pp. 146–57 (English). Note the recent useful analysis of this text by Francis Bradley, "Moral Order in a Time of Damnation: The *Hikayat Patani* in Historical Context," *Journal of Southeast Asian Studies* 40, 2 (June 2009): 267–93.

[6] Ibrahim Syukri, *History of the Malay Kingdom of Patani*, trans. Connor Bailey and John Miksic (Athens, OH: Ohio University Center for International Studies, 1985), pp. 3–9.

[7] Hsü Yün-ch'iao, *Pei-ta-nien Shih* [*History of Patani*] (Singapore, 1946), is cited by Teeuw and Wyatt in *Hikayat Patani*, p. 225, with acknowledgement to Professor Wang Gungwu for making it available to them. The chapter of this book on Lin Daoqian is fortunately now available in translation in Geoff Wade, "From Chaiya to Pahang: The Eastern Seaboard of the Peninsula as Recorded in Classical Chinese Texts," in *Etudes sur l'histoire du sultanat de Patani*, pp. 75–8.

[8] Kwan Wai So, *Japanese Piracy in Ming China during the 16th Century* (East Lansing, MI: Michigan State University Press, 1975). On the other hand, the "piratic"

however acknowledge the importance of one such "pirate," Lin Daoqian, whose 2,000 Cantonese followers made their base in Patani in or after 1566, effectively dominating the city for the next generation. There are also diverse local Chinese traditions about this man, including a Teochew story that he married the daughter of the sultan but then fell out with him and fled, and others that he cast bronze cannons for Patani's wars but was blown up in testing them. Other stories center on the legendary figure of Lin Guniang or Lim Kor Niaw, a Chinese woman whose tomb is adjacent to the old Kreu Se mosque (and bears the recently-inscribed date 1574). Many stories make her the sister of Lin Daoqian, who committed suicide by hanging herself from a tree after protesting in vain against her brother's adoption of Islam, marriage to a local woman, and organizing the building of Patani's then principal mosque.[9] This lady's cult was already known locally in the late 19th century, but in the nationalist 20th century, she (the upholder of a pure "Chinese" tradition) rather than the *peranakan* Lin Daoqian (the founder of local Chinese identity and fortune) became a hero for the Chinese of Singapore and Malaysia. As Askew and Cohen have pointed out, a busy cross-border religious tourism has arisen since the 1960s, whereby certain shrines have become ways of celebrating Chineseness in a way that would be ill-advised, politically incorrect or more expensive in Malaysia and Singapore. Chinese from south of the border, perceiving South Thailand as "a substitute Chinese homeland," have funded two new and gaudy shrines — one at her tomb and the other the flamboyant San Jao Lim Kor Niaw in the northern part of the modern town (Figure 1.1).[10]

---

background of Patani appears to have been to some extent accepted locally, to judge from van Neck's report: "the people of this place used to be great pirates (*zeerovers*), and people say that the richest men in the city got most of their wealth from that." J. van Neck, "Journaal," 1604, in *De Vierde Schipvaart der Nederlanders naar Oost-Indië onder Jacob Wilkens van Neck (1599–1604)*, Vol. I, ed. H.A. van Foreest and A. de Booy (The Hague: Nijoff for Linschoten-Vereeniging, 1980), pp. 217–8.

[9] Teeuw and Wyatt, eds., *Hikayat Patani*, pp. 224–5; Hsü, in Wade, "From Chaiya to Pahang," pp. 75–8; Francis R. Bradley, "Piracy, Smuggling, and Trade in the Rise of Patani, 1490–1600," *Journal of the Siam Society* 96 (2008): 27–50; Daniel Perret, "Patani dans les grands réseaux marchands du XVIIe siècle," in *Etudes sur l'histoire du sultanat de Patani*, ed. Daniel Perret, Amara Srisuchat, and Sombun Thanasuk (Paris: EFEO, 2004), pp. 236–7.

[10] Quotation from Mark Askew and Erik Cohen, "Pilgrimage and Prostitution: Contrasting Modes of Border Tourism in Lower South Thailand," *Tourism Recreation Research* 29, 2 (2004): 94–5. Also Paul Gray and Lucy Ridout, *Rough Guide to Thailand's Beaches and Islands* (London: Rough Guides, 2001), p. 426.

Figure 1.1 The image of Lin Guniang ("Lim Kor Niaw"), sister of the legendary Chinese cannon-builder of Patani, Lin Daoqian ("Lim Toh Khiam"), from the shrine in her honor in Pattani town (also known as the Leng Ju Kiang shrine).

Plural Rise

In terms of the internal or local memory of Patani's early history, therefore, we must give due justice at least to these three traditions which originally borrowed from one another, though later hardening into rival ethnicized versions. For a more adequate record of how Patani in fact emerged, we must also consult the archeological record (conveniently collected in the volume of Daniel Perret and colleagues) and the foreign accounts, relatively abundant during the time of Patani's commercial prominence before and after 1600. They show a port of gradually increasing significance in the late 15th century, gaining importance after the fall of Melaka to the Portuguese in 1511. It served what might be called the "alternative" trade between China and Southeast Asia, labeled smuggling by the Ming court. For its first two centuries, 1368–1568, the Ming court permitted no foreign maritime trade as legitimate except that conducted in connection with "tribute" missions from the southern kingdoms it acknowledged. Siam and Melaka both played this tribute card with skill, using it to monopolize the legal trade of the Gulf of Siam and the Peninsula with China. Except for Pahang, which briefly played a similar role in the second decade of the 15th century, no port between Siam and Melaka (or indeed between Siam and Java once Melaka fell in 1511) was acknowledged as a legitimate tributary (read trading partner) by the Ming. Of course, in reality a large amount of trade was carried on at rival ports, and "smuggled" to China by various means. The Ming took a dim view of its Chinese subjects who defied the bans on private trade, forcing them to make their bases at non-tributary ports outside the reach of Chinese power — notably Singapore before 1400, and Palembang until it was invaded and "punished" by Zheng He in 1407.

Patani only later became a major haven for this "alternative" trade, and may have attracted refugees from those two centers. It naturally appears very little in Chinese court records, but begins to appear in those of Ryukyu (Okinawa) from the 1490s. Ryukyu provided a safe alternative means of trading with both China and Japan, since it sent "legitimate" tribute missions to both powers laden with Southeast Asian produce.[11] After the fall of Melaka, Patani became one of the major Southeast Asian exporters to use the Ryukyu connection to send pepper, spices, gold, tin and aromatic woods to China, while the Sino-Javanese trade that had intensively used Melaka also shifted much of its entrepôt trade for southern China to Patani. Daniel Perret summarizes the rise of Patani as in no sense depending on a productive hinterland, but rather "a Sino-Javano-Malay nucleus that developed Patani into an emporium where Chinese products were exchanged principally for pepper, sandalwood and Moluccan spices."[12] By the mid-16th century, these alternative networks formed the key commercial links between the southern Chinese coast and the Peninsula, and comprised a hybridized mix of Chinese, Portuguese, Malays, Chams and Japanese. The scale and efficiency of this alternative, even if considered smuggling by the Ming court, made the Ryukyu detour unnecessary. Private Portuguese and Eurasian traders were able to participate more fully and profitably in the East Asian trade in association with these networks than in the officially licensed Portuguese trade out of Melaka.[13] Already by the 1520s, Barros noted, there was a sizable settlement of Portuguese traders in Patani, where "many ships of the Chinese, Ryukyus and Javanese come, as well as from all the surrounding islands."[14]

---

[11] Atsushi Kobata and Mitsugu Matsuda, *Ryukyuan Relations with Korea and the South Sea Countries: an Annotated Translation of Documents in the Rekidai Hoan* (privately printed, 1969), pp. 177–80.

[12] Perret, "Réflexions," p. 31.

[13] Bradley, "Piracy, Smuggling, and Trade in the Rise of Patani, 1490–1600."

[14] João de Barros, *Da Asia* (Lisbon: Regia Officina, 1563; reprinted 1973), III, i, p. 183.

The internal ethnic divide that came to dominate the 20th century is not mentioned in these varied early Asian sources. The *Hikayat Patani*, indeed, seems oblivious to ethnicity of any kind, acknowledging "only three parties … [in his story], the people of Patani, those of Johor, and the Siamese."[15] The external sources record communities of Chinese, Japanese, Javanese and Indian Muslims, but no source informs us about "Malay" or "Thai" as ethnic categories. The ruling elite are simply Patani people. At most a Chinese source of 1617 will allow: "Originally it was subject to Java, but now it is under Siam."[16] Only with the coming of the northern Europeans at the peak of Patani's prosperity does Patani's intense internal plurality come to be expressed in ethnic terms.

Patani's Heyday, 1580–1620

Chinese sources make clear that the hybrid commercial networks they identified as bandits reached a peak of effectiveness in the 1550s in moving goods in and out of China through the Fujian coast, with Patani one of the networks' important southern bases. "Legal" means of trading to China had effectively died, the tribute trade by the mid-15th century and the Ryukyu alternative by the 1540s (the last recorded to Patani was 1543).[17] A rethink of Chinese trade policy was overdue. The violence and bribery of officials that often accompanied the alternative "smuggling" networks itself became too much for the Ming bureaucracy, and in 1557 measures were begun to co-opt some of the "smugglers" to help suppress the more obdurate network leaders. As one reforming official pointed out, "When trade is permitted, pirates become merchants. When trade is prohibited, merchants convert to pirates."[18] In 1567, local authorities in Fujian were finally permitted to license private trading vessels to trade legally to the south, a watershed in China's adjustment to economic reality. Patani was still too notorious an alternative center for ships to be licensed officially to trade to it at this stage (though four a year were cleared officially for Siam in the 1580s), but by

---

[15] Teeuw and Wyatt, eds., *Hikayat Patani*, p. 251.

[16] *Dong-xi-yang Kao* (1617), as translated in Wade, "From Chaiya to Pahang," p. 56.

[17] Kobata and Matsuda, *Ryukyuan Relations with Korea and the South Sea Countries*, p. 182. This period is now best covered in Bradley, "Piracy, Smuggling, and Trade in the Rise of Patani, 1490–1600."

[18] *Chouhai tubian* (1562), cited in Wang Tai Peng, *The Origins of the Chinese Kongsi* (Petaling Jaya: Pelanduk Publications, 1994), p. 39.

the time of Floris' reporting in 1613 there were three large Chinese ships unloading at Patani in each February-May "season."[19]

Lin Daoqian, mentioned above as the central figure of official Chinese memory in Patani, was the principal hold-out against this shift, at times negotiating to join the new Ming system but ultimately settling in Patani around the 1570s (1566 is mentioned in some sources, 1578 in others) as a refugee from it. He brought with him about 2,000 hardened mariners and fighters, as well as a set of commercial connections around the South China Sea. This undoubtedly made him the dominant military and economic factor in Patani in the troubled years that followed, up until the commencement of female rule in 1584. On the basis of many contradictory legends about him, Bradley speculates that the Patani woman he married (thereby officially becoming Muslim) may have been Raja Ijau, sister of the last male sultan of the *Hikayat Patani* record, Bahadur, assassinated in 1584.[20] Such a marriage might have recognized Lin Daoqian as the effective strong man of the state, enabling van Neck to understand Raja Ijau to be the widow rather than the sister of the last king: she "remained Queen after the death of the King, her husband."[21]

This injection of hybrid Chinese wealth and manpower underlay the rise of Patani to one of the leading Southeast Asian entrepôts by the time of the arrival of the Dutch in 1601. Even if the initial Chinese settlement was peaceful, it is indeed likely that there were sooner or later conflicts between those who declared their local identity by becoming Muslim, and those who retained enough Chinese language and cultural tradition to do business with

---

[19] Anthony Reid, *Southeast Asia in the Age of Commerce c.1450–1680. Volume II: Expansion and Crisis* (New Haven: Yale University Press, 1993), pp. 18–9. Anthony Farrington and Dhiravat na Pombejra, The English Factory in Siam 1612–1685 (London: British Library, 2007), II: 104, 112–3. H. Terpstra, *De Factorij der Oostindische Compagnie te Patani* ('s-Gravenhage: Nijhoff for KITLV, 1938), pp. 131–6.

[20] Bradley, "Piracy, Smuggling, and Trade in the Rise of Patani, 1490–1600," n72. Also Hsü in Wade, "From Chaiya to Pahang," pp. 75–8. Another candidate for a husband of Raja Ijau may be the Hokkien merchant surnamed Zhang who in the *Dong-xi-yang Kao* is said to have been declared an influential Datu by the sultan, but then fled during Patani's "troubles," to be brought back in honor once the Queen had assumed the throne — Wade, "From Chaiya to Pahang," p. 57.

[21] J. van Neck, "Journaal," in *De Vierde Schipvaart der Nederlanders naar Oost-Indië onder Jacob Wilkens van Neck (1599–1604)*, Vol. I, ed. H.A. van Foreest and A. de Booy (The Hague: Nijoff for Linschoten-Vereeniging, 1980), p. 226, and see Appendix.

Figure 1.2 The remains of the Krue Se mosque, Pattani province, flanked by flags of the King and Queen and the Thai national flag.

the ships from China which had become the biggest factor in Patani's trade by 1600. To this extent the stories around the death of the "sister," Lim Kor Niaw, reflect a cultural reality.

Hsü Yun-tsiao claimed in the 1940s that "The Malay people of Kase [Krue Se, or Gresik, the 17th-century capital] all claim that Lim Toh Khiam [Lin Daoqian] was their progenitor and they frequently say that their ancestors were Chinese."[22] The Chinese tradition that Lin built the Krue Se mosque (see Figure 1.2) around which this community settled is confirmed by van Neck's account, which reports that the then principal mosque of the city "was very neatly constructed by Chinese workers from red bricks."[23] Certainly it was utterly unlike the traditional square wooden mosques of the earthquake-prone Archipelago. In Patani, even more than earlier in Melaka, a Malay identity was eventually forged among those who made Patani their home, Islam their religion, and Malay their lingua franca. When the Dutch fleets arrived, in pursuit first of pepper and later of Chinese manufactures, this Malay identity was perceived as a fact, distinguishing this local elite

---

[22] Hsü, in Wade, "From Chaiya to Pahang," p. 77.
[23] J. van Neck, "Journaal," p. 222, and see Appendix.

group from Chinese identifying with the Ming, and Thais identifying with Ayutthaya (Siam). The beginning of direct shipping from Fujian ports to Patani at the end of the 16th century had ensured a continuing presence of "Chinese" Chinese, in relation to whom the hybridized followers of Lin Daoqian must have appeared not Chinese at all. Wybrandt van Warwyck's Dutch fleet were the first visitors to Patani, in 1602, to specifically describe as "a Malay of Chinese origin" the most important man in the city, Datu Seri Nara.[24]

The other major elements in the population of Patani at its peak were Javanese, Japanese, Portuguese and Indian Muslims. Javanese and Gujaratis are the only commercial minorities mentioned in the *Hikayat Patani*, when their sections of the city were destroyed during the Siamese invasion of 1633.[25] Perret has made a case that "the Javanese played an important role in the foundation and emergence of Patani during the second half of the fifteenth century."[26] He instances several Portuguese references to Javanese ships frequenting Patani, and presumes that the umbilical cord that tied Melaka with its large (Sino-) Javanese community to Java before 1511, would have shifted to Patani thereafter. Like Melaka, Patani appeared to be partly dependant on Java for its rice and other food supplies, and Floris' 1612–1613 journal shows that most of the Patani-owned "junks" that left the city during his time there touched at Banten or Jortan on Java's north coast on their way to and from Maluku to collect spices.[27] Floris is also the source for the revolt of the Javanese slaves, particularly those in the service of three *orangkaya* (merchant-aristocrats) — Datu Besar, Datu Laxamana and Raja Schey — after Datu Besar had killed their leader (*panglima*).[28] These *orangkaya* may themselves have been Javanese or Sino-Javanese who came to Patani with their numerous retinues, as had been the case with the many Javanese "slaves" of Melaka.

Japanese "red-seal" ships (as opposed to the earlier Ryukyu connection) began sailing directly to Patani at the end of the 16th century, and in the

---

[24] Wybrandt van Warwyck, "Historische Verhael vande Reyse gedaen inde Oost-Indien, met 15 Schepen voor Reeckeningh van de vereenichde Gheoctroyeerde Oost-Indiscvhe Compagnie," 1604, in *Begin ende Voortgangh van de Vereenighde Neederlandtsche Geoctoyeerde Oost-Indische Compagnie*, ed. Isaac Commelin (1646, reprinted Amsterdam 1974), p. 43.

[25] Teeuw and Wyatt, eds., *Hikayat Patani*, p. 113 (Malay) and p. 184 (English).

[26] Perret, "Patani dans les grands réseaux marchands du XVIIe siècle," p. 239.

[27] Farrington and Pombejra, *The English Factory in Siam 1612–1685*, pp. 106–7.

[28] Ibid., pp. 118–9.

first years after 1600 there appeared to be about two a year, using Patani preeminently as a place to buy the Chinese silk and other manufactures they were prohibited from acquiring directly. As van Neck put it, "from Japan they come also every year bringing Japanese swords, costly woodwork, which those from China buy, also copper and other small things."[29] Two such ships arrived in Patani in 1605, and again in 1614, with Dutch captains employed by Japanese merchant-aristocrats to pilot their vessels to the south.[30] Japanese however were treated with great caution, especially since they had twice burned large sections of the town in response to some affront, according to Floris.[31] In 1614, they were "prohibited to come without license within the walls, for breach whereof 8 were killed in one day, all Japonders."[32] The Gujerati, as noted above, were mentioned by the *Hikayat Patani* as having their *kampong* burned in the Siamese attack of 1633. They, as well as the South Indian (Chulia) Muslims from Coromandel, also feature prominently in English trade reports as both competitors and partners in trading ventures across the Bay of Bengal and in Southeast Asia.

The Dutch reports on Patani in its commercial and political heyday are the most revealing, and have not yet been fully exploited. Because a Dutch dissertation was published on the Dutch trade in Patani as early as 1938, no modern study has been undertaken, even though Leonard Blussé's paper on the Patani Chinese merchant Inpo showed how fruitful that might be.[33] Terpstra's study was surprisingly little concerned to explicate the social dynamics of the city, summarizing the Dutch reports in hardly more than a page. Patani was a city of about 10,000 people [a conservative view given van Neck's estimate of 4–5,000 armed men following a royal procession[34]] with three large communities — Chinese, Malay and Siamese — and many lesser ones, Malay was the most widely spoken *lingua franca*, but three other

---

[29] Van Neck, "Journaal," p. 229; see also Appendix below.

[30] Terpstra, *De Factorij der Oostindische Compagnie te Patani*, pp. 30–1; Farrington and Pombejra, *The English Factory in Siam 1612–1685*, pp. 139–40.

[31] Farrington and Pombejra, *The English Factory in Siam 1612–1685*, p. 119. It seems likely that these were Siam-based Japanese emigrés, much feared as mercenaries for either Siam or the Portuguese.

[32] Ibid., pp. 139–40.

[33] Leonard Blussé, "Inpo, Chinese Merchant in Pattani: A Study in Early Dutch-Chinese Relations," in *Proceedings of the Seventh IAHA Conference, Held in Bangkok, 22–26 August 1977* (Bangkok: Chulalongkorn University, 1978), Vol. I, pp. 290–309.

[34] Van Neck, "Journaal," p. 226, and Appendix below.

languages, Chinese [in fact probably Hokkien for the most part], Siamese and what he calls Patani-ese were much in evidence.[35]

The Dutch primary sources however tell us much more, and show how profoundly plural Patani was, even by the standards of "the plural peninsula."[36] The commander of the fleet, Jacob van Neck, reached Patani in November 1601 and spent the next nine and a half months there. His description of Patani is particularly valuable ("a classic document," say its editors[37]) — even if the Patani section was written by a scribe after van Neck's own hand was badly injured in Ternate. Though morsels of it have been used previously, his full Patani description is translated for the first time in the Appendix below. It gives a vibrant and highly favorable account of the mixed community of Patani — "the most suitable place in East India to trade with all the nations of the whole Orient." Nowhere the Dutch had been in the Indies had they been treated "more courteously or more uprightly than in this city."[38] Another of the journal-writers of his fleet believed the inner city to be "as extensive as Old Amsterdam [along the coast] but not so broad … It is in East Indian terms a very fine city, and also strong, and well-provided with metal guns," including one cannon by the castle gate bigger than any in Amsterdam.[39]

As van Neck pointed out, the three major languages of Patani — Malay (written in Arabic script from right to left), Thai (in an Indic-derived Thai script written from left to right), and Chinese (written vertically in characters) — were so astonishingly different that he could not help but divide the population into the three groups, while conceding also "many other languages."[40] This was the beginning of the ethnic stereotypes. The Malays he considered the natives of Patani, above all a maritime people skilled in handling boats and fishing, but also engaged in agriculture. Chinese, by which van Neck appears to have meant those who had been arriving in the

---

[35] Terpstra, *De Factorij der Oostindische Compagnie te Patani*, p. 3.

[36] Anthony Reid, "A Plural Peninsula," in *Thai South and Malay North: Ethnic Interactions on a Plural Peninsula*, ed. Michael Montesano and Patrick Jory (Singapore: NUS Press, 2008), pp. 25–38.

[37] H.A. van Foreest and A. de Booy, eds., *De Vierde Schipvaart der Nederlanders naar Oost-Indië onder Jacob Wilkens van Neck (1599–1604)*, p. 112.

[38] Van Neck, "Journaal," pp. 217, 229.

[39] "Journael van Roelof Roelofsz," in *De Vierde Schipvaart der Nederlanders naar Oost-Indië onder Jacob Wilkens van Neck (1599–1604)*, Vol. I, ed. H.A. van Foreest and A. de Booy (The Hague: Nijoff for Linschoten-Vereeniging, 1980), p. 258.

[40] van Neck, "Journaal," p. 223 — and Appendix below.

trading ships from China since 1567, not the hybridized local Chinese now considered Malay, dominated trade and manufacture, and were as numerous in the city as the Malays. The Siamese were a markedly less important and sizable third element, except in their religious role.

The great *orangkaya* of Patani, who sent their "junks" to Ayutthaya, Java, Jambi, Palembang, Brunei, Makassar, and Banda in this period, and whom the Dutch and English dealt extensively with in matters of trade and investment, appear to have been localized enough to be seen as "Malays of Chinese descent," like Sirinara. These included besides Sirinara himself, Orangkaya Raja Indra Muda and Datuk Laksamana (confirming the unusual Chinese role in military affairs at Patani), both of whom traded extensively around Southeast Asia, as did some other junk-owners described as Nakhoda — the "Nachoda Sanqua" and "Nachoda Hascan" mentioned favorably by the British in 1613.[41] However, although these Chinese and part-Chinese traders were identified as closest to the Queen, there must have been other *orangkaya* in the small oligarchy who had a more passive or rentier role in the commercial prosperity of the port, enjoying their share of the substantial "sombaye" (*sembah*, or tribute as a customs charge) which those who traded had to pay to the oligarchy as a group. Datuk Besar, whose Javanese began the slave revolt described by Floris, may have been of Javanese or Sino-Javanese origin himself. Other *orangkaya* responsible particularly for court protocol and Islamic observance (the world of particular interest to *Hikayat Patani*) may have had origins in the Malay world or India.

Thanks to the Queen's enlightened rule in consultation with the trading class, van Neck opines, foodstuffs and other necessities were abundant and cheap in the city, and "there is such a great trade done here as in no other city in the vicinity."[42] Traders came there from everywhere with the goods they had for exchange — silks, velvet, metalware and all kinds of manufactures including the essential "peddlar's wares" from China; swords and fine craft articles from Japan, cloth from India and the local entrepôt of Melaka, rice, salt, gold and lead from Siam, slaves from Cambodia, Champa and Borneo, spices and rice from Java. The Patani-based traders also sent their own ships out, as far afield as the Spice Islands (Banda and Maluku)

---

[41] Farrington and Pombejra, *The English Factory in Siam 1612–1685*, pp. 106, 109. For the role of *orangkaya* in Southeast Asia, and particularly for *nakhoda* as a true entrepreneur category of shipowner-traders, see Reid, *Southeast Asia in the Age of Commerce c.1450–1680*, II, pp. 114–25. For the *orangkaya* of Patani specifically, see Perret, "Patani dans les grands réseaux marchands du XVIIe siècle," pp. 231–5.

[42] Van Neck, "Journaal," p. 229, and Appendix below.

for cloves and nutmeg, Timor for sandalwood, Sumatra and the Peninsula for pepper. Undoubtedly, the key factor was that Patani was in this period a major hub, perhaps for a time the largest, for the vast Chinese supply of manufactures and demand for raw materials, a role that no Chinese port was permitted by the Ming authorities to play. As van Neck put it, Patani ships went "to all the surrounding countries, except China, where no foreigners may go."[43]

The Dutch were in the capital long enough to see much of its architecture. The houses, reported van Neck, "are of wood and reeds, as in almost all the surrounding countries, inexpensive, airy, and suitable for the heat of the sun." But the citadel which the Dutch officers appear to have visited often, was surrounded by a high wooden palisade, and contained the grander houses of the oligarchy. At its center was the royal palace, the most elegant of all the dwellings though still in wood, "worked with gold panels and other carved woodwork."[44]

Sex and Religion

Perhaps the most important insights from the Dutch come in the areas of sexual relations and religion, issues glanced only obliquely in other sources, whether local or foreign. I long ago found van Neck's information helpful in forming my own views about Southeast Asian gender patterns,[45] though it is useful to look at this evidence again with care to the local Patani context. In general, van Neck presents a picture not unlike that enlightenment writers gave to Polynesia two centuries later, of a relaxed and pragmatic attitude to sexuality intended to contrast with a puritanical Europe. He reported the surprising freedom allowed to unmarried women, particularly in forming temporary marriages with visiting male traders, who were typically in the city for several months waiting for the change of monsoon. He depicts the practice in benign terms, claiming that when the man is ready to depart "he gives her whatever is promised, and so they leave each other in friendship, and she may then look for another man as she wishes, in all propriety, without scandal."[46] Besides this convenience there was a system of prostitution operated particularly by slaves of the great lords, and

---

[43] Van Neck, "Journaal," p. 230, and Appendix below.

[44] Van Neck, "Journaal," p. 222, and Appendix below.

[45] Reid, *Southeast Asia in the Age of Commerce c.1450–1680. Volume I: The Lands below the Winds* (New Haven: Yale University Press, 1988), pp. 149–55.

[46] Van Neck, "Journaal," p. 225, and Appendix below.

perhaps even the numerous handmaidens of the Queen (of whom he reports that they may sleep with anyone but may not marry). Since the ethnic and religious orientation of the women in question is not mentioned, these may have been luxuries the women could not afford. The Siamese however are considered particularly unchaste, most of all because of the penis-bells worn by their men and allegedly much appreciated by their women. Van Neck is, again, one of the most valuable sources on this peculiar practice, widespread in Southeast Asia until banished by the rise of Islam and Christianity.[47]

By contrast with this freedom for the unmarried, van Neck portrays adultery among the married as being punished very severely, "but it happens there often nevertheless."[48] Although he states this as a generality, his example is among the very highest class of Muslim *orangkaya*, no doubt exceptional both for the cosmopolitan cast of its Islam but more importantly for the importance of marriage for inheritance and alliance among the property-holders. While the political implications of this particular adultery among the ruling class are clear, van Neck is by no means alone among early travelers in characterizing Southeast Asian women as, by European standards, "very constant when married, but very loose when single."[49]

The early Dutch voyages also tell us more about popular religion in Patani than we hear at any other time before the late 19th century. In regard to Islam, van Neck and the leading clergyman in his fleet, Roelof Roelofszoon, mention only one mosque ("the church of the [Muslim] inhabitants of the city"), the handsome Chinese-built one near the palace. Of this, Roelofszoon reports that "it was on the inside very splendidly gilded, and the pillars were ingeniously painted after their fashion. In the middle and against the wall stood a great gilded chair, with four stairways up to it, extremely magnificently and cleverly made.[50] No-one was permitted to ascend into this chair except only the priests of the country, who were there held in very great esteem."[51] The Dutch accounts do not mention

---

[47] Reid, *Southeast Asia in the Age of Commerce c.1450–1680*, I: 148–50.

[48] Van Neck, "Journaal," p. 224, and Appendix below.

[49] Reid, *Southeast Asia in the Age of Commerce c.1450–1680*, I: 151–7. The quotation (p. 154) is from Beeckman, referring to Banjarese a century later than van Neck.

[50] This was presumably an elaborate variant of the *minbar* (pulpit), the elevated platform from which the Prophet spoke in the first mosques. Because of these sacred roots, preachers (*khatib*) in modern times have regarded the top level as too sacred, and have spoken from one of the lower stairs, which may have confused Roelofszoon. A chair is not part of the *minbar* in modern mosques, but was in some older ones.

[51] "Journael van Roelof Roelofsz," pp. 259–60.

other Islamic public expressions which appeared a little later in Aceh, such as a royal procession to the Friday prayer or other Muslim feasts, fasting (although Ramadan of 1010H fell in February–March 1602 while the Dutch were there) or other publicly noticeable applications of Islamic law. They do report the presence of a Muslim eminence called "their bishop," who swiftly translated an Arabic document that had been drawn up in Holland for the fleet's use.[52]

The Dutch were more struck by the religious systems of the Chinese and Siamese, whom they put in the category of "heathens" and "idolators." It is striking that the only role ascribed to Siamese in the European sources is a religious one. Van Neck noted that Chinese and Siamese were "great idolators, not of one mind but of diverse sects."[53] While the Siamese (Theravada) monks were already distinguished by their yellow robes, it was the Chinese popular religion of spirit possession that made the biggest impression on van Neck (see Appendix). The adepts of this cult appear particularly to have been among the transient China-based traders, some of whom departed the city because of the medium's prophesying about a fire.

The most information about Siamese religion comes from the pen of the pastor, Roelofszoon.

> In one of the Heathen churches, which the people of Siam had there, was a gilded statue in the figure of a man, as big as a horse, but seated, with one hand pointing downward and the other upward. On each side stood a gilded dragon, and beside each dragon a stone statue, one of a man, the other of a woman, with their hands together as if they were praying. In the second church we found similar statues, but not more than half were gilded, the other half painted red. In the third and last church was again such a statue, with a gilded stripe across the chest, and behind the altar of this last statue stood a smaller statue made of stone in the figure of a man, with a very large spout on its head, which appeared to be like a horn. The priest,[54] who received us as guests and was very friendly, when asked what these statues represented, said it was the great God; he also had in his house three small metal statuettes standing on a small *Outaerken* [shrine?] with a little curtain in front. His name, he said was Brahala.[55] He was a Siamese, and so did not understand the

---

[52] Van Neck, "Journaal," p. 218.

[53] Van Neck, "Journaal," p. 223, and Appendix below.

[54] *Paep*, see note note 63 below.

[55] In Malay usage, *berhala* is idol, and Chinese or Thai temples are sometimes called *rumah berhala*. It is probable therefore that the Siamese monk in question was attempting to make himself understood in Malay.

Malay language, hence our people could not speak with him as much as they wished.[56]

This description of three temples together with Van Neck's information about the different sects among Siamese and Chinese, helps us to understand a process of interaction between Chinese or part-Chinese traders and the earliest Thai Theravada monks of the area. Although the primary direction of assimilation appears to have been toward a Malayo-Muslim identity, through acceptance of Islam and the Malay language, we should also expect a substantial accommodation of Chinese, Japanese and others toward Thai Buddhism. Presumably most of the worshippers and patrons of the earliest Theravada monasteries were Chinese, while Chinese monks or religious specialists were scarce at this early period.[57] We may presume multiple religious options for the Chinese settlers, before the harder lines of the 20th century separated Thai, Malay and Chinese modes of worship as necessarily different.

Female Rule

Patani was at its commercial height under its first queen, Raja Ijau (1584–1616), with Datuk Sirinara as a kind of chancellor. It was then one of the leading entrepôts of Southeast Asia, although producing very little on its own account for the export market. Because it was already such a key center for the exchange of goods from China, Japan and Southeast Asia, and because it then had a more trade-friendly environment than bigger pepper-producers like Aceh, Jambi and Palembang, the Dutch and English, new players from 1600, also made it an important base in the period, adding to both supply and demand in its market. In this period, pluralism was of its essence, enabling traders from all parts of Asia to interact in an orderly atmosphere. While many Chinese, Javanese and Japanese became hybridized, speaking fluent Malay as well as, or eventually in place of, their own languages, others retained their roots in their respective traditions. Olivier van Noort encountered a group of Patani traders in Brunei in 1601, who represented themselves as a community that had fled or been banished from China, but were still "Chinese" enough in Patani to have their own "king," with "the same laws as exist in China."[58] Since this process of cultural interaction was

---

[56] "Journael van Roelof Roelofsz," p. 259.

[57] Thai Buddhist temples in Singapore and Malaysia in modern times have also enjoyed majority support from Chinese worshippers.

[58] *De Reis om de wereld van Olivier van Noort 1598–1601*, ed. J.W. Ijzerman (The Hague: Nijhoff for Linschoten-Vereniging, 1926), p. 124.

dynamic, however, the Patani traders who became an important diaspora with the decline of Patani's trade after about 1618, became another kind of Malay, not unlike the Melaka refugees of a century earlier, who became Malay in diaspora where they may have been seen as Javanese, Gujerati, Chinese or Luzon in an earlier Melaka context.

The European element in Patani's variegated cultural interaction should not be ignored either, in the form of first Portuguese and then the big Dutch fleets. Patani was one of the early sites of encounter between Europe and China, as with the Malay world and Siam; the Europeans bought Chinese manufactures here, consumed Chinese food, and studied how to penetrate further the China market. Europeans themselves at that stage had fewer manufactures of interest to the Asians, but an intriguing insight is provided by a list of 140 European artworks, in the form of engravings sold in the Patani marketplace by that first Dutch voyage in 1602.[59] Many of them were representations of popular biblical stories, or famous events from classical or Dutch history. In the marketplace of Patani in those days, cultural encounters of world-historical significance were taking place, between the world's civilizations and religions.

In Patani, as in Aceh half a century later, female rule was a brilliant constitutional innovation, a tribute to the flexibility and imagination of the key players. The traders, especially the hybridized "Chinese" traders with no hope of return to China, needed a stable and secure base, where their property could be secure. The Kings of maritime states of the region, whether Muslim or Buddhist, were not inclined to acknowledge restraints to the new money and power that came their way through trade. As males in the gendered pattern of early modern Southeast Asia, they were expected to be concerned with maximizing their status, not the "women's business" of money. Foreign traders knew very well the commercial advantages of acquiring a local wife, since marketing and finance was largely in female hands. Placing a woman on the throne was a remarkable experiment, but the merchant oligarchs who did this had reason to expect her to be more businesslike and pragmatic than her male predecessors, and this proved to be the case. Raja Ijau loaned money at reasonable interest to the leading merchants including the Europeans, and invested in voyages, but there is no evidence of her having squeezed or expropriated the merchants or seen them as dangerous rivals to her own authority.

---

[59] J.W. Ijzerman, "Hollandse Prenten als Handelsartikelen te Patani in 1602," in the KITLV's *Gedenkschrift uigegeven ter gelegenheid van het 75-jarig bestaan* ('s-Gravenhage: Nijhoff, 1926).

Southeast Asian kingship needed a new constitutional framework within which the new mercantile wealth could be accommodated. Islamic sultanates were new, and had merits over their Indic predecessors in a certain inherent cosmopolitanism that recognized an Islamic ecumene of states. But the strongest of them quickly developed into "gunpowder empires," breaking all conventions in the personal accumulation of arbitrary power. Female rule represented a new constitutionalism. When historians begin to write Southeast Asian history as they have European, as a long struggle to expand the rights of citizens, they will see these queens as a very important indigenous experiment. It was successful enough to be repeated in Patani over more than a century, and to be emulated in Aceh, the biggest Archipelago port to escape Dutch control through the 17th century.

APPENDIX

Jacob van Neck's account of Patani in 1602,[60] translated by Anthony Reid

[222] The city of Patani lies on the Siam Sea, at 7 degrees north of latitude and 149 degrees of longitude, between Malaca and the mighty kingdom of Siam, which lies to the north and Malaca to the south. This city is the capital of the kingdom, which therefore takes its name, as does the ruler, as is the case with almost all the surrounding countries and islands, who follow this practice. The city lies close by the sea for about a half-mile in length, without a port where ships may berth. The closest anchorage is less than a mile from the city, in four fathoms of water, with a muddy bottom. This place is built from wood and reeds, as in most of the surrounding countries, inexpensive, airy, and suitable for the heat of the sun. The place where the king [sic] has his palace, and where the most powerful people of the city live, is surrounded by a high palisade of tightly joined posts. The principal church or *muskita*, as they call it, was very neatly constructed by

---

[60] Although published in part in early collections such as that of Comenius (1646), a reliable modern edition of van Neck's account had to wait for the Linschoten Vereeniging edition, *De Vierde Schipvaart der Nederlanders naar Oost-Indie onder Jacob Wilkens en Jacob van Neck (1599–1604)*, ed. Jhr H.A. van Foreest and A. de Booy, Vol. I (The Hague: Martinus Nijhoff, 1980). The translated passage, embracing the description of Patani, is at pages 222–31. Only fragments have previously been translated into English.

Chinese workers from red bricks.[61] The king's [*sic*] dwelling is more elegant than that of the other nobles, worked with gold panels and other carved woodwork.

The people of this country are between black and white in color, not unpleasant, loose of limb, very proud of bearing, magnificent and making much of themselves, especially those of standing. They go out accompanied by many servants and slaves; they are friendly and familiar in conversation, with foreigners as among themselves; in their clothes not very extravagant. Their daily practice is to sit among their women and amuse them. If any of their acquaintance comes to visit, they receive them in a friendly way and arrange a place for them to sit in the entryway of the house. They do not allow anyone to come among their women. They regale those who visit them with betel and areca.[62] For that they have beautiful, well-made boxes, of which all its little dishes and equipment are of fine gold, sometimes silver, or the lesser of copper. Each according to his state, but in every case the entertainment is betel.

The ordinary people here go to sea often, and indeed are skilled in few other trades, even agriculture which they engage in. They know nothing of handicrafts, and if something of fine workmanship is made, that is from the people of China. This nation I consider to be as numerous in the city as the inhabitants themselves, [223] as traders, craftsmen and laborers. They are very eager to earn something, and they spare no difficulty, labor, nor falsehood, thievery or any vile thing to make some money. Most of the commerce here is done by them, and the greatest wealth is found among them. There are whole districts which belong to them, and they are among the most influential with the King [*sic*]. Their language is as common here as the language of the country, but there are in this city (besides many other languages) three very common languages, namely Malay (as native), Siamese, and also Chinese.

These three languages are so different that each has nothing in common with the others, and especially in the writing. The Malays, or the people of Patani, write like the Hebrews, or Arabs, beginning from the right side and ending where we begin; those of Siam as people of Europe, with the letters

---

[61] The Krue Se mosque, all that remains today of the 17th-century capital, east of the modern city. *Muskita* is from Portuguese *mesquita*, very likely more current at the time in the polyglot port than Arabic *masjid*.

[62] The *sirih* (leaf) and *pinang* (nut) combination, chewed together with lime to form a mild stimulant.

almost Roman; those of China begin on the right side, and the line goes down under that. These differences are astonishing since the countries are so close to one another.

These three nations are also very different in belief; those of China and Siam are all heathens, great idolators, not of one mind but of various sects; they have their temples there in the city decorated with golden idols to which they sacrifice in various ways. They have also a great many priests (*papen*),[63] especially those of Siam, who are always dressed in yellow. Those of China have young men who prophesy, which is accompanied with many superstitious ceremonies.[64] They constantly sit on the ground in great numbers, some distance from the idol, and have a high regard for the prophesying young man, who with unbound hair (which they wear long like women in our country) hanging over his eyes, lies down before the mute image, like one who is in ecstasy. Meanwhile all those who stand around play along. The one who will prophesy then lifts himself up from the ground, like a man who is possessed by an angry ghost, and flies hither and thither with a distracted look and a bloody sword in the hand, as if he wanted to destroy himself and all those around. Those who lay on the ground with great devotion, beseech the young man to tell them what is desired by the dead; he then at last comes to himself after a long period of frenzy, and tells them what the gods have revealed.

When we were in Patani and a religious ritual of this kind took place, they were warned that they should leave, because a great fire would come [224] which would destroy all their houses. They were obedient to their gods, and sailed away from the place, though no fire had damaged them. The superstitious idolatry of these people and many other nations who frequent the place, would take too long to explain; also we have not been able to perceive the basic drift of their sects, since we do not understand their strange languages.

As regards the people of Patani, who follow the Mohammedan faith and have many women, both concubines and wives, as the Mahommedan practice is; they nevertheless have very strict laws about adultery, for it is punished by death, especially among the most powerful, and the execution is carried out by the father himself, so long as he is still alive and in good

---

[63] The Protestant Reformation and the long struggle against Spain had made the Pope (*paap*, or plural *papen*) the popular epitome of false religion, so that Dutch writers regularly called Hindu or Buddhist priests *papen*.
[64] These are presumably spirit mediums in the tradition of Chinese popular religion.

health, otherwise by his closest friend. This happened while we were in Patani with two of the principal *menteri* [ministers] of the kingdom, whose son and daughter had committed adultery. The woman in question was married to a son of the *Syabandar* [minister for the port], who came to know of it through an old woman, who had carried to his son's wife as a present some small cups made of gold (which they use to eat betel from). When he had caught her in this and by threatening her had come to know what had taken place, he then informed the father of the daughter, who immediately summoned his daughter to him. Once she had acknowledged the misdeed, he gathered all his friends, and brought the woman there with much ceremony and tears of farewell. That done, the father strangled her with his own hands, which was the death that she had chosen, for the custom is that she is given the choice of what manner of death she will suffer. Many ask to be stabbed, while some while we were there were killed by shooting, and they are free to choose whether they will receive the fatal wound in the breast or the throat. As for the young nobleman who had committed adultery with her, he at first concealed himself but was eventually found, and with similar ceremony was stabbed by his own father (who is one of the greatest men there). This good man was still mourning this event with great grief when I took leave of him before my departure.

Cruel punishments like this are imposed in this country for adultery, but it happens there often nevertheless, since the women are very unchaste.

As for the unmarried women, they have great freedom, [225] for no penalties are imposed on their business, no enquiry is made into it, nor is it in the least regarded as immodesty. It is a custom in Patani that when foreigners come there from other lands to do their business, or to conduct trade, men come and ask them whether they do not desire a woman; these young women and girls also come and present themselves, from whom they may choose the one most agreeable to them, provided they agree what he shall pay for certain months. Once they agree about the money (which does not amount to much for so great a convenience), she comes to his house, and serves him by day as his maidservant and by night as his wedded wife. He is then not able to consort with other women or he will be in grave trouble with his wife, while she is similarly wholly forbidden relations with other men, but the marriage lasts as long as he keeps his residence there, in good peace and unity. When he wants to depart he gives her whatever is promised, and so they leave each other in friendship, and she may then look for another man as she wishes, in all propriety, without scandal.

As regards those who are not satisfied with few women, they have the convenience in almost all parts of the city, where the greatest nobles allow those of their female slaves who are suited for it to ply their trade for money, provided that they yield a profit. But this type of whoring is held in contempt, and is not indulged in by the people of consequence, who consequently have such a surfeit of women in their houses.

In this city there are Chinese traders who have married wives and acquired children there. The same is the case in Chinceo [Quanzhou],[65] from which they mostly come and to which they go back and forth, so that wherever they come they find house, wife and children. The people from Siam are also burdened with many wives; they are exceedingly inclined to wantonness. They carry gold bells beneath the skin of their manhood, some one, others two, some three, each one being about as big as a small cat-bell [*caetsbal*], and very sweet of sound, although that appears rather incredible. Nevertheless I have seen this myself with various men, having not wished otherwise to speak of such a strange thing. [226] If one asks these people what purpose these bells serve, they say that those who are not thus equipped with bells and want to consort with women, will not enjoy the opportunity to copulate, and moreover the women obtain inexpressible pleasure from it. They tell of weird and strange things there, which out of modesty I will refrain from relating. The Mahometans consider these bells as a thing against nature; so that this is practiced only by the heathens, by nobles as well as commoners, yes even the Queen herself.

This land of Patani is ruled by a woman, who remained Queen after the death of the King, her husband, and has reigned very peacefully with her counselors (whom they call *menteri*) for 13 to 15 years, so that all the subjects consider her government better than that of the dead king. For all necessities are very cheap here now, whereas in the king's time (so they say) they were dearer by half, because of the great exactions which then occurred. This queen is about 50 years old; she always stays in her palace among her women, whom she has in large number. Many of these because they are in the service of the queen may not marry, but may sleep with whoever they please. Others are given in marriage to those who request them, if the queen gives permission. One sees these women very seldom and only when they go out to amuse themselves, which happens only once every two or three years, though it happened twice while we were there. We were told (when this was going to happen) the Queen would be particularly pleased if we along with

---

[65] Quanzhou, or in older English spellings Chinchew, in southern Fujian, was China's leading port in the Song and Yuan dynasties, labeled Zayton by Marco Polo. In the 17th century, it was eclipsed by Amoy (Xiamen) to its north.

others accompanied her, which also happened. She went out accompanied by all the lords of the land, with 4 or 5,000 armed men, who spread out behind her in troops all over the riverbanks, and with fully 150 elephants, some of which were equipped for battle, others carrying the weapons of deceased kings, and most a crowd of the Queen's women. [227] She herself sat on a large elephant, that was all royally equipped. When she arrived at the appointed place, she called us to her, and bid us sit down at some distance from her (as their custom is), while food and drink were provided.

After this we once went out with her by water, up the river. She was accompanied by a great many oared vessels, and had us informed that we should not stay back but should go with her. Once everyone had arrived at the place they intended to stay the night, they had us come to her, right next to her galley, which was fitted out in a very pretty and elegant manner. She spoke with us in a friendly way, asking when we intended to depart, and she said that next time we came to the Indies we should not sail past Patani, because we would always (as on this occasion) be received and entertained well there. Also that the reason she had not invited us regularly to court to amuse us there was only that this would not be appropriate for her (as a woman). After we had thanked her for her good disposition toward us, she had our barge provided with a superfluity of banquet and all kinds of food, and we asked leave to sail back to the city to continue our journey, which was our settled intention. After that she traveled further up the river, and it was 20 days before she returned to the city. I will leave at that the description of the manners and customs of this unmanned nation, with their Queen Pratiau[66] (which is her name), although (to avoid long-windedness) I have not told a tenth of it, and say a little about the potential of the country.

This country has a great abundance of produce, and very good and agreeable air, although it lies rather close to the equator, and is consequently rather subject to the great heat of the sun, but you should know that for a good eight months, from February to the end of October, there are winds off the sea around midday and off the land at night, with an enviably cool and fair weather. Moreover the months of November, December and January are their winter when it rains steadily, with a very strong northeast wind, so that no one puts to sea until February. Then the winds begin to blow from the east, and the rains to cease [228] and it is again summer, so that the fruits begin to ripen, because it is richly endowed through the fertility of the soil, which they till and plough with buffalos and oxen, and sow with rice, as

---

[66] This was in fact her Siamese title, *Phra Chao*.

people do in our country with wheat and rye. This rice is also very abundant and cheap there, so that it is exported to various places. As for Indian fruits, this place is as richly endowed as any country in India, for it has a new fruit every month of the whole year, each more delicious than the last.

Turning to their daily foods like meat and fish, they are numerous there. Oxen, bulls, buffaloes, *cabrito* [goats; Portuguese] are numerous there, and chickens so abundant that they are exported from there in thousands without their appearing to be any fewer. There are also geese and ducks so prolific that they lay their eggs twice within one night and day. The woods are full of game, such as wild bulls, wild pigs, deer, hares, wild fowl, white herons and turtledoves. With these the fields are plentifully spread, some so beautifully feathered that they exceed the parrots. There are also quails, and still more birds unknown to us, but little of all this game is caught because of the indolence of the inhabitants. The most destructive beasts there are tigers, and apes or long-tailed monkeys; the former cause great losses to the villagers in their cattle, and the latter in their fruits. The wild elephants which are numerous there stay off in the wilderness, so they suffer no damage from them. These are captured in the following way: they take a tame elephant, a large strong one, with a man seated on it, and they go off into a grove. If they come across some wild ones, they make the tame one fight against one. Their fighting (as I have seen myself) is by locking their tusks with each other's so that their trunks are wound together, and then putting their strength to work so that one forces the other to fall to the ground. As they stand against each other struggling, some people appointed to the job come and shackle the rear legs of the wild one to each other, which is easily done since he is held so constrained by the tame one (which is a match for him) that he cannot move the legs quickly without falling to the ground. Once he is thus bound, if they want to keep him alive they must tame him through great hunger, so as to bring him out of the wilderness. If they want to kill him, they can bring this about with little difficulty, [229] which happens only for the tusks, which are their value, and are sold to the people from China.

That is enough on the animals. As for the fish, they are very abundant and of various sorts, but none of them like ours either in appearance or taste. There are also crabs and lobsters, turtles, various mussels, shrimps, and many other shellfish. These are all caught here in great quantities, so that almost all the common people can be fed by them. In short, this city lacks little of the things that are necessary for life.

There is such a great trade done here as in no other city in the vicinity. Those of Melaka and Bengal bring their cloths and clothing, those of Java sandalwood, those of Borneo slaves, camphor, sago, wax and *lapis besar*,[67] those of Siam gold, rice, salt, lead and Benjamin, those of Champa or Cambodia bring their slaves, calves and the valuable wood *calamba*, the best in the world; the people of China come every year with many kinds of merchandise, they bring white and yellow raw silk, also velvet, damask, and other silkwork of various colors, porcelain in quantity, iron, copper, and various peddlers' wares which people in these countries need, and from Japan they come also every year bringing Japanese swords, costly woodwork, which those from China buy, also copper and other small things. Besides these foreign nations that come from those places in their ships, those of Patani themselves trade in various directions; they sail to Banda and Cambodia for nutmeg, mace and cloves, to Timor for sandalwood, to Jambi and Indragiri for pepper, which they bring back on their return, also from Kampar, Johor, Pahang, Bordelong [Phatthalung] and Ligor [Nakhon Sithammarat], [230] places lying in the vicinity of about 130 miles, and they also travel to all the surrounding countries, except China, where no foreigners may go.

Since I have explained what goods are brought to Patani, I will now relate where these goods are sent. Those from Johor and Pahang take back rice, salt, oxen, chickens and other foodstuffs; those of Melaka the same, but also Benjamin, *lapis besar* and tortoiseshell, those of Borneo iron, steel and copper, those of Siam cloth and bad pepper, those of China fine pepper, camphor, yellow and white sandalwood, hides, elephant tusks, wax, buffalo horns, and other small things, those of Japan deerskins, lead, and roe skins[68] which are so desired they sell dear there; they also buy silk that the Chinese bring.

In these ways trade is conducted in Patani, which would make it the most suitable place in East India for our country to trade with all the nations of the whole Orient, if Dutch merchandise was in demand there. But these goods are bought by nobody there, except the people of Siam and that very modestly, which in the end is the reason that silver will fall to a low price there (as in many places in India), and the trade will fall almost to nothing, while those from other countries will forcefully increase, and especially the people of China, which is nearby, and whose merchandise is cheaper there than in China itself. For even if our nation had the freedom to trade there, they would have to pay such heavy tolls which the inhabitants themselves

---

[67] Malay, literally "big layer," here evidently referring to something in thick sheets.
[68] Roe (Dutch *rogge*) is a small species of deer, the skin of which was particularly sought in 17th-century Japan.

would not, that we would find it more profitable to buy the wares in Patani than there. Moreover other countries would also be eager then to bring in their goods, for in Siam indigo grows in such abundance that whole ships could be loaded with it and at a low price, but they can still not dry it, so that when it is in demand they must take it by hand.

Those of Borneo and Pegu, nearby countries, bring their precious stones, and each year [231] will be able to provide seven or eight hundred *last*[69] of pepper.

Not much pepper is grown in Patani, but it is brought in from the surrounding places; the pepper of Patani is, after that of Kedah, the finest in India, but there is each year no more than 60, or 70 *last*; but since we began to sail there, they have planted out many times that, so that undoubtedly within three or four years the harvest will be much increased.

---

[69] One *last* is roughly two metric tons.

Gates, Elephants, Cannon and Drums: Symbols and Sounds in the Creation of a Patani Identity

Barbara Watson Andaya

The ongoing conflict in southern Thailand has spawned increased interest in the historical processes by which a sense of being "Malay/Muslim" as opposed to "Thai/Buddhist" developed in the contemporary provinces of Yala, Narathiwat, Satun and especially Pattani. Because these processes have been analyzed primarily in terms of the relationship between Patani and the Siamese (later Thai) state, discussions about a growing sense of "Malayness" have focused on Patani resistance to the assertion of Thai authority. This tendency, however, has raised questions about the extent to which the people of Patani felt themselves to be "Malay" in premodern times; it has recently been argued, for instance, that the juxtaposition of "Malay" versus "Thai" has only assumed prominence over the last hundred years.[1]

Although it would certainly be misleading to apply contemporary understandings of ethnicity to Patani's earlier history, this chapter contends that a sense of "Patani-ness" can still be detected in pre-19th-century sources.[2] While acknowledging the depth of oral memory in the Patani region, it draws primarily on the *Hikayat Patani*, approaching the text as a "site of memory," a record of the participatory experiences that contributed

---

[1] Michael J Montesano and Patrick Jory, "Introduction," in *Thai South and Malay North: Ethnic Interactions on a Plural Peninsula*, ed. Michael J. Montesano and Patrick Jory (Singapore: NUS Press, 2008), p. 8.

[2] See Chuleeporn Virunha, "Historical Perceptions of Local Identity in the Upper Peninsula," in *Thai South and Malay North*, ed. Montesano and Jory, pp. 52, 67.

to group cohesion.[3] The memories of these experiences — at once plural, collective, and individual — were intimately connected to places, objects and sounds that communicated compelling messages about the relationship between locality and ancestral origins.[4]

People and Place, Symbols and Sound

The phrase "*orang Melayu*" (Malay people) occurs relatively rarely in court chronicles, but the customary coupling of "*orang*" with a place, a *negeri*, be it Siak, Pahang, Kedah, Johor, or Patani, testifies to the self-conscious relationship between locality and community.[5] Despite its central position in the Malay *imaginaire*, historians have long encountered difficulties in identifying an appropriate English term for *negeri* and its more courtly form, *negara* (both introduced into Malay via Sanskrit). In appreciating a sense of "*negeri*-ness" as manifested in the *Hikayat Patani*, it is therefore useful to consider the association between spiritual forces and a specific locality as they have been described in other areas of Southeast Asia. Among the Chams, for example, certain objects regarded as manifestations of the soil deity apparently generated a cult of propitiation that formed the basis for a communal polity. A recent study of Laos similarly contends that the "power of place" is vitalized through a community's memory of noteworthy events attached to a particularly territorial domain.[6] Accordingly, while the *Hikayat Patani* contains no specific assertion of being "Malay," it does convey a strong

---

[3] A Teeuw and D.K. Wyatt, eds., *Hikayat Patani: The Story of Patani* (Nijhoff: The Hague, 1970), 2 vols. For references to oral accounts, see Pierre Le Roux, "*Bedé kaba'* ou les derniers canons de Patani," *Bulletin de l'École Française d'Extrême-Orient* 85, 1 (1998): 125–62. Ibrahim Syukri, *Sejarah Kerajaan Melayu Patani* [*History of the Malay Kingdom of Patani*] (Bangi: Universiti Kebangsaan Malaysia, 2002), p. 13.

[4] Pierre Nora, "Between Memory and History: *Les Lieux de Mémoire*," *Representations* 26, Special Issue: Memory and Counter-Memory (Spring 1989): 9.

[5] I wish to acknowledge the invaluable access to Malay texts offered by the Malay Concordance Project, begun by Dr. Ian Proudfoot of the Australian National University.

[6] Paul Mus, *Cultes indiens et indigenes au Champa, l'Inde vue de l'Est* (Hanoi: Imprimerie de l'Extrême-Orient, 1934). Ian Mabbett and David Chandler, trans., "India Seen from the East," Monash Papers on Southeast Asia, Clayton, Victoria, 1975, pp. 11–2, 15, 23; John Clifford Holt, *Spirits of the Place: Buddhism and Lao Religious Culture* (Honolulu: University of Hawai'i Press, 2009), pp. 21–53, especially 24–5; Virunha, "Historical Perceptions," p. 67.

connectivity with a place, "our country" — *negeri kita*, as one ruler puts it.[7] In recounting "a story told (*diceterakan*) by old people about the origins of the *raja* who established the *negeri* of Patani, the Abode of Peace" — the opening episode vehemently asserts the interlocking links between community, ruler, and locality.

The explicit reference to oral transmission contained in the word *diceterakan* is a reminder that this "text" was never intended to be perused silently but was recited in public presentations where the intent was to instruct, inform and recall as well as entertain. The contemporary scholar is thus faced with the impossible task of resuscitating the aural context in which such works operated as well as the complicated interaction between visual images, symbolic representation and spoken words. Does the English rendering of *gilang gemilang* as "luminous sheen," for instance, adequately convey the way in which written Malay uses assonance and alliteration to project a visual image of glint and sparkle? As yet we have no Southeast Asian equivalent to Richard Rath's study of the sonic environment of early America, but Malay material offers a promising field for exploring the notion that premodern societies sensed the world more through their ears that we do today.[8] Furthermore, although noises such as a clap of thunder, the trumpeting of an elephant, or the firing of a cannon, may "sound" more or less the same today as they did in 18th-century Patani, we do not hear them in the same way as did the audiences of this text. In other words, attitudes and beliefs about sounds have changed, and while many have been lost, or can only be partially recovered, even those that have retained acoustic permanency no longer inform the lives of modern Malays or Thais as they did in the past. The perception of thunder as supernatural speech alerting the community to the perpetration of some immoral act, for example, has a long history in Southeast Asian societies but has now largely disappeared.[9] Yet thunder provided the benchmark and the basis of comparison for awe-inspiring sounds. Drums, *serunai* and *nafiri* (types of oboe) should be played so loudly that they sounded like thunder; a crowd of people acclaiming their ruler shout like rolling thunder; the noise of thunder is replicated

---

[7] Teeuw and Wyatt, eds., *Hikayat Patani*, pp. 85, 160.

[8] Richard Cullen Rath, *How Early America Sounded* (Ithaca, NY and London: Cornell University Press, 2003), p. 174.

[9] Rath, *How Early America Sounded*, p. 174. For anthropological perspectives on attitudes to thunder in the Malay world, see Marina Roseman, *Healing Sounds from the Malaysian Rainforest: Temiar Music and Medicine* (Berkeley: University of California Press, 1991), pp. 137, 146.

in the firing of cannon.[10] Particularly relevant is Rath's argument that in the premodern soundscape, noises of many kinds could often function "as embodied acts of identity," helping to define the community's cultural parameters by drawing elite and commoner together.[11]

Pintu Gajah: "The Power of Place"

In the *Hikayat Patani*, the way in which a people's memory could so infuse a specific place that it became a node of cultural orientation is nicely illustrated by the sights and sounds associated with the Elephant Gate, the Pintu Gajah. Like most Southeast Asian centers, the complex of buildings associated with the ruler and the "aristocratic core," the *kota raja*, was surrounded by a wall of thick wooden beams, as described in 1601 by the first Dutch traders.[12] The most prominent feature was the two entrance gates. In the western wall, the main gate, the Pintu Gerbang, is even mentioned in the classic Malay text, *Hikayat Hang Tuah*, and was said to be carved with a *naga*, a serpent, representing the sun.[13] On the eastern side was the Elephant Gate, the Pintu Gajah, a name apparently unique to Patani that is usually explained by the nearby stabling of the royal elephants. Nonetheless, the tissue of folklore, legend and religious traditions through which outside influences and local ideas percolated presents other possibilities. For example, in many cultures it was common for gates to be guarded by statues of animals, and the Pintu Gajah may have displayed some representation of an elephant, in the same fashion as the *naga* of the Pintu Gerbang. The pairing would be

---

[10] For example, A.H. Hill, "Hikayat Raja-Raja Pasai," *Journal of the Malaysian Branch of the Royal Asiatic Society* 33, 2 (1960): 82, 142; 104, 163; 68, 129.

[11] Rath, *How Early America Sounded*, pp. 7, 61, 174–5. See further: Barbara Watson Andaya, "Distant Drums and Thunderous Cannon: Affirming Identity and Sounding Authority in Traditional Malay Society," *International Journal of Asian and Pacific Studies* 7, 2 (July 2011): 19–35.

[12] H.A. van Foreest and A. de Booy, eds., *De Vierde Schipvaart der Nederlanders naar Oost-Indië onder Jacob Wilkens en Jacob van Neck (1599–1604)* (The Hague: Linschoten Vereeniging, 1980), 1: 222, 258; Wayne A. Bougas, "Patani in the Beginning of the XVIIth Century," *Archipel* 39 (1990): 119–24; Daniel Perret, Amnat Sombatyanuchit and Siriporn Limwijitwong, "Sites fortifiés du cours inférieur due fleuve Pattani," in *Études sur l'histoire du sultanat de Patani*, ed. Daniel Perret, Amnat Sombatyanuchit and Siriporn Limwijitwong (Paris: EFEO, 2004), p. 87.

[13] Kassim Ahmad, ed., *Hikayat Hang Tuah* (Kuala Lumpur: Dewan Bahasa dan Pustaka, 1975), pp. 416–7.

quite appropriate since elephants, like the *naga*, are associated with symbols of fertility, in this case clouds and monsoon rain. Associations may have been even more localized, for in the past certain Malay sites were thought to be the domain of *gajah keramat*, supernatural and ghostly elephants who could also act as the guardian spirit of a particular shrine.[14] Or we may simply be talking about a gate that was specifically constructed to allow an elephant and rider to pass through comfortably.

Whatever the reasons behind the designation "Pintu Gajah," in all human societies, gates are heavy with symbolic meaning, representing points at which friends and foes are identified and occupying a prominent place in royal ceremonial and religious ritual. Within the *Hikayat Patani*, both the Pintu Gerbang and the Pintu Gajah play a significant role in maintaining the distinction between "*orang Patani*" and people from other *negeri*, such as Kelantan, Aceh, and Pegu.[15] A careful reading suggests that the Pintu Gajah was particularly associated with legends and events that made it a nexus of concentrated power, a centerpoint of *negeri*-ness, since it had been constructed on the very site where the community was thought to have its origins. According to Patani legend, the founder-king, mounted on his elephant, goes hunting by the shore, but without success. Only when he releases his dogs does the "sound of their voices" alert him to the finding of game. His men tell him that the dogs had started up an albino mousedeer (Tragulus javanicus, *pelanduk* or *kancil*) as large as a goat with a body that glinted and sparkled. It had been chased as far as the beach, where it suddenly vanished into thin air.[16]

Although the motif of a mousedeer whose appearance helps determine the location of a capital recurs in other Malay histories, the associated details always display local variations. A text from Sumatra, for instance, describes how the barking dog and the mousedeer embrace each other; in the Melaka version, a white mousedeer demonstrates his courage by kicking the much larger dog; by contrast, the Patani *pelanduk* simply runs away and disappears from sight. However, its unusual size and glittering white coat provided clear

---

[14] W.W. Skeat, *Malay Magic* (New York: Dover, 1967, reprint of 1900 edition), p. 153.

[15] It is significant that in 1641 the Patani queen delayed an audience with a Dutch envoy because the main gate to her compound had fallen down and had to be repaired. H.T. Colenbrander, ed., *Dagh-Register gehouden int Casteel Batavia vant passerende daer ter plaetse als over geheel Nederlandts-India Anno 1641–1642* (The Hague: Nijhoff, 1900), p. 154.

[16] Teeuw and Wyatt, eds., *Hikayat Patani*, pp. 69–70, 146–8.

evidence of its supernatural qualities. Not only are normal mousedeer about as small as a cat; they are typically brown in color, and any albino, human or animal, was popularly attributed with magical powers.[17] In addition, the *pelanduk* episode would have reverberated with other "established patterns of meaning" underlying Malay culture.[18] Over the centuries, the mythology that emphasized the mousedeer's cunning sagacity had absorbed many influences from outside, including Islamic credentials. In a context where Patani was faced with increasing demands from its overlord Ayutthaya, the oft-told story of how the white mousedeer (the Wise Syeikh of the Jungle) successfully overcame stronger jungle animals, notably the lion and elephant, to establish his own kingdom must have been intensely relevant.[19] The *Hikayat Patani* records that the new settlement, Patani Darussalam, the Abode of Peace, was established on the site spot where the *pelanduk* had so mysteriously vanished, with a landing stage known as Jambatan Kedi leading to the Elephant Gate.[20]

The Elephant Gate also appears to have had a particular link to the Patani rulers, for it adjoined a Muslim religious building and a cemetery where members of the royal family were buried, and adjoined the pavilion containing the great drum from which emanated the beat of royal authority.[21] Simultaneously, however, the Elephant Gate and the Jambatan Kedi stood as silent spectators of the heinous crimes of *derhaka* — regicide and rebellion — that had been played out in the vicinity.[22] Infused with the vibrations of the ancestral past, the Pintu Gajah acted as a cultural prompter, a historical prop for the mental re-enactment of events demonstrating that kings and queens were still subject to God's ordinance. For instance, the *Hikayat Patani* records that a Minangkabau trader renowned as an Islamic teacher and his pupil-assistant were put to death at the Elephant Gate because they had flouted the ruler's orders and illegally sold copper intended to build a cannon. It was the will of Allah, however, that their corpses did not sink, but for three days stood upright in the water, drifting back and forth so that they appeared to be walking. Though the bodies were finally removed for burial, again "by the will of Allah," they began to lengthen and their extraordinary height thus required elongated burial plots. Still today in

---

[17] Skeat, *Malay Magic*, p. 51.

[18] Graham Allen, *Intertextuality* (London and New York: Routledge, 2000), p. 18.

[19] C.A. Mees, ed., trans., *Hikayat Pelanduk Jinaka* (Santpoort: C.A. Mees, 1929).

[20] Teeuw and Wyatt, *Hikayat Patani*, pp. 70, 148.

[21] Ibid., pp. 97, 100, 109, 170, 172, 181.

[22] Ibid., pp. 96, 101, 170, 174.

a village at the end of Patani Bay, the tombs of two "giants" remain a *keramat* site of popular veneration.[23]

Elephants

Like places, objects could also be saturated with an accumulation of cultural and symbolic memories that infused them with a social agency which, argues Alfred Gell, could be "exercised by things (and also animals)."[24] As cultural agents in their own right, the paraphernalia of royalty in premodern societies was never regarded as the personal possession of individual kings or queens. Because these objects — unusual animals, images, daggers, religious texts, musical instruments — embodied protective powers, they were directly linked to the welfare of the people at large. Their existence not only fostered a general sense of security but inculcated a sense of identity that helped infuse a community with self-perceptions of coherence and uniqueness. Nonetheless, the very tangibility of these sacral objects made them vulnerable to destruction or loss, while capture by some enemy meant that the power vested in them would be transferred to another presumably hostile individual and his/her associated group.

The place of elephants in the *Hikayat Patani* can be profitably discussed within this framework. We can reasonably assume that elephant mythology in Southeast Asia developed in very ancient times, but it is evident that these ideas were reinforced by Indian influence. Because of their size, color and shape, elephants were often compared to clouds, and thus popularly associated with the onset of monsoon rains, and fertility itself. The association between elephants and the gods in Hindu traditions also finds its counterpart in Buddhism. According to the Buddhist Birth-stories, the Buddha had once been born as an elephant; indeed, before giving birth, the mother of the historic Buddha dreamed that a white elephant entered her womb, which made the finding of such animals an extraordinarily auspicious event.[25] Although the symbolism of elephants in the Malay world has yet to be thoroughly explored, they are given a prominent place in most texts, including localized Islamic traditions. Despite their unlikely appearance

---

[23] Ibid., pp. 76, 153; Syukri, *Sejarah Kerajaan Melayu Patani*, p. 55; Le Roux, "*Bedé kaba'*," pp. 147–8.

[24] Alfred Gell, *Art and Agency: An Anthropological Theory* (Oxford: Oxford University Press, 1998), pp. 17–8.

[25] S.K. Gupta, *Elephant in Indian Art and Mythology* (New Delhi: Abhinav 1983), pp. 20, 31, 36ff.

in an Arabian environment, for instance, elephants in their hundreds are included in the armies of the Prophet's uncle Amir Hamzah as he battles in defense of the faith.[26] A person of high status virtually always rode on a splendidly decorated elephant, and in 1602 the Dutch in Patani were greeted ceremonially by the Queen accompanied by 4,000 armed men and 150 elephants, with many magnificently caparisoned.[27]

In the *Hikayat Patani*, the relationship between rulers and the beasts they ride is often depicted as a metaphor for the ordering of social status and royal hierarchy. Sultan Bahadur, the youngest child of Sultan Mansur, rides on the shoulders of his attendants, Wan Jajarullah and Alung In as he would elephants.[28] His father even gives him a golden elephant goad with which he strikes his human mounts, sometimes drawing blood. Though the two men are rewarded with gifts of cloth, the text conveys a clear message that this was not appropriate behavior. Furthermore, other courtiers are concerned about Sultan Bahadur's age, and some influential nobles believe that Raja Bima, Sultan Mansur Syah's son by a secondary wife, would be a more suitable successor. On one occasion, after Sultan Bahadur's installation as ruler, he passes Raja Bima's residence while riding on his elephant Seri Negeri, a title that could hardly have been chosen lightly. Raja Bima joins the convoy on foot, but Sultan Bahadur's mahout, Wan Jaharullah suggests that he should join his brother and mount another royal elephant, Jarum Perak ("Silver Needle," or possible "Needle from [the state of] Perak"). On seeing his brother riding Jarum Perak, Sultan Bahadur is clearly infuriated. He "pushes Wan Jaharullah with his foot," ordering him to tell Raja Bima to dismount. Weeping at this public humiliation, Raja Bima obeys but seeks support to usurp the throne. On Friday, after the drum for the morning prayers has been sounded, Raja Bima rides into the royal compound on his own elephant and kills Sultan Bahadur. As he returns, however, Raja Bima is in turn stabbed by one of his trusted associates, and falls from his elephant to the ground. When his eldest sister, Raja Ijau, succeeds to the throne she

---

[26] A. Samad Ahmad, ed., *Hikayat Amir Hamah* (Kuala Lumpur: Dewan Bahasa dan Pustaka, 1987), pp. 226, 628, 630.

[27] H. Terpstra, *De Factorij der Oostindische Compagnie te Patani*, Verhandelingen van het Koninklijk Instituut voor de Taal-, Land- en Volkenkunde van Nederlandsch-Indië 1 (The Hague: Nijhoff, 1938), p. 8; van Foreest and de Booy, eds., *De Vierde Schipvaart*, pp. 226–7, 258.

[28] The image of a boy riding an elephant conjures up descriptions of the elephant Bujang Sekalis and his boy rider, founder of a dynasty, in the *Hikayat Raja Pasai*. Hill, "Hikayat Raja-Raja Pasai," p. 111.

installs Wan Jajarullah and Alung In, the two elephant specialists, as senior court officials in apparent recompense for their past service.[29]

The *Hikayat Patani* is by no means alone recording that those who were skilled in attending to animals were accorded great respect. The *Sejarah Melayu*, for example, records that one ruler customarily sent his young courtiers to study "*ilmu gajah*" the science of elephants, with experts.[30] In an obviously inserted section, the *Hikayat Patani* proudly traces the origins of the Bendahara line to a royal "elephant doctor" (*mau gajah*) who founds a new *negeri*, and similar stories of "elephant doctor" founder figures are found among other communities in southern Thailand (notably Nakhon Si Thammarat or Ligor), and among Thai villages in Kelantan.[31] These stories encode important messages about the capacity of certain individuals (in this case evidenced by their ability to tame elephants) to ensure fertility, prosperity, and communal well-being. By the same token, specific elephants could be credited with extraordinary qualities because they were thought to have contributed to success in battle, or were associated with some momentous event. Like other "objects," they could embody the memories of a people's collective experience. The female elephant Jarum Perak plays a key role in the defense of Patani against a besieging Siamese force because her trumpeting tricks the Siamese army into believing that Patani is defended by an army of elephants.[32]

The episode in which Seri Negeri is involved in a "status battle" between Sultan Bahadur and his half-brother Raja Bima can be usefully juxtaposed with the actions of a previous ruler, possibly Sultan Bahadur's uncle. The *Hikayat Patani* describes a failed coup attempt by the Patani ruler, Sultan Muzaffar, in Ayutthaya, but additional details are supplied by the royal chronicles of Siam. The Phraya of Tani, we are told, had contributed forces to the Thai campaign against the Burmese, but while in Ayutthaya he rebelled, "and led all of the Tani men into the royal palace. After they managed to enter the royal palace, he brought out a white elephant to mount and it stood in the middle of the palace plaza. Then he descended from the elephant and

---

[29] The trusted court official who kills Raja Bima, is himself later put to death with the Queen's implicit order; Teeuw and Wyatt, *Hikayat Patani*, pp. 91, 95, 97–8, 104, 163, 169, 171, 176.

[30] Brown, *Sejarah Melayu*, p. 94.

[31] Barbara Watson Andaya, *Perak: The Abode of Grace: A Study of an Eighteenth Century Malay State* (Kuala Lumpur: Oxford University Press, 1979), pp. 401–3; Teeuw and Wyatt, eds., *Hikayat Patani*, pp. 70, 132, 148, 202, 262–3, 278–9.

[32] Teeuw and Wyatt, eds., *Hikayat Patani*, pp. 109–10, 181.

left the palace. The inhabitants of the capital stretched out large ropes and fought with the Tani men, many of whom died. The Phraya of Tani boarded a junk and was able to escape."[33]

In the first instance, one must ask how this textual version of events might have been interpreted in the Thai context. Presumably for the people of Ayutthaya, as for their Malay counterparts, the sight of a Patani ruler riding a white elephant, the discovery of which had been greeted with universal delight because of its auspicious connotations, was shocking in the extreme. White (albino) elephants were not meant to be ridden except by the World Ruler, the Cakkavatti. Because of the belief that that the Buddha himself had once taken this form, they were to be venerated as a communal treasure, a sign that this historical moment and the king himself were especially favored.[34] One must also ask whether accounts of an action that Thais would have viewed as appalling, desecrating, and flagrantly insolent were ever retold to Patani audiences. If so, would they have recalled the defiant mousedeer of legend, who defeated the lordly elephant, running up the latter's trunk, leaping on to his neck and finally sitting on his head?[35] Would they have seen Sultan Muzaffar's appropriation of the Thai equivalent of an elephant like Seri Negeri, as a deliberate act by which the Patani ruler publicly rejected his vassal status? In adopting Arjun Appadurai's felicitous phrase, a modern historian might see in this episode a "tournament of value," a contest that signified not merely the claims of the actors to status, rank, fame or reputation, but was a profound statement about the "the disposition of central tokens of value" in both Malay and Thai society.[36] It is revealing that still today, in some highland villages in southern Thailand, the story of the mousedeer has survived, though it is now transformed into a "white elephant with black tusks" that appears on the beach and disappears in the forest. Its return is linked to the revival of "Jawi" society, the return of the golden age of the sultanate, and ultimately, after an interregnum of Thai superiority, the triumph of Islam itself.[37]

---

[33] Richard Cushman, trans., and David K. Wyatt, ed., *The Royal Chronicles of Ayutthaya* (Bangkok: The Siam Society, 2000), p. 49.

[34] Frank and Mani Reynolds, *Three Worlds according to King Ruang: A Thai Buddhist Chronology* (Berkeley: Asian Humanities Press, 1982), pp. 160–2.

[35] Mees, *Hikayat Pelanduk Jinaka*, p. 54.

[36] See Arjun Appadurai, "Introduction: Commodities and the Politics of Value," in *The Social Life of Things: Commodities in Cultural Perspective*, ed. Arjun Appadurai (Cambridge: Cambridge University Press, 1988), p. 21.

[37] Pierre Le Roux, "To Be or Not to Be … the Cultural Identity of the Jawi," *Asian Folklore Studies* 57 (1999): 223–55.

Cannon

The last chapter in the *Hikayat Patani* manuscript contains a lengthy description of the valuable "state objects" (*perkakas kerajaan*) that comprised the Patani regalia — the swords, the standards, the spears, all plated or decorated with gold.[38] Scholars have been far more interested, however, in Patani's three cannon because of the details given about their casting, the contrasting role played by Chinese and Turk artisans, and their subsequent capture by the Siamese. European sources add further material, for in 1602 a Dutch report noted that a large cannon, "bigger than any found in Amsterdam" was placed in a prominent position near the port.[39] Such information can be combined with additional insights about the place of cannons in Southeast Asian cultural life. Sometimes placed upright around a palace or fortification, or even reproduced in miniature, their phallic shapes, resonant with ideas of fertility, invoked ancient beliefs in procreative powers.[40] If the spirits who animated these venerated objects were appropriately propitiated, they would ensure that the monsoons came in time and that the harvests flourished. A greatly revered cannon cast under King Narai, for example, was called Phra Pirun, in honor of the Rain God. The belief that its loss would be disastrous is clearly indicated in 1767, when the Burmese approached the walls of Ayutthaya. On this occasion, Phra Phirun was thrown into a lake near the palace in an effort to evade the Burmese invaders, but it was eventually located and blown up. Significantly, its remains were taken back to Burma to contribute to the Burmese storehouse of power. In 1777, after the reconstitution of the kingdom under Taksin, another Phra Phirun was cast and engraved with the inscription "a hundred thousand measures of rain" as a sign "that the kingdom had regained its former greatness."[41]

In island Southeast Asia, we can also locate repeated evidence of the conviction that the destinies of sacralized state "objects" were linked to that

---

[38] Teeuw and Wyatt, eds., *Hikayat Patani*, pp. 141, 211.

[39] J.W. Ijzerman, "Hollandsche Prenten al Handelsartikel te Patani in 1602," *Koninkiljk Instituut voor de Taal-, Land- en Volkenkunde van Nederlandsch-Indië. Gedenkschrift uitgegeven ter gelegenheid van het 75-jarig bestaan op 4 Juni 1926* (The Hague: Koninklijk Instituut, 1926), p. 88.

[40] C.A. Gibson-Hill, "Notes on the Old Cannon Found in Malaya and Known to Have Been of Dutch Origin," *Journal of the Malayan Branch of the Royal Asiatic Society* 26, 1 (1953): 145–71; F.W. Douglas, "The Penang Cannon Si Rambai," *Journal of the Malayan Branch of the Royal Asiatic Society* 21 (1948): 117–8.

[41] C.A. Seymour Sewell, "Notes on Some Old Siamese Guns," *Journal of the Siam Society* 15, 1 (1922): 21–3.

of the community itself, and of the belief that their presence strengthened the country's spiritual power. In communities where superior size and weight indicated spiritual strength, the firing of a cannon was equally a sign of power, a "speech act" that linked their "owners" (the ruler and his/her subjects) to cosmically charged sounds such as thunder. Across Southeast Asia, the titles given to cannon — "Si Jimat (Lord Talisman)," "The Bugis who runs amok," "The Demon that rends and devours," Java's husband and wife "Kyai Satoma" and "Nyai Satomi," "Child of Makassar" — registered their animation by supernatural powers that tied them to legendary individuals, animals, nature, powerful spirits or even entire ethnic groups.[42] Because the representation of the human figure was rare in most of the region's Islamic societies, the anthropomorphic metamorphosis of awe-inspiring objects like cannon into powerful and protective patrons was doubly significant. At their very birth, such sacral but personified objects are set apart from ordinary things and designated for special use because exceptional skills were required to give them life.[43] In the Patani case, although a man from the legendary kingdom of Rum (Istanbul) casts the first cannon, it was too thin to be fired. It was only through the extraordinary powers (*daulat*) possessed by Patani's founder king that the three cannon were cast — Seri Negeri, Tuk (Datuk) Buk and Nang (Lady) Liu-Liu.[44]

The names accorded Patani's cannon are central to the corpus of legends that comprised their biographies. As with Sultan Bahdur's royal elephant, the title "Seri Negeri" is freighted with associations of place and the identity attached to a locale. Simultaneously, however, it was also animated by the spirit of the individual who had caused it to come into being; in other words, its physicality indexed the moment and the primary agent in its manufacture.[45] The great cannon that bears the inscription Phaya Tani,

---

[42] Sewell, "Notes on Some Old Siamese Guns," p. 10.

[43] On this line of thought, see further William H. Davenport, "Two Kinds of Value in the Eastern Solomon Islands," in *The Social Life of Things: Commodities in Cultural Perspective*, ed. Arjun Appadurai (Cambridge: Cambridge University Press, 1988), p. 106.

[44] Teeuw and Wyatt, eds., *Hikayat Patani*, pp. 224–6; Frances R. Bradley, "Moral Order in a Time of Damnation: The *Hikayat Patani* in Historical Context," *Journal of Southeast Asian Studies* 40, 2 (June 2009): 271. Ibrahim Syukri places the casting of Patani's cannon in the reign of the queen Raja Biru, noting that the larger two were called Seri Negara and Seri Patani and the smallest one Maha Lela. Syukri, *Sejarah Kerajaan Melayu Patani*, pp. 55–6.

[45] Gell, *Art and Agency*, pp. 23–4.

captured in 1785 and still standing outside the Ministry of Defense in Bangkok, was said to have been named "Nang Tani," Lady Patani, after the queen who ordered it cast.[46] The personification of cannon as female is not uncommon in Southeast Asia, possibly because they are thought to have an almost sexual relationship with the [normally male] ruler, and a maternal concern for the welfare of those living under her protection. Certainly, the *Hikayat Patani* gives particular attention to the protective powers of Nang Liu-Liu, who was taken to Ayutthaya by Sultan Muzaffar when he went to make a marriage proposal, an appropriate companion given the role of women in marriage negotiations. When the Patani attempt to seize power in Ayutthaya failed, Nang Liu-liu accompanied Sultan Muzaffar's brother, Sultan Mansur Syah, as he fled from the Siamese.[47] Standing at the stern of the boat, the prince held Nang Liu-liu (*dipegang*, as one might a dear friend or lover) and promises her great rewards if she assists him to return safely to Patani. She then fires her shots, sinking many of the Siamese *perahu* and frightening off the remainder.[48] Sultan Mansur delays the ceremonies for his own installation, during which time Lady Liu-Liu is celebrated like royalty with a fringed umbrella, while the drums are beaten for her alone for three days and nights. Only after she has been thus honored is the king himself drummed in.[49] Subsequently, Lady Liu-liu joins Seri Negeri and Datuk Buk in defending Patani against an attack by the Sumatran state of Palembang. On this occasion, the firing of the three cannon killed a large number of the enemy "and those wounded were innumerable, lying in heaps." The audience was obviously meant to be impressed by cannon's force and its capacity to wreak destruction on any opposing force. "When the gun Seri Negeri was fired its cannon balls fell as far as Kuala Bang Pelemu; the cannon balls of Nang Liu-Liu fell on the other side of Kuala Bekah, and those of Tuk Buk fell into the village Mendaharan." Implicitly, however, the text represents this show of military might as a reflection of the *daulat* of Sultan Mansur, to whom the victory is attributed.[50]

Contemporary descriptions that speak to the awe with which certain cannon were regarded suggest that in Patani, as elsewhere in Southeast Asia, the biographies of "things" are inextricably linked to the history of locality

---

[46] Sewell, "Notes on Some Old Siamese Guns," pp. 16–7.

[47] Teeuw and Wyatt, eds., *Hikayat Patani*, pp. 82, 158.

[48] Ibid., pp. 86, 161.

[49] Ibid., pp. 87, 162.

[50] Ibid., *Hikayat Patani*, pp. 89, 164.

Figure 2.1 The captured "Phaya Tani" cannon, known among Patani Malays as "Seri Patani," now situated outside the Ministry of Defence building, Bangkok.

and community. The depth and
longevity of such relationships
makes any parting not merely
"unthinkable" but culturally un-
bearable.[51] The capture of Patani's
cannon by Bangkok's forces in
1785 thus represented far more
than the loss of ordnance or the
humiliation of defeat. Syukri
puts the matter simply: of all the
items that were looted, he writes,
"the most valued was the great
cannon made in the reign of
Raja Biru of former times."[52] The
psychological and cultural trauma
resulting from their loss finds

Figure 2.2 The Thai government's official seal
of Pattani province since 1939.

a parallel in the western Malay state of Selangor, where it was commonly
believed that Selangor would only return to its former greatness when the
cannon Si Rambai, confiscated by the British, was returned from Penang.[53]

The Nobat

Although Malay textual studies accord little attention to the auditory sense,
sounds of many kinds permeate the *Hikayat Patani*. The firing of guns
announces the return of a ship from an overseas mission; elephants trumpet
as Patani forces defend their *negeri*; the beautiful singing of Dang Sirat
entrances the prince of Johor; the royal troupe sings of legendary heroes
like Rama, of Melaka's battle against the Portuguese, of Johor's invasion
of Jambi.[54] One body of sound to which the text gives special attention
is that of the *nobat*, a word that can connote the entire royal orchestra, or
specifically the main drum. The original term *naubat* (from Arabic *nauba*),
apparently reached the Malay world from the Middle East via Indian-
Muslim connections. In Mughal India, it referred to an orchestral style
using drums and other instruments such as the *nafiri* (small oboe), the
surnāī (oboe, Malay *serunai*) and *nagārā* (kettledrum) that was performed at

---

[51] Kopytoff, "The Cultural Biography of Things," p. 80.

[52] Syukri, *Sejarah Kerajaan Melayu Patani*, p. 74.

[53] Douglas, "The Penang Cannon Si Rambai," p. 118.

[54] Teeuw and Wyatt, eds., *Hikayat Patani*, pp. 68, 94, 116, 186.

the gateways of palaces and mausoleums at fixed hours of the day. Though heralding the arrival and departure of visiting dignitaries, the *naubat* tradition was especially associated with rulers and the music produced was considered particularly auspicious by both Hindus and Muslims.[55]

The *nobat* of Patani was said to have been received from the Sultan of Melaka, and the *Sejarah Melayu* reminds us that this was no small gift, since "in former times" umbrellas, drums and *nafiri* were expensive.[56] As the history of Selangor demonstrates in a later period, possession of a *nobat* that could trace its lineage back to the very origins of Malay culture endowed a ruler with extraordinary status.[57] It was not merely that these musical instruments, especially the drums, were very old; more specifically, they were redolent with supernatural powers that could bring sickness and even death should they be touched or played by any unauthorized person.[58] In comparison with other Malay states, it would seem that Patani's orchestra was not only relatively large but extremely valuable. According to the *Hikayat Patani*, it comprised four golden and four silver trumpets (*nafiri*), two gold and two silver *serunai*, 12 two-sided drums (*gendang nobat*) and eight one-sided drums (*negara*).[59]

In the pages that follow, the chronicler undertakes a challenging task; the compilation of a reference text for musicians that explains not merely how instruments should relate to one another but which attempts to record in writing the sounds of *ragam* (tunes) considered unique to Patani's acoustic history. For the most part, scholars have been puzzled as to how this section can be incorporated into a "historical" analysis, although several authorities have emphasized the importance of music in Malay culture.[60] In terms of affirming group identity, it is worth noting that in every court the tunes played and the instruments themselves were weighted with legendary

---

[55] Nazir A. Jairazbhoy, "A Preliminary Survey of the Oboe in India," *Ethnomusicology* 14, 3 (September 1970): 377; Nazir A. Jairazbhoy, "The South Asian Double-Reed Aerophone Reconsidered," *Ethnomusicology* 24, 1 (January 1980): 147–56.

[56] Brown, *Sejarah Melayu*, pp. 57, 151.

[57] Andaya, *Perak, the Abode of Grace*, p. 42.

[58] Skeat, *Malay Magic*, p. 40.

[59] Teeuw and Wyatt, eds., *Hikayat Patani*, pp. 141, 211.

[60] Takeshi Ito, "The World of the Adat Aceh: A Historical Study of the Sultanate of Aceh," Unpublished ANU thesis, 1984, pp. 228, 247; Amirul Hadi, *Islam and State in Sumatra: A Study of Seventeenth-Century Aceh* (Leiden and Boston: Brill, 2004), p. 125n146; Bradley, "Moral Order in a Time of Damnation," p. 289, gives music in Patani some attention.

associations. Perak's royal chronicle, the *Misa Melayu*, thus notes that eight arrangements for its *nobat* came "out of the sea" and the royal drum of Aceh was personalized with the name Ibrahim Khalil (i.e, the prophet Abrahim, friend of God — Ibrahim Khalilullah).[61] The Patani *ragam* also possessed sacred power and symbolic authority because of the *nobat*'s antiquity and its association with *negeri* origins. More particularly, its auditory reach invoked far more than royal status; as Rath has emphasized, in premodern societies, "instrumental sounds were often used to constitute community."[62] If sounds were somehow "incorrect," if a gong sounded dull or cannon did not fire, it could well be a warning of some impending disaster and was therefore a matter of public concern. Because music was communication, the tunes, notes, beats, rhythms all helped establish a reciprocal relationship between player and listener, addresser and addressee within a specific cultural and social environment. The "noise" of a drum or gong could thus summon the Muslim community to prayer or call men to arms; such sounds could also mark the consummation of a royal marriage, the birth of a prince, or the ruler's entry and exit from the palace. In effect, the beating of the *nobat* became an auditory metaphor for the religious and social order; like bells in early America, its sounding marked out the extent of local identity and royal authority by giving it a public hearing.[63] In this mode, the *Sejarah Melayu* tells us that a ruler of Pahang, abdicating in favor of his son, moves upstream "until he could no longer hear the royal drum."[64]

Historical comparisons also indicate that the musical context could bring together actors from different cultural systems as the sounds of a new environment were interpreted and explained. An early conversational guide intended to help Dutch speak Malay, for instance, includes a dialogue noting that the "*boenji namfieri dengan seroney*" (the sound of the *nafiri* and *serunai*) was a sign the sultan is coming.[65] As originators of Europe's first "national

---

[61] Raja Chulan, *Misa Melayu* (Kuala Lumpur: Pustaka Antara, 1968; reprint of 1919 edition), p. 194; Ito, "The World of the Adat Aceh," p. 219; Hadi, *Islam and State in Sumatra*, pp. 126–37. See the *nobat* Ibrahim Khalil, mentioned in Panuti H.M. Sudjiman, ed., *Adat Raja-Raja Melayu* (Jakarta: Penerbit Universitas Indonesia, 1983), p. 7, and Hill, "Hikayat Raja-Raja Pasai," p. 119.

[62] See further Rath, *How Early America Sounded*, pp. 3, 5, 7, 46–7, 68; Appadurai, "Introduction," p. 15.

[63] Rath, *How Early America Sounded*, p. 51.

[64] Brown, *Sejarah Melayu*, 151.

[65] Denys Lombard, ed., *Le "Spraek ende Woord-Boek" de Frederick de Houtman* (Paris: École Française d'Extrême-Orient, 1970), p. 37.

anthem," the Dutch were well aware that ceremonial sound was not merely central to a display of status, but that music could also help proclaim group identity. During his first meeting with the Patani queen, the Dutch factor thus put his best trumpeters on display to perform the *Wilhelmus*, the song of the House of Orange-Nassau.[66] One observer noted that the queen and her nobles were "very surprised," because they had never before heard this type of sound. "When our people passed close by her elephant, she put her head out of the tent in order to see [and presumably hear] better."[67] In sonic terms, a Patani identity had been restated merely by its juxtaposition to a non-Patani sound.

As in most of the non-European world, Patani musicians would have learned to reproduce sound through aural transmission rather than by reference to a written score. The *Hikayat Patani* stands out among Malay texts because it represents an attempt by a literate man to produce a musical manual that would convey the percussive structures of various *ragam* through the onomatopoeia of drum mnemonics.[68] This itself is of interest, because drums and gongs usually do not carry the melody, and because notation through techniques such as numbers are not possible. Since music was an audible expression of royal authority and status, it was critical that the rhythm, tempo and instrumental coordination be followed precisely, and it is quite possible that the original text was written out in musical phrases that ended on a vibration ("m" or "ng"), rather than in a continuous text.[69] For example, one particular song (*Dondang Anak*, "A Lullaby for a [Royal] Child") is notated thus:

> *kemitang gegar kam–kam*
> *titang gar gam–gam*
> *titang gar gam*
> *titang–titang kam*

---

[66] Since the 1560s, the *Wilhelmus* ("William of Nassau/I am of Dutch blood/Loyal to the fatherland/I will remain until I die") had been sung on many official occasions and was usually accompanied by trumpets or church bells. Available at http://en.wikipedia.org/wiki/Het_Wilhelmus [accessed October 14, 2009].

[67] Van Foreest and de Booy, eds., *De Vierde Schipvaart*, 1: 258.

[68] David W. Hughes, "No Nonsense: The Logic and Power of Acoustic-Iconic Mnemonic Systems," *British Journal of Ethnomusicology* 9, 2 (2000): 93–120; Judith Becker, "Percussive Patterns in the Music of Mainland Southeast Asia," *Ethnomusicology* 12, 2 (May 1968): 173–91.

[69] I am grateful to Mayco Santaella and my colleague Ricardo Trimillos for these insights, and to Judith Becker for looking over this section.

> *titang kam*
> *titang kam*
> *titang gam*
> *tang kekar kam*
> *titang gam*[70]

The musician is instructed that this is to be repeated, presumably several times since the notation ends (*balik pulang*, back and forth). In this context, improvisation could only be permitted to a very limited extent. Though lexically meaningless, written phrases like "*gemitang gam tit*" make eminent sense when we understand that they were intended to be sung or recited in order to provide vocal cues for the drummer to imitate. For example, the "g" is a hard stroke, but the "ng" and "m" indicates vibration; a final "b" represents a stopped sound; short notes, possibly struck around the rim, are specified by words such as "tit."

A second section of the "manual" stresses the coordination necessary between the drum and the trumpet in the total *nobat* performance.

> This paragraph explains (what happens) when people want to strike up the royal band; when the drummer has taken the drum (*gendang*) and begins to tap it, then we (*kita*) blow the *nafiri* — blow it long twice; when blown long it sounds *uting-uting*. Then blow it short three times, then long once more, and then stop. Then begin again, five times, in turns; the five times being over; when the resounding has subsided it should coincide with the sound of the drum. When the *gendang* is tapped, blow two trumpets; if there are four blow all of them long. When the drum is to be stopped, blow three times and let it stop at the same time as the drum.[71]

Given the argument that words and music stand in a reciprocal relationship between speaker and audience, it would be tempting to speculate about the "addressivity" of the inclusive *kita* ("we") and the extent to which it points to a common sense of "Patani-ness." More solid evidence of the local character of royal music is provided by the various *ragam* listed, for even though the basic instruments were similar, the rhythms and tunes seem to be quite distinct from those of Perak or Aceh.[72] Although Malays shared many musical traditions, local performances operated under established expectations of style and rendition. In the *Adat Aceh*, for instance, every stage

---

[70] Teeuw and Wyatt, eds., *Hikayat Patani*, pp. 142, 212.

[71] Ibid., pp. 143, 213–4.

[72] Ibid., p. 287.

of a royal procession is signaled by a different drum rhythm.[73] It is only in this context that we can appreciate the detailed instructions provided in the *Hikayat Patani* for blowing the trumpets, since a feature of the *nafiri* and the *serunai* is the double reed (tongue or *lidah*), which changes not only pitch (like the single reed) but also produces a more intense volume. "Anyone wanting to learn to blow the trumpet should blow as hard as possible so that the sound is 'round.' … The sound should be loud. If the blowing is not strong enough, then the sound is insufficient."[74] Like the roll of thunder, the trumpeting of elephants, the noise of cannon, the decibel level itself establishes the criteria by which majesty can be measured.

Despite the standing of the *serunai* and *nafiri*, due in part to their Indian origins, the key instrument in the Malay orchestra was always the indigenous *gendang*. Its prominence in Patani's musical arrangements recalls a long Southeast Asian tradition in which gongs and drums were central in rituals intended to ensure the land's fertility and energize protective forces. In the Malay world, the beating of the *nobat* drum was always heard during a ruler's installation, but it could also be played when he went to war, during a royal procession, or to recognize high status, wherever it might reside. As we have seen, the protection given by the cannon Nang Liu-Liu was recognized by the three-day beating of the *nobat* drum in her honor. Carrying with it the power of the state — and thus an enactment of authority — drumming could be used to summon people for battle, to an assembly, to attend the ruler, for labor projects. The sound of the drum and the blowing of the *nafiri* and *serunai* also became an integral part of ceremonies that marked the Muslim calendar; the daily prayers, Friday worship, the feast of the pilgrimage,[75] the final days before the commencement of the fasting month. In Patani, as in other Malay states like Aceh, the "bedlam of noise" that struck Europeans was intimately linked to the celebration of an Islamic identity and a mosque community that even a royal challenger must honor.[76] About to confront the queen of Patani, for instance, the Bendahara briefly halts his advance when he hears the sound

---

[73] Ramli Harun and Tjut Rahma M.A. Gani, eds., *Adat Aceh* (Jakarta: Departemen Pendidikan dan Kebudayaan, Proyek Penerbitan Buku Sastra Indonesia dan Daerah, 1985), p. 37; Ito, "The World of the *Adat Aceh*," pp. 218, 269n82.

[74] Teeuw and Wyatt, eds., *Hikayat Patani*, pp. 145, 216.

[75] Hari Raya Haji, 10 Zulhijjah.

[76] Anthony Reid, *An Indonesian Frontier: Acehnese and Other Histories of Sumatra* (Sigapore: NUS Press, 2005), pp. 119–22; Ito, "The World of the *Adat Aceh*," p. 227.

of the drum signaling the Friday prayer, and only continues to the palace when this stops.[77]

Several references in the *Hikayat Patani* reinforce the idea of an ongoing interaction between drum sounds, royal power and the coherence of a *negeri*. When Sultan Muzaffar goes to Ayutthaya, he sees the "great drum" hanging in front of the palace, and tells a young boy to "make a hole" in the tympanum, and thus destroy its instrumental capacity. But the boy strikes the drum instead, a move that symbolically and practically invokes Siamese authority by summoning troops. It also dooms the Patani plan to usurp power in the Thai capital.[78] In another episode, the Johor *raja* does not play his *nobat* when he visits Patani, an explicit recognition of the queen's status.[79] The most revealing incident, however, concerns the debates over the installation by beat of drum (*tabalkan*) of Dang Sirat, with whom the prince of Johor is infatuated. She asks that the *nobat* of Johor be played in her honor. However, the prince recognizes that if she were to be installed in her own house, which was close to the palace, the *ragam* of the Johor *nobat* would sound discordant when juxtaposed with those of Patani. He suggests Kedi, which, as I have argued, is a vicinity of particular importance in the Patani environment. The ministers remind him that any drumming in this area will compete or be compared with that of the Patani Queen, and the "*nama*," the reputation of the Johor ruler, could well be diminished.[80] In a text where the statement "Johor and Patani are very much alike, but there are differences in customs and rules" makes the sense of local identity quite explicit, it is significant that a possible translation for the first Patani *ragam* is "primordial beginnings."[81]

Conclusion

In her recent essay, Chuleeporn Virunha has suggested that the *Hikayat Patani* was composed at a time of crisis when there were major challenges from both Ayutthaya and other Malay states and that it was intended to promote a sense of cultural unity. She has gone on to argue that a "Patani

---

[77] Teeuw and Wyatt, *Hikayat Patani*, pp. 143, 174.

[78] Ibid., pp. 83–6, 159–61.

[79] Ibid., pp. 109, 181.

[80] On "*nama*," see A.C. Milner, *Kerajaan: Malay Political Culture on the Eve of Colonial Rule* (Tucson, AZ: University of Arizona Press, for the Association of Asian Studies, 1982), p. 104, *passim*.

[81] Teeuw and Wyatt, *Hikayat Patani*, pp. 123, 141, 193, 211.

identity" shaped by experiences was closely related to the sense of locality.[82] As a number of scholars have pointed out, the *Hikayat Patani* conveys little sense of incorporation into a wider "Malay" world. On the other hand, the notion of a place, a "*negeri* Patani" is clearly embedded in the text. Much academic work on mainland Southeast Asia has focused on the idea of a ritual center in a settlement or city, and while such sacred places are less evident in Malay material, I have suggested here that the function of Patani's Pintu Gajah, the elephant gate, was not dissimilar. Marking the site of the extraordinary events associated with the founding of the *negeri*, the gate stood as a witness to momentous events in Patani's collective memory. In the same mode, the *Hikayat Patani* provides telling testimony to the potency of the sacral objects (drums, cannon) and animals (elephants) and the sounds they emit as visual and oral representations of the essence of Patani-ness. Subsumed within the text is also a lesson about the management of a *negeri*, for despite the unique powers associated with royal *daulat*, rulers are themselves fallible and their actions are often damaging to the country's well-being. A king pays lip service to his conversion to Islam; another fails to reciprocate favors shown by the Ayutthaya ruler; a queen appears indifferent to the death of a loyal and holy man; quarrels between a king and his brothers bring about Patani's ruin.[83] By contrast, the spiritually charged drums, elephants, cannon, swords, trumpets never fail to stand as guardians and protectors, rightly honored by titles that incorporate the word *negeri*. As social agents in historical action, they are far more than symbols; rather, as presented in the text, they become quintessential "sites of memory" in the Patani consciousness.

---

[82] Chuleeporn Virunha, "Historical Perceptions of Local Identity in the Upper Peninsula," in *Thai South and Malay North*, ed. Montesano and Jory, pp. 46, 52, 67.
[83] Teeuw and Wyatt, *Hikayat Patani*, pp. 82, 104, 133, 159, 176, 202.

The Patani Region in Chinese Texts of the 6th to the 19th Centuries

Geoff Wade

While numerous studies have drawn attention to the importance of Chinese texts for the study of the major Thai polities,[1] very little has yet been written on how Chinese sources might be drawn upon to elucidate aspects of the Patani past.[2] This is due both to the paucity of materials available and to the fact that identifications of toponyms and polity names in earlier texts are not

---

[1] Some of the better-known works which employ Chinese sources in examining Thai history include: Chan Hok-lam, "Xian-luo gong-shi 'Xie Wen-bin' shi-jian pou-xi" [An Analysis of the Incident Involving the Siamese Tribute Envoy Xie Wen-bin] in his *Ming-dai Ren-wu yu Chuan-shuo* [*Essays on Ming Personages and Legends*] (Hong Kong: Chinese University of Hong Kong, 1997); Chan Hok-lam, "Ming Cheng-hua Lin Xiao Yao Long chu-shi Xian-luo zhi mi" [The Mystery of the Mission to Siam by the Envoys Lin Xiao and Yao Long During the Cheng-hua Reign of the Ming Dynasty], *Wen-shi* 3 (1999): 91–101; Chen Lu-fan, *Whence Came the Thai Race? — An Enquiry* (Kunming, 1990); E.T. Flood, "Sukothai-Mongol Relations," *Journal of the Siam Society* 57, 2 (1969): 1–20; T. Grimm, "Thailand in the Light of Official Chinese Historiography: A Chapter in the History of the Ming Dynasty," *Journal of the Siam Society* 49, 1 (1961): 1–20; Hsieh Yu-jung, *Hsien-lo Kuo Chih* [*An Account of the Country of Siam*] (Bangkok, 1949); Hoshino Tatsuo, *Pour une Histoire Médiévale du Moyen Mékong* (Bangkok, 1986); Li Dao-gang, "Can-lie Bao Bi-ya Cuan-wei wei wang" [The Usurpation of the Throne by Samtec Pū Brahyā], *Dong-nan-ya Xue-kan* [*Southeast Asian Studies Journal*] 1 (1999) and "Can-lie Zhao Bi-ya chung-deng wang-wei" [Samtec Chao Brahyā Resumes the Throne], *Dong-nan-ya Xue-kan* 3 (1999); Li Zhang-fu, "Zhong-Tai Gu-dai Jiao-tong-shi kao" [A Study of the History of Ancient Communication Between China and Thailand], *Nan-yang Xue-bao* 1, 1 (1940); G.H. Luce, "The Early Syam in Burma's History," *Journal of the Siam Society* 46, 2 (1958): 123–214; G.H. Luce, "The Early Syam in Burma's History:

always free from dispute. Below, are provided in translation references to the Patani region found in classical Chinese texts. This collection is not exhaustive but attempts to provide all successive texts where new information was

A Supplement," *Journal of the Siam Society* 47, 1 (1959): 59–101; P. Pelliot, "Deux Itineraires de Chine en Inde a la Fin du VIIIe Siècle," *Bulletin de l'Ecole Française d'Extrême-Orient* IV (1904): 131–413; G.W. Skinner, *Chinese Society in Thailand: An Analytical History* (Ithaca, 1957); Sarasin Viraphol, *Tribute and Profit: Sino-Siamese Trade 1652–1853* (Cambridge, MA, 1977); Suebsaeng Promboon, "Sino-Siamese Tributary Relations: 1282–1853," Unpublished PhD thesis, University of Wisconsin, 1971; O.W. Wolters, "Chen-li-fu, a State on the Gulf of Siam at the Beginning of the 13th Century," *Journal of the Siam Society* 48, 2 (1960); O.W. Wolters, "The Khmer King at Basan (1371–3), and the Restoration of the Cambodian Chronology During the Fourteenth and Fifteenth Centuries," *Asia Major* XII, 1 (1966): 80–4; O.W. Wolters, "Ayudhya and the Rearward Part of the World," *JRAS* (1968): 166–78; Yamamoto Tatsuro, "Dawara-koku-ko" [A Study of Dvaravati], *Shirin* 28, 4 (1943): 347–68; Yamamoto Tatsuro, "Thailand As It is Referred to in the Da-de Nan-hai zhi at the Beginning of the Fourteenth Century," *Journal of East-West Maritime Relations* 1 (1989): 47–58; Zou Qi-yu, "Zhong-Tai guan-xi shi shang de yi-ge yi-an" [A Mystery in the History of Sino-Thai Relations — On the Issue of Whether Khun Ramkhamhaeng, the Ruler of Sukothai, Ever Visited China], *Li-shi Yan-jiu* [*Historical Research*] 5 (1980): 171–85. Further references, not seen by the present author, include Likhit Hootrakul, *The Historical Relations of the Siamese-Chinese Relations*, Vol. 1 (Dhonburi, 1975) (noted by Zou); Chaloem Yongbunkoet, trans., "Muang Thai nai chotmaihet Chin" [Thailand in Chinese Records], *Sinlapkorn* 7, 2 (July 1963): 50–65 (noted by Charnvit Kasetsiri), and the three articles by Sugimoto Naojiro quoted in Flood's bibliography. Details of many other Chinese-language articles on Thailand, which make use of Chinese sources, can be found in: *Index to Chinese Periodical Literature on Southeast Asia 1905–1966*, edited by the Institute of Southeast Asia, Nanyang University (Singapore, 1967), p. 2; Austin G.W. Shu and William W.L. Wan, *Twentieth Century Chinese Works on Southeast Asia: A Bibliography* (Hawai'i: East-West Center, 1968). The Institute of Southeast Asian Studies of Zhongshan University in Guangzhou, PRC has compiled a new collection of classical Chinese references to areas which are today part of Thailand and this is to be published in the near future.

[2] Two exceptions are: Hsü Yun-tsiao, *Bei-da-nian shi* 北大年史 [*A History of Patani*] (Singapore, 1946); and Geoff Wade, "From Chaiya to Pahang: the Eastern Seaboard of the Peninsula as Recorded in Classical Chinese Texts," in *Études sur l'histoire du sultanat de Patani*, Études thématiques, ed. Daniel Perret, Amara Srisuchat, Sumbun Thanasuk (Paris: École française d'Extrême-Orient, 2004), pp. 37–78. Some Chinese references can also be found in Chaloem Yongbunkoet, trans., "Muang Thai nai chotmaihet Chin" [Thailand in Chinese Records], *Sinlapkorn* 7, 2 (July 1963): 50–65; and Li Dao-gang, *Tai-guo gu-dai shi-di cong-kao*, 泰國古代史地叢考 (北京: 中華書局, 2000).

provided on the region. These include geographies, histories, ethnographies and reign annals. While the toponym Patani is a relatively recent term, classical Chinese texts have been examined herein to find materials relating to the coastline from Chaiya down to what is today Kelantan. The aim of this study is to draw attention to references in, or translations from, a range of Chinese texts noting toponyms and polities which have been associated with this region. These have not been drawn on previously in studies of the region's past, although Hsü Yun-tsiao has employed some of the later texts in his study of 17th–19th-century Patani.[3] How the textual references might be collocated with sources from other traditions in the writing of histories of Patani will necessarily be left to others to investigate.

References to the Patani Region from the First Millennium CE

The *Liang shu* [*History of the Liang Dynasty*], an official Chinese history compiled in the seventh century, but which refers to the preceding century, contains references which suggest the existence of polities along the eastern coastline of the Isthmus of Kra during the early centuries of the Christian era. Following a voyage to what is now known as Southeast Asia, the Liang court officials Kang Tai and Zhu Ying, who had been sent as envoys to the early Khmer polity of Fu-nan, reported that they had visited or heard of 100 countries in the region. The text also informs us that the Fu-nan ruler had, sometime in the third century, sent his ships across the Chang-hai (the Gulf of Siam), to attack more than 10 polities including Qu-du-kun (Hokkien: Kut-doo-kun; Cantonese: Wat-to-kwan), Jiu-zhi (Hokkien: Gao-di; Cantonese: Kau-chi) and Dian-sun (Hokkien: Dian-sng; Cantonese: Tin-suen).[4] The fact that these polities lay across the Gulf of Siam from Fu-nan, suggests the possibility that they were located on the peninsula. There is no firmness in identifying any of these polities with references from other traditions. All we can posit is that one or more of these polities possibly controlled areas which are today in the Patani area.

Langkasuka (I)

The *Liang shu* also contains the earliest reference to a country ("*guo*") named Lang-ya-xiu 狼牙脩 (Hokkien: Long-gga-siu; Cantonese: Long-nga-sau).

---

[3] Hsü Yun-tsiao *Bei-da-nian shi* 北大年史 [*A History of Patani*] (Singapore, 1946).
[4] Paul Wheatley, *The Golden Khersonese: Studies in the Historical Geography of the Malay Peninsula before A.D. 1500* (Kuala Lumpur, University of Malaya Press, 1961), p. 15.

This and other Chinese textual references to Lang-ya-xiu 狼牙修, Lang-jia-shu 郎迦戍, Lang-jia-xu 郎迦戌, Ling-jia-xiu 棱枷修, Ling-ya-si-jia 凌牙斯加 or Long-ya-xi-jiao 龍牙犀角 have been associated by many with a polity named Langkashuka in Arabic texts, Ilaṅgāśōka in a Cōla inscription, Lengkasuka in the Javanese court poem *Nāgarakṛtāgama*, and Langkasuka in the Malay *Hikayat Marong Mahawangsa*.[5] The precise location of the polity remains a topic of debate.[6] That it lay on the peninsula, however, appears to be beyond doubt. Wheatley was quite firm in his conclusion that "[...] *Langkasuka*, a kingdom of considerable importance during the first fifteen hundred years of the Christian era, was situated in the vicinity of modern Patani."[7] Michel Jacq-Hergoualc'h also suggests that we should look to the former estuary of the Menam Patani around Yarang for Langkasuka, since it is "on the banks of this vanished estuary that the various entrepôt ports of this city state were located."[8] I will also locate Langkasuka in the vicinity of modern Patani for reasons discussed in a later section of this chapter.

The *Liang shu* tells us about this place, and Paul Wheatley has translated the account of the country.[9] The account begins:

> The country of Lang-ya-xiu is in the Southern Ocean. East to west its territory extends for a distance which requires 30 days to traverse on foot, while south to north, it requires 20 days to traverse. From Guang-zhou, it is a distance of 24,000 *li*.[10]

In another part of the *Liang shu* in a notice dated to the ninth month of the 14th year of the Tian-jian reign (equivalent to July/August 515 CE), it is noted: "The envoy sent by the country of Lang-ya-xiu presented local products."[11] Elsewhere in the same work, the reader is informed:

> Other missions by this polity to the Liang court in China are recorded for the years 523, 531 and 568 C.E.[12] Texts by or about Buddhist

---

[5] Wheatley, *The Golden Khersonese*, pp. 256–63.

[6] See, for example, the works by Groeneveldt, Schlegel, Huber, Pelliot, Gerini, Blagden, Braddell, Ferrand and Wheatley cited in Wheatley, *The Golden Khersonese*, pp. 252–3.

[7] Wheatley, *The Golden Khersonese*, p. 265.

[8] M. Jacq-Hergoualc'h, *The Malay Peninsula: Crossroads of the Maritime Silk Road (100 BC–1300 AD)*, trans. Victoria Hobson (Leiden: Brill, 2002), pp. 168–9.

[9] Wheatley, *The Golden Khersonese*, pp. 253–4.

[10] Yao Si-lian, *Liang shu, juan* 54.

[11] Yao Si-lian, *Liang shu, juan* 2.

[12] For which see Wang Gungwu, *The Nanhai Trade: The Early History of Chinese Trade in the South China Sea* (Singapore: Times Academic Press reprint, 1998), pp. 47, 119.

pilgrims who travelled through Southeast Asia on their way to or from India also include references to this place. We read that to the north it adjoined another polity named Pan-pan,[13] and that it lay in the ocean south-west of Śrikṣetra, between that place and Dvāravatī.[14] The 'country of Chi-tu,' 赤土 or the Red-Earth Country, inhabited by 'another Fu-nan people,' lay to Langkasuka's south.

---

[13] The first mention of the polity of Pan-pan (Hokkien: *Puan-puan*; Cantonese: *P'oon-p'oon*) is made in the Fu-nan section of the seventh-century *Liang shu*. Missions from the polity to China include a number from the fifth and sixth centuries. Its location is recorded as being to the southwest of Lin-yi (Champa), and adjoining Lang-ya-xiu. According to the Chinese texts, Pan-pan was a center of Buddhist studies, and the city was built by the waterside. The most detailed account of the polity is contained in the *Wen-xian tong-kao*, and Wheatley has provided a translation of this (Wheatley, *The Golden Khersonese*, pp. 48–9). The Tang histories also inform us that Pan-pan was located to the south of a polity known as Duo-he-luo, which is universally recognized as Dvāravatī. Given that Dvāravatī influence extended well down the peninsula, it is most likely that Pan-pan lay somewhere on the peninsula, possibly along the coast which this chapter is examining. This is supported by the note in the *Wen-xian tong-kao* which mentions that Pan-pan lay across the "small sea" (Gulf of Siam) from Lin-yi (Champa). The possibility that the polity name has been retained in the town of Phoon-phin which lies close to the mouth of the Ban Don River, one of the major trans-peninsular routes, should not be ignored. This is in accord with the conclusions of Groeneveldt, Pelliot, Ferrand, Luce, Fujita Toyohachi and Briggs, who all locate Pan-pan on or near the Bay of Bandon (Wheatley, *The Golden Khersonese*, p. 50). Jacq-Hergoualc'h also sees Pan-pan as having been the major influence in the southernmost section of the Isthmus of Kra (Jacq-Hergoualc'h, *The Malay Peninsula*, p. 103), and he has detailed the cultural remains which he associates with this polity (ibid., pp. 107–60). The various accounts of Pan-pan indicate that the polity's chief officials bore various titles, including Bo-lang-so-lan, Kun-lun Ti-ye, Kun-lun Bo-ho and Kun-lun Bo-di-so Gan. The recurrence of the "Kun-lun" element in these official titles suggests that the polity may have been Khmer-speaking, as it likely represents the title *Kloñ/Khloñ*, arguably the most widespread official title in pre-Angkorian and Angkorian Cambodia. The final title noted above could be a variant of *"khloñ bhūtāśa."* Chamic influence should likewise not be ruled out, as the "Bo-lang" in the first-mentioned title could well be the title *"Pu neng,"* a Chamic title used in pre-Angkorian Cambodia (Michael Vickery, *Society, Economics, and Politics in Pre-Angkor Cambodia: the 7th–8th Centuries* [Tokyo: Toyo Bunko, 1998], p. 221), and likely linked with the *"pu lyang"* attested as a title in Cham inscriptions. Such investigations, however, fall beyond the immediate scope of the present chapter.

[14] As recorded in Xuan-zang's *Da Tang Xi-you-ji*. See Wheatley, *The Golden Kher-sonese*, p. 256.

In one of the very few illustrations of Southeast Asian persons from the sixth century, a Chinese scroll entitled *Liang zhi-gong tu* 梁職工圖 [*Illustrated Tributaries of the Liang*] completed *circa* 539 CE and now only partially extant provides us with an illustration of an envoy from the country of Langkasuka. Next to the illustrated figure of the envoy is a brief description of the country, which reads:

> *An envoy of the country of Lang-ya-xiu.* Lang-ya-xiu is situated in the Southern Ocean, 21,000 *li*[15] from Guang-zhou. The territory of the country extends a 30-day journey east to west, and a 20-day journey north to south. Its climate is constantly hot and its plants and trees always flourish. There is no snow or frost. There is much gold and silver, Barus camphor, and gharu-wood. Both men and women go about with exposed bodies and untied hair. They use cotton which they wrap around themselves. The king of the country uses *yun-xia*[16] cloth to cover his body, while the officials and ministers wear sandals of straw and gold waist cords and have gold rings in their ears. The women wrap cloth, decorated with fringes, around themselves. The city wall is made of piled bricks, and there is a double gate, towers and pavilions. The pavilions are of three storeys. When the king goes out, he is mounted on an elephant, and is accompanied by pennants, fly-whisks, flags and drums, and is shaded by a white umbrella. The military forces are well-established. The people of the country say that their country was first established over 400 years ago, but that those who succeeded to the throne gradually became weaker. Within the king's family there was a man of integrity and the people gave their allegiance to him. The king thus captured and chained him, but the locks broke apart by themselves. The king thus dared not execute him, and instead exiled him beyond the borders. He then fled to India where he married the daughter of the ruler. Not long after the king of Lang-ya-xiu died, and the whole country welcomed back the exile and established him as ruler. After more than twenty years this king also died and his son, Po-jia-da-duo,[17] ascended to the throne. In the 14th year of the Tian-jian reign [515 C.E.], he sent his envoy, A-sa-duo, to present to the Court a memorial and tribute products.[18]

---

[15] One *li* is equivalent to approximately 0.5 kilometers.

[16] An unidentified textile. The term *yun-xia* refers to red clouds, which may have some reference to the color of the cloth.

[17] Possibly a representation of Bhagadatta.

[18] Translated from the Chinese text provided in Enoki Kazuo, "The Liang chih-kung-t'u," *Memoirs of the Research Department of the Toyo Bunko* 42 (1984): 75–138. The text is given on p. 111 and in an appended illustration of the scroll.

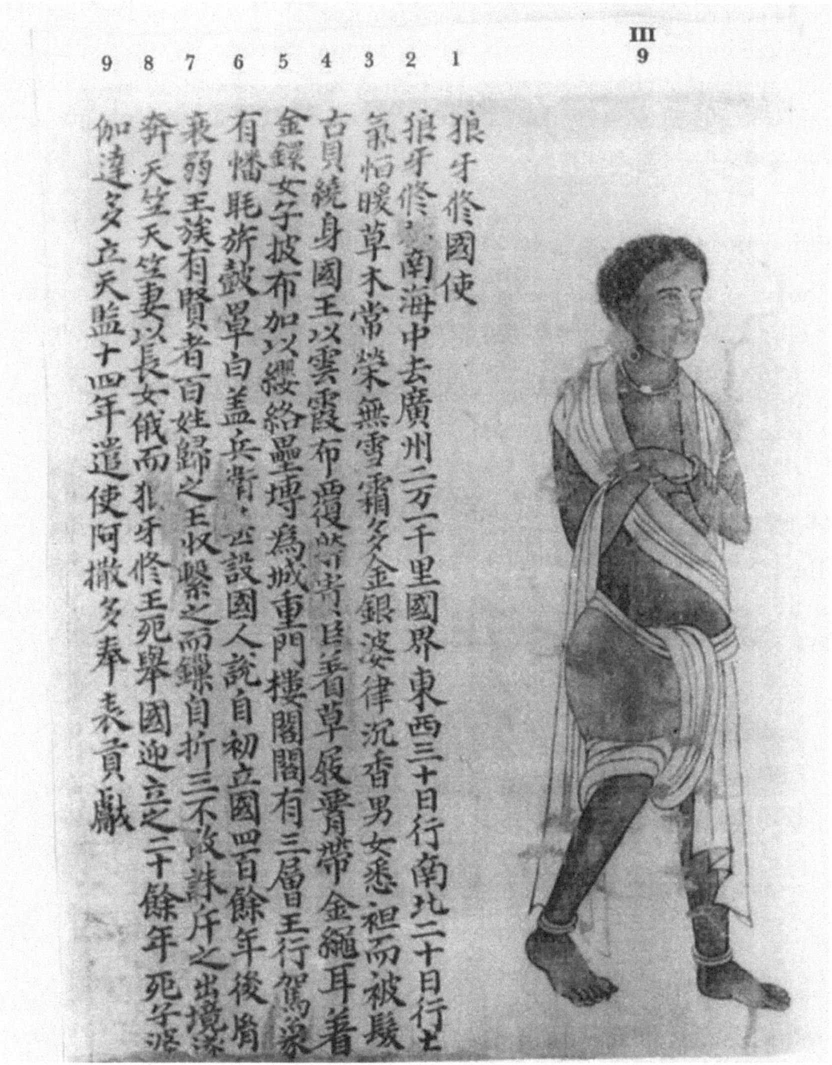

Figure 3.1 Envoy to Liang China from the country of Lang-ya-xiu in the sixth century CE.

What do these early texts suggest about Langkasuka in the sixth century? First, it was a polity of a considerable size which lay on the east coast of the peninsula between Pan-pan to its north and Chi-tu to its south. It had a political hierarchy, a bureaucracy, a military and a walled capital. It was a rather wealthy polity and appears to have been a trading mart. That it was Indianized to some degree is suggested by both the flight of the exile to

India and the reconstruction of his son's name. The polity was also visited by Chinese monks on their way to India,[19] suggesting some Buddhist affiliation. The mention of gold as a standard for assessing the value of products suggests that the metal was available in some quantity, certainly a phenomenon suggested by later sources.[20]

References from the Early Second Millennium CE

The major Chinese texts providing information on polities and toponyms in Southeast Asia from the 12th to the 14th centuries are *Ling-wai dai-da* 岭外代答, compiled in 1178, *Zhu-fan-zhi*, completed in 1225, the *Song shi* 宋史 of the early 14th century, and the *Dao-yi zhi-lue* 岛夷志略 of the mid-14th century.[21]

Langkasuka (II)

The *Zhu-fan-zhi* 诸蕃志 of 1225 CE records a polity named as Ling-ya-si-jia 淩牙斯加 (Hokkien: Ling-gga-su-ga; Cantonese: Ling-nga-sz-ka). It notes the following:

> The Country of Ling-ya-si-jia can be reached sailing with a good wind from Dan-ma-ling [Tambralinga] in six days and nights. There is also an overland route. The local ruler wraps around himself a piece of cloth and goes barefooted. The people of the country cut their hair and also wrap themselves with a piece of cloth. Local products of this place are elephant tusks, rhinoceros horn, 'su' gharu wood, 'zan' gharu wood, musk, and camphor. The *fan*[22] merchants do business in wines, rice, 'he-chi'[23]

---

[19] Wheatley, *The Golden Khersonese*, pp. 255–6.

[20] See, for example, Eredia on Patani as cited by Wayne Bougas in "The Early History of Sai," in *Études sur l'histoire du sultanat de Patani*, ed. Perret *et al.*, pp. 259–80; and the references to Patani contained in the Chinese text *Hai-lu* below.

[21] For translations of many of the relevant references from these texts, see Hirth and Rockhill, 1967; Wheatley, *The Golden Khersonese*; Almut Netolitzky, *Das Ling-wai tai-ta von Chou Chu-fei: e. Landeskunde Sudchinas aus d. 12. Jh. / von Almut Netolitsky* (Wiesbaden: Steiner, 1977); W.P. Groeneveldt, "Notes on the Malay Archipelago and Malacca from Chinese Sources," *VBG* 39 (1880): i–x, 1–144; and W.W. Rockhill, "Notes on the Relations and Trade of China with the Eastern Archipelago and the Coasts of the Indian Ocean During the Fourteenth Century," *T'oung Pao* 15 (1914): 419–47 and 16 (1915): 61–159, 236–71, 374–92, 435–67, 604–26.

[22] "Foreign."

[23] Apparently either a type or origin name.

silks, porcelain and such products. In each case they first determine the standard value of the particular class of product in gold or silver and then engage in barter. For example, one *deng*[24] of wine is valued at one *liang*[25] of silver or two mace of gold. Two *deng* of rice are valued at one *liang* of silver, while ten *deng* of rice are valued at one *liang* of gold and so on. Annually [Ling-ya-si-jia] gives tribute to San-fo-qi.

Langkasuka is here depicted as being a dependency of San-fo-qi, to which it offered annual tribute.[26] The commercial nature of the place is also in evidence. Most scholars see this polity as a successor of the sixth-century Lang-ya-xiu (and related later toponyms) noted above. Wheatley also associates the Long-ya-xi-jiao (Hokkien: Liong-gga-se-gak; Cantonese: Lung-nga-sai-kok) as recorded in the *Dao-yi zhi-lue*[27] with Langkasuka. Daniel Perret, after examining Malay texts and other evidence, further endorses the association of Langkasuka with Patani.[28]

One of the key pieces of evidence fixing Langkasuka in the Patani region comes from a collection of Chinese maps showing, *inter alia*, the maritime routes connecting China and Southeast Asia. These undoubtedly derive from the Zheng He voyages of the early 15th century, despite this

---

[24] This term *deng* 燈 as a unit does not seem to be a Chinese term.

[25] A Chinese ounce or *tahil*.

[26] Translations of this reference can be found in Friedrich Hirth and W.W. Rockhill, *Chau Ju-Kua: His Work on the Chinese and Arab Trade in the Twelfth and Thirteenth Centuries, entitled Chu-fan-chï* (St. Petersburg: Imperial Academy of Sciences, 1911; Taipei: Ch'eng-wen Publishing Company, 1970), pp. 68–9, and Wheatley, *The Golden Khersonese*, pp. 67–8. While frequently translated as "Srivijaya," the name San-fo-qi remains somewhat of an enigma in early Southeast Asian history. It seems to be impossible not to equate it with the Arab Zabaj. Sumio Fukami considers that the term refers to a region conquered by the Chola rulers in the 11th century, and draws a convincing correlation between San Fo-qi's dependencies and those claimed by the Cholas. He suggests that different polities within this grouping employed the name or were referred to in the Chinese texts by the term "San Fo-qi." See Sumio Fukami, "San-fo-qi, Srivijaya, and the Historiography of Insular Southeast Asia," in *Commerce et navigation en Asie du Sud-Est*, ed. Nguyễn Thế Anh and Yoshiaki Ishizawa (*XIVe–XIXe siècle*) (Paris: L'Harmattan, 1999), pp. 31–45.

[27] Wheatley, *The Golden Khersonese*, pp. 80–1; and Su Ji-qing in Wang Da-yuan, *Dao-yi zhi-lue jiao shi*, annotated by Su Ji-qing (Beijing: Zhong-hua shu-ju, 1981), pp. 181–4.

[28] Daniel Perret, "Réflexions sur l'émergence du sultanat de Patani" in *Études sur l'histoire du sultanat de Patani*, Études thématiques, ed. Daniel Perret, Amara Srisuchat, Sumbun Thanasuk (Paris: École française d'Extrême-Orient, 2004), pp. 17–36.

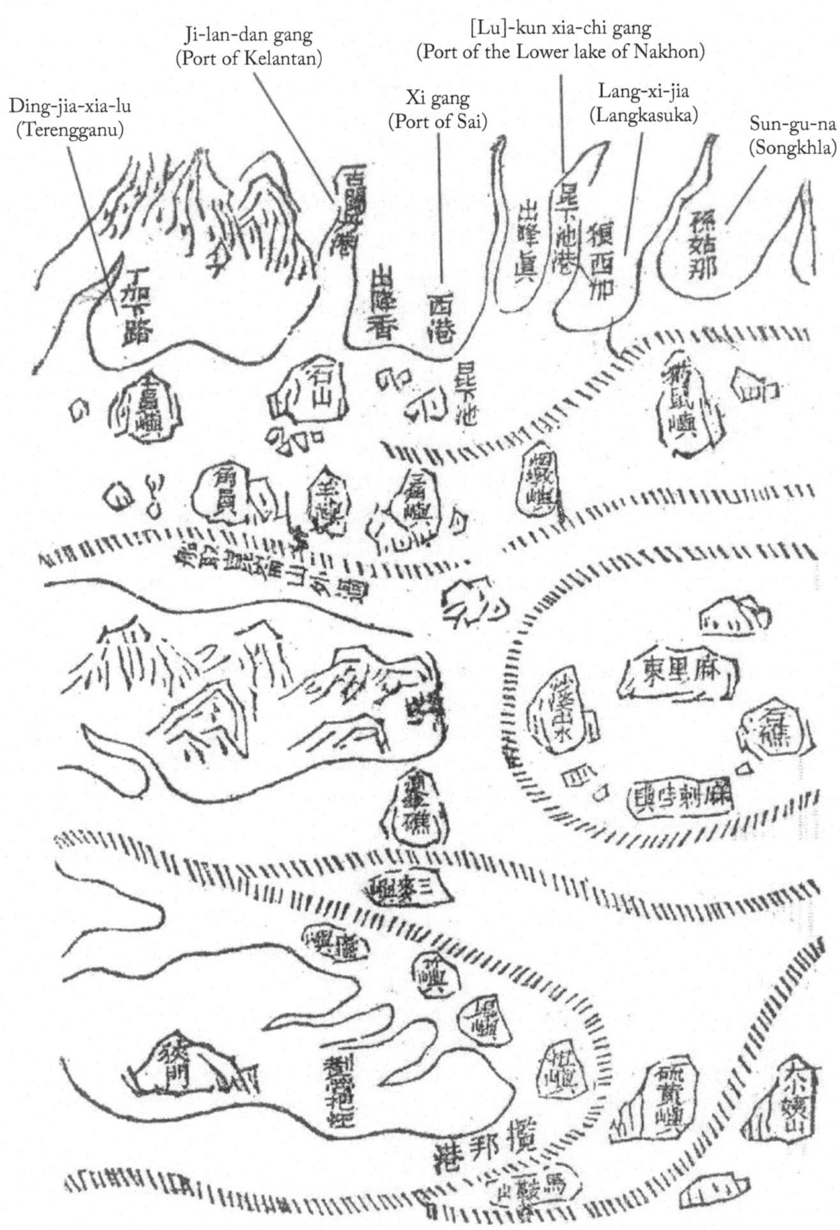

Figure 3.2 One of the maps from the *Wu-bei-zhi* 武备志 dating probably to the early 15th century (Roman script identifications added by author).

version having been published in 1628. Known as the Mao Kun 茅坤 or *Wu-bei-zhi* 武备志 [Records of Military Preparations] maps — from the author and name of the text in which they were published respectively — they comprise maps from the China coast, through Southeast Asia, to South Asia, the Middle East and the East coast of Africa. Going south in the region with which this chapter is concerned, the place names on these maps read: Sun-gu-na (Songkhla), Lang-xi-jia (Langkasuka), [Liu]-kun xia-chi Port (the port of the lower Nakhon lakes), Xi-gang (or Xi [Sai] port — the port of the Sai River), and Ji-lan-dan port (Kelantan). There is no name which can be related to "Patani." In the Patani area, we find the toponym Lang-xi-jia 狼西加, which is a close representation of the name Langkasuka. This suggests that even in the early 15th century, the Chinese recognized a place called Langkasuka in the area of modern Patani.[29] The Arab navigators of the 15th and 16th centuries also located their Langashukā between Singor and Kelantan.[30]

On the basis of both textual and archaeological evidence, Michel Jacq-Hergoualc'h suggests that the area of dense archaeological sites around Yarang in Patani should be further explored for evidence of Langkasuka.[31] He suggests that the whole area between Patani, Saiburi and Yala was part of "Langkasuka."[32] This identification and correlation is certainly in accordance with the information provided in the Chinese texts.

Chinese References to Early Modern and Modern Patani

Between the 16th and the 19th centuries, we see in diverse Chinese texts a range of references to a polity known as Patani. The earliest use of the name "Patani" in Chinese that I have been able to locate is an abbreviated version, "Da-ni," which appears in the late 16th-century text *Si-yi-guan kao*, below. It is worthy of note that neither of the 15th–16th-century Arab geographical works by Shihāb al-Dīn Ahmad ibn Mājid or by Sulaimān bin Ahmad al-Mahrī[33] uses the term Patani. Might the name itself, or Patani as the center of the polity, have emerged only in the 16th century? Below, I

---

[29] Wheatley, *The Golden Khersonese*, pp. 257–65.
[30] See G.R. Tibbetts, *A Study of the Arabic Texts Containing Material on South-East Asia* (Leiden: Brill, 1979), p. 242.
[31] Jacq-Hergoualc'h, *The Malay Peninsula*, pp. 161–71.
[32] Ibid., Document 7.
[33] For which see G.R. Tibbetts, *A Study of the Arabic Texts Containing Material on South-East Asia* (Leiden: Brill, 1979), pp. 194–229.

will detail what the Chinese texts of the 16th to the 19th centuries tell us of Patani. Unless otherwise noted, the Chinese texts refer to Patani by the name Da-ni (大泥).

1. Si-yi-guan kao 四譯館考 [An Account of the Translator's Institute] (Late 16th Century)

Under the account of the Siam Department within the Si-yi-guan, or Translators Institute, in Beijing, it is noted: "To the east this country [Siam] links with Da-ni, to its south it shares a border with Dong-niu (Toungoo), to its west it adjoins Lan-chang, and to its north it borders the great Ocean." Despite the skewed geography represented by this statement, it can be affirmed that, in this period Da-ni (Patani) was seen, at least by the Chinese, as being beyond the borders of Siam, only adjoining it to its east.

2. Tsang-wu zong-du jun-men-zhi 蒼梧總督軍門志 [Account of the Military Defences of the Guangdong/Guangxi Commander] (1581)

This military encyclopaedia includes a short passage referring to "pirates" from Patani:

> In the intercalary fourth month of the eighth year of the Wan-li reign [May/Jun 1580], the *fan*[34] bandits came from the country of Da-ni (Patani) and gathered together thousands of followers in order to attack Qiong-zhou and Ya-zhou.[35] Their power expanded enormously.[36]

It is worthy of note that maritime operators based in Patani were in 1580 engaging in raids on Hai-nan island. This was indeed a period of intense maritime raiding in East Asia, with repeated attacks on the China coast by maritime operators who based themselves in what are today Japan, Taiwan, the Philippines and the peninsula.[37] This reference is undoubtedly to the

---

[34] A generic reference to non-Chinese persons. Sometimes translated as "barbarians."

[35] Both were administrative divisions on Hainan Island.

[36] Ying Jia *et al.*, *Cang-wu zong-du jun-men-zhi*, Beijing photolithograph reprint (Beijing: Quan-guo tu-shu-guan wen-xian su-wei fu-zhi zhong-xin, 1991), *juan* 21.52a. See p. 225.

[37] For further details of the maritime raiding during this period, see So Kwan-wai, *Japanese Piracy in Ming China during the Sixteenth Century* (East Lansing, MI: Michigan University Press, 1975).

events recorded in the *Ming shi-lu* (for which see *Ming Shen-zong Shi-lu* below) of the same date, whereby the fleets of the Chinese "pirate" Lin Dao-qian were using Patani as one of their bases.

3. Tu-shu-bian 圖書編 [An Illustrated Compendium] (Late 16th Century)

This encyclopedia repeats the statement that Siam is contiguous on its east with Da-ni.[38]

4. Dong-xi-yang kao 東西洋考 [Account of the Eastern and Western Oceans] (1617)

The account of Da-ni contained in the *Dong-xi-yang kao* is a hodge-podge of confusing references. This is due to the belief of the compiler, current at that time, that Da-ni was formerly known as Bo-ni, a polity generally equated with Brunei. However, later sections of the account undoubtedly refer to Patani, for example:

> Da-ni was anciently the country of Bo-ni. Originally it was subject to Java but now it is under Siam. The country uses planks to make its city walls [...].[39] During the Wan-li reign [1573–1620 C.E.] the king of the country died of illness. As he was without a son his relatives all fought for the throne and there were killings all over the country until none of the relatives was left. Thus they enthroned a female chief as queen.
>
> [...]
>
> Formerly, a Zhang-zhou[40] person surnamed Zhang[41] was appointed as a Datuk.[42] Datuk is the title of a senior chieftain. When the country's troubles erupted, the Datuk fled to avoid the dangers. After the queen assumed the throne, she sent people to invite the Datuk back and she

---

[38] See *juan* 51, pp. 17–9 of the woodblock edition of *Tu-shu-bian* dated 41st year of the Wan-li reign.

[39] Here then follows a section relating ancient references to the country of Bo-ni.

[40] Zhang-zhou was a major port in Fu-jian during the Ming dynasty. It is located near the modern Xiamen.

[41] Hokkien pronunciation is "Teo."

[42] "Na-du" 哪督. This is the representation of the Malay honorific Datuk. The use of Datuk as a title in Patani is confirmed by its frequency in the *Hikayat Patani*; see A. Teeuw and D.K. Wyatt, eds., *Hikayat Patani: The Story of Patani* (The Hague: Nijhoff, 1970), pp. 312–3.

restored his title. The Datuk's daughter was able to come and go within the palace, but she was mentally ill. One day she spoke to the queen saying that her father intended to rebel against her. The queen was greatly angered and she immediately sent people to arrest the Datuk and his family. The Datuk thereupon killed himself. Not long after this the people of the country submitted a plaint noting that the Datuk had not been planning to rebel. The queen was greatly contrite. She had the Datuk's daughter strangled and appointed his son as a chieftain. Recently, the "red-haired *fan*"[43] who built mud storehouses there and plotted to go to Peng-hu[44] to trade, carried letters from the country of Da-ni. The events are detailed in *Hong-mao-fan kao*.[45]

The *Dong-xi-yang kao* is a valuable text as it incorporated diverse new materials, many of which were obviously based on accounts brought back from Southeast Asia. In respect of Patani, we read that by the beginning of the 17th century, the polity was regarded as subject to Siam. The narrative of the ruler dying, of contention for the throne among relatives, and the eventual enthroning of a queen, reflects quite closely the account contained in *Hikayat Patani* which relates the story of Sultan Mansur Syah dying of illness, of contention among his sons until all had died, and the installation of the Queen Raja Ijau.[46] These events, Teeuw and Wyatt inform us, occurred between 1572 and 1584, a chronology with which the Chinese text well accords.[47]

The account of the Chinese Datuk, his daughter, and his death given in the *Dong-xi-yang kao* text appears not to be contained in or confirmed by any other source. However, the use of Chinese merchants and others by Southeast Asian rulers has a long history. The reference to the "red-haired *fan*" (the Dutch) who had "recently" arrived in Patani, is certainly corroborated by the account of Peter Floris, a Dutchman who lived in Patani over the period 1612–1613.[48]

---

[43] Referring to the Dutch.

[44] An island group situated between Taiwan and Fu-jian. Known to Europeans as the Pescadores.

[45] Zhang Xie, *Dong-xi-yang kao*, annotated by Xie Fang (Beijing: Zhong-hua Shu-ju, 1981), pp. 55–9.

[46] Teeuw and Wyatt, eds., *Hikayat Patani*, pp. 169–73.

[47] Ibid., pp. 9–13.

[48] For his account, see W. Moreland, ed., *Peter Floris, His Voyage to the East Indies in the Globe, 1611–1615*, Hakluyt Society series II, Vol. 74 (London, 1934). See also Teeuw and Wyatt, eds., *Hikayat Patani*, pp. 14–5, for further references to the Dutch in Patani in the first two decades of the 17th century.

5. *Ming Shen-zong Shi-lu* 明神宗實錄 *[The Veritable Records of the Wan-li Reign] (1630)*

This text, which constitutes part of the Ming imperial annals, relates to events in and around Ming China over the period 1572–1620. A number of references from this annalistic work refer to Patani. These are provided below in the order in which they occur.

> [26 May 1580] The pirate Lin Dao-qian[49] had occupied islands in the ocean and brought calamities through his sudden attacks and disappearance. The generals and troops were unable to apprehend him and he used Siam and Da-ni as his lairs. Subsequently, he threatened Da-ni and engaged in violent attacks on Siam. An interpreter noted that those countries wished to offer their services by capturing him. Liu Yao-hui, the supreme commander of Guang-dong/Guang-xi, proposed that a reward for him be again established, as he would thereby certainly be captured. The ministry re-submitted this request and the Emperor approved it.[50]
>
> [...]
>
> [1 May 1623] The Assistant Censor-in-Chief of the Right Shang Zhou-zuo, grand coordinator of Fu-jian, reported advice that the 'red *yi*' had respected the instructions, demolished their walls and moved away in their ships. It was ordered that the Ministry be informed. Note: The 'red-hair *yi*' are distant *yi* from the country of Holland in the south-west and in the past they had not had contact with China. The Fu-jian merchants were each year issued warrants for trading with the country of Patani and with Batavia and these *yi* traded with them at these places. In the *jia-chen* year of the Wan-li reign [1604/05] the evil person Pan

---

[49] Lin Dao-qian was one of the most famous late-Ming maritime marauders and he appears to have played a prominent role in the history of 16th-century Patani. For the various accounts of his activities and exploits, see Hsü Yun-tsiao, *Da Bei-nian shi* [*A History of Patani*] (n.p., 1946); see especially pp. 111–21. Hsü records legends among the Chao-zhou people in Thailand suggesting that Lin Dao-qian had helped Siam fight off Annam (Dai Viet) and for his achievements was given the king's daughter to marry (ibid., p. 118). Hsü records various other legends and accounts of Lin Dao-qian and his younger sister (after whom a temple in Patani is named), and notes the claims that Lin Dao-qian formerly resided at Kase (Krue Se), six kilometers east of the city of Patani, which is where the grave of his younger sister is located. He is also reputed to have built a large cannon foundry. For the *Hikayat Patani* references to the cannons of Patani, see Teeuw and Wyatt, eds., *Hikayat Patani*, pp. 152–4, 224–8.

[50] *Ming Shen-zong shi-lu, juan* 99.4a. See Geoff Wade, "The Ming Shi-lu (veritable records of the Ming Dynasty) as a Source for Southeast Asian History, 14th to 17th Centuries," PhD diss., University of Hong Kong, 1994, VII: 2221–2.

Xiu traded to the country of Patani, linked up with these people and brought them here [to China]. They occupied Peng-hu and sought to trade with China. This was not permitted and it was ordered that they trade at Patani as before. Subsequently, due to the long voyage very few trading ships went there. Those who were given the warrants to trade to that port preferred a shorter route and higher profits and thus they traded secretly with Luzon [...].[51]

[...]

[23 September 1623] Also, the *yi* had despatched five 'pressed plank' ships to go directly to Peng-hu with the intention of coming to trade. Huang He-xing firmly refused permission and he assigned seven *fan* [foreigners] to them. With their two ships they sailed to Patani together with the *yi* ships. Chen Shi-ying and others then visited the ruler of Patani. The Patani chieftains advised that the Batavia chieftain had ordered the recall of the 'pressed plank' ships from various places and intended to proceed to Peng-hu. They noted that if those from Batavia were not allowed to trade they would certainly use their weapons. Holland is the country of the 'red *yi*,' while Batavia and Patani are both *fan* tribes. Their confederacy is obvious [...].[52]

The reference of 1580 shows the concern which the Ming administration felt over Lin Dao-qian and how they perceived his relationship with both Patani and Siam (Ayutthaya). The 1623 entries are of interest in several respects. They inform us that Chinese ships had been licensed by the Fu-jian authorities to trade to Patani. This was a system which had been instituted after 1567 when Chinese ships were first licensed to trade with Southeast Asian ports. The Dutch had obviously used Patani as a staging post for their trade with China, something already known from other sources. However, it is worth noting that this text suggests that when the Dutch were pushed out of Peng-hu, the islands located between Taiwan and Fu-jian, that Chinese trade moved away from Patani to Luzon. The last entry also suggests the arrival of a Chinese official in Patani to discuss trade issues and notes his conclusion that Patani, Batavia and the Dutch were colluding to achieve trading rights along the Chinese coast.

6. Hou-jian-lu 後鑒錄 [Second Half of 17th Century]

This history of insurrections and collection of biographies of insurgents during the Ming dynasty, compiled by Mao Qi-ling 毛奇齡, contains several

---

[51] *Xi-zong shi-lu, juan* 33.3a-b. See Wade, 1994, VII: 2486–7.
[52] *Xi-zong shi-lu, juan* 37.20a–21a. See Wade, 1994, VII: 2496–8.

references to Lin Dao-qian and Patani (necessarily relating to the period prior to 1575, when Yin Zheng-mao was promoted away from Guang-dong), as follows:

> The Guang-dong/Guang-xi Regional Military Commissioner Yin Zheng-mao instructed Siam and Annam that they should coordinate in punishing him [Lin Dao-qian]. Siam then sent an envoy Wu-kun Na-la[53] with a request, stating: 'Dao-qian has changed his name to Lin Wu-liang and he is now operating in our coastal bays. He desires to join with those of the country of Da-ni (Patani) in order to engage in plunder. We have already despatched troops to key places.' Zheng-mao, together with the Fu-jian Regional Military Commissioner Liu Yao-hui, thus despatched Wu Zhang from Xiang-shan[54] together with the Fo-lang-ji,[55] Shen-ma-luo-shu[56] and the ship captain, Luo-ming-chong-wen-shi-nu,[57] to jointly attack Dao-qian. Dao-qian thereupon fled to the islands of Fo-chou.[58]

This suggests that even in the first half of the 1570s, Lin Dao-qian was operating in the seas around Patani, and that the Ming were utilizing Portuguese ships as well as Thai naval forces against him. Could these events have played a role in the extension of Thai power over the Patani region?

7. Tôsen Fusetsu-gaki 渡船風說書 [1674–1723]

This Japanese work is a collection of reports made by Chinese ship captains who sailed to Nagasaki from ports in China and Southeast Asia. In Nagasaki, they were interrogated about events in ports through which they passed or

---

[53] Perhaps Ok Khun Nara?

[54] A Chinese administrative division in today's Guangdong, just to the north of Macau.

[55] Referring here to the Portuguese at Macau.

[56] An unidentified Portuguese name.

[57] An unidentified Portuguese name.

[58] The name "Fo-chou" has given rise to much debate. It has been suggested that the characters may have been reversed and the original term was Chou-fo, or Johor. This would then have referred to the islands off Johor, perhaps the Riau Archipelago. Another suggestion is that it referred to an island Fo-yu, near Ko Samui. See Chang Tseng-hsin, *Maritime Activities on the Southeast Coast of China in the Latter Part of the Ming Dynasty* (Taipei: China Committee for Publication Aid and Prize Awards, 1988), p. 90. It is also possible that the character "*chou*" is a copyist error for "*ni*." Fo-ni (or But-ni) was one of the names used for Patani. The issue remains unresolved at present.

of which they had heard. Their accounts are included in this work. The references to Patani contained within this text have been translated by Ishii Yoneo.[59] Ishii translates accounts from 18 ships which arrived in Nagasaki from Patani between the years 1675 and 1709.[60] The accounts provided are useful adjuncts to existing historical sources as they are reports by eyewitnesses of events in Patani. A report from August 1675 is particularly useful in understanding how the rulers of Ligor (Nakhon Si Thammarat), Songkhla and Patani came to be involved in long-lasting warfare:

> A country called Dai-ni [Patani] is especially barbaric and they have an inferior moral order. Since olden days their hereditary ruler has been a Queen who rules nominally regardless of the actual government of the country. The regent is called 'Third King.' The last 'Third King' was so unjust that one of his subjects revolted against him, killing him in the Year of the Ox [the year before last] and usurping the 'Third Kingship' himself. He calls himself the 'Third King' as well. The children of the murdered king fled to *liu-kun* [Ligor] in Siam and asked the ruler of Ligor for help. To avenge their dead father they recruited an armed force of 10,000 men from that ruler and travelled across land and water to attack the usurper who was defeated and secretly fled to Song Ju Lao (Songkhla), which is located between Patani and Ligor. The late 'Third King's' heir assumed the 'third Kingship.' The ruler of Songkhla, deeply sympathetic with the deposed 'Third King,' lent him an army and a navy and 10,000 men to challenge the former 'Third King's' heir. At the time of our departure from Patani the navy had reportedly arrived but the army was yet to come. We have had no news about subsequent developments in this incident. There is nothing else to add. Due to these disturbances, we had a difficult time trading there and barely managed to come here.[61]

Here, then, we have the background to the battles between Patani and Songkhla described in various sources which appear to have continued at least until the end of the 1670s.[62] In 1683 and 1684, Chinese ships sailed to

---

[59] Yoneo Ishii, ed., *The Junk Trade from Southeast Asia, Translations from the Tosen Fusetsu-gaki 1674–1723* (Singapore: Institute of Southeast Asian Studies, 1998), pp. 103–29.

[60] He also provides a short note on these texts in: Yoneo Ishii, "A Note on Pattani recorded in late 17th and Early 18th Century Japanese Documents," in *Études sur l'histoire du sultanat de Patani*, ed. Daniel Perret *et al.*, pp. 255–7.

[61] Ishii, ed., *The Junk Trade from Southeast Asia*, pp. 105–6.

[62] For some accounts of the fighting from other sources, see Teeuw and Wyatt, eds., *Hikayat Patani*, pp. 19–20.

Patani, did business there, each for more than three months, and returned to China.[63] A ship in 1686, after trading to Patani, reported to the Nagasaki authorities that: "In Patani whence we came nothing unusual happened and peace prevailed. It is also quiet in the neighbouring countries and the other 'inner' countries."[64] The situation is confirmed by the French visitors to Patani in 1684–1689 who likewise made no mention of any conflict at the time.[65]

The 1687 report provided by a ship from Xiamen which had visited Patani gave a detailed account of the polity, noting the political structure comprising a great queen, a secondary queen and a third king, and the secondary queen who would ascend the throne at the death of the great queen. It even provides an etymology for the name Da-ni 大泥 (Great Mud), suggesting that this Chinese name for the place derived from its muddy beach with mud flats extending about 900 meters out to sea. These mud flats posed difficulties for landing cargoes and the report notes that this was the reason why the Dutch and other European ships had stopped trading to it. Only small ships sailed there and only 40 Chinese resided there at this time.[66] The 17th-century decline of Patani may thus well have been in part associated with this reduction in the facility of its port.

A further report from 1689 details some of the key political events of Southeast Asia in that year. It noted that the king of Siam had died the year before[67] without an heir and that a Siamese official had usurped the throne. "To show her protest about the usurpation of the Siamese throne by this senior official, Patani sent a punitive expedition of approximately 15,000 soldiers to Siam. It was crushed by the powerful Siamese army." The report detailed separately how the regent of Johor[68] had fled to Patani to escape the efforts by the prince of Johor to destroy him. The regent was captured at sea but his family found safe haven in Patani. This resulted in Johor considering Patani an enemy polity, and that it needed to defend itself.[69] Could either of

---

[63] Ishii, ed., *The Junk Trade from Southeast Asia*, pp. 106–9.

[64] Ibid., p. 110.

[65] Teeuw and Wyatt, eds., *Hikayat Patani*, pp. 19–20.

[66] Ishii, ed., *The Junk Trade from Southeast Asia*, p. 112–3.

[67] This was the year of the death of King Narai (1656–1688) of Ayutthaya.

[68] The Laksamana (Paduka Raja) of Johor, who was captured and eventually executed by the Johor forces; see Ishii, ed., *The Junk Trade from Southeast Asia*, p. 116; and Leonard Andaya, *The Kingdom of Johor, 1641–1728* (Kuala Lumpur: Oxford University Press, 1975), pp. 138–61.

[69] Ishii, ed., *The Junk Trade from Southeast Asia*, p. 115–7.

these events have been the cause of the emergence of the Kelantan Dynasty, which is the subject of the second part of the *Hikayat Patani*?

A Chinese ship which reached Nagasaki in 1690 added further to the story of Patani's relations with Siam. It noted that

> an English official killed the king secretly and ascended the throne himself. A Siamese minister disliked the English minister's disloyal deeds which had alienated the vassal states. Eventually he killed the treacherous English official who had betrayed the king.[70] The Siamese minister usurped the Siamese throne himself with his powerful army. Taking advantage of the turmoil in Siam described above the ruler of Patani invaded Ligor with an army of 10,000 soldiers and took control of it. To counter the invasion Siam despatched reinforcements to fight Patani's army. The combined forces of Ligor and Siam easily defeated Patani's army, which was forced to withdraw. Siam despatched no further reinforcements but instead sent an ambassador who conveyed a royal command admonishing Patani for her disloyalty and made a proposal for peace negotiations. This impressed Patani greatly and she agreed to the resumption of tributary relations with Siam. Since then nothing has happened. Siam, Ligor and Patani are all at peace.[71]

An account provided by a ship which reached Nagasaki in 1693 provided new details of the invasion of Patani by Siamese forces. It noted:

> Traditionally the ruler of Patani is a queen. No man has ever ruled. On hearing the news about the Siamese forces' attack she hid in the mountains and dared not come out. The Siamese army, being unfamiliar with the topography of the mountains, had to stay at the foot of the hills. The Queen of Patani's prolonged absence made the Siamese army restless. The Queen frequently ordered the contamination of the river water which repeatedly killed Siamese soldiers. […] If her land was in disorder and eventually ruined the Chinese merchants would cancel their trading trips to Patani which would amount to the destruction of the country […] Having realized this the Queen of Patani came out of her mountain hideaway, surrendered, and promised to resume her traditional tribute to Siam. The Siamese army retreated. Soon afterwards a tributary ship was sent to Siam and both countries are at peace.[72]

---

[70] Presumably, this is a reference to the battle between Phaulkon and Phra Petracha on King Narai's death. For background to these events, see E.W. Hutchinson, *1688: Revolution in Siam. The Memoir of Father de Blèze, S.J.* (Hong Kong: Hong Kong University Press, 1968).

[71] Ishii, ed., *The Junk Trade from Southeast Asia*, pp. 117–8.

[72] Ibid., pp. 120–1.

This report is interesting in that it records the continuing existence of a queen of Patani in the early 1690s. Was this Raja Kuning[73] or a queen not mentioned in the *Hikayat Patani*?

As for accounts given by ships arriving in Japan in 1694, 1695, 1696, 1697 and 1709, all reported that Patani was at peace.[74]

8. Ming shi 明史 *[History of the Ming Dynasty] (1739)*

This *Ming shi*, the standard Chinese history of the Ming dynasty, includes several references to Patani. In *juan* 323, which gives an account of Ji-long port in Taiwan, we read:

> At the end of the Jia-jing reign (1522–1566), the *wo-kou*[75] harassed Fu-jian, and the senior general Qi Ji-guang defeated them. The *wo-kou* fled and came to live at this place. The gang member Lin Dao-qian followed them. However, Dao-qian was frightened that his forces would be absorbed by the *wo-kou* and that the imperial army would attack him. Thus he hoisted his sails and sailed directly to Bo-ni.[76] There he appropriated some land on the borders and resided there. It thus came to be known at Dao-qian port.

This obviously refers to the 1570s or 1580s and adds only the information that some Chinese knew Patani as Dao-qian Port.

9. Hai-guo wen-jian-lu 海國聞見錄 *[Account of Things Heard and Seen in the Maritime Countries] (1730)*

In this account of the maritime realm written by Chen Long-jiong 陳倫炯, based on the personal experiences of his father, we read:

> From Jian-pu-zhai (Cambodia) the main mountain range curves to the south-west into Xian-luo (Siam). From Siam, following the mountains and coast south, one reaches Xie-zai (Chaiya), Liu-kun (Nakhon), Da-nian (Patani), Ding-ge-nao (Trengganu) and Peng-heng (Pahang). The

---

[73] Teeuw and Wyatt, eds., *Hikayat Patani*, p. 20, suggest that Raja Kuning could not have reigned long after 1688.

[74] Ishii, ed., *The Junk Trade from Southeast Asia*, pp. 121–9.

[75] A generic term for "Japanese pirates," many of whom were actually Chinese or otherwise not Japanese.

[76] The Chinese name for Brunei, but as noted above, because of phonetic similarity to Patani, frequently confused in Chinese texts. Here it refers to Patani.

mountains join to China and extend directly to the south end here. Then, following the coast beyond the mountains one proceeds west. Beyond the mountains across from Pahang lies Ruo-fo (Johor). Further west from Ruo-fo lies Ma-la-jia (Malacca). This is situated across the mountains from Trengganu [...]. The various countries which lie along the coast from Siam to Johor all have their own rulers but are all under the jurisdiction of the country of Siam.[77]

In a later section of the same text, we read,

South from Siam, there are Xie-zai (Chaiya), Li-kun (Nakhon), and Song-jiao (Songkhla), which are all countries subordinate to Siam. The countries of Da-nian (Patani), Ji-lien-dan (Kelantan), Ding-ge-nao (Trengganu) and Peng-heng (Pahang) continue to the south along the mountain chain. They are all reached by travelling west from Shang-zhen Island (Poulo Obi). The sea distances vary between 150 and 160 *geng*.[78]

In the first extract, this text suggests that all of the countries from Siam to Johor were under the jurisdiction of Siam, while the second extract suggests that Siam's relations with Patani, Kelantan, Trengganu and Pahang were to some degree different from those with Chaiya, Nakhon and Songkhla, which appear to have been more directly under the control of Siam. We also see here appearing for the first time the Chinese name Da-nian 大年 being used for Patani.

10. Qing-chao tong-dian 清朝通典 [General Statutes of the Qing Court] (1780s)

The account of Patani appearing in this work is found under that of Songkhla. All of the countries noted in the account are stated to be subject to Siam.

Da-ni, or Da-nian (Patani) lies in the South-west Ocean. To the north-east it links to Liu-kun (Nakhon). The men and women wear short shirts

---

[77] For an alternate translation, see Jennifer W. Cushman and Anthony C. Milner, "Eighteenth and Nineteenth-Century Chinese Accounts of the Malay Peninsula," *JMBRAS* 52, 1 (1979): 9.

[78] A *geng* (literally a watch) was a time/distance unit used for sea voyages, generally considered to be equivalent to 60 *li* (or approximately 36 kilometers). See J. Needham, Wang Ling and Lu Gwei-Djen, *Science and Civilisation in China*, Vol. 4, part III, "Civil Engineering and Nautics" (Cambridge: Cambridge University Press, 1971), p. 564, note e. See also J.V.G. Mills, "Chinese Navigators in Insulinde about 1500," *Archipel* 18 (1979): 69–93. See pp. 24, 32.

and go barefooted. They wear knives and carry spears. The local products include pepper, dried prawns, birds nests, bees-wax, and dried buffalo and deer meat. This country is 150 *geng* distant from Xia-men.

11. Hai-lu 海錄 [Account of the Seas] (Early 19th Century)

The account of Patani contained in this text informs us that Patani lay five to six days south of Songkhla by land, or a day by sea. This account has been translated and annotated by Cushman and Milner,[79] and needs no further explication here, other than to note that much attention is given to the gold mines in Ulu Sai.

12. Yue-hai-guan-zhi 粵海關志 [Account of the Canton Customs] (1838)

This text brings together a vast range of materials from the Ming and Qing dynasties relating to countries which traded to Canton. In *juan* 22, there is a short reference to Patani, as follows:

> During the Wan-li reign (1573–1619) Fu-jian merchants were annually provided with tallies and proceeded to trade in Ta-ni (Patani), Lu-song (Luzon) and Jiao-liu-ba (Kelapa = Batavia). The Dutch then traded these goods among the various countries but dared not spy on China.

13. Hai-shang ji-lue 海上紀略 [A Short Account of the Seas] (19th Century)

This work is contained in a late 19th-century collection, but it was obviously compiled much earlier. It contains a short account of Lin Dao-qian:

> Lin Dao-qian, was a pirate band leader at the end of the Ming. Prior to the time of Zheng Zhi-long and Liu Xiang-lao he tried to occupy places in Fu-jian and Guang-dong but was unsuccessful. He then proceeded to Ryukyu, Luzon, Siam, Tonkin and Jiao-zhi, but was unable to find openings he could take advantage of. He thus proceeded to Da Kun-lun (Poulo Condore) and seeing the beauty of the place he decided to remain there […]. He then left and proceeded to Da-nian (Patani) which he attacked and captured. The current Da-nian (Patani) ruler is a descendant of his.[80]

---

[79] Cushman and Milner, "Eighteenth and Nineteenth-Century Chinese Accounts of the Malay Peninsula," p. 15.

[80] *Xiao-fang-hu-zhai yu-di cong-chao*, fasc. 9: 163.

This is the only account which claims that Lin Dao-qian had genetic input into any of the rulers of Patani.

From the information we have from Chinese texts between the 15th and the 19th centuries, Patani appears to have been a more or less independent kingdom that was drawn into the Siamese tributary system only in the 18th century. It seems that some trade shifted from Melaka to Patani following the fall of the former in 1511. In the 1560s, there appears to have been an influx of Chinese and the place appeared to have flourished for the rest of the 16th century. "Patane" appears on Portuguese charts from at least the 1560s[81] while Ishii suggests that the port declined rapidly from the end of the 17th century.[82]

Chinese Inscriptions in Patani

Chinese epigraphic texts relating to Patani are provided by Franke.[83] Evidence that a Chinese community existed in Patani from at least the late 16th century is demonstrated by a tombstone of a Chinese woman named Chen Shu-qin (Tan Siok-kin in Hokkien), dating to the *ren-zhen* year of the Wan-li reign (1592). This is, to date, the second oldest Chinese tombstone recorded for Southeast Asia.[84]

Patani in Chinese Navigation Guides and Routiers

Shun-feng xiang-song 順風相送 (sixteenth century)

This collection of sailing directions dates, in its extant form, from the 16th century, but some materials appear to have been based on earlier materials — perhaps early 15th-century sailing data collected during the Zheng He voyages. The sole manuscript of this work is held in the Bodleian Library at Oxford University. It was given to the library by an Archbishop Laud in 1639, apparently having been purchased from a Jesuit University in Europe.

---

[81] Armando Cortesao and Avelino Teixeira da Mota, *Portugaliae monumenta carto-graphica* (Lisbon: 1960–1962). See map by Anónimo-Sebastião Lopes c.1565 (Plate 401) depicting "Patane."

[82] Ishii, ed., *The Junk Trade from Southeast Asia*, p. 105.

[83] Wolfgang Franke *et al.*, *Chinese Epigraphic Materials in Thailand* (Taipei: Shin Wen Fung, 1988), pp. 640–64.

[84] For a fuller account of the stone, see Wolfgang Franke, "A Chinese Tombstone Found in Pattani," *Nan-yang Xue-bao* 39 (1984): 61–2.

Figure 3.3 Tombstone of a Chinese woman named Chen Shu-qin (Tan Siok-kin in Hokkien), dating to the *ren-zhen* year of the Wan-li reign (1592), found in Patani.

Some of the voyages contained within this collection have been translated by J.V.G. Mills.[85] It is possible that many of these maritime routes were in use for centuries before the date of this written compilation.

The routes which mention Patani and which illuminate the many maritime links it enjoyed during the sixteenth century include the following:

Voyage from Wu-yu to Patani and Kelantan[86]

Sailing out from Wu-yu,[87] one adopts a course of 205 degrees[88] and then 195 degrees for 7 *geng* […]. Then adopting a course of 215 degrees for 15 *geng* the ship will make Kun-lun-shan,[89] and you should pass on the outer side. Then proceed on a bearing of 235 degrees and then 265 degrees for 30 *geng*, and the ship will make the port of Kelantan. There is a muddy bottom and you can cast anchor. Adopting a course of 240 degrees for 7 *geng* the ship will make Liu-kun's[90] Kun-shen-wei[91] where there are shallows. Travelling further to the west, one will enter a port which is Da-ni (Patani).[92]

Return Voyage from Patani to Wu-yu and Xia-men

Leaving the shallows at Da-ni one adopts a course of 65 degrees. Passing the mountain adopt a course of 85 degrees and then 90 degrees for 10 *geng*. Then follow a course of 65 degrees for 20 *geng* after which you will make Kun-lun-shan,[93] where you should pass to the outside of the island […]. Then following a course of 55 degrees for 7 *geng* you will reach Tai-wu[94] and home.

---

[85] J.V.G Mills, "Chinese Navigators in Insulinde about 1500," *Archipel* 18 (1979): 69–93.

[86] Xiang Da, *Shun-feng xiang-song* (Beijing : Zhong-hua shu-ju, 1982), p. 53.

[87] The island of Jin-men or Quemoy in Fu-jian, from where Chinese junks set out.

[88] The compass directions given in the Chinese texts are taken from a compass divided into 24 segments, each equivalent to 15 degrees of the Western compass. For this translation, the navigational directions are converted to Western equivalents from the Chinese compass bearings. An illustration of a reconstructed Chinese compass is given in Wheatley, *The Golden Khersonese*, p. 100.

[89] Poulo Condor, off the coast of today's southern Vietnam.

[90] Nakhon Si Thammarat.

[91] Literally "The Tail of Kun-shen." "The end of the coast" (?).

[92] The port of Patani.

[93] Poulo Condore, off the coast of today's southern Vietnam.

[94] Mt. Tai-wu at the entrance to the port of Xiamen (Amoy).

Voyage from Cambodia to Patani[95]

After departing from the port [of Cambodia] and the ship leaves the shallows, when the water is 7 to 8 *tuo* in depth proceed on a bearing of 185 degrees for three *geng* and then a course of 240 degrees for five *geng* and 225 degrees for four *geng*. One will come into sight of Zhen-ci [Pulo Obi]. Then adopt a course of 225 degrees for 10 *geng*, 240 degrees for five *geng* and then 245 degrees for 10 *geng*. You will then sight Zhai-li Da-shan.[96] Adopting a bearing of 295 degrees for four *geng*, proceed along the Kun-shen[97] and follow the mountains, plumbing to find water of 16 to 17 *tuo* in depth. Proceeding ahead one reaches Kun-shen-wei [lit. the tail of Kun-shen: Possibly the entrance to the lakes]. This is Liu-kun xia-chi,[98] and there are shallows. From there, one proceeds to the west, following the mountains and enters the port of Da-ni.[99]

Return Voyage from Patani to Cambodia

Setting sail from Da-ni adopt a bearing of 75 degrees for 8 *geng* until you make Shi-bei Shoal.[100] Passing to the south-west adopt a bearing of 72.5 degrees for 22 *geng* and you will make Zhen-ci (Pulo Obi). Then adopt a bearing of 52.5 degrees for 8 *geng* and 67.5 degrees for 7 *geng*. The minor Kun-lun islands will lie to the stern of the ship and you will make the southern port of Cambodia.

Voyage from Siam to Pahang and Melaka[101]

After leaving the shallows in Siam proceed on a bearing of 172.5 degrees for 10 *geng* and you will make Bi-jia-shan.[102] There plumbing will indicate a water depth of 15 *tuo*. Passing beyond it there is a small island. There, adopt a bearing 165 degrees for 5 *geng* and one will make

---

[95] Xiang Da, *Shun-feng xiang-song*, p. 60.

[96] This place is obviously a major mountain on the east coast of the peninsula. The Chinese scholar Xiang Da identifies it as being six *geng* south of Nakhon Si Thammarat, but does not give a modern name. See Xiang Da, *Shun-feng xiang-song*, p. 262.

[97] Unidentified. Possibly a generic reference to the mainland coastline.

[98] Literally "The Lower Lake of Nakhon."

[99] The Port of Patani.

[100] Unidentified.

[101] Xiang Da, *Shun-feng xiang-song*, pp. 61–2.

[102] An important navigation point on various maritime routes recorded in *Shun-feng xiang-song*, but as yet not firmly identified.

Gui-shan.[103] Plumb the depth and pass by in waters of 12 *tuo*. Then when the water reaches a depth of 18 *tuo* there will be an island beyond. From there, use a bearing of 172.5 degrees for 3 *geng*, whereupon one will make Wan-die Island.[104] There the water will be of a depth of 3 to 4 *tuo*. Then adopt a bearing of 180 degrees for 5 *geng* and one reaches Chuan-xin-shan,[105] where the water is 24 *tuo* deep. Then proceed on a bearing of 172.5 degrees for 5 *geng* and one will make Fo Island.[106] There, the water is 25 *tuo* deep and the land is muddy. Proceed on the bearing of 172.5 degrees for 3 *geng* and one makes Lan-shan,[107] where the water is 27 *tuo* in depth. Employing the same bearing of 172.5 degrees for a further 5 *geng*, one makes Tang-shan,[108] where the water is 24 *tuo* in depth. Facing here, Su-mei-shan[109] lies to the port side.[110] The water is 20 *tuo* in depth. Adopting a course of 172.5 degrees for 5 *geng*, one arrives at Lesser Su-mei-shan,[111] where on the port side, the water depth is 20 *tuo*. Adopting a bearing of 172.5 degrees for five *geng*, one makes the Greater Su-mei-shan.[112] Ships can pass through all of the three channels, inner and outer. On the 'kun-shen'[113] side, there is a mountain called Mount Hu-lu.[114] On the starboard side[115] there are many small islands. Adopting a bearing of 180 degrees for five *geng* one makes Xi-shan,[116] which has a flat estuary where the water is 12 *tuo* in depth. Then, following a bearing of 157.5 degrees for 3 *geng*, one will make Gong-po-shan.[117] These are both on the mainland coast.[118] Here the water is 16 *tuo* in depth. By following a bearing of 172.5 degrees for five *geng*, one will arrive at the port of Liu-kun.[119] Here the water is 9 *tuo* in depth. Off the coast there is an island called Dai-mei-zhou[120]

---

103 Literally "Turtle Island." Unidentified.

104 Unidentified.

105 Unidentified.

106 Literally "Buddha Island." Unidentified.

107 Unidentified.

108 Possibly the Ang Thong Islands.

109 A generic term for Ko Samui and Ko Pha Ngan.

110 "*Zai fan pu bian*" (在帆鋪邊).

111 Koh Phangngan.

112 Koh Samui.

113 The coastal side?

114 Literally "Mt. Gourd." Unidentified.

115 "ma-hu" bian (馬戶邊).

116 Possibly Ban Sichon.

117 Literally "Husband-and-Wife Mountain/Island." Unidentified.

118 Again a tentative translation of "Kun-shen."

119 The port of Nakhon Si Thammarat.

120 Literally "Turtle-Shell Island." Possibly Koh Krah.

where the water is 15 *tuo* in depth. Proceeding along a bearing of 172.5 degrees for 3 *geng* one will make Liu-kun. Proceed carefully with your ship here as the water is only 6 to 7 *tuo* in depth. Employing a bearing of 172.5 degrees one makes Jiao Nu[121] and Miao-shan,[122] and the port of Sun-gu-na.[123] This is Qu-tou-long.[124] The water is 12 *tuo* in depth, and passing inside the water is 5 to 6 *tuo* in depth. By adopting a bearing of 157.5 degrees for 3 *geng* one makes Jiao-nu-shan[125] where the water is 12 *tuo* in depth. By adopting a bearing of 157.5 degrees for 7 *geng* one makes the Liu-kun xia-chi.[126] Following the coastline along and heading west around the mountains one enters the port of Da-ni.[127] The central channel has shallows and one cannot enter through it. Bear this in mind. From the port of Da-ni sailing along the mountains the ship will make the port of Ji-lan-dan.[128] Then, proceeding on a bearing of 172.5 degrees for 4 *geng* one arrives within the San-jiao islands.[129] At the entrance sits a large island as the central point and it is named Jiao-yuan-shan.[130] One can pass through both the inner and outer channels. By adopting a course of 180 degrees for three *geng* one makes Mian-hua Island.[131] Then, proceeding for a further 5 *geng* along a bearing of 180 degrees one makes Duo Island.[132] Then, following the same bearing for another 5 *geng* one makes the port of Peng-heng […].[133]

Voyage from Melaka to Siam[134]

[…] Adopting a bearing of 360 degrees for 5 *geng* one makes the port of Peng-heng.[135] A further five *geng* along the same bearing and one

---

[121] Koh Gnu.

[122] Koh Mu.

[123] Songkhla.

[124] Phatthalung, a polity slightly to the north of Songkhla. In Cantonese, the characters are read Wat-t'au-lung.

[125] Koh Gnu.

[126] Literally "The Lower Lake of Nakhon."

[127] The port of Patani.

[128] The port of Kelantan.

[129] Pulau Perhentian.

[130] Pulau Perhentian Besar.

[131] Possibly Pulau Redang.

[132] Possibly Pulau Tenggol off Kuala Dungun.

[133] The port of Pahang, situated on the Sungei Pahang.

[134] Xiang Da, *Shun-feng xiang-song*, p. 62.

[135] The port of Pahang.

will make Mian-hua Island.[136] In the south-west direction there are sunken shoals. Adopting a bearing of 360 degrees for 3 *geng* one reaches San-jiao Island[137] and the port of Ji-lan-dan.[138] Proceeding of a bearing of 360 degrees for 7 *geng* one reaches the Liu-kun xia-chi[139] which is the port of Da-ni.[140] Following a course of 352.5 degrees for 5 *geng* one will make the port of Sun-gu-na.[141] This is Qu-tou-long.[142] Pursuing the same course of 352.5 degrees for a further 10 *geng* one will make Dai-mei-zhou.[143] Pass to the inner side. Then, assuming a course of 360 degrees for 15 *geng* one will make the Greater and Lesser Islands of Su-mei-shan.[144] Pursuing a course of 352.5 degrees for 10 *geng* one will make Fo Island.[145] A further 10 *geng* along the same bearing of 325.5 degrees will bring one to Gui-shan.[146] A further 5 *geng* along the same bearing will bring you to Bi-jia-shan.[147] Then, along a bearing of 360 degrees for 5 *geng* one will reach Chen-gong island.[148] Then, adopting a bearing of 7.5 degrees for 5 *geng* one will make Zhu-yu[149] on the coast.[150] When the stern of the ship lies across from Zhu-yu enter and you will find the port [of Siam] …

Voyage from Patani to Timor[151]

Leaving the port [Patani], adopt a course of 172.5 degrees and you will make San-jiao Island.[152] Then pursue a course of 180 degrees for 5 *geng* and you will make Mian-hua Island.[153] Then by assuming a course of 157.5 degrees for 5 *geng* one will make Duo Island.[154]

---

136 Possibly Pulau Redang.

137 Pulau Perhentian.

138 The port of Kelantan.

139 Literally "The Lower Lake of Nakhon."

140 The port of Patani

141 The port of Songkhla.

142 Phatthalung.

143 Literally "Turtle-Shell Island." Possibly Koh Krah.

144 Koh Phangngan and Koh Samui.

145 Literally "Buddha Island." Unidentified.

146 Literally "Turtle Island." Unidentified.

147 Unidentified.

148 Possible identities include Koh Pai and Koh Lan.

149 Literally "Bamboo Island."

150 Again, a tentative translation of "Kun-shen bian" (崑莘邊).

151 Xiang Da, *Shun-feng xiang-song*, p. 62.

152 Pulau Perhentian.

153 Possibly Pulau Redang.

154 Possibly Pulau Tenggol, off Kuala Dungun.

Conclusion

Chinese texts provide the earliest references to the area which is today known as Patani. It is not unlikely that the area had been attacked and perhaps administered by the Khmers from the third century, although this suggestion remains speculative. The first polity name associated with this region which we can glean from Chinese texts is Langkasuka, recorded in a wide variety of historical traditions from at least the sixth century CE. This polity was extensive. It likely included what is today the region of Patani, but comprised territories extending far beyond it. It appears clear that it was a major center of Buddhism and was a transit point for monks traveling between China and India, as well as a key trading center. This polity or a successor was still in existence and was an influential trade center in the 13th century, albeit in some sort of subordinate relationship with Zabaj/Sri Vijaya. The location of Langkasuka in the Patani region is confirmed by Chinese maps showing maritime routes in the early 15th century.

It appears that a certain amount of trade shifted from Melaka to Patani following the fall of the former to the Portuguese in 1511. Chinese texts provide no evidence for the introduction of the polity name Patani, although they do indicate that the area was known to the Chinese by the name "Da-ni" by the late 16th century. The Portuguese had recorded "Patane" on their charts from at least the 1560s. In the 1560s, there was an influx of Chinese and apparently the place flourished for the rest of the 16th century. A late 16th-century text suggests that Da-ni lay to the south of Siam, beyond the political boundaries of that state. It was also recorded as a base for Chinese maritime operators who engaged in raids on southern China. The historical existence of the figure of Lin Dao-qian as a maritime operator based in Patani is affirmed by several Chinese texts relating to the late 16th century.

Patani was also one of the ports to which Chinese ships were licensed to trade in the late 16th century. The enthroning of a queen in Patani in the late 16th or early 17th century is recorded in the *Dong-xi-yang kao* (1617), as is the prominence of a Chinese official under the queen and the arrival of the Dutch in Patani in the early 17th century. The *Tōsen Fusetsu-gaki*, which recorded statements from the captains of Chinese ships entering Nagasaki, provides an independent source on political events in the polity of Patani during the 17th to the early 18th century, often unrecorded in other texts. The progress of warfare between Patani and Songkhla, involving Johor, Kelantan and Siam, is also detailed in these reports. The port appears to have declined swiftly from the end of the 17th century. *Hai-guo wen-jian-lu*, an early 18th-century text, suggests that even in that period Patani was seen as basically independent of Ayutthaya.

Like any historical text, the Chinese records need to be read in the context of their compilation and the concerns of their intended audience. Their contents are not always congruent with the texts of other traditions, but they do provide valuable materials for illuminating the historical evolution of polities in the Patani region.

PART TWO

Patani's Place in Southeast Asian and Middle Eastern Islamic Networks

CHAPTER 4

The Patani *'Ulamâ'*: Global and Regional Networks

Azyumardi Azra

Geographically, the Muslim area in Southeast Asia, also conveniently called the Malay-Indonesian world, is often viewed by scholars as being at the periphery of the Islamic world centered in Mecca, Medina, and even Cairo. Situated far from the region known today as the Middle East, the area of Muslim Southeast Asia represents one of the least Arabized parts of the Islamic world. Despite this, however, the development of Islam in Southeast Asia is inseparable from that in the Arab world. Since the introduction of Islam into Southeast Asia, the development of Islam in the Middle East has affected the course of Islam in the Malay-Indonesian world. Within this context, throughout the 17th and 18th centuries, international scholarly (*'ulamâ'*) networks centered in the Haramayn (Mecca and Medina) played a crucial role in continually sending renewal and reform impulses to the Malay-Indonesian world. Within these networks, Patani scholars had a prominent position.

There is a tendency among scholars of Islam to exclude Southeast Asian Islam in any discussion of Islam. This kind of treatment is largely based on an assumption that the area did not have single stable core of Islamic tradition in the early period to serve as a dominant focal point, in relation to which scholars can find some points of orientation. Furthermore, the evidence that survives for the arrival and development of Islam in Southeast Asia is fragmented among a large number of languages and cultural traditions. The combination of these factors has, until recent times, placed the study of Southeast Asian Islam outside of the mainstream of Islamic studies. However, recent works on Southeast Asian Islam, together with the fact that this area now contains the most populous Muslim country (Indonesia) in the world, have brought a new impetus to the study of the nature of the relationship between Middle Eastern and Southeast Asian Islam.

Strong links between Southeast Asian Muslims and their Middle Eastern counterparts have existed since the very early period of Islam in the Malay-Indonesian world. Contact between Southeast Asia and the Arab world existed even in the pre- and early Islamic period, and took place mostly by way of trade. Later, from the late 12th century, wandering Sufi teachers from the Arab world frequented the harbor-cities of Southeast Asia and introduced Islam to the native population. The increasing prosperity of the Muslim states in the Malay world in the 16th and 17th centuries due to the rise of a lucrative trade in gold, pepper, and other spices, increased these contacts and expanded relations even further. A massive penetration of Islam was carried out mainly by these wandering Sufi teachers from the Middle East and South Asia who were attracted both by the spirit to spread Islam and the prosperity of the Muslim courts in this region. As a rule, they came and lived under the patronage of the sultans. The latter provided for them not only peaceful and convenient shelters as well as a good deal of material reward, but also crucial facilities which enabled them to carry out their mission to improve Islamic life among the population.[1]

The prosperity of the Southeast Asian Muslim states provided opportunities for the Muslim population in this area to travel to the centers of Islam in the Arab world. Most of them, of course, went to the Hijâz or more precisely the Haramayn to make the *hajj* — the fifth pillar of Islam. But there were also those who stayed there and studied various Islamic sciences for years. This led to the rise of what the Meccans and Medinese called the "*Jâwî*" community in the Holy Land. The term '*As̲h̲âb al-Jâwîyyîn*' literally refers to the Javanese people, but more than that it came to signify the whole Malay-Indonesian people[2] regardless of their original homelands or ethnic origins. Thus, the Javanese, Sumatranese, the

---

[1] On the presence of scholars from the Arab world in the courts of the Malay-Indonesian states during the early days of Islam in Southeast Asia, see B. Schrieke, *Indonesian Sociological Studies*, part 2 (The Hague and Bandung, 1957), pp. 237–67; HJ. de Graaf and TH.G.TH. Pigeaud, *De eerste Moslimse vorstendommen op Java: studien over de staatkundige geschiedenis van de 15e en 16de eeuw* (The Hague: KITLV, Verhandelingen 69, 1974); R.O. Winstedt, "Early Muhammadan Missionaries," *JSBRAS* 81 (1920).

[2] Ibn Battûta in the 14th century also used the term, "Jâwâ," to signify the whole Malay archipelago. See Ibn Battûta, *Travels in Asia and Africa 1325–1354* (London, 1983), pp. 271–6, 367.

peninsular Malays and even the Patani of southern Thailand were all called the *'Jâwî'*. The phenomenon of the Jâwî community in the Middle East has been commented upon by numerous scholars. In his biographical dictionary, *Fawâ'id al-Irtiḥâl wa Natâ'ij al-Safar*,[3] compiled in the 11th/17th century, Mustafâ al-Hamâwî (d. 1171/1757), a pupil of Ibrâhîm al-Kûrânî, one of the most important figures in the global *'ulamâ'* networks, provides us with the earliest yet known Arabic reference to the *Jâwî* students in Medina. Two centuries later, Snouck Hurgronje also vividly described the lives of the *Jâwî* students and their community in Mecca.[4]

Considering the extensive economic, diplomatic and socio-religious relations between the Muslim Malay-Indonesian and the Arab world, it is very likely that *Jâwî* students had pursued Islamic learning even before the 17th century in various places along the trade and *ḥâjj* routes in the Middle East. Unfortunately, on this subject we have only very sketchy and fragmentary information. The scarcity of source materials makes the effort to reconstruct the early history of the *Jâwî* students in the Arab world difficult. The effort must be made, however, for even if the evidence uncovered is fragmentary, it provides a picture of various networks which articulated not only the nature of the religious and intellectual relationships between the Arab and Southeast Asian Muslims but also reflected the development of Islam in the region, thus presenting a clearer picture of Islam in the Malay-Indonesian world.

Western records, particularly those of the Portuguese from the 15th century, are an important source of knowledge. They, however, present a picture of Islam as an economic and political rival and offer little about Islam's religious face, representing the extension of a world community. To discover this dimension, it is necessary to turn from the political and the economic faces of Islam, those encountered by its political and economic enemies, toward the intellectual and spiritual products of Muslim life and civilization. To do this, one must seek the lines of intellectual tradition exemplified in the study and pursuit of Islamic learning — either inside or outside of the

---

[3] For biographies of Mustafa b. Fath Allâh al-Hamâwî, see Muhammad Khalîl al-Murâdî, *Silk al-Durar fi a'yân al-qarn al-thânî 'ashar* (henceforth *Silk al-Durar*) (Baghdad: 1302/1883–1834), pp. 3–4: 178; 'Abd al-Rahmân al-Jabartî, *'Ajâ'ib al-âthâr fî al-tarâjim wa al-akhbar* (henceforth *'Ajâ'ib al-âthâr*), ed. Hasan Muhammad *et al.* (Cairo, 1957–1958), 1: 181. A copy of the *Fawâ'id al-Irtiḥâl* is available as Ms. Dâr al-Kutub, Cairo, tarîkh 1093, folio 166–7.

[4] Snouck Hurgronje, *Mekka in the Latter Part of the Nineteenth Century* (Leiden, 1970), pp. 215–92.

Southeast Asian region — and attempt to see their distribution among and influence upon the various focal points of Islam in the Malay-Indonesian world. Unless this is done, it is not possible to isolate the crisscrossing networks of lines of tradition and lines of authority which stimulated and maintained the pulse of Islamic belief and social life in this area.

A clearer picture of the lineages of intellectual tradition in the 17th- and 18th-century Malay-Indonesian world is provided by the networks of Aḥmad al-Qushâsî and Ibrâhîm al-Kûrânî, then the leading *'ulamâ'* in the Haramayn, and their students. There are at least two branches of the network of the above *'ulamâ'* in the Malay-Indonesian world. The first can be traced down to 'Abd al-Ra'ûf al-Sinkilî of Aceh and Yûsuf al-Makassâri of Sulawesi (formerly Celebes). The second was through Abû al-Ṭâhir ibn Ibrâhîm al-Kûrânî, Muḥammad Ḥayyâ al-Sindî, originally of India, and Muḥammad 'Abd al-Karîm al-Sammânî and the latter's *Jâwî* students in the 18th century including Dâwûd ibn 'Abd Allâh al-Faṭânî, the main figure of this chapter.

The main purpose of this chapter is to uncover the intellectual and religious networks of the Patani *'ulamâ'* with their Arab and Southeast Asian counterparts, specifically those originating from Aḥmad al-Qushâsî, Ibrâhîm al-Kûrânî, 'Abd al-Ra'ûf al-Sinkilî, Yûsuf al-Makassâri and their students in the 17th and 18th centuries. This discussion is confined to the Patani branch in the networks. We do not include in this discussion the branches of the network in the other parts of the Malay-Indonesian world in the period discussed which included al-Palimbânî and al-Banjarî and the latter's *Jâwî* disciples.

The chapter also aims to assess the impact of those networks upon the Islamic renewal movements in the Malay-Indonesian world which gained momentum from the 17th and 18th centuries. By concentrating upon these themes, we will hopefully have a better grasp of the development of Islam, not only in the Patani area but also in Southeast Asia in general. As we will see, the Patani region, like many other areas in the Malay-Indonesian archipelago, constantly received numerous impulses — mainly through the networks of the *'ulamâ'* — from the centers of Islam in the Arab world which to a great degree influenced the dynamic of Southeast Asian Islam.

The Global *'Ulamâ'* Networks

Before discussing the global and regional networks of the Patani *'ulamâ'*, it is necessary to give some account of religious developments in the Muslim world, since these developments had a profound influence on the character of Islamic scholarship in Patani. The spiritual situation of Islam in the late medieval period can be said to be broadly characterized by the tension between so-called orthodox Islam and Sufism. From the fourth/tenth and fifth/tenth centuries onward, there emerged among the *tarîqas* a new doctrine largely opposed to the spirit of orthodox Islam. The contrast, not only with orthodox Islam but even with the early Sûfî practices, is remarkable. Whereas during the first three centuries, seekers of the Sûfî path displayed a striking independence of spirit, resourcefulness and creativity, later on a rigorous discipline was imposed and an absolutely unquestioning submission to the spiritual dictatorship of the Shaykh or the master was emphasized. And whereas in the third/ninth century, Junayd al-Baghdâdî, for instance, taught that a seeker should behave vis-à-vis God as a puppet, it was now said that he should be in the hands of his preceptor as a "dead body in the hands of its washers."[5]

In the meantime, however, efforts had already begun in the third/ninth century within Sûfî circles like al-Kharrâz and Junayd to bridge the gulf between orthodox Islam and Sufism and to keep the latter within reasonable limits. A powerful instrument in this whole *rapprochement* were the new *ahâdith* (the Prophet Muhammad tradition) put into circulation throughout the third/ninth century and fourth/tenth centuries with the double purpose of promoting the cause of Sûfism and bringing it into the orthodox fold. In the last quarter of the fourth/tenth century, a number of men such as al-Sarrâj (d. 377/987) and al-Kalâbâdhî (d. 385/995), through their writings pleaded the cause of a moderate Sufism with a structure of ideas consistent with and even lending support to orthodoxy. This movement culminated in the monumental life-work of al-Ghazâlî (d. 505/1111), who proved to be its genuine cornerstone. He succeeded in achieving a synthesis between Sufism and *kalâm* which was largely adopted by orthodoxy and confirmed by *ijma'*. The strength of the synthesis lies in the fact that it gave a spiritual basis for the moral practical *elan* of Islam and thus brought it back to its original religious dimensions. Al-Ghazâlî, therefore, not only reconstituted orthodox Islam, making Sufism an integral part of it, but also was a great reformer of Sufism, purifying it of un-Islamic elements and putting it at the service of orthodox religion.

It is clear that after the Sûfî movement had captured the Muslim world during the sixth/12th and seventh/13th centuries, emotionally, spiritually and intellectually, among the *'ulamâ'* — even the pure *muhaddithûn* (traditional-

---

[5] Fazlur Rahman, *Islam*, 2nd ed. (Chicago: University of Chicago Press, 1979), p. 137.

ists) — there was a growing awareness that it was almost impossible for them to neglect the Sûfî forces entirely. Now, instead of refuting it, they tried to incorporate as much of the Sûfî legacy as could be reconciled with orthodox Islam and which could be made to yield a positive contribution toward it. The moral motive of Sûfîsm was emphasized and some of its techniques such as *dhikr* or *murâqaba*, "spiritual concentration," were also adopted. But the object and the content of this concentration were now identified with the orthodox doctrine and the goal redefined as the strengthening of faith in dogmatic tenets and the moral purity of the spirit.

This type of Sufism, or "neo-Sufism" as Fazlur Rahman calls it, tended to generate orthodox activism and fostered a more positive attitude to this world.[6] Henceforth, often a great *'ulamâ'* and a great Sûfî were one and the same person. The involvement of the *'ulamâ'* in the Sûfî movement resulted in continual emphasizing and renewal of the original moral factor and puritanical self-control in it, especially at the expense of the extravagant features of popular ecstatic Sufism. This was the spiritual situation of Islam when, beginning in the 11th/17th century, a sense of anxiety and urgency for religious-social moral reform gripped the greater part of the Muslim world, expressing itself in different areas in reform movements and schools which exhibited a fundamentally similar character.

It appears that scholarly communities, particularly those centered in Mecca and Medina, played a crucial role in the abovementioned developments. Due the central role of these Holy Cities in the religious life of the Muslims, it is not surprising that both cities increasingly became the crucial focal points and meeting places of *'ulamâ'* from all over the Muslim world. Since the early 11th/17th century, changing patterns of communication and exchange among various parts of the Muslim world produced a significant increase in the interaction among scholars in the Holy Cities. The growing presence of European trade shipping and naval power, especially in the Indian Ocean, made travel between the Indian Ocean region and the Hijâz even more direct and convenient.[7] Similar growth in commercial activity also increased the facility of travel within the Mediterranean Basin. As a result, more *'ulamâ'* were able to come together more frequently from the widely

---

[6] Ibid., p. 195.

[7] For an interesting account of the growing European trade shipping and naval presence in the Indian Ocean since the early 17th century, see Willem Floor, "The Iranian Navy in the Gulf during the Eighteenth Century," *Iranian Studies* 20, 1 (1987): 31–53. Cf. Auguste Toussant, *History of the Indian Ocean* (Chicago: University of Chicago Press, 1967), pp. 118–44.

scattered parts of the Islamic world. Thus, a cosmopolitan network of *'ulamâ'* emerged out of the Haramayn.

The core of this network was the popular and influential *'ulamâ'* of Mecca and Medina, both the natives and those from other parts of the Islamic world who had resided permanently there. In other words, the birthplaces and areas of early study of members of this network, both teachers and students, ranged from the Hijâz, Persia, India, Indonesia to Egypt, Morocco and beyond. The group as a whole was widely traveled and very few among them received their full education in just one or two places. The increased cosmopolitanism of the international network of *'ulamâ'* helped knowledge seekers like the Jâwî students broaden their intellectual horizons. Such a network helped to bring together different sources of information and different traditions of study. It provided students with a wider ranging education. Furthermore, in addition to studying with their main teachers as a rule the students also took advantage of contact with scholars coming to the Holy Cities on the *hâjj* pilgrimage.

Further analysis of this intellectual community reveals an even more interesting picture. It appears that this group was not defined by *tarîqa* membership or *madhhab* affiliation. However, it does seem that this group had some relationship to the legal schools. As Voll suggests, the core of this group was Shâfi'î, with a solid leaven of Mâlîkî scholarship.[8] Moreover, the community represented the continuation of the strong trend toward a renewed emphasis on various Islamic disciplines, particularly *hadîth* studies. In accordance with the trends mentioned earlier beginning in the late 10th/16th century, there were efforts among the *'ulamâ'* in the Haramayn and Egypt to go beyond the six standard collections of the *hadîth* and the later medieval manuals based on them. More than simply preserving, explaining and reorganizing the materials found in these collections, more and more *'ulamâ'* showed an increasing interest in searching new *ahâdîth*, examining and putting them into use. Thus, there was a gradual shift of emphasis in *hadîth* studies; now most *'ulamâ'* studied *hadîth* more for practical purposes rather than for academic reasons. *Hadîth* studies were now utilized more and more to provide a standard for judging current practices among Muslims.[9]

---

[8] John O. Voll, "Muhammad Hayyâ al-Sindî and Muhammad ibn Abd al-Wahhab: An Analysis of an Intellectual Group in Eighteenth Century Haramayn," *BSOAS* 38 (1975): 35.

[9] John O. Voll, "Hadith Scholars and Tariqahs: An *Ulama* Group in the Eighteenth Century Haramayn and their Impact in the Islamic World," *JAAS* 15, 3–4 (1980): 264–7.

This development in *hadîth* studies was clearly related to the intention to reform Sufism. *Hadîth* studies were viewed as a discipline supporting attempts at the socio-moral reconstruction of Muslim society, and thus had a scripturalist tone. For many of those in the international community of *'ulamâ'* who developed a commitment to the socio-moral reconstruction of society, the content of the thought that they shared came out of their *hadîth* studies; the model of the ideal society used was the community described by *hadîth*. Furthermore, *hadîth* studies provided strong linkages among the *'ulamâ'*. In addition, Sûfî *turuq* gave them a more personal tie and a common set of affiliations that helped to give the informal groupings of *'ulamâ'* a greater sense of cohesion. Even among the reformist *muhaddithûn* in the Haramayn and their students, *turûq* affiliation was almost always an important part of their self-identification.

To sum up, the network consisted of international *'ulamâ'* who had a variety of contacts with one another and shared educational experiences. The picture that emerges from the pattern of relationships is one of a relatively closely intertwined intellectual community. There is no evidence to show that this network was in any way formally organized. However, it seems safe to assume that these *'ulamâ'* had some basic common views and either knew the other personally or were well-known to one another by reputation. The lines of connection can also be traced through the chains of student-teacher relations. However, the ideal of the socio-moral reconstruction of society and the enthusiasm imparted by the teachers within the network were more important in linking them together in this revivalist network than any uniformity of doctrinal position.

The Patani *'Ulamâ'* in the Networks of the 19th Century

If al-Rânîrî, al-Sinkilî and al-Maqassârî — who were central figures in the Malay-Indonesian *'ulamâ'* networks in the 17th century — have commanded attention from many modern scholars, the *'ulamâ'* in the 18th century have been less studied. Furthermore, the few sources that are available, mainly in Malay and Indonesian, simply narrate biographies without a critical examination of their positions vis-à-vis Islamic develop-ments in the Malay-Indonesian world or their relationship to the teachings introduced by al-Rânîrî, al-Sinkilî and al-Maqassârî. No attempt has been made to trace their connection to the scholarly networks of the larger Muslim world, which would allow us to gain a better picture of the con-tinuing religious and intellectual relations between the archipelago and the Middle East.

The *'ulamâ'* involved in the 18th century scholarly networks did indeed have traceable connections with the earlier networks. While they did not have direct teacher-student connections with al-Rânîrî, al-Sinkîlî and al-Maqassârî, their teachers in Mecca and Medina were among the prominent figures of the networks in their period and had direct connections with earlier scholars to whom the three predecessors had also been linked. Malay-Indonesian scholars in the 18th century, moreover, were well aware of the teachings of their three precursors, and they established their intellectual connections with them by making references to their works.

In the 17th-century *'ulamâ'* networks we can see how through al-Maqassârî and his disciples the regions of South Sulawesi and West Java, following Aceh, came into the picture of Islamic learning in the archipelago. In the 18th century, South Sumatra, South Kalimantan (Borneo), and the Patani region in the south of modern Thailand (or in the northern part of the Malay Peninsula), came to prominence. I would argue that the birthplaces and ethnic origins of Malay-Indonesian scholars reflect the historical course of Islam in the archipelago through the centuries. It points to the fact that appreciation of the importance of Islamic learning as well as the need for renewal and reform began to gain ground among various ethnic groups in the archipelago. These scholars, having acquired substantive credentials in Islamic learning, in turn stimulated a further intensification of Islamization, particularly among their respective ethnic groups. In the 18th century, such developments continued, so as to become one of the most distinctive features in the transmission of Islam in the archipelago.

There were several major Indonesian-Malay *'ulamâ'* who came from various regions and ethnic groups in the archipelago in the period of the 18th to the early 19th centuries. A prominent group came from the Palembang region of South Sumatra. The most important among them were Shihâb al-Dîn b. 'Abd Allâh Muhammad, Kemas Fakhr al-Dîn, 'Abd al-Samad al-Palimbânî, Kemas Muhammad b. Ahmad, and Muhammad Muhyî al-Dîn b. Shihâb al-Dîn. Then came Muhammad Arshad al-Banjârî and Muhammad Nafîs al-Banjârî from South Kalimantan; 'Abd al-Wahhâb al-Bugisî from Sulawesi; 'Abd al-Rahmân al-Batâwî al-Masrî from Batavia, and Dâwûd b. 'Abd Allâh b. Idrîs al-Fatânî from the Patani region — the subject of this chapter.

Although information about these scholars is sketchy, their careers and teachings make it clear that they were involved both socially and intellectually in the networks. Taken together, they constitute the most important scholars of the archipelago in the 18th and early 19th centuries. I will in this chapter deal only with Dâwûd b. 'Abd Allâh b. Idrîs al-Fatânî, the prototype of the Patani *'ulamâ'* who were involved in both regional and global *'ulamâ'* networks.

Dâwûd b. 'Abd Allâh Al-Faṯanî and the Rise of Patani Scholarship

For the purpose of this chapter, I will examine those Patani scholars who, by the end of the 18th century, increasingly came into the picture of Islamic learning in the archipelago. With the rise of Patani scholars, we can observe not only the proliferation of the tradition of Islamic learning at both local and regional levels, but also the further dissemination of renewal and reformism in the Malay-Indonesian world as a whole.

We should again mention briefly the conversion of the Patani region in South Thailand to Islam, which took place roughly from the 12th to the 15th century. The Patani Sultanate was a populous and prosperous Muslim kingdom on the Malay peninsula until it fell under Thai control in 1202/1786. Its harbor was also an important center of commerce for Asian and European traders.[10] There have been numerous studies of Patani Muslim separatism after the Second World War, but less attention has been paid to the growth of Islamic tradition and institutions among the Patani Muslims in the earlier period.[11]

Despite Patani's political weakness as a border state, wandering teachers, mainly Sûfîs, continually frequented the Patani region. The *Hikayat Patani*, for instance, reports the coming of scholars such as Shaykh Gombak and his student 'Abd al-Mu'mîn from Minangkabau,[12] and Shaykh Faqîh Shâfî al-Dîn from Pasai in the second half of the 16th century. They played crucial roles in the religious life of the sultanate. Shâfî al-Dîn, for instance, urged the construction of a royal mosque and later became the advisor of Sulṯân Muẕaffar Shâh in religious matters.[13] Again, in the middle of the 17th century, a number of scholars came to Patani: Sayyid 'Abd Allâh from Jerusalem via Trengganu, Ḥâjî 'Abd al-Raḥmân from Java, Faqîh 'Abd al-Manân, a Minangkabau from Kedah, and Shaykh 'Abd al-Qâdir from

---

[10] For the classic treatment of the rise and decline of the Patani Sultanate, see Ibrahim Syukri, *History of the Malay Kingdom of Patani*, trans. C. Bayley and J.N. Miksic (Athens, OH: Center for International Studies, 1985), pp. 13–62.

[11] See Syukri, *History of the Malay Kingdom of Patani*, pp. 21–38; A. Teeuw and D.K. Wyatt, eds., *Hikayat Patani* (The Hague: Nijhoff, 1970), pp. 10–20.

[12] Ibid., pp. 76–7.

[13] Ibid., pp. 78–9.

Pasai.[14] They were reported to have carried out concerted efforts to spread further the *hukum Allâh* (*sharî'ah*) into Patani.[15]

An important point conveyed by these accounts is that the Patani Muslims were not isolated among their fellow Muslims in the archipelago. With the coming of scholars to their region, Patani Muslims were made aware of developments in religious ideas and institutions in other parts of the Malay-Indonesian world. It is highly plausible that it was such scholars who stimulated the establishment of the traditional Islamic educational institution known in Patani as the *pondok*.[16] Furthermore, it has been suggested that the *pondok* system which also developed in other parts of the Malay Peninsula, may have originated from Patani.[17] It is said that al-Palimbânî had his early education in Patani, probably in the *pondoks* there, but little is known about them in the period before the 19th century. Matheson and Hooker point out that the *pondoks* in Patani were very prestigious and that their more advanced students were welcomed as teachers elsewhere in the Malay-Indonesian archipelago.[18] I would argue, however, that this was only true in the 19th century, when native Patani scholars increasingly came onto the scene and contributed significantly to the further growth of the *pondoks*.

---

[14] Ibid., p. 131.

[15] Ibid.

[16] "*Pondok*" literally means "hut" but it is also generally used to refer to a cluster of buildings used collectively as a center of Islamic education. The *pondok* is thus similar in characteristics to the *surau* and *pesantren* existing in other parts of the archipelago. For further discussion of these terms, see Azyumardi Azra, "The Rise and Decline of the Minangkabau Surau," Unpublished MA thesis, Columbia University, 1988, especially pp. 19–21.

[17] Virginia Matheson and M.B. Hooker, "Jawi Literature in Patani: The Maintenance of an Islamic Tradition," *JMBRAS* 61, I (1988): 43. Cf. R.L. Winzeler, "The Social Organization of Islam in Kelantan," in *Kelantan: Religion, Society and Politics in a Malay State*, ed. W.R. Roff (Kuala Lumpur: Oxford University Press, 1974), p. 266n7; Cf. A.A.H. Hasan, "The Development of Islamic Education in Kelantan," in *Tamaddun Islam di Malaysia*, ed. Khoo Kay Kim (Kuala Lumpur: Persatuan Sejarah Malaysia, 1980), pp. 190–6. For an account of the Patani *pondok* in recent years, see W.K. Che Man, "The Thai Government and Islamic Institutions in the Four Southern Muslim Provinces of Thailand," *Sojourn* 5, II (1990): 263–70.

[18] Matheson and Hooker, "Jawi Literature in Patani," p. 43; and Hamdan Hassan, "Pertalian Pemikiran Islam Malaysia-Aceh," in *Tamaddun Islam*, ed. Kim, pp. 53–5.

Wan Mohd Shaghir Abdullah, a grandson of Aḥmad Zayn al-'Âbidîn al-Faṭânî — a leading Patani scholar[19] — lists Muḥammad Ṭâhir b. 'Alî al-Faṭânî (914–978/1508–1578), the author of the famous *Tadhkirât al-Mawḍû'ât*,[20] as among the earliest and most famous scholars of Patani. This is incorrect, since Muḥammad Ṭâhir also had a *laqab* (nickname) of al-Hindî (from India), to be exact, from Patan in the Gujarat region.[21] If this claim were true, Muḥammad Ṭâhir al-Faṭânî would have been the earliest *Jâwî*/Malay scholar to have been involved in the scholarly networks of the Haramayn, that is, a century ahead of al-Rânîrî, al-Sinkilî and al-Maqassârî.

The best known Patani scholar was Dâwûd b. 'Abd Allâh b. Idrîs al-Faṭânî, however he was neither the earliest nor the only scholar from this region to be involved in the networks. From Dâwûd al-Faṭânî's *silsilah* of the Sammâniyyah *ṭarîqa*, we know that he received the order not directly from Muḥammad al-Sammânî but by way of two other Patani scholars, namely 'Alî b. Isḥâq al-Faṭânî and Muḥammad Ṣâliḥ b. 'Abd al-Raḥmân al-Faṭânî.[22] They probably came to the Haramayn earlier than Dâwûd al-Faṭânî. Abdullah suggests that the three were contemporaries although Dâwûd al-Faṭânî was the youngest among them.[23]

Thanks to research done by Abdullah published in his *Syeikh Daud bin Abdullah al-Fatani*, we know more about Dâwûd al-Faṭânî's life and career. According to Abdullah, records kept by families related to Dâwûd al-Faṭânî give differing dates of birth of this great scholar, that is 1724, 1153/1740 and 1183/1769. He died in Ta'if, and one of the records states that the date of his death was 1265/1847.[24] There is no way that we can be certain which date

---

[19] H.W.M. Shaghir Abdullah, *Syeikh Daud bin Abdullah al-Fatani: Ulama dan Pengarang Terulung Asia Tenggara* (Kuala Lumpur: Hizbi, 1990), p. 3; Matheson and Hooker, "Jawi Literature in Patani," pp. 19, 28.

[20] This work deals with *ḥadîth* forgeries, see a Beirut reprint of the Cairo (?) edition, 1343.

[21] For a biography of Muḥammad Ṭâhir al-Hindî al-Faṭânî, see Abû al-Fallâḥ b. 'Abd al-Ḥayy Ibn al-'Imâd, *Shadharât al-Dhahab fî Akhbâ man Dhahab*, 8 vols. (Cairo: Maktabat al-Qudsî, 1350–1351/1930–1931), VIII: 410; Ṣiddîq b. Ḥasan al-Qannûjî, *Abjad al-'Ulûm*, 3 vols. (Beirut: Dâr al-Kutub al-'Ilmiyyah, n.d.), III: 222–3; al-Kattânî, *Fahras*, I: 171; al-Zarkalî, *al-A'lâm*, VII: 42–3; Brockelmann, *GAL*, II: 548; S. II: 601.

[22] See, Dâwûd al-Faṭânî's *silsilah* of the Sammâniyyah *ṭarîqa*, in Abdullah, *Syekh Daud bin Abdullah*, pp. 36–7.

[23] Ibid., pp. 37–8.

[24] Ibid., pp. 23–4.

is correct. But on account of the fact that he studied with certain teachers, I believe that al-Fatânî was most probably born in 1153/1740. He is reported to have studied with al-Barrâwî (d. 1182/1768). Furthermore, his earliest dated work was completed in Mecca in 1224/1809, when he would have been 69 years old and had established himself as a learned scholar. The date of his last work is 1259/1843.[25] This means that he lived a relatively long life. The height of his career was certainly in the early decades of the 19th century — beyond the period of our discussion. However, since he had direct connections with the 18th-century scholarly networks, he must be included in this discussion.

According to Abdullah, Dâwûd al-Fatânî was born in Kresik (also spelled Gresik), an old harbor in Patani, where Mawlânâ Malik Ibrâhîm, one of the famous *Wali Sanga*, reportedly preached Islam before proceeding to East Java. There he built a center of Islamic propagation also named Gresik. It is said that Dâwûd al-Fatânî had ancestral relations with Malik Ibrâhîm.[26] Abdullah believes that Dâwûd al-Fatânî's grandfather was a certain Faqîh 'Alî or Datuk Andi Maharajalela, a prince of the Bone Sultanate, South Sulawesi, who came to Patani in 1047/1637 from the court of Bone as a result of political unrest. Later he married a Patani woman and rose to influence in the Patani Sultanate.[27] Although it is difficult to substantiate these accounts, they at least indicate that in addition to intellectual connections among various Muslim ethnic groups in the archipelago, there also existed blood relations among them.

It is certain that Dâwûd al-Fatânî acquired his early education in his own region, apparently from his father. Abdullah suggests that Dâwûd al-Fatânî also studied in *pondoks* in Patani.[28] He later traveled to Aceh where he studied for two years with Muhammad Zayn b. Faqîh Jalâl al-Dîn al-Ashî.[29] According to Hasjmi, Muhammad Zayn al-Ashî was a leading scholar of the Acehnese Sultanate during the period of Sultân 'Alâ' al-Dîn Mahmûd Shâh (r. 1174–1195/1760–1781). Al-Ashî appears to have inherited his father's expertise in *fiqh*, for he wrote several works in this field. There is strong evidence that al-Ashî also studied in the Haramayn. Two of al-Ashî's known

---

[25] P. Voorhoeve, "Dâwûd b. 'Abd AllÂh b. Idrîs al-Fatânî or Fattânî," *EI²*, II: 183.

[26] Abdullah, *Syeikh Daud bin Abdullah*, p. 22.

[27] Ibid., pp. 10–3. Neither the *Hikayat Patani* nor Syukri's *History of Patani* mentions Faqîh 'Alî or Datuk Maharajalela. The *Hikayat Patani* makes mention only of Faqîh or Shaykh Safî al-Dîn (pp. 78–9) and Faqîh 'Abd al-Manân (p. 131).

[28] Abdullah, *Syeikh Daud bin Abdullah*, p. 32.

[29] Ibid., p. 32.

works, the *Bidâyat al-Hidâyah* and *Kashf al-Kirâm*, were prepared in Mecca in 1170/1757 and 1171/1758 respectively and were apparently completed in Aceh.[30]

In all probability, Dâwûd al-Fatânî traveled from Aceh directly to the Haramayn, but I have found no evidence when he reached the Holy Land. In the Haramayn, he immediately joined the circle of *Jâwî* students already there. Among them were Muhammad Sâlih b. 'Abd al-Rahmân al-Fatânî, 'Alî b. Ishâq al-Fatânî, al-Palimbânî, Muhammad Arshad, 'Abd al-Wahhâb al-Bugisî, 'Abd al-Rahmân al-Batâwî, and Muhammad Nafîs. Abdullah tells us that Dâwûd al-Fatânî was the youngest of these scholars.[31] All the older students were also teachers of Dâwûd al-Fatânî or at least assisted him in his studies with non-Malay teachers.

Abdullah asserts that Dâwûd al-Fatânî, like al-Palimbânî, Muhammad Arshad, 'Abd al-Rahmân al-Batâwî and 'Abd al-Wahhâb al-Bugisî, studied directly with al-Sammânî.[32] He is also reported to have learned as well from 'Isâ b. Ahmad al-Barrâwî, who died in 1182/1768, seven years earlier than al-Sammânî (d. 1189/1775). In other words, when Dâwûd al-Fatânî studied with al-Barrâwî, presumably in the last years of his life, al-Sammânî was at the height of his career. On account of the fact that he had studied with al-Barrâwî and al-Sammânî, Dâwûd al-Fatânî must have reached the Haramayn in the second half of the 1760s, or when he was in his late twenties.

Who were these teachers? 'Isâ b. Ahmad (b. 'Isâ b. Muúammad al-Zubayrî al-Shâfi'î al-Qâhirî al-Azharî), better known as al-Barrâwî, was a *muúaddith* and *faqîh* who had a special expertise in legal *hadîth* and in the comparative study of schools of Islamic law.[34] He lived mainly in Cairo where he died in 1182/1768. He was also a frequent visitor to the Haramayn,

---

[30] See A. Hasjmi, "Pendidikan Islam di Aceh dalam Perjalanan Sejarah," *Sinar Darussalam* 63 (1975): 20; *Sejarah Kebudayaan Islam di Indonesia* (Jakarta: Bulan Bintang, 1990), p. 230; Abdullah, *Syeikh Daud bin Abdullah*, p. 32; "Syekh Muhammad Zain bin Faqih Jalaluddin Aceh" in his *Perkembangan Ilmu Fiqh*, pp. 62–74; Amir Sutarga *et al.*, *Katalogus Koleksi Naskah Melayu Museum Pusat* (Jakarta: Departemen P&K, 1972), pp. 264, 276.

[31] Abdullah, *Syeikh Abdush Shamad*, p. 6; Syeikh Muhd. Arshad, pp. 8–9; *Syeikh Daud bin Abdullah*, pp. 32–3.

[32] Abdullah, *Syekh Abdush Shamad*, p. 6; *Syeikh Daud bin Abdullah*, p. 33.

[33] Abdullah, *Syeikh Daud bin Abdullah*, p. 39.

[34] For al-Barrâwî's biography and works, see Muhammad Khalîl al-Murâdî, *Silk al-Durar*, III: 273; al-Jabartî, *'Ajâ'ib al-Athâr*, I: 366–7; al-Baghdâdî, *Hadiyyat al-'Ârifîn*, I: 811; Brockelmann, *GAL*, S II: 445; al-Zarkalî, *al-A'lâm*, V: 283–4; al-Kattânî, *Fahras*, I: 223.

performing pilgrimage and involving himself in scholarly activities. He received *hadîth* through *isnads* which included 'Abd Allâh al-Basrî among others. Al-Barrâwî was also a teacher of Murtadâ al-Zabîdî, and Muhammad b. 'Alî al-Shanwânî.[35] Al-Shanwânî, as we shall see shortly, was also a teacher of Dâwûd al-Fatânî. Al-Fatânî mostly studied *Usûl al-Dîn* (literally "roots of religion") with al-Barrâwî. He possessed an *isnâd* in this science which ran from al-Barrâwî to include such major network scholars as 'Abd Allâh al-Basrî, 'Alâ' al-Dîn al-Bâbilî, Shams al-Dîn al-Ramlî, and Zakariyyâ al-Ansârî.[36] Taking into consideration the fact that al-Fatânî wrote a number of works on *fiqh*, it is highly probable that he also learned this science from al-Barrâwî.

More than any other Malay-Indonesian scholar who preceded him, Dâwûd al-Fatânî had many teachers either of Egyptian origin or with a strong Egyptian connection. Since there is no evidence that he ever traveled to Cairo, he must have studied with them during their visits to the Haramayn. In addition to studying with al-Barrâwî, Dâwûd al-Fatânî continued his studies with al-Sharqâwî,[37] the Shaykh of al-Azhar and celebrated Khalwatiyyah reformist mentioned earlier as a teacher of Muhammad Nafîs. Since al-Sharqâwî was an expert in *hadîth*, *sharî'ah*, *kalâm* and *tasawwuf*, it is probable that Dâwûd al-Fatânî also learned these sciences from him.

The next teacher Dâwûd al-Fatânî studied with was the successor of al-Sharqâwî as Shaykh of al-Azhar. He was Muhammad b. 'Alî Al-Shanwânî (d. 1233/1818), better known simply as al-Shanwânî, who was elected President of al-Azhar University upon al-Sharqâwî's death.[38] During his youth, Al-Shanwânî studied with most of the leading scholars of Egypt, including Ahmad al-Damanhûrî, al-Barrâwî, al-Sharqâwî and Murtadâ al-Zabîdî. He was an outstanding scholar of *hadîth*, *fiqh*, *tafsîr* and *kalâm*. Although he taught mostly in Cairo, he had a number of students in Mecca who studied with him during his visits there.[39] With al-Shanwânî, al-Fatânî advanced his studies in *fiqh* and *kalâm*.

---

[35] See al-Kattânî, *Fahras*, I: 102, 197, 535, 1078.

[36] For Dâwûd al-Fatânî's complete *isnâd* of the Usûl al-Dîn, see Abdullah, *Syeikh Daud bin Abdullah*, p. 39.

[37] Ibid., p. 38.

[38] See Al-Shanwânî's biography in al-Jabartî, *'Ajâ'ib al-Athâr*, III: 588; Al-Baytâr, *Hilyat al-Bashar*, III: 1270–1; al-Zarkalî, *al-A'lam*, VII: 190; al-Kattânî, *Fahras*, II: 10789.

[39] See al-Kattânî, *Fahras*, I: 229; II: 578, 777, 796.

In addition to studying with the scholars mentioned above, al-Fatânî learned from Muhammad As'ad, Ahmad al-Marzûqî, and Ibrâhîm al-Ra'îs al-Zamzamî al-Makkî.[40] The latter was also a teacher of al-Palimbânî. Dâwûd al-Fatânî studied various branches of Islamic discipline with Ibrâhîm al-Ra'îs as well as receiving the Shâdhaliyyah *tarîqa* from him. It is interesting that Ibrâhîm al-Ra'îs in turn took this *tarîqa* from Sâlih al-Fullânî, who received it from his teacher Ibn Sinnah.[41]

"Muhammad As'ad" was most probably Muhammad As'ad al-Hanafî al-Makkî, a *muhaddith* who is said to have been very proud of having a *hadîth isnâd* which went back to 'Abd Allâh al-Basrî.[42] Interestingly enough, al-Fatânî did not take the *isnâd*, but instead took the Shattâriyyah *tarîqa* from Muhammad As'ad al-Makkî, who took it from Muhammad Sa'îd b. Tâhir, who took it from his father, Abû Tâhir, who in turn took it from his father, Ibrâhîm al-Kûrânî, who took it from Ahmad al-Qushâshî, who took it from Aúmad al-Shinnâwî, who took it from Sibghat Allâh.[43] This *silsilah* is different from that of al-Sinkilî, who received the *tarîqa* not from al-Kûrânî, but from al-Qushâshî.

We have little information about "Ahmad al-Marzûqî," the last in the list of al-Fatânî's teachers. This scholar very likely was Ahmad al-Marzûqî [al-Makkî al-Mâlikî], a student of al-Shanwânî. Ahmad al-Marzûqî was known as a *muhaddith* who taught mostly in Mecca.[44] Both Muhammad As'ad al-Hanafî and Ahmad al-Marzûqî al-Mâlikî were al-Fatânî's teachers of non-Shâfi'î *madhhab*. This indicates that the differences among scholars in their adherence to schools of Islamic law, as in the previous century, were not barriers in the networks of *'ulamâ'* in the 18th century.

Taking into account all the teachers he studied with and the sciences he obtained from them, it is clear that Dâwûd al-Fatânî's education was complete and comprehensive. He possessed more than sufficient knowledge to earn him fame as a major Malay-Indonesian scholar in the period of transition between the 18th and 19th centuries. Al-Fatânî seems to have never returned to Patani or elsewhere in the Malay-Indonesian archipelago. Instead he devoted himself to teaching and writing in the Haramayn until he died in Ta'if. His numerous Malay-Indonesian students came from all over

---

[40] Abdullah, *Syeikh Daud bin Abdullah*, pp. 34–5, 39.

[41] See al-Fatânî's *silsilah* of the Shâdhiliyyah order in Abdullah, *Syeikh Daud bin Abdullah*, p. 41. For Sâlih al-Fullânî and Ibn Sinnah, see again 4: 2.

[42] al-Kattânî, *Fahras*, I: 198–9.

[43] Abdullah, *Syeikh Daud bin Abdullah*, p. 35.

[44] Al-Kattânî, *Fahras*, I: 122–3; II: 1079.

the archipelago.[45] He has been claimed as a pivotal figure for the history of Islam in Patani.[46]

There can be no question that al-Fatânî was one of the most prolific of all Malay-Indonesian scholars. He wrote at least 57 works, dealing with almost all branches of the Islamic disciplines.[47] The works themselves, however, some printed in various places in the Middle East and the Malay-Indonesian world, have not been sufficiently studied.

The careers of Malay-Indonesian scholars in the 18th century such as al-Fatânî and many others have shown us that the scholarly networks among Malay-Indonesian and Middle Eastern scholars continued to gain momentum. More importantly, they indicate the incessant transmission of reformism from the centers of learning in the Middle East to various parts of the archipelago. The wide circulation of the writings of these Malay-Indonesian scholars pushed Islamic reformism in this part of the Muslim world even further.

Dâwûd al-Fatânî made a substantial contribution to the further spread of Islamic reformism through legal doctrines not only in the Patani area but also in other parts of the Malay-Indonesian archipelago. He is one of the best examples of scholars who were successful in their attempts to reconcile the legal and mystical aspects of Islam.

While we will discuss Dâwûd al-Fatânî's main works on *tasawwuf* later, we now focus our attention on those works dealing with various aspects of the *sharî'ah* or *fiqh*. The most important among them are the *Bughyat al-Tullâb al-Murîd Ma'rifat al-Ahkâm bi al-Sawâb* which discusses religious observances (*fiqh al-'ibâdah*), and *Furû' al-Masâ'il wa Usûl al-Masâ'il* which deals with rules and guidelines in daily life. Smaller epistles then follow, such as the *Jâmi' al-Fawâ'id* on the various obligations of a Muslim towards his fellows and others, *Hidâyat al-Muta'allim wa 'Umdat al-Mu'allim* on *fiqh* in general, *Munyat al-Musallî* on prayer (*salât*), *Nahj al-Râghibîn fî Sabîl al-Muttaqîn* on commercial transactions, *Ghâyat al-Taqrîb* on inheritance

---

[45] See a partial list of his students in Abdullah, *Syeikh Daud bin Abdullah*, p. 42, followed by accounts of the activities and roles of these students in furthering reformism in the archipelago on pp. 43–50. Cf. Matheson and Hooker, "Jawi Literature in Patani," pp. 26–35, which give the names of the most important Patani scholars together with their works in the period after Dâwûd al-Fatânî.

[46] Matheson and Hooker, "Jawi Literature in Patani," p. 19.

[47] For lists of his works and descriptions of their contents, see Abdullah, *Syeikh Daud bin Abdullah*, pp. 55–99; Matheson and Hooker, "Jawi Literature in Patani," pp. 21–6; and Winstedt, *A History of Classical Malay*, pp. 153–4.

(*farâ'id*), *Idah al-Bâb li Murîd al-Nikâh bi al-Sawâb* on matters relating to marriage and divorce, and a number of other shorter writings on particular sections of *fiqh*.[48]

Coming out of the same intellectual milieu, it is hardly surprising that al-Fatânî also derived most of his teachings from the important scholars referred to earlier. His major sources for *Bughyat al-Tullâb* are, among others, the *Minhâj al-Tâlibîn* of al-Nawawî, *Fath al-Wahhâb* of Zakariyyâ al-Ansârî, *Tuhfat al-Muhtâj* of Ibn Hajar al-Haytamî, and *Nihâyat al-Muhtâj* of Shams al-Dîn al-Ramlî. Al-Fatânî's *Bughyat al-Tullâb* consists of two volumes of 244 and 236 pages, and was printed several times in Mecca, Istanbul, Cairo and various places in the archipelago. Delineating the details of various Muslim religious obligations (*'ibâdah*), this work has been claimed as the most complete book on this particular aspect of *fiqh*. The *Bughyat al-Tullâb* was as popular as the *Sabîl al-Muhtadîn* of Muhammad Arshad, and it is still used in many parts of the Malay-Indonesian world.[49]

The *Furû' al-Masâ'il* is also an ample work on *fiqh*; a reprinted Meccan edition (1257/1841), based on an earlier edition published in Cairo (n.d.), consists of two volumes of 275 and 394 pages. The work is an adaptation of both Shams al-Dîn al-Ramlî's *al-Fatâwâ* and Husayn b. Muhammad al-Mahallî's *Kashf al-Lithâm*, and was written in the form of questions and answers. By adopting this style of writing, al-Fatânî introduced a new method of delineating the intricacies of *fiqh* to produce what he considered an attractive and effective way to teach *fiqh* to his Malay-Indonesian audience.

Al-Fatânî, through his works listed above, played a major role in the history of *fiqh* in the archipelago. Even though the works bore Arabic titles, they were in fact written in Malay. This reflects al-Fatânî's concern that his Malay-Indonesian co-religionists be able to understand the precepts of the *sharî'ah*. He underlines the importance of the *sharî'ah* or *fiqh* for Muslims by citing a *hadîth* of the Prophet which states that a good *faqîh* can better defend himself against evils than a thousand Muslims who perform religious obligations without sufficient knowledge of *fiqh*. It must be kept in mind, however, that al-Fatânî was not simply a great *faqîh* or an expert on the

---

[48] See Abdullah, *Syeikh Daud bin Abdullah*, pp. 55–99; Matheson and Hooker, "Jawi Literature in Patani"; Winstedt, *A History of Classical Malay*, pp. 153–4.

[49] Abdullah, *Syeikh Daud bin Abdullah*, pp. 99–100; Matheson and Hooker, "Jawi Literature in Patani," p. 21; M.B. Hooker, *Islamic Law in South-East Asia* (Singapore: Oxford University Press, 1984), p. 32; van Bruinessen, "Kitab Fiqh di Pesantren," pp. 48–9.

sharî'ah. He was also a Sûfî *par excellence*, devoting a number of writings to *taṣawwuf* and *kalâm*.

A comprehensive study of Dâwûd al-Fatânî's mystical teachings is not yet available, but it is clear that he was also a great proponent of al-Ghazâlî's *tasawwuf* as well as a prominent defender among Malay-Indonesian scholars of Ibn 'Arabî's tradition. Al-Fatânî is known to have written several works along the same lines as the doctrines of al-Ghazâlî, bearing such titles as the *Tarjamah Bidâyat al-Hidâyah* and *Minhâj al-'Âbidîn*.[50] For al-Fatânî, al-Ghazâlî was the greatest Sûfî. As he put it: "Imâm al-Ghazâlî is like a very deep sea, containing precious pearls which cannot be found in other seas."[51]

In al-Fatânî's view, the greatest Sûfî next to al-Ghazâlî was al-Sha'rânî. He points out in the introductory notes to his Malay translation of al-Sha'rânî's *Kashf al-Ghummah* that al-Sha'rânî was his "*penghulu*" (master) who guided him in the path of God.[52] It is no surprise, therefore, that al-Fatânî, like al-Sha'rânî, staunchly defends the doctrine of Ibn 'Arabî's *waḥdat al-wujûd* and the seven grades of being in a little known but important work entitled *Manhal al-Sâfî fî Bayân Zumar Ahl al-Sûfî*.[53]

Al-Fatânî was very critical of people who styled themselves Sûfîs, while in fact they were simply pseudo-Sûfîs (*berlagak seperti sufi*), ignorant of the true teachings of Sufism. According to al-Fatânî, among the groups of pseudo-Sûfîs were people who claimed to have complete union (*ittiḥâd*) with God. He bitterly denounces them, "The people of *ittiḥâd* believe that their essence (*dhât*) becomes the Essence of God. This is a gross infidelity (*kufr*). Those who worship idols are much better than they are ... they think that they gain the true vision ... [by contrast] they have come to the presence of *iblîs* (devil)."[54]

---

[50] See, Matheson and Hooker, "Jawi Literature," p. 24; Abdullah, *Syeikh Daud bin Abdullah*, pp. 61, 77.

[51] Abdullah, *Syeikh Daud bin Abdullah*, p. 109.

[52] Ibid., pp. 74, 111, 168. The *Kashf al-Ghumma* is listed among al-Sha'rânî's works. See Michael Winter, *Society and Religion in Early Ottoman Egypt: Studies in the Writings of 'Abd al-Wahhâb al-Sha'rânî* (New Brunswick: Transaction Books, 1982), p. 8.

[53] Abdullah, *Syeikh Daud bin Abdullah*, p. 62. For a lengthy exposition of the contents of the *Manhâl al-Sâfi*, see Abdullah, "Syeikh Daud bin Abdullah al-Fathani," in his *Perkembangan Ilmu Tasawwuf*, pp. 121–46.

[54] Al-Fatânî, *Ward al-JawÂhir*, p. 55, cited in Abdullah, *Syeikh Daud bin Abdullah*, p. 107.

In connection with this view, al-Faṭânî conceives the *Manhal al-Ṣûfî* as an answer and explanation of various concepts and terms in *taṣawwuf.* In addition to discussing such concepts as *waḥdat al-wujûd, martabat tujuh* and other mystico-theological matters, al-Faṭânî complemented the work with a list of key terms in Ṣûfî vocabularies and their meanings. In the introductory notes to the *Manhal al-Ṣûfî*, the author again criticizes pseudo-Ṣûfîs who misunderstood the concept of, for instance, *waḥdat al-wujûd*, because they simply embraced its literal meaning. For that reason, he reminds the Muslims that books dealing with such topics should be read only by experts or by those who have solid grounding in the "*ṭarîqa Muḥammadiyyah.*"[55]

The fact that al-Faṭânî was a scholar of *fiqh* makes it no surprise that he was a leading proponent of the *jihâd* among Malay-Indonesian scholars in the 18th century. This is not surprising, since his period saw increasing attempts by the Thais to tighten their grip over the Muslim region of Patani. It is hardly surprising, therefore, that this sorry political situation in his homeland also became a main concern of al-Faṭânî.[56] Abdullah[57] even asserts that al-Faṭânî returned home to lead *jihâd* himself against the Thais before he finally returned and settled permanently in the Haramayn. We cannot support this assertion for there is no evidence to corroborate it. Al-Faṭânî never returned to Patani from the time he left it in search of knowledge, and seems to have spent the rest of his life teaching and writing in the Haramayn.

Al-Faṭânî appeals to Muslims, especially those in Patani, through his writings. However, he did not write a special work on the *jihâd*, nor did he send letters to the Muslim rulers of Patani. He delineated his ideas on the *jihâd* in his various works. It is known, for example, that his work on prayer (*ṣalât*), entitled *Muniyyat al-Muṣallî* in Malay, completed in Mecca in 1242/1827, has some political overtones. Matheson and Hooker[58] suggest that the work was written particularly for the Muslims in Patani in order to support them in their struggles against the Thai.

Al-Faṭânî's teachings on *jihâd* appear to have some relation to his idea of the Islamic state. In his opinion, an Islamic state (*dâr al-Islâm*) should be

---

[55] For further discussion of al-Faṭânî 's *taṣawwuf*, see Abdullah, "Syeikh Daud bin Abdullah al-Fathani," pp. 24–58; *Syeikh Daud bin Abdullah*, pp. 106–11.

[56] See Syukri, *History of the Malay Kingdom of Patani*, pp. 39–56, on Thai renewed attacks on Patani.

[57] Abdullah, *Syeikh Daud bin Abdullah*, pp. 94–5.

[58] Matheson and Hooker, "Jawi Literature in Patani," p. 25; bin Ngah, *Kitab Jawi*, pp. 29n12, 41n3, 41n5, 42n8–9.

based on the Qur'ân and the *hadîth*, otherwise it would be called a state of unbelievers (*dâr al-kufr*).[59] We have no details about his notion of the Islamic state, particularly with regard to its system of administration. However, an Islamic state must function to protect Islam and the Muslims. Therefore, apostasy (*murtadd*) from Islam is not allowed, and those who so deviated should be killed.[60]

In connection with the protection of Islam and the Muslims, according to al-Fatânî, it is an essential obligation (*fard al-'ayn*) for every Muslim to wage *jihâd* against hostile unbelievers (*kafîr al-harb*). If an Islamic state is attacked and annexed by unbelievers, the Muslims are obliged to fight them until they regain their freedom. As for the *jihâd* to expand the realm of Islam, which involves the subduing of the unbelievers, it is only a *fard al-kifâyah*, an obligation which is acquitted in the name of all as long as it is performed by some. In both cases of the obligation of *jihâd*, al-Fatânî stresses the need for Muslims to have fighting strategies; they must not wage *jihâd* if they are ill-prepared militarily.[61]

Viewing al-Fatânî as the prototype of the Patani *'ulamâ'* in the networks, the Patani *'ulamâ'* were no exception in the tradition of Islamic scholarship in the Malay-Indonesian world. By the early to mid-19th century, scholarship coming from this area was overwhelmingly concerned with *fiqh* and *usûl al-dîn*; *tasawwuf* is poorly represented in the surviving material.[62] In part, this may be explained as a reflection of what was happening in Mecca where, as Snouck Hurgronje explains,[63] the chief branches of learning had been reduced to these three. However, there is also a local factor to take into account.

Patani in the 19th century was arguably a pawn in the power struggle between Britain and France for political control in Southeast Asia. Siam itself was desperately trying to retain its status as an independent state, and part of its success lay in convincing European powers (in this case Britain) of its actual exercise of sovereignty over its southern, and Malay-populated,

---

[59] Abdullah, *Syeikh Daud bin Abdullah*, pp. 34, 95.

[60] Al-Fatânî, *Hidâyat al-Muta'allîm*, p. 17, cited in Abdullah, *Syeikh Daud bin Abdullah*, p. 95.

[61] Al-Fatânî, *Furû' al-Masâ'il wa Usûl al-Masâ'il*, MS., Jakarta, National Library, Ml. 779, 945ff.; *Bughyat al-Tullâb*, I: 95, cited in Abdullah, *Syeikh Daud bin Abdullah*, pp. 97–8.

[62] Matheson and Hooker, "Jawi Literature in Patani," p. 36.

[63] C. Snouck Hurgronje, *Mekka in the Latter Part of the Nineteenth Century* (Leiden: E.J. Brill, 1931), p. 160.

territorial possessions. The Patani *'ulamâ'* were not unaware of this and their priority became the protection of a Malay-Muslim identity. In this effort, *tasawwuf* had little obvious practicality to offer. This does not mean to say that it was neglected — it was not — but the prior emphasis was elsewhere.

An excellent example of this line of argument is of course the work of Shaykh Dâwûd b. 'Abd Allâh al-Fatânî, the subject of this chapter. But we can also give an illustration of the later extent of the genealogy in the life and work of Shaykh Ahmad Muhammad Zayn (1856–1906), one of the greatest Patani *'ulamâ'* in the post-Dâwûd ibn 'Abd Allâh period. His grandfather, two of his three uncles and two cousins were all well-known scholars.[64] In Mecca, Shaykh Ahmad studied medicine and later became supervisor of the Malay (*Jâwî*) printing press which published many of Shaykh Dâwûd's works. He was also a noted teacher and his students went on to fill high positions in politics, as Mufti in various parts of Malaya, Kalimantan and Cambodia, and as teachers and founders of *pondok*. His influence has extended into the 20th century. One of the most prominent of his students was Che Muhammad Yusuf, better known as Tok Kenali (1868–1933), who established the Majlis Ugama Islam in Kelantan and was a leading commentator and teacher of religion in the Malay world. Shaykh Ahmad's own writing is distinguished, in particular his *al-Fatâwâ al-Fatâniyyah*. This is a long and complex collection of *fatâwâ* (religious rulings) and the material shows just how great the pressure on the 19th century *'ulamâ'* was, and initially at least, how the responses were written.

Conclusion

I have attempted to show that the Patani region was not a separate entity in the Malay-Indonesian archipelago or in the Muslim world. Though the Patani Muslims seem to be geographically peripheral, they in fact continually received impulses from the centers of Islam in the Arab world which influenced the development of Islam in their area and other parts of Southeast Asia.

From the 17th century onward, the most crucial link between Islam in the Arab world and Southeast Asian Islam — Patani included — was the international network of *'ulamâ'*, centered in the Haramayn. Consisting of *'ulamâ'* from various parts of the Muslim world, this network proved to be one of the most important training grounds for the *Jâwî* students (including

---

[64] For genealogy, see Matheson and Hooker, "Jawi Literature in Patani," p. 28.

those coming from Patani) who since the early 17th century increasingly came to the Arab world to pursue the Islamic disciplines. Through this network, the *Jâwî* students received not only various branches of Islamic learning but also the renewed spirit of Islamic renewal and reform. Given this fact, it is not surprising that when they returned to the Malay-Indonesian world, these *Jâwî* students became prominent figures in the Islamic renewal and reform movements in Southeast Asia.

With respect to Islam in the Malay-Indonesian world, the period from the 17th century onward was a crucial stage of its development. Following mass-conversion in the previous centuries, it was only after the second half of the 17th century that we observe the rise of Islamic renewal movements which brought about the purification of Islam from the remnants of Hindu-Buddhist and animistic belief and practices. This renewal tendency continued down to the 18th and 19th centuries during which time European colonial powers increasingly penetrated the Malay-Indonesian world. In these later stages, the ever-growing Western encroachment was also in part responsible for a further crystallization of the Islamic renewal movements among the Muslim population.

This chapter has dealt with just one of the branches of the global networks of *'ulamâ'*, that is the Patani *'ulamâ'* networks. As one might expect, this branch of the scholarly network proved to be the most important vehicle for the transmission of the spirit of renewal in Islam from the Haramayn to the Malay-Indonesian world. With respect to the extended international network of Patani scholars in the Malay-Indonesian world, further research is needed in order to better explicate the nature of the transmission and diffusion of the new understanding of Islam. In this context, one should deal not only with the genealogy of the scholars in the network but also with their intellectual posture as reflected in their works. It is only after studying their works that we may have a clearer picture of Islam in Patani and Southeast Asia as a whole and its relationship to Islam in the Arab world and other Muslim areas.

CHAPTER 5

The Intellectual Network of Patani and the Haramayn

Numan Hayimasae

Since the 17th century, the Haramayn (the holy cities of Mecca and Medina in present-day Saudi Arabia) played a crucial role in disseminating Islamic knowledge to Southeast Asian Muslims, among them the Muslims of Patani. Previous studies of Patani that discuss the influence of the Haramayn tend to focus on the religious scholars who resided there for the purposes of acquiring and disseminating knowledge, but do not describe in any detail the intellectual phenomena they experienced.[1] This chapter argues that the intellectual experience of religious scholars in the Haramayn played a direct role in the shaping of educational institutions in Patani. It will examine the origins of the intellectual network linking the Haramayn and Patani. It discusses the development of the tradition of Malay-Muslims journeying to the Haramayn for their education, the role of Patani's *ulama*, and the study patterns of the Malay-Muslims from Patani. The chapter concludes by reflecting on the impact that Patani's intellectual network with the Haramayn had on the establishment of the *madrasah* system in southern Thailand.

Patani Malay-Muslims in the Haramayn

There is no clear evidence to show who the first individual or group from Patani was to have traveled to the Haramayn. Generally, apart from the purpose of education, the trip to the Haramayn was undertaken in order

---

[1] See, for instance, works by Ahmad Fathy al-Fatani and Wan Mohd. Shaghir Abdullah.

to perform the *Hajj*. Among the Malays from the Malay peninsula, Syeikh Abdul Malik Abdullah of Trengganu (1650–1736) was regarded as having been the first individual to have reached the Haramayn (Mecca).[2] Linkages between Patani and the Haramayn appear to have begun following Patani's conversion to Islam around the middle of the 15th century. The coming of Islam had a considerable impact on Patani's intellectual development as Islam began to penetrate the daily lives of the lay persons to create a new Muslim community. Syed Muhummad Naquib al-Attas compares the coming of Islam to the Malay-Indonesian world with the impact of Islam upon Europe, when the advent of Islam and the consequent culture of knowledge it fostered pushed the Europeans into the "Modern Era."[3]

Numerous sources point to the early significance of Patani as a prominent place of learning in the Malay-Indonesian world. For example, the *Sejarah Melayu* describes a Malay noble from Patani who had instructed Sri Lanang to write the *Hikayat*.

> The person who supported me to write the *Sejarah Melayu* is Raja Dewa Said Nara Wangsa whose name is Tun Bambang, a son of the King of Patani, who was the most honourable man with a high-ranking status compared to others in an assembly of nobles …[4]

Patani's intellectual prestige in the 18th century is also well-described in the *Hikayat Patani*:

> Some time later Alung Yunus became King in Air Lilih for a period of eleven months. While he was reigning as King he was called Yang Dipertuan by the people. He was the man who built the mosque in the port, and this mosque was originally the palace which Raja Dajang constructed in the town. Alung Yunus had it pulled down and transferred to the port where it was rebuilt as a mosque. It was at that time that Sayyid Abdullah came to Patani from Trengganu. Sayyid Abdullah was a descendent of the prophet of God, and he originally came from Jerusalem; and Haji Yunus was a Malay from Patani. Sheikh Abdul Kadir was a man from Pasai and Haji Abdurrahman a Javanese; on his way back from a pilgrimage to Mecca he took a wife here in Patani,

---

[2] Mohammad Redzuan Othman, "The Role of Makka-Educated Malays in the Development of Early Islamic Scholarship and Education in Malaya," *Journal of Islamic Studies* 9, 2 (1998): 147.

[3] Syed Muhammad Naquib Al-Attas, *Islam dalam Sejarah dan Kebuyadaan Melayu* (Kuala Lumpur: UKM Press, 1972), pp. 18–9.

[4] W.G. Shellabear, *Sejarah Melayu* (Kuala Lumpur: Fajar Bakti Sdn. Bhd, 1979), p. 2.

> Fakih Abdul Mannan was a Minangkabau who came from Kedah and took a wife in Pujut. All these wise men took counsel on the sufferings of the people of Patani in accordance with the law of God as it is to be found in the holy book of God. So the people in the port of Patani were very contented and tranquil at that time. And the name of the king was famous in the countries in both east and west.[5]

A succession of Patani scholars from the latter half of the 18th century shows a strong linkage between Patani and the Haramayn. Like a number of others from the Malay-Indonesian region, several well-known *'ulama* of Patani origin became renowned scholars — the most prominent among them being Syeikh Daud Abdullah al-Fatani. These *'ulama* had accumulated considerable learning after many years of living and studying in the Haramayn. Later, their knowledge and experience were adapted and developed into a unique style of religious instruction in Southeast Asia. The *Halaqah* method gradually became dominant and developed into a new institution of religious education known as *pondok* in Patani and Malaysia and *pesantren* in Java.[6]

Syeikh Daud al-Fatani was synonymous with Patani, which subsequently became one of main locations in Southeast Asia for the study of Islam. Through his initiative, many *'ulama* from Patani rose to prominence in the Haramayn and in Patani. His contribution in terms of writings and teaching in many disciplines made him well-known among the intellectual community in the Haramayn and Southeast Asia. Syeikh Daud began his studies under his family members, especially his uncle Syeikh Safiyuddin.[7] He then traveled to Aceh where he spent two years, 1780–1781, under the instruction of the famous Acehnese *'ulama*, Syeikh Muhammad Zayn al-Asyi.[8] Based on Ahmad Fathy al-Fatani's calculation, he left for Mecca in 1787 at the age of 18, journeying directly from Patani to Mecca.[9]

---

[5] A. Teeuw and D.K. Wyatt, *Hikayat Patani: The Story of Patani* (The Hague: Martinus Hijhoff, 1970), pp. 199–200.

[6] Abdul Latif Hamidong, "Institusi Pondok Dalam Tradisi Budaya Ilmu," *Kertas kerja Persidangan Antarabangsa Mengenai Tamadun Melayu*, Anjuran Kementerian Kebudayaan, Belia dan Sukan, Malaysia, November 11–13, Kuala Lumpur, 1986, p. 2.

[7] Ahmad Fathy al-Fatani, *Ulama Besar dari Patani* (Bangi: Universiti Kebangsaan Malaysia Press, 2002), p. 26.

[8] A. Hasjmi, *Sejarah Kebudayaan Islam di Indonesia* (Jakarta: Bulan Bintang, 1990), p. 230.

[9] Ahmad Fathy al-Fatani, *Ulama Besar dari Patani* (Bangi: Universiti Kebangsaan Malaysia Press, 2002), pp. 26–7.

Although Syeikh Daud was not the first person from Patani to have reached the Haramayn — a number of Patani *'ulama* and students had been there before him — he was the first to achieve great renown. In Mecca, he mixed with a group of Southeast Asian students, many of whom later became famous *'ulama*, including Muhammad Shalih 'Abdul al-Rahman al-Fatani, 'Ali Ishaq al-Fatani, al-Falimbani, Muhammad Arsyad, Abdul al-Wahab al-Bugisi, 'Abdul Rahman al-Batawi and Muhammad al-Nafis.[10] They were both senior friends and his teachers. Syeikh Daud was often referred to as the youngest student from Southeast Asia in Mecca.[11] In the Haramayn, Syeikh Daud studied for many years under many well-known scholars from the Middle East (especially Egypt) and from "Jawah." It is commonly accepted that he resided in Mecca for 30 years and in Medina for five years.[12] Syeikh Daud studied the *Hadith* with 'Isa Ibn Ahmad al-Barrawi (d. 1768), al-Syarqawi (1737–1812) and Muhammad Ibn 'Ali Syanwani (d. 1818) who became the Rector of al-Azhar University after al-Syarqawi.[13]

Syeikh Daud had also studied under notable teachers like Muhammad As'ad, Ahmad al-Marzuqi and Ibrahim al-Ra'is al-Zamzami al-Makki.[14] Both Muhammad As'ad and Ahmad al-Marzuqi were well-known as *muhaddithin* or experts in Prophetic Tradition.[15] The knowledge obtained from myriad *'ulama* transformed Syeikh Daud into one of the most prominent *'ulama* from Southeast Asia during this period. His scholarship is impressive as seen from the breadth of his published works which total 57 Arabic-and-Malay treatises covering a range of fields of religious subjects.[16]

Azra accurately describes the golden era of *'ulama* from Southeast Asia during the 18th century as follows:

> The careers of Malay-Indonesian *'ulama* in eighteenth century, from al-Palimbani to al-Fatani, show that the linkages of *'ulama* of the Middle

---

[10] Wan Mohd. Shaghir Abdullah, *Syeikh Daud bin Abdullah al-Fathani: 'Ulama dan Pengarang Terulung Asia Tenggara* (Kuala Lumpur: Hizbi, 1990), pp. 32–3.

[11] Ibid.

[12] Ahmad Fathy al-Fatani, *Ulama Besar dari Patani*, p. 33.

[13] Azyumardi Azra, *Jaringan Ulama Timur Tengah dan Kepulauan Nusantara Abad XVII dan XVIII* (Bandung: Mizan, 1995), pp. 262–3.

[14] Ibid., pp. 34–5, 39.

[15] Ibid., p. 263.

[16] Virginia Matheson and M.B. Hooker, "Jawi Literature in Patani: The Maintenance of an Islamic Tradition," *JMBRAS* 61 (1988): 21–6.

East and Southeast Asia had grown considerably. Most importantly it shows that the reformist pulse from the centre of knowledge and Islamic sciences in the Middle East to the various regions of the Malay-Indonesian archipelago had never ceased. The dissemination of such *'ulamas'* works stimulated the tempo of reformist Islam in this region.[17]

Patani experienced much political turmoil from the 18th until the 20th century including the Patani-Siam wars of 1785–6, 1791, 1832 and 1838. This political disorder had a considerable affect upon local intellectuals.[18] Based on their permanent settlement, the Patani Malay-Muslim intellectuals can be classified into three major groups, namely: (i) those who had migrated to the neighboring Malay States of Kelantan, Trengganu, Perak, Kedah, and Penang; (ii) those who had migrated or decided to stay longer or permanently in the Haramayn, especially Mecca; and (iii) those who had returned or stayed in their homeland, Patani. For all three groups, the Haramayn remained the center for the pursuit of knowledge, and almost all of them had experienced a study sojourn in the Haramayn for a certain period. The career of Syeikh Daud al-Fatani encouraged other Patani Malay-Muslims to seek Islamic knowledge in the Haramayn. It had become the center for the study of Islam with the presence of a large number of local or overseas *'ulama*, especially the *"'ulama Jawi."* As a result, the number of Patani students began to increase annually. Their success in the Haramayn was crucial to sustaining the *pondok* system in Patani and the northern Malay states, while those who did not return, for instance, Syeikh Nik Mat Kechik al-Fatani (1844–1915), Syeikh Nik Dir al-Fatani (+1829–1898) and Syeikh Wan Ahmad bin Muhammad Zain al-Fatani (1856–1908), contributed to intellectual life in the Haramayn itself.

Patani *'Ulama* in the Haramyn

By the early 19th century Patani *'ulama* had become involved in a range of activities that deepened relations between Patani and the Haramayn. They provided services relating to the pilgrimage (*Hajj*), taught in the precinct of the Masjid al-Haram and other educational institutions in the Haramayn, became involved in setting up printing presses and publishing the *"kitab*

---

[17] Azra, *Jaringan Ulama*, p. 266.
[18] A. Bangnara, *Patani Dahulu dan Sekarang* (Pattani: Penal Penyelidikan Angkatan al-Fatani, 1977), pp. 34–9.

jawi," and, finally, they composed their own *kitab* to be used as textbooks for religious studies both in the Haramayn and Southeast Asia.

The role of Patani *'ulama* as pilgrimage volunteers began with Syeikh Daud Abdullah al-Fatani, who may have been one of the first individuals from the Malay peninsula to have done so. They were known as "Syeikh Haji Melayu." The services include familiarizing the pilgrims with *Hajj* procedures, introducing them to important places relating to the *Hajj*, organizing accommodation, and various other services. Syeikh Daud bought a house in Medina for the use of pilgrims from the Malay peninsula, especially Patani. In 1824, his house became a center for *Hajj* pilgrims under his supervision. Syeikh Daud was assisted by his relative, Syeikh Wan Musa, who became the Syeikh Haji Melayu after his death.[19] After Syeikh Wan Musa returned home in the 1860s, the position was taken over by a son of Syeikh Idris, Tok Wan Zainab. Syeikh Idris was one of Syeikh Daud's nephews. Tok Wan Zainab was later succeeded by his son Syeikh Nik Mat Kechik, a well-known Patani *'ulama* based in Mecca.[20] The position of Syeikh Haji was a significant one, and was usually filled by those considered to be highly accomplished in Islamic knowledge and who were based in Mecca. The Syeikh Haji Melayu required assistants as their services covered both Mecca and Medina. For example, Syeikh Nik Mat Kechik was helped by his sons in Mecca, while in Medina his son-in-law, Syeikh Daud bin Idris, provided assistance there. The services of the Syeikh Haji Melayu were offered to all Malay-Muslim pilgrims. Syeikh Nik Mat Kechik himself had to serve Sultan Zainal Abidin III of Trengganu, who went on the *Hajj* in 1913.[21]

Over time, the position of Syeikh Haji Melayu underwent a transformation. By the first half of the 20th century, the growing number of pilgrims led to an increase in the number of Syeikh Haji Melayu. The original voluntary nature of the task was gradually transformed into a permanent vocation that promised a substantial financial reward. Undertaking to organize the pilgrimage now became a business venture, notably with the increasing participation of the Saudi Arabia government. Records of the Thai Ministry of Foreign Affairs show an annual increase in the number of Syeikh Haji. In 1957, there were 20 who dealt with only Thai Muslims from

---

[19] Ahmad Fathy al-Fatani, *Ulama Besar dari Patani*, p. 36.

[20] Ibid.

[21] Ibid.; Mohd. Saleh bin Haji Awang, Dato' Haji, *Haji di Semenanjung Malaysia: Sejarah dan Perkembangannya Sejak Tahun 1300–1405H. (1896–1985)* (Kuala Terengganu: Syarikat Percetakan Yayasan Islam Terengganu Sdn. Bhd., 1986), p. 139.

all over Thailand. In that year, the record shows that 1,686 Thai pilgrims went on the *Hajj*, with most of them from the south — the region of the former Patani sultanate.[22]

With regard to their contribution to the transmission of Islamic knowledge, Patani *'ulama* were equally prominent. Quite often, they had a large followings of students. Syeikh Daud Abdullah al-Fatani began active teaching during the early 19th century. Many of his pupils became well-known and influential *'ulama* not only in Patani but also in the regions of what are now Malaysia and Indonesia. The list includes Syeikh Hasan bin Ishak (Besut, Trengganu), Syeikh Wan Musa (Kelantan), Syeikh Zainuddin (Aceh), Syeikh Ismail bin Abdullah (Minangkabau), Syeikh Muhammad Zainudin bin Muhammad Badawi (Sumbawa) and Sultan Muhammad Safiyudin (Sambas).[23]

In the pursuit of their studies in the Haramayn, the student did not study under only one teacher or just one subject. The pre-eminent study location was in the precinct of the Masjid al-Haram, Mecca, and the nearby areas. Students could follow as many classes as possible from early morning until midnight.[24] Due to their poor linguistic skills, new students would learn basic subjects with *Jawah 'Ulama* before taking classes in the Arabic language with either *Jawah* or Arab *'ulama*. The basic knowledge included *Nahw* (Arabic Grammar), *Sarf* (Arabic Words), *Fiqh* (Islamic Jurisprudence), *Tawhid* (Islamic Doctrine, Faith) and *Tasawwuf* (Islamic Ethics) while the higher level covered the same subjects in more depth besides new ones like *Tafsir* (*Qur'anic* Interpretation), *Hadith* (Prophetic Tradition), *Mantiq* (Rhetoric), *Adab* (Arabic Literature) and *Falak* (Astrology).[25] The learning style was dependent on each individual *'ulama*, while the study timetable coincided with the times of the daily prayers

---

[22] National Archives of Thailand, Ministry of Interior 3.1.4.19/52. "Kan chuai leua thai islam pai prakorp satsanakit na muang mecca, Dec. 21, B.E. 2498-Aug. 11, B.E. 2503" [Assistance to Islamic Thais Going to Perform the Pilgrimage in Mecca, December 21– August 11, 1955–1960].

[23] Ahmad Fathy al-Fatani, *Ulama Besar dari Patani*, pp. 35–6.

[24] Interview Haji Abdul Rahman Jehsae, President of Islamic Council of Yala Province at his office on April 29, 2007.

[25] This is based on Babo Yeh's experience in Mecca from 1949 to 1968 during which time he studied almost every religious discipline under *Jawah* and Arab scholars. For more details, see Abdul Ramae Sulong, "Botbart Khong Tok Khru: Korani Serksa Hayi Wan Idris bin Wan Ali" [Role of Tok Guru: A Case Study of Haji Wan Idris bin Haji Wan Ali], Masters thesis, Prince of Songkhla University, 2000, pp. 45–6.

with lessons starting after each prayer. It is likely that students had their preferred or main instructor. Teaching and learning in the Haramayn relied considerably on the credibility of each individual *'ulama*, with students congregating around knowledgeable and charismatic teachers. To achieve the status of a learned individual in the Haramayn, experience was dependent on one's efforts to memorize and understand the lessons and the texts; understanding of the basic Islamic knowledge (*Nahw, Sarf, Adab, Usul al-Fiqh*, and *Usul al-Hadith*); in-depth discussions with *'ulama* and fellow students; expertise in Islamic subjects; and the ability to relate the various fields of knowledge to one another. Each Haramayn *'ulama* had his own timetable with time allocated for teaching, worship, rest, family life and for writing.[26] Writing was meant to enlighten and train students, to simplify and to explain.

Educated Patani Malay-Muslims played another significant role in the print media. Printing technology arrived in Istanbul and Cairo prior to its appearance in Mecca. Arabic printing was introduced in Istanbul in 1729 while in Cairo the first presses were established in 1822. In Mecca, there is no obvious evidence when the printing technology was first used but Snouck Hurgronje, who visited Mecca in 1885, mentions that Syeikh Nawawi al-Bantani sent his works both in Arabic and *Jawi* to the press in Cairo.[27] The most productive period for Malay printing in Mecca coincides with the career of the scholar Syeikh Ahmad Ibn Muhammad Zain al-Fatani. Born in Patani in 1856, Syeikh Ahmad al-Fatani was one of the most famous Southeast Asian scholars during the 1870s–1900s. Due to his exceptional understanding of religious knowledge and proficiency in the Malay language he was appointed by the Ottoman Caliphate as supervisor and "Malay Manuscript" editor of the newly established government press in Mecca in 1884.[28]

Besides editing *Jawi* Malay works, Syeikh Ahmad was also entrusted to edit Arabic materials.[29] Some of his edited Arabic scripts included: *I'anatut Thalibin* by Sayyid Abu Bakar Syatha; *al-Ajrumiyah* by Imam Shanhaji; *Nuz-hatun Nazhirin* by Sayyid Ja'afar Ibn Ismail al-Barzanji; *al-Kharidatul Bahaiyah* by Syeikh Abdullah Ibn Usman Makki; *Kitab Dara-ilul*

---

26 See, for instance, Ahmad Fathy al-Fatani, *Ulama Besar dari Patani*, p. 75.

27 C. Snouck Hurgronje, *Mekka in the Latter Part of the 19th Century* (Leiden: E.J. Brill, 1970), p. 271.

28 Ibid., pp. 87, 286.

29 The term "*tash-hih*" (edit/edition) was widely used by the 1880s; Wan Mohd. Shaghir Abdullah, *Syeikh Daud bin Abdullah al-Fathani*, p. 48.

Khairat by Syeikh Sulaiman al-Jazuli; *Tafsir al-Qur'an Juz Amma* by Syeikh Muhammad Amin Bugis; and *Ibirizud Dari fi Maulidis Saiyidi Adnanni* by Syeikh Nawawi. Such Arabic treatises became important textbooks studied by Southeast Asian students in the Haramayn and in Islamic education in Southeast Asia. His *Jawi* editions included works written by Syeikh Abdur Rauf Ibn Ali al-Fansuri; Syeikh Naruddin ar-Raniri; Syeikh Muhammad Nafis Ibn Idris al-Banjari; Syeikh Abdus Shamad al-Falimbani; Syeikh Daud Ibn Abdullah al-Fatani; Syeikh Muhamad Zaib Ibn Faqih Jalaluddin Aceh; Syeikh Muhammad Arshad Ibn Abdullah al-Banjari; Syeikh Muhammad Ibn Ismail Daud al-Fatani; and Syeikh Wan Ali Ibn Abdur Rahman Kutan al-Kelantani.[30] These scholars were among the most knowledgeable and productive Southeast Asian scholars of Islam. In 1884 alone, Syeikh Ahmad managed to edit 30 treatises in Arabic and 20 in *Jawi*. His initiative in editing manuscripts encouraged other *Jawi 'ulama* to produce and publish their own works in the Middle East, especially Mecca.[31]

Syeikh Ahmad also established the Maktabah Fataniyyah ("Patani Store"), whose aim was the promotion, storage, and distribution of the *kitab jawi*. One of the largest branches of the store was located in Qhashah, Mecca. Until the end of the 19th century, it played an important role in the distribution of the *kitab jawi*. It is most likely that the institution also operated as a publisher. Many of the books listed in several of its advertisements were printed by the Matba'ah al-Miri'ah.[32]

Following the death of Syeikh Ahmad al-Fatani in 1908 at Mina, Saudi Arabia, it was not clear who succeeded him at the printing press. However, the Maktabah al-Fataniyyah continued to be the leading Malay publisher in Mecca until the early 20th century. With the proliferation of publishers and printers in Malaya in the 1930s, the Middle Eastern publishers for *kitab jawi* became less important. Although the publishing houses of the Halabi

---

[30] All *kitab* in Malay or Jawi Literature that had been published in Mecca, Egypt and Turkey during 1877–1889 were edited by Syeikh Ahmad al-Fatani. *Kitab* that were published after 1889 included two kinds, namely his original works and works edited by his two outstanding students, Syeikh Daud bin Ismail al-Fatani and Syeikh Idris bin Husein al-Kelantani. See Wan Mohd. Shaghir Abdullah, *Syeikh Daud bin Abdullah al-Fathani*, pp. 50–2.

[31] Wan Mohd. Shaghir Abdullah, *al-'Allamah Syeikh Ahmad al-Fathani: Ahli Fikir Islam dan Guru kepada Hampir Semua Ulama dan Tokoh Asia Tenggara Abad ke 19–20* (Kuala Lumpur: Khazanah Fathaniyah, 1992), pp. 40–1.

[32] Md. Sidin Ahmad Ishak and Mohammad Redzuan Othman, *The Malays in the Middle East* (Kuala Lumpur: Universiti Malaya Press, 2000), p. 61.

brothers still exist to this day and continue to be significant publishers of Arabic books, its Malay department has lost its importance. New editions of Malay titles rarely appear while many Malay students, particularly those based in Cairo, are no longer interested in writing.[33]

The publication of religious treatises in Malaya was a continuation of the earlier activities that had taken place in the Middle East inspired by Syeikh Ahmad al-Fatani. Indeed, several establishments like the Matbaah Riawwiyah in Sumatra and the Matbaah al-Ahmadiyyah in Singapore, were an extension of the Maktabah al-Fataniyyah.[34] According to Hasan Madmarn, most of the *kitab jawi* written by the leading *ulama* of Patani were initially printed either in Mecca or Cairo besides Bombay and Istanbul.[35] Subsequent printings were produced by the printing presses of Sulaiman Mar'i in Singapore and the Maktabah Dar al-Ma'rif of Penang.[36] The printing press in Patani was initiated in the 1910s while its most active period was in the 1940s and the 1950s. The 1950s in Patani was a period of strong support for the *pondok* although it was also a period of economic hardship for the Malay-Muslims of Patani.[37]

The final major role of the Patani *'ulama* was to produce treatises in the various fields of Islamic knowledge. Comparing those who settled in Patani and those who had stayed permanently or for long periods in the Haramayn, the latter were more productive as they had more time and a superior intellectual and religious environment, while the former spent most of their time with the community and on their teaching duties. The Haramayn also provided more opportunities for publication. Patani *'ulama* who were domiciled mostly in Mecca conducted their teaching within the precinct of the Masjid al-Haram or in their house. Patani settlements in Mecca were mainly located in Shu'ib 'Ali, Ma'la, Misfalah, Jiyad, Sukalil and Yaruwal.[38] Malay-Muslims from the South also resided outside Mecca including in Taif, Riyadh and Medina. The most learned men, however, preferred Mecca.

Political events in the Arabian peninsula in the early decades of the 20th century resulted in significant changes in administration and teaching

---

[33] Ibid., p. 67.

[34] Ibid.

[35] Hasan Madmarn, *The Pondok and Madrasah in Patani*, p. 52.

[36] Ibid.; Virginia Matheson and M.B. Hooker, "Jawi Literature in Patani," p. 53.

[37] Matheson and Hooker, "Jawi Literature in Patani," p. 54.

[38] National Archives of Thailand, Ministry of Foreign Affairs 43.2/82. "Ngop ngoen kha chai jai nai kan dulae nak rian thai nai saudi arabia, B.E. 2505–B.E. 2509" [Budget of Expenditure for Organizing Thai Students in Saudi Arabia, 1966–1966].

in the Haramayn.[39] It was a time of war between the Wahabiyyah forces led by Ibn Saud and those of Syarif Husain, the protector of the Haramayn, who had been appointed by the Ottoman government. Ibn Saud's victory by 1925 saw the end of the long history of the *Syarif* descendants (descendants of the Prophet Muhammad SAW) in the Haramayn. Subsequent major changes imposed by the new ruler began to affect the organization of teaching in the Masjid al-Haram. The new government allowed only registered teachers who had obtained the official permission of the new Saudi government to teach in the Masjid al-Haram. They were also required to teach all four major Islamic legal schools (*madhhab*) — the Maliki, Hanafi, Shafi'i and Hanbali, although the leader for daily prayers was to be only from one *madhhab*, the Hanbali, the school to which the new Saudi regime formally adhered.[40]

Patani scholars who were from the Shafi'i school began to use their own houses for teaching purposes. Although the location of instruction had changed, they still applied the old methods of teaching. By 1966, the number of Thai Muslims who were involved in education in Saudi Arabia had increased tremendously. Of the total number, it appears that more than 80 percent came from the former region of Patani, judging by their homeland origin recorded in official documents. The Thai Consulate in Jeddah identified at least three groups of Thais, including these Patani Muslims, who were involved in religious education in the Haramayn, namely the students, teachers who were attached to *madrasah*, and teachers based in their private residences. Of a total of 598 Thais, two were teaching in the Masjid al-Haram area, one at the Madrasah Indonesia, one at the Madrasah Sulaimaniyyah, one at the Madrasah Dar al-'Ulum, and 192 in their own residences. The rest were students scattered among different locations.[41]

With the growing popularity of the *madrasah* system[42] and increasing official control, the role of the individual *'ulama* in the Haramayn also

---

[39] For details, see Hamka, *Ayahku* (Jakarta: Umminda, 1992), pp. 153–5; see also William R. Roff, "Kaum Muda-Kaum Tua: Innovation and Reaction amongst the Malay," in *Reading on Islam in Southeast Asia*, ed. Ahmad Ibrahim *et al.* (Singapore: Institute of Southeast Asian Studies, 1985), p. 124.

[40] Mohd. Sarem Haji Mustajab, "Gerakan Islah Islamiyah di Tanah Melayu 1906-1948," in *Sejarah dan Proses Pembangunan* (Kuala Lumpur: Persatuan Sejarah Malaysia, 1979), p. 161.

[41] National Archives of Thailand, Ministry of Foreign Affairs 43.2/82.

[42] *Madrasah* generally means a place of learning and studying, however, here it refers to a hierarchically structured educational curriculum with sequential learning generally attuned with the formal education system.

increased. A number were given Saudi citizenship, especially those who had remained in the Haramayn for a long period of time, such as Syeikh Tok Gudang al-Fatani, Syeikh Nik Mat Kechik al-Fatani and Syeikh Nik Dir al-Fatani. From this time, the *madrasah* became known by the names of famous individual scholars attached to them, like Muhammad Yasin Haji Isa al-Pandani, from Sumatra, and Tunku Abdul Jalil, from Java. The *Isnad* method of learning and the *halaqah* teaching style were gradually reduced. The modernization of education was also signaled by the establishment in 1957 of the first university in Saudi Arabia.[43] It was the start of a new era in the propagation of Islamic knowledge in Saudi Arabia, since the new system of education began to integrate technical skills and other academic subjects designed to help students adjust to the modern world.

Study Patterns of the Patani Malay-Muslims in the Haramayn

The "circle" pattern of learning, or *halaqah*, had long been the most practical form of instruction used in the major religious institutions in the Haramayn. The *halaqah* instructional approach placed the teacher at the center surrounded by pupils. Instruction began with the reading of an opening *doa'* while the texts used were set by the teacher or upon request of the pupils. The instruction went into a certain depth (*tahqiq*) page by page until the students comprehended the subject matter. Textual explanation was quite detailed with the teacher providing additional explanation on certain issues. To fully understand, students had to have sufficient knowledge of Arabic grammar, Arabic literature, the Arabic word system, reading (*Qira'at*), the prophetic tradition, the *Qur'an* and its interpretation. Following the completion of one book or one subject, the lesson moved on to another book, either on the same subject or a subject at a higher level. In the *halaqah* instructional model, pupils accorded great respect to their teachers who practiced a conservative system of teaching known as *Isnad*. The *Isnad* system gave emphasis to the narration of transmitted knowledge. The sciences of *Qur'anic* recitation, *Hadith* (prophetic tradition), Islamic history, Arabic language, and Islamic jurisprudence, are all based on narration. This generation of teachers was linked to their teachers before them and so on back in an unbroken chain to the Prophet Muhammad and the *Qur'anic* verses. The quality of the student in the *halaqah* system depended much more upon the individual teachers rather than the institution. Besides acquiring as much knowledge as possible from

---

[43] The first university, known as King Saud University, was founded in Riyadh in 1957.

the teachers they chose to study under, students would obtain a certificate of transmission called *Ijazah*. Students needed to study with as many teachers as possible to acquire the maximum knowledge. These teachers would give their classes either in the area of the Masjid al-Haram or at their residence. Pupils could set their schedule of daily study and were free to attend the *halaqah*. The amount of knowledge that the student gained depended on their diligence in attending the various *halaqah*, proper revision, memorizing the core of each subject, as well as the length of the period of study since there was no formal time limit. The *halaqah* as practiced in the Haramayn was applied to the Malay-Muslim educational institutions in Patani, which already had its own religious educational institution, the *pondok*. The *halaqah* method was used in the *pondok* with instruction conducted in the prayer hall (*balai* or *surau*) daily. It survives in *pondok* in southern Thailand today.

The *halaqah* style of instruction persisted until the introduction of the new mode of education, known today as the *madrasah*, toward the end of the 19th century. *Madrasahs* received a positive response from students and later became the predominant form of instruction. The new style of education was first introduced by Indian Muslims through the Madrasah Shaulatiyyah, which was built in Mecca in 1874 by an Indian woman, Shaulah al-Nisa. Its management was led by Rahmatullah Ibn Khalil al-'Uthmani, a well-known Indian *'ulama* and leading anti-British Muslim cleric in India, who had migrated to Mecca after his involvement in failed efforts to resist British rule in India.[44]

A major problem faced by the Malay-Indonesian students in the Madrasah Shaulatiyyah was language. Students at Shaulatiyyah were required to use only Arabic, including in their living quarters, which caused considerable difficulty for the Malay-Indonesians. Due to their large number, the students were likely to communicate with one another in their own language. This caused discomfort to some teachers and others, even resulting in clashes between Malay-Indonesian students and their teachers. Finally, almost all the Malay-Indonesians from Shaulatiyyah decided to leave and establish a new *madrasah* based on their own resources and management.[45] It is recorded that more than 100 students moved out from Shaulatiyyah at this time.[46] The new *madrasah* was called Madrasah Dar al-'Ulum al-Diniyyah and became the new destination for many Malay-Indonesian students,

---

[44] Martin van Bruinessen, *Kitab Kuning, Pesantren dan Tarekat: Tradisi-tradisi Islam di Indonesia* (Bandung: Mizan 1995), p. 35.
[45] Ibid.
[46] Ibid., p. 37.

including Malays from Patani. It was established in 1934 by Haji Majid Zainuddin, the Malay Pilgrimage Officer in Jeddah, in association with some leading Indonesian scholars. It was located at Shu'ib Ali, not far from the Masjid al-Haram. The building was donated by Toh Puan Sharifah, the wife of Dato' Panglima Kinta.[47] The first *madrasah* principal (*mudir*) was Sheikh Zubir bin Ahmad, a graduate of the Madrasah al-Mashhor of Penang. He was later succeeded by Muhammad Yasin Haji Isa al-Pandani of Sumatra at the end of the Second World War.[48]

Classes in the Madrasah Dar al-'Ulum were divided into four levels, namely elementary (*tahdiri*), primary (*ibtidai'*), secondary (*thanawi*) and upper secondary (*'aliy*), with each level lasting for three years. An important difference with other *madrasah* was that besides Arabic, the Malay language was also used as a medium of instruction, particularly in the elementary classes. Under the leadership of Syeikh Zubir, the *madrasah* managed to gain considerable support from Malay students who came to the Haramayn to further their education. Many graduates of Madrasah Dar al-'Ulum later established *madrasah* of their own after they returned to their homelands.[49]

Besides Madrasah Dar al-'Ulum, Patani Malay-Muslim students also studied at other *madrasah* institutions, both private and public, in the Haramayn and the nearby region. Such *madrasah* included Madrasah al-Falah, Ma'had al-'Ilmi al-Saudi, Madrasah al-Lailiyyah, Madrasah Jeddah, Madrasah Asasiyyah, Madrasah Rahmaniyyah, Kulliyyah Syar'iyyah, Madrasah al-Sahir al-Mutawassitah, Madrasah Khalid Ibn Waleed and Madrasah al-Sa'ah (al-Sa'ab).[50] These *madrasah* were mostly located near the areas where Patani Malay-Muslim communities settled.

There were two early generations of *madrasah* in Patani. The first generation began in the 1930s and 1940s, while the second generation followed during the 1950s–1960s. Madrasah Dar al-Ma'arif al-Wataniyyah was established in 1933 by the well-known scholar Haji Sulong Abdul

---

[47] Md. Sidin Ahmad Ishak and Mohammad Redzuan Othman, *The Malays in the Middle East*, pp. 30–1.

[48] Ibid., pp. 33, 42.

[49] Some of the *madrasahs* built in Malaysia and Thailand that were influenced by the Madrasah Dar al-'Ulum are Madrasah al-Khairiyyah al-Islamiyyah, Pokok Sena in Perak, Madrasah al-Ulum al-Syari'ah, Batu 20, Bagan Datoh, Ma'had al-Tarbiyyah, Bandar, Pattani, and Ma'had al-Ba'that al-Diniyyah, Yala.

[50] "Ngop ngoen kha chai jai nai kan dulae nak rian thai nai saudi arabia, B.E. 2505–B.E. 2509"; National Archives of Thailand, Ministry of Foreign Affairs 43.31/4, "Kan khuapkhum nakrian thai nai prathet Saudi Arabia, B.E.2502–B.E.2505" [Control of Thai Students in Saudi Arabia, 1959–1962].

Kadir, while in the subsequent decade a number of other *madrasah* were established. Since the *madrasah* system was a new kind of institution, it drew a poor response from both the Thai government and locals. They were also considered by the government to be an obstacle to national integration due to suspicions that they were seed-beds for anti-government movements. Hence, the operations of numerous *madrasah*, such as the Madrasah Dar al-Ma'arif al-Wataniyyah, Madrasah Dar al-Anwar, and Madrasah al-Islah al-Diniyyah, were terminated. The *madrasah* established in the late 1960s up to the 1970s, however, received a more positive response from both the Malay Muslim population and the government. A major change took place in the first half of the 1970s when *madrasah* were transformed as a result of a government initiative to introduce academic subjects and the Thai language into the *madrasah* curriculum. These newly-styled "Islamic Private Schools" gradually lost their original character as *madrasah* which they had received directly from the Haramayn.

The number of Muslim students from Thailand in the Haramayn increased annually, especially after the Second World War. In 1949, the Thai Ministry of Foreign Affairs sent a representative, Ari Wongsan, to monitor Thai Muslims residing in Saudi Arabia. He later recommended that the Thai government set up a Thai consulate to service Thai citizens. Following the establishment of the consulate in Jeddah in the early 1950s, data on Thai citizens in the country began to be collected. In 1956, it was recorded that a total of 679 Thais were then living in Saudi Arabia, all classified as "students" by profession, of which an estimated 90 percent came from Patani.[51] The number of Thai nationals involved in education in Saudi Arabia in 1966

---

[51] This estimate is made on the basis of the names listed in the record. The names of students from Patani and southern Thailand are likely to show the original Muslim name and Malay-or-Muslim surnames, while the names of the Muslims from other regions are either in Thai, or slightly-distorted Malay or Thai slang. National Archives of Thailand, Ministry of Interior 3.1.4.19/52, "Kan chuai luea thai islam pai prakorb satsanakit na muang mecca, Dec. 21, B.E.2498–Aug. 11, B.E.2503" [Assistance to Thai Islam Going to Perform the Pilgrimage in Mecca, December 21, 1955–August 11, 1960]. It is likely that the category "students" covered other groups. It was reported in 1949 that there were three different groups of Thais residing in Saudi Arabia, namely those who had come for the *Hajj* and who would return home after the pilgrimage; those who stayed to study religious knowledge; and those who were working there; National Archives of Thailand, Ministry of Foreign Affairs 94.4/1, "Kan jat kan hai chao thai islam doenthang pai prakorp satsanakit na makka, B.E. 2504" [Arranging for Islamic Thais to Make the Pilgrimage to Mecca, 1961].

was reported to be 466 students and 17 teachers.[52] The list indicates that Thai students, especially those from the three southern Thai provinces (i.e., the former region of Patani), were attending both formal instruction in the *madrasah* scattered throughout Saudi Arabia, and informal modes of study, the latter including the residences of individual *'ulama*, mosques, and the teaching areas around the Masjid al-Haram.

The Masjid al-Haram has always attracted Muslims from around the world. Here, Malay-Muslims from Patani undertook religious instruction in the Masjid al-Haram by attending classes given by well-known Arab or Asian religious scholars. Apart from following religious scholars in the mosques, many also attended instruction at public (i.e., those supported by the Saudi Arabian government) and private *madrasah*. The two most popular *madrasah* were Madrasah Dar al-'Ulum al-Diniyyah and Madrasah Indonesia, both located in Mecca. They had 75 and 70 Thai students respectively. The rest were scattered at the Madrasah Shaulatiyah, Ma'had al-'Ilmi al-Saudi, Madrasah Rahmaniyyah, Madrasah al-Lailiyyah, Madrasah 'Assasiyyah, Madrasah al-Falah, Madrasah Jeddah, and Madrasah Madinah.[53]

The Saudi government was reluctant to support private education since public *madrasah* had already been built with governmental support. The Madrasah Madinah had been established by the Saudi government. Those who wished to attend a government *madrasah* had to obtain official approval through a competitive entrance examination. It became more difficult for Malay-Indonesian students to enter these schools since the examination was open to both Arab and non-Arab students. Yet some Patani students continued to do well. During the 1950s, Haji Abdul Rahman bin Ahmad, founder of the Madrasah Mu'assasah al-Islamiyyah in Panare district, Pattani province, was the only student from Southeast Asia to place in the top 500 out of 10,000 applicants.[54] The *madrasah* provided students with a secondary education certificate which enabled them to continue their studies to bachelor and postgraduate level in Arab countries, notably in Egypt,

---

[52] "Kan chuai luea thai islam pai prakorb satsanakit na muang mecca."

[53] "Kan khuapkhum nakrian thai nai prathet Saudi Arabia, B.E.2502–B.E.2505." Of the number of Thai students who studied at Madrasah Dar al-'Ulum al-Diniyyah and Madrasah Indonesia, judging by their names, almost all were from the former region of Patani. Thai students from other regions who were not familiar with the Malay language tended to study in *madrasah* where the medium of instruction was Arabic; interview, Dr. Hasan Madmarn, 2009.

[54] Interview, Haji Abdul Rahman Jehsae, April 29, 2007.

Sudan, Syria, Lebanon, Morocco, Jordan and Libya, as well as at European and American universities.

The curriculum for secondary education provided by the Saudi Arabia government in the 1960s was a mixture of religious and academic subjects, namely Religion, Arabic Language, Mathematics and General Knowledge (GK), including Health Science, Skill/Craftsmanship, Physical Education, History and Geography. This classification ran from primary until upper secondary level. Private *madrasah* had to follow the requirements of the Saudi educational curriculum in order to receive government approval. In 1960, 10 primary schools (*madrasah*) and five secondary schools (*madrasah*) had been approved by the Thai government based on a report prepared by the Thai Foreign Ministry and acknowledged by the Saudi government.[55] At the tertiary level, only one university in the Saudi capital Riyadh provided instruction in Islamic Studies and some fields of Humanities.[56] Students from Patani could sit for the entrance examination to further their studies in this university or in institutions in other Arab countries, or else simply study according to the traditional *halaqah* system in the Masjid al-Haram or its precincts.[57]

Following the 1925 surrender of Syarif Hussein to Ibn Saud and the ascendancy of the *Wahabiyyah*, there were significant changes to the mode of instruction in religious education. The *Wahabiyyah* focused on purity of belief and faith in God, with religious practice based strictly on the *Qur'an* and the *Sunnah* (the way of the Prophet Muhammad), rather than the teachings of the *'ulama* who came after the Prophet. *Tawhid* (Faith in God) received considerable attention while the thought of Muhammad Abdul Wahab, the founder of the *Wahabiyyah*, was also emphasized. This resulted in a degree of official control over the teaching of *Tawhid* and other religious disciplines by scholars within the precincts of the Masjid al-Haram. Those without formal permission to teach had to use their private residences for teaching purposes. Thus *Tawhid* came to be instructed by qualified professionals who were mostly Saudi citizens. In other subjects, the Saudi authorities still depended

---

[55] National Archives of Thailand, Ministry of Foreign Affairs 43.31/4, "Kan khuapkhum nakrian thai nai prathet saudi arabia, B.E.2502–B.E.2505" [Control of Thai Students in Saudi Arabia, 1959–1962].

[56] Ibid.; interview Haji Abdul Rahman bin Ahmad (Tok Guru Pombing), founder of Mu'assasah al-Saqafah al-Islamiyyah, at Pondok Darussalam, Kuala Ibai, Terengganu, dated April 23, 2007.

[57] Interview Haji Abdul Rahman Jehsae, April 29, 2007.

on foreign instructors because there were not enough teachers to meet the needs of the increasing student numbers.[58]

Depending on their ability and diligence, a student might follow separate classes. Some might study in certain classes of the *madrasah* while others followed only informal education in the Masjid al-Haram. The majority of students, however, attended both types of instruction. After graduating from the *madrasah*, some Patani students would remain in the Haramayn for further studies with the various *halaqah*. After the opening of universities in Arab countries, many of these students left the Haramayn and transferred to these universities to take degrees in various disciplines such as Arabic Language, Islamic Jurisprudence, Economics, Business, History, Literature, and Political Science.

The *halaqah*-led *'ulama* remained in existence through the first half of the 20th century. Southeast Asian Muslim students who took this form of education would attend those *halaqah* led by *'ulama* from Patani, Malaya, and Indonesia, as well as those led by Arabs. There was a considerable number of *'ulama* from Patani and southern Thailand teaching in Mecca during this time, including Pok Doe Ae (1882–1965), Syeikh Wan Daud bin Wan Mustafa al-Fatani (1866–1936), Syeikh Muhammad Nur bin Muhammad al-Fatani (1873–1944), and Tok Senggora (1850s–1930).[59] Other well-known Malaya-Indonesian *'ulama* included Syeikh Abdul Kadir bin Abdul Mutthalib al-Mandili, Syeikh Muhammad Yasin bin Isa al-Pandani (born in 1916), Syed Abdul Karim Baryar, Muhsin bin Ali Musawwa (the first principal of Madrasah Dar al-'Ulum in Mecca, who died in 1935), and Ali Banjar (who died in 1951).[60]

Conclusion

The significance of the Haramayn as the center of the *Hajj* pilgrimage, one of the five pillars of Islam, was the vital factor for the development of the relationship between Patani and the Haramayn. Muslims from all around the

---

[58] Interview Haji Abdul Rahman bin Ahmad, at Pondok Darussalam, Kuala Ibai, Terengganu, dated April 23, 2007; interview Haji Abdul Latif bin Haji Wan Muhammad (Babo Teh Cerangbatu), member of the Islamic Committee of Pattani Province, April 25, 2007.

[59] Abdul Ramae Sulong, "Botbat khong tok khru: korani sueksa hayi wan idris bin wan ali" [Role of Tok Guru: A Case Study of Haji Wan Idris bin Haji Wan Ali], M.A. Thesis, pp. 45–6; van Bruinessen, *Kitab Kuning, Pesantren dan Tarekat*, p. 39; Ahmad Fathy al-Fatani, *Ulama Besar dari Patani*, p. 7.

[60] Van Bruinessen, *Kitab Kuning, Pesantren dan Tarekat*.

world, including those of the Malay-Indonesian archipelago, gathered there every year not only for the purposes of pilgrimage but also for intellectual exchange. The Malay Muslims from Patani themselves were part of that process and constituted one element in a wider network of Muslims from the Malay-Indonesian archipelago.

A combination of factors, including the unstable political situation in their homeland, access to the most prominent Islamic scholars, both *Jawah* and Arabs, besides the Haramayn's special environment as the location of the holy places of Islam, attracted large numbers of students from the Malay-Indonesian archipelago to acquire knowledge there. For those from Patani, the names of major scholars began to appear in the 18th century, and in the Haramayn — especially in Mecca — Patani Malays played major roles in teaching, composing religious treatises in both *Jawi* and Arabic, organizing the printing and publication of religious works, and providing services for the increasing numbers of Muslims undertaking the *Hajj* pilgrimage. To serve the *Hajj* pilgrims meant not only leading them to the locations fixed by the conditions of the *Hajj* pilgrims, but also teaching them and accompanying them at every stage of the pilgrimage.

The restrictions placed by the new government of Saudi Arabia in the 1920s on those visiting the country for the *Hajj* pilgrimage and for other purposes, including for education, was a major factor leading to the decrease in the number of Patani Malay Muslims studying in the Haramayn. At the same time, other Arab countries began to accept overseas students, especially those from minority groups like the Patani Malays in southern Thailand and the Moros in southern Philippines. The intellectual experience of students who had studied in the Haramayn had a direct impact on Islamic education in Patani, as those who returned to Patani brought back their knowledge and educational methodologies and applied them to the Patani community. Yet the cumulative result of these changes was that by the early 1980s the Haramayn had lost its time-honored place for Patani students as the most attractive center for a religious education — although it retained its importance as the place of the *Hajj* pilgrimage.

CHAPTER 6

Patani's Creole Ambassadors

Christopher M. Joll

Claims and counterclaims have been made concerning Patani's uniqueness vis-à-vis other Southeast Asian port city-states. Wayne Bougas argues that Patani's history and culture have been shaped by its location between the Thai and Malay *mandalas* of Ayutthaya/Bangkok and Melaka.[1] While Islam typically supplanted and eventually replaced Hindu-Buddhist predecessors elsewhere in the Malay world (SM. *dunia Melayu*), these faiths coexisted and interacted with one another in Patani. As such, Islam was heavily influenced by Buddhism, acquiring a "unique character of its own, quite different from that encountered in the rest of the Peninsula and Archipelago."[2] Less measured claims are made by Paul Dowsey-Magog, who argues for Patani's isolation from the southern and eastern Malay states, and the Thai kingdom to the north.[3] While its current location is at the northern extremity of the Malay world, Siamese influence once extended

---

[1] Wayne A. Bougas, "Patani in the Beginning of the XVII Century," *Archipel* 39 (1990): 115.

[2] Bougas cites an unnamed Dutch source from the 1600s which claims that Buddhists (who comprised 30 percent of the population) continued to worship in their temples in Patani; *The Kingdom of Patani: Between Thai and Malay Mandalas* (Bangi: Institute of the Malay World and Civilization, University Kebangsaan Malaysia, 1994), p. 37. Ibrahim Syukri mentions that 60 Burmese slaves given to the Raja by the Thai king were allowed to remain Buddhist; Ibrahim Syukri, *History of the Malay Kingdom of Patani*, trans. C. Bailey and J. Miksic (Athens, OH: Center for International Studies, Ohio University, 1985), p. 20.

[3] P. Dowsey-Magog, "Popular Culture and Traditional Performance: Conflicts and Challenges in Contemporary Nang Talung," in *Dynamic Diversity in South Thailand*, ed. Wattana Sungannasil (Chiangmai: Silkworm Books, 2005), p. 111.

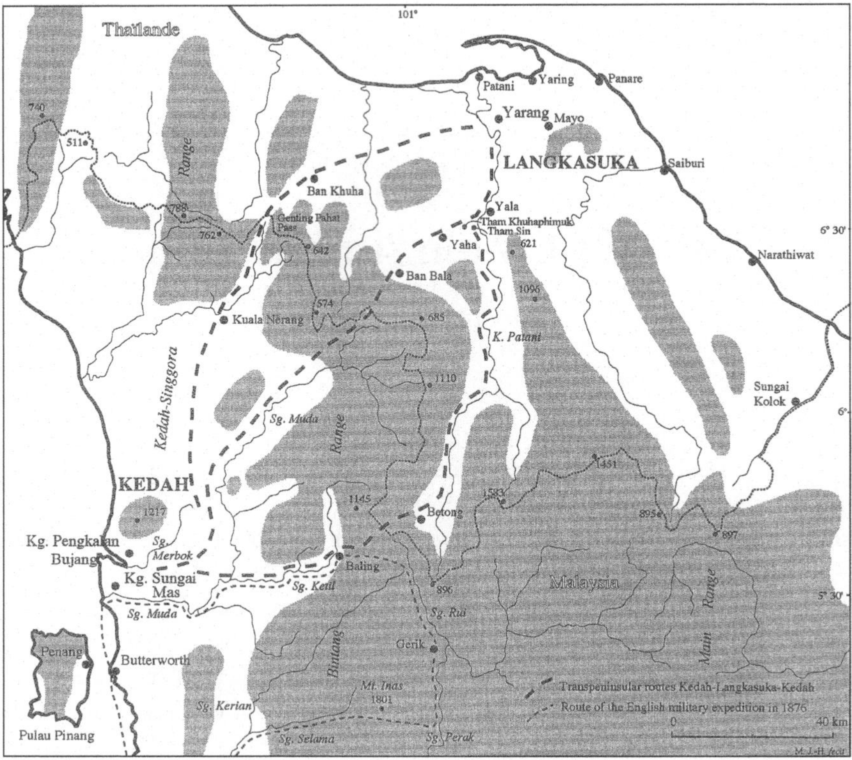

Figure 6.1 Historical location of trans-peninsula trade routes in the Langkasuka/Patani region.

into present-day Kedah, Kelantan, and Trengganu. Patani should be viewed as more similar to, rather than distinct from, other Southeast Asian port city-states with which it was connected through trading networks. Patani's harbor not only provided protection from north-eastern and south-western monsoon winds, but was also located in close proximity to trans-peninsula trading routes that linked it with the outside world. The importance of these routes increased once sailing technology permitted Chinese ships to reach the Malay peninsula directly from southern Vietnam. Preferring ports closer to China, Patani became the favored port of Chinese traders.[4] In addition to the unreliable winds in the Straits of Melaka and the threat of pirates, the Portuguese presence after 1511 led more traders to take overland routes to

---

[4] Bougas, "Patani in the Beginning of the XVII Century," p. 115.

east coast conduits such as Patani. The fall of Melaka in 1511, therefore, was a significant factor contributing to Patani's prosperity.[5] As is well-known, goods were traded alongside ideas, the most important of which was Islam. During the period that Werner Kraus refers to as the "magical" epoch in Patani's history, Sheikh Said of Pasai convinced Raja Phaya Tu Antara to adopt Islam.[6] Sheikh Safiuddin al-Abbasi was another "Arab" from Pasai, who advised the recently renamed Sultan Ismail Syah Zillulah Fil-'Alam, of the need to construct a royal mosque.[7] The *Hikayat Patani* also mentions wandering sages who visited Patani in the second half of the 16th century. This included one of the famous *wali sanga*, Mawlana Malik Ibrahim, who preached at an Islamic propagation center in Kruese before proceeding to East Java.[8]

Neither Sheik Said nor Sheikh Safiuddin al-Abbasi was from Patani, nor were they described as "Malay." The central contention of this chapter is that while Patani's most famous *'ulama besar* Sheikh Daud al-Fatani (1769–1847), Sheikh Ahmad al-Fatani (1856–1908), and Haji Sulong (1895–1954) are routinely referred to as Malays, they were no ordinary Malays. These important personalities were distinguished from the Malay population in Patani by more than their Arab ancestry and Arabic literacy. They were born into families possessing the financial resources and family connections required to travel across the Indian Ocean to Islam's spiritual and intellectual centers. This chapter considers the "creole" credentials of Patani's best-known *'ulama* and how they functioned as ambassadors for Islam during a tumultuous period in both the Hijaz and on the Thai/Malay Peninsula. The term "creole ambassador" was coined by Michael Laffan to describe Muslims born to parents from either shore of the Indian Ocean

---

[5] Francis R. Bradley, "Moral Order in a Time of Damnation: The Hikayat Patani in Historical Context," *Journal of Southeast Asian Studies* 40, 2 (2009): 281.

[6] Werner Kraus, "Islam in Thailand: Notes on the History of Muslim Provinces Thai Islamic Modernism and the Separatist Movement in the South," *Journal of Muslim Minority Affairs* 5, 2 (1984).

[7] Hasan Madmarn, *The Pondok and Madrasah in Patani* (Bangi: UKM, 1990), p. 23, Perayot Rahimmula, "The Patani Fatawa: A Case Study of the Kitab Al-Fatawa Al-Fataniyyah of Shaykh Ahmed Bin Muhamad Zain Bin Mustafa Al-Fatani," PhD diss., University of Kent, 1990, p. 161.

[8] Azyumardi Azra, *The Origins of Islamic Reformism in Southeast Asia: Networks of Middle Eastern 'Ulama' in the Seventeenth and Eighteenth Centuries* (Honolulu: University of Hawai'i Press, 2004), pp. 123–4.

who played prominent roles in the propagation of Islam in Southeast Asia.[9] I use "creole" to denote mobile, multilingual members of cosmopolitan coastal trading communities who are inadequately described as simply "Arab," "Indian" — or even "Malay."[10] Such creole communities were created through the circulation of Islam east and west of the Thai/Malay peninsula, and played a key role both in Islam's initial Southeast Asian expansion and subsequent consolidation.

Circulating Islam and Creole Communities

Scholarship on how Islam was transmitted to and assimilated in Southeast Asia has tended to dwell on the question of origins. Was Islam only capable of flowing eastward to receptive markets? Did trading guilds and Sufi orders resemble nothing more than supply chains?[11] Recent studies into Islam's Southeast Asian expansion that have moved from a focus on comparison to attention to connections are better equipped to comprehend the mediated nature of Islamic transmission and networking.[12] Far from acting as simple conduits between the poles of supply and demand, the trading systems of Southeast Asian port-cities were complex and multi-circuited systems, described by Ali as "multiple circuits of cultural exchange rather than [...] unidirectional transmission."[13] Torsten Tschacher proposes the concept of "circulating Islam": the multi-directional movement of ideas, some of which

---

[9] Michael F. Laffan, *Islamic Nationhood and Colonial Indonesia: The Umma Below the Winds* (London: Routledge, 2003), pp. 9, 400. On hybridity and cosmopolitanism, see: Carool Kersten, "Islam, Cultural Hybridity and Cosmopolitanism: New Muslim Intellectuals on Globalization," *The Journal of International Studies* 1, 1 (2009); R. Michael Feener, "Hybridity and the 'Hadhrami Diaspora' in the Indian Ocean Muslim Networks," *Asian Journal of Social Science* 32, 3 (2004).

[10] On the vexed question of "Malayness," see Timothy P. Barnard, ed., *Contesting Malayness: Malay Identity Across Boundaries* (Singapore: Singapore University Press, 2004).

[11] See Daud Ali, "Connected Histories? Regional Historiography and Theories of Cultural Contact Between Early South and Southeast Asia," in *Islamic Connections: Muslim Societies in South and Southeast Asia*, ed. R. Michael Feener and Terenjit Sevea (Singapore: Institute of Southeast Asian Studies, 2009), pp. 10, 14; R. Michael Feener, "Introduction: Issues and Ideologies in the Study of Regional Muslim Cultures," in Feener and Sevea, *Islamic Connections*, p. xvi.

[12] Feener and Sevea, *Islamic Connections*, p. xiv.

[13] Ali, "Connected Histories?", p. 14.

were transformed by the people who transported them.[14] Through his work on the connections between Ma'bar and Nusantara, Tschacher reveals patterns of convergence and divergence in Islamic texts, ritual practices, and material culture that did not follow ethnic, linguistic, or economic fault-lines. For example, Malay borrowed more Arabic words through Tamil than it borrowed actual Tamil words, and encounters between Arabic and South and Southeast Asian languages had transformative effects on both.[15]

Replacing the model of one-way diffusion with one of multi-directional circulation permits a more nuanced understanding of the development of Islamic traditions in South and Southeast Asia, where "shared customs were transformed and inflected in divergent ways in dispersed geographical settings and fed back into the circulatory regime."[16] Such connections and circulations explain why the Malay world's greatest Sufi poet, Hamzah Fansuri (d. 1590–1604), was in fact a Persian hailing from Barus (Fansur) in northwest Sumatra. From there, he traveled widely both east and west. In addition to having studied in the Middle East (which explains his fluency in Persian and Arabic), he also spent time in Ayutthaya, which was known to its sizeable Persian population as "*Shahr-i Nav*," Persian for "city of boats and canals." Whilst Marcinkowski claims that Hamzah Fansuri was born in Ayutthaya, van Bruinessen argues that Ayutthaya was where he experienced his most profound mystical insights.[17] He was fluent in Persian, Malay, and Arabic. As is well-known, Hamzah Fansuri was the first scholar writing in

---

[14] Torsten Tschacher, "Circulating Islam: Understanding Convergence and Divergence in the Islamic Traditions of Mabar and Nusantara," in Feener and Sevea, *Islamic Connections*, p. 49.

[15] Ibid., pp. 50, 55–6.

[16] Ibid., p. 62.

[17] See M. Ismail Marcinkowski, "Selected Historical Facets of the Presence of Shi'ism in Southeast Asia," *The Muslim World* 99, 2 (2009): 397; Martin van Bruinessen, "Origins and Development of the Sufi Orders (Tarekat) in Southeast Asia," *Studia Islamika* (1994): 114. For more on Hamzah Fansuri, see: Syed Muhammad Naguib Al-Attas, *The Mysticism of Hamzah Fansuri* (Kuala Lumpur: University of Malaya Press, 1970); Syed Muhammad Naguib Al-Attas, "New Light on the Life of Hamzah Fansuri," *Journal of the Malaysian Branch of the Royal Asiatic Society* 40 (1967); Lobe Brakel, "The Birth Place of Hamza Pansuri," *Journal of the Malaysian Branch of the Royal Asiatic Society* 42 (1969); Vladimir I. Braginsky, "Towards the Biography of Hamzah Fansuri. When Did Hamzah Live? Data from His Poems and Early European Accounts," *Archipel* 57, 2 (1999); Peter G. Riddell, "Breaking the Hamzah Fansuri Barrier: Other Literary Windows into Sumatran Islam in the Late Sixteenth Century CE," *Indonesia and the Malay World* 32, 93 (2004).

Malay to have articulated the monist doctrine of *wahdat al-wujud* (Ar. the unity of being) associated with Ibn 'Arabi (d. 1240).[18]

The doctrines that were established (or perhaps continued) by Hamzah Fansuri in Sumatra were famously opposed by Nur al-Din Muhammad b. Ali. b. Hasanji al-Hamid al-Shafi'i al-Ashari al-'Aydarusi al-Raniri, another creole personality produced by this circulating Islam. Scarcity of information about Nur al-Din al-Raniri has led scholars to attempt to deduce something about his background from the large number of *nisba* (Arabic references to tribal or geographical affiliation) in his name.[19] A general consensus exists that Al-Raniri belonged to a diasporic family of the Hamid clan in Ranir (present-day Rander) in India's state of Gujerat. Claiming to be a Hadrami descended from the Quraysh clan, he also studied in the Hadhramaut. Van Bruinessen proposes that al-Raniri represents the last documented case of direct Indian influence on the Rifa'iyya Sufi order in the archipelago. Although other Indian branches of prominent Sufi orders subsequently reached Indonesia, they came via the Honjas, where Indonesians had been initiated.[20] Riddell notes that Al-Raniri had traveled both west and east of India; he had journeyed to Mecca where he performed the *Hajj* in 1620–1621 before visiting the Hadhramaut, while Al-Raniri's connections to the east were through his uncle, Muhammad Jilani Hamid, who had visited the Sultanate of Aceh in the 1580s.

A number of claims have been made by scholars about Al-Raniri's contacts with the Malay world. These range from his mastery of the Malay language before his residency in Aceh between 1637 and 1644, perhaps due to the influence of the significant Malay community in Gujerat, to assertions by Naguib Al-Attas that his mother was Malay.[21] On the last point, Azyumardi Azra agrees. Al-Raniri is included in his study of 17th- and 18th-century networks (Ar. *silsilah*) and chains of transmission (Ar. *isnad*)

---

[18] Anthony H. Johns notes the monistic treatises by Ibn 'Arabi (d. 1240) being among the earliest extant manuscripts from north Sumatra; A.H. Johns, "Sufism in Southeast Asia: Reflections and Reconsiderations," *Journal of Southeast Asian Studies* 26, 1 (1995): 78, 169.

[19] Azra, *The Origins of Islamic Reformism in Southeast Asia*, p. 54. For more on Al-Raniri and his rejection of Hamzah Fansuri, see Riddell, "Breaking the Hamzah Fansuri Barrier."

[20] Van Bruinessen, "Origins and Development of the Sufi Orders (*Tarekat*) in Southeast Asia," p. 2.

[21] Peter G. Riddell, "Sharia-Mindedness in the Malay World and the Indian Connection: The Contributions of Nur al-Din al-Raniri and Nik Abdul Aziz bin Haji Nik Mat," in Feener and Sevea, *Islamic Connections*, p. 176.

that laid the foundations of Islamic reformism in Southeast Asia. Although Azra claims that his Hadrami father moved between South and Southeast Asia, he insists that al-Raniri was neither an Arab nor an Indian *'alim* (Ar. scholar), but a Malay-Indonesian.[22]

Highly ethnicized debates over the relative importance of Arab and Indian Sufis in Islam's Southeast Asian expansion have been engaged in by Arab and Indian scholars such as Al-Attas and Sastri, and their respective students.[23] Absent in discussions of the personalities that played a role in Islam's expansion to and embedding in Southeast Asia, is the fact that many of these figures are only inadequately described as "Arab," "Indian," or "Malay." They were mobile, multilingual members of cosmopolitan coastal trading communities. They were creoles. Such figures also played important roles in mediating the processes of Islam's initial adoption and subsequent development. They were Islam's ambassadors.

The origins of the first Arab-Indian creole communities on the southwest coast of India were male Hadrami immigrants who married Indian women. These mixed communities were rejuvenated by new arrivals from the Hadhramaut. This dynamic distinguished them from the "Mappila" communities located inland who practiced a more syncretic form of Islam. Increased immigration during the 13th century caused the population to swell leading local Malabari Muslims and Hadrami immigrants to move further and further east, which partly explains why southern Arabia, South India, and Southeast Asia all follow the Shafi'i school of Islamic jurisprudence.[24] Far from the pristine Islam of the *Salaf al-Salih*, these

---

[22] Azra, *The Origins of Islamic Reformism in Southeast Asia: Networks of Middle Eastern 'Ulama' in the Seventeenth and Eighteenth Centuries*, p. 54.

[23] See Amri Baharuddin Shamsul, "Islam Embedded: Religion and Plurality in Southeast Asia as a Mirror for Europe," *Asia Europe Journal* 3 (2005): 164. See also: K.A. Nilakanta Sastri, *South Indian Influences in the Far East* (Bombay: Hind Kitab Ltd, 1949); Syed Muhammad Naguib Al-Attas, *Preliminary Statement on a General Theory of the Islamisation of the Malay-Indonesian Archipelago* (Kuala Lumpur: Dewan Bahasa dan Pustaka, 1969).

[24] Andrew D.W. Forbes, "Southern Arabia and the Islamization of the Central Indian Ocean Archipelagoes," *Archipel* 21 (1981). For more on the Hadrami Immigration, see: Ulrike Freitag and W.G. Clarence-Smith, "Hadrami Traders, Scholars, and Statesmen in the Indian Ocean, 1750s–1960s," in *Social, Economic, and Political Studies of the Middle East and Asia*, v. 57 (Leiden and New York: Brill, 1997); Natalie Mobini-Kesheh, *The Hadrami Awakening: Community and Identity in the Netherlands East Indies, 1900–1942* (Ithaca, NY: Cornell University Southeast Asia Program Publications, 1999).

ambassadors introduced a range of interpretations of Islam that had been embedded in the Arab-Indian-Malay creole communities. The selective appropriation and application of a range of "Islams" resulted in the presence in Southeast Asia of all major streams of Islamic thought and practice, although often in a mediated and modified form. As a result, the *"umma below the winds"* resembled its Middle Eastern antecedents, but with distinguishing local features.

While Islam was once regarded as peripheral to Southeast Asia, and the region as peripheral to Islam, recent studies by Laffan and Azra have emphasized Southeast Asian Islam's connection to — not separation from — the Middle East via the Indian Ocean. The cosmopolitan characteristics of Southeast Asian port city-states that served as conduits for the spread of Islam from the 14th century are well-known.[25] Ali claims that from the 13th century, "Arab" traders and religious leaders active in Southeast Asia originated not from the traditional Arab heartlands but from important ports along the Indian Ocean's trading circuits. One of the earliest Western accounts of Southeast Asia is provided by Marco Polo, whose description of Sumatra in 1291 mentions the many *Idrîsî's* (Indian Muslim middle-men), who were also observed by Ibn Battûta (1304–1377) on the Malabar Coast. Laffan suggests that the toponyms used by Marco Polo may indicate that he sailed with Sino-Muslim sailors.[26] Jan van der Putten refers to Southeast Asia's coastal settlements as "intermediary communities" where "creative foreigners" who were receptive to new influences resided. In addition, to be active in the localization of various activities, as polyglots they were able to maintain "contacts with people in the land of origin of their forebears."[27]

The opening of the Suez Canal in 1869 and introduction of steamships greatly increased the connectedness between the Middle East and Southeast Asia that had circulated Islam and created these creole communities. By the 1890s, the small sailing vessels transporting independent pilgrims had disappeared from the Indian Ocean, replaced by steamers that made the

---

[25] See Anthony Reid's chapter in this volume.

[26] M.F. Laffan, *Finding Java: Muslim Nomenclature of Insular Southeast Asia from Śrîvijaya to Snouck Hurgronje*, WP 52 (Singapore: Asia Research Institute, 2005), p. 49. For a recent discussion of the role of Chinese in Islam's Southeast Asian expansion, see Tan Ta Sen, *Cheng Ho and Islam in Southeast Asia* (Singapore: Institute of Southeast Asian Studies, 2009).

[27] Jan van der Putten, "Wayang Parsi, Bangsawan and Printing: Commercial Cultural Exchange between South Asia and the Malay World," in Feener and Sevea, *Islamic Connections*, p. 89.

previously arduous trip in two weeks. Before these developments, it was not the forest dwellers of the interior, but the mobile, multilingual men of mixed ethnicity from coastal towns who possessed the financial means to perform the *Hajj*. These advances in transport had a number of effects. More Southeast Asian Muslims returned with greatly increased religious knowledge, and consequently enhanced status and authority. More traveled to the Middle East, primarily to further their Islamic education. Immigration from the Middle East to Southeast Asia also increased.[28] Many of these mainly Hadrami immigrants were revered as saints possessing supernatural powers that enabled them to rise to the highest ranks of Malay society. Intermarriage with Malays and management of the *Hajj* traffic further strengthened the Islamic element of Malayness.[29] Finally, these advances in transport also coincided with developments in communication technology — the most important of which was the printing press.

Creole Ancestries

The circulation of Islam throughout the region between the Middle East and China created a range of communities populated by mobile, multilingual Arab-Indian-Malay creole figures who played key roles in Islam's Southeast Asian expansion. In addition to being a conduit of circulating Islam, Patani both attracted and produced a range of such creole Muslim figures. Some became influential ambassadors for Islam. In Figure 6.2 below, I delineate the genealogies of some of Patani's most famous scholars: Sheikh Daud b. Abdullah b. Idris al-Fatani (Sheikh Daud al-Fatani) (1769–1847), Sheikh Zain al 'Abidin (Tuan Minal) (1820–1913), Sheikh Wan Ahmad b. Muhammad Zain Mustafa al-Fatani (Sheikh Ahmad al-Fatani) (1856–1908), and the modernist leader Shaykh Muhammad Sulong bin Abdul Kadir bin Muhammad al-Fatani (Haji Sulong) (1895–1954). With the exception of Tuan Minal, I provide brief descriptions of these below. The reputation of these great scholarly figures was bolstered by claims that they were descended from Arab religious figures from the Hadhramaut. For example, the daughter of Sheikh Ibrahim al-Hadhrami bin Abar, Wan

---

[28] Laffan, *Islamic Nationhood and Colonial Indonesia*, p. 36.

[29] See: Syed Mhd. Khairudin Aljunied, "Making Sense of an Evolving Identity: A Survey of Studies on Identity and Identity Formation of Malays in Singapore," *Journal of Muslim Minority Affairs* 26, 3 (2006): 375; Syed Mhd. Khairudin Aljunied, "The Role of Hadramis in Post-World War Two Singapore: A Reinterpretation," *Immigrants and Minorities* 25, 2 (2007): 164.

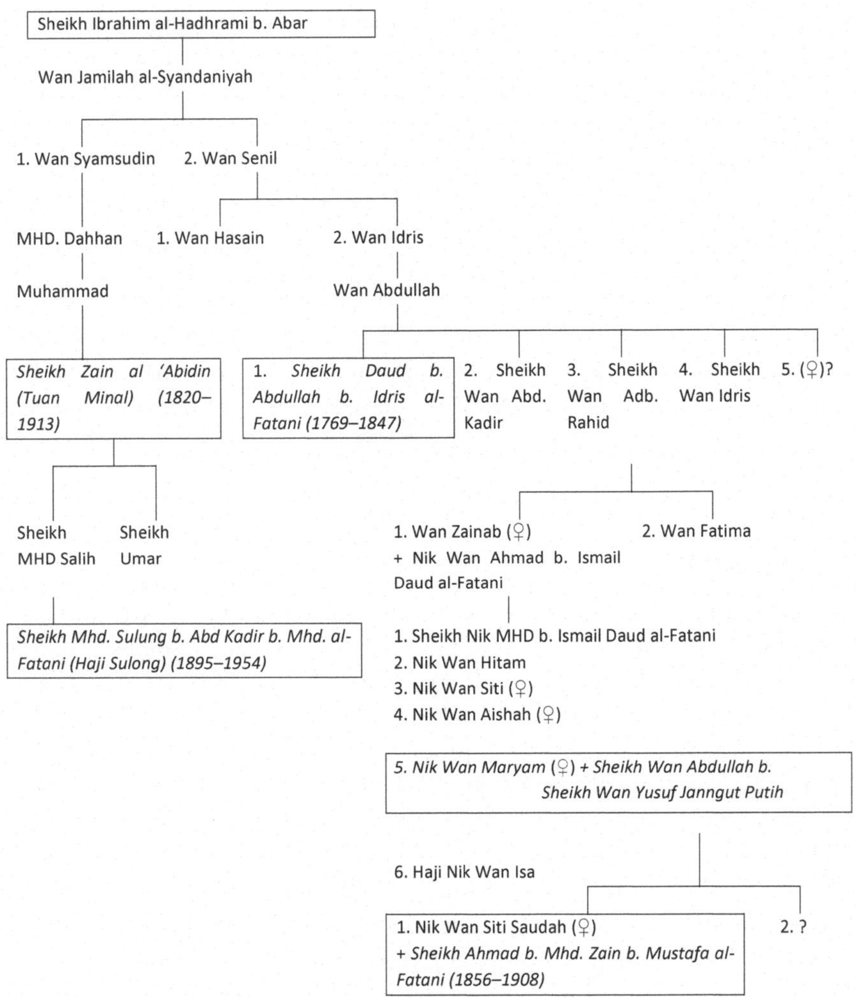

Figure 6.2 Genealogies of Patani's creole ambassadors.[30]

Jamilah al-Syandaniyah is said to have been the great-great-grandmother of a number of Patani's *'ulama besar*. Another Hadrami involved in the spice trade by the name of Sheikh Usman had three sons, all of whom played important roles in Islamic education in Patani. The eldest was the great-grandfather of Sheikh Daud while the second eldest was the great-

---

[30] This genealogy is based on information provided in the following: Ahmad Fathy Al-Fatani, *Ulama Besar Dari Patani* (Bangi: Penerbit Universiti Kebangsaan Malaysia, 2002), p. 63; and Rahimmula, "The Patani Fatawa," pp. 201, 231, 355.

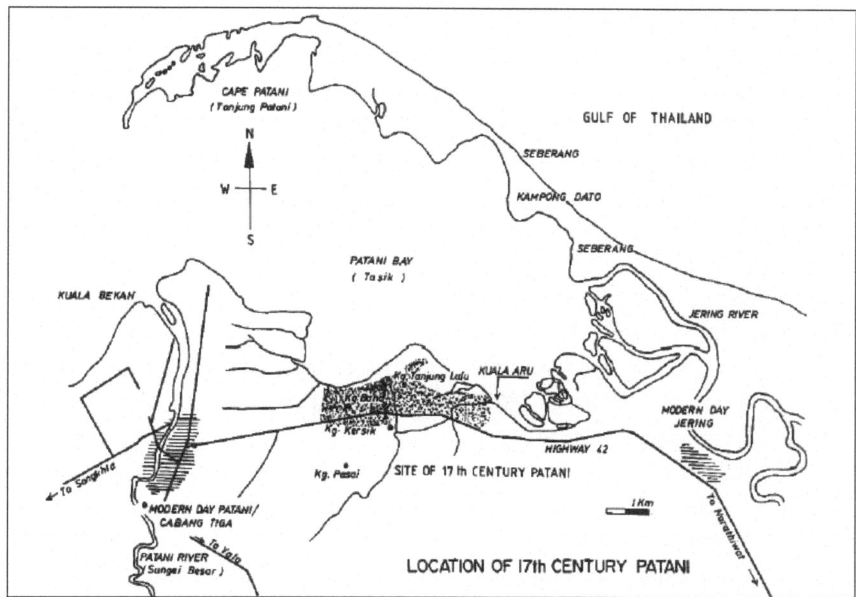

Figure 6.3 Site of the former location of the palace in Krue Se in relation to modern-day Pattani and Cabetigo.

grandfather of Sheikh Ahmad.[31] Sheikh Abdul Razak, the great-grandfather of Sheikh Wan Mustafa al-Fatani, was another Hadrami. Having witnessed a miraculously overflowing well on a night at the end of Ramadan, he asked Allah to bless his four sons and their descendants by making them great *'ulama*. Patani's *'ulama besar* shared three common attributes: Hadrami ancestry; an early Islamic education provided by their fathers and grand-fathers; and the financial means, connections, and linguistic skills which enabled them to make the trip to Mecca via Aceh.

Sheikh Daud b. Abdullah b. Idris al-Fatani was born in Krue Se in 1769 and died in Ta'if in 1847.[32] His grandfather, Sheikh Wan Idris al-Fatani, and father, Sheikh Wan Abdullah al-Fatani, are both known to have been involved in his early religious education. According to Rahimmula,

---

[31] Hasan Madmarn notes that Sheikh Ahmad al-Fatani's grandfather was a descendent of a Hadrami missionary who settled in Patani; Hasan Madmarn, *The Pondok and Madrasah in Patani*, p. 23.

[32] For a discussion of Sheikh Daud, see Francis R. Bradley, "The Social Dynamics of Islamic Revivalism in Southeast Asia: The Rise of the Patani School, 1785–1909," PhD diss., University of Wisconsin-Madison, 2010, pp. 189–337.

"the young Sheikh Daud had taken his traditional Islamic education in Patani under Malay and Arabic *'ulama*, many of whom were related to each other."[33] Following his early education in Patani, Daud al-Fatani spent time in a *pondok* before traveling to Aceh where he studied for two years with Muhammad Zayn bin Faqih Jalal al-Din al-Ashi, a leading Acehnese scholar during the period of Sultan 'Ala' al-Din Mahmud Shah (r. 1760–1781). Azra believes that Sheikh Daud reached the Hijaz via Aceh in his late twenties. Although he joined other scholars from Patani residing there, they were all his seniors. He also joined the Shattariyyah *tariqah*.[34] Interestingly, Sheikh Daud's earliest known work was only completed in Mecca in 1809. As one of the leading Malay-Indonesian scholars residing in Mecca, he was honored with the title of al-'Alim al-'Allamat al-'Arif ar-Rabbani by the Ottoman authorities.[35] His reputation was based on his output of more than 57 works which covered many branches of the Islamic disciplines and which were printed not only in many parts of the Middle East but throughout the Malay-Indonesian world.[36]

Sheikh Daud's teachings are acknowledged as having been "preserved and extended" by another of Patani's best known scholars, his great nephew Sheikh Wan Ahmad bin Muhammad Zain Mustafa al-Fatani (Sheikh Ahmad). The connection between these two famous *'ulama besar* began with Sheikh Ahmad's father, who, after performing the *Hajj*, settled in Mecca to work as Sheikh Daud's copyist.[37] Sheikh Ahmad was born in 1856 in Kampung Sena Janjar, Patani, and died in Mina on January 14, 1908. Like Sheikh Daud, Sheikh Ahmad received his early Islamic education from his Mecca-educated father who taught at Pondok Bendang Daya, which was renowned as one of the largest *pondok* schools in Southeast Asia.[38] Born a generation after the final subjugation of Patani by the Siamese in 1838, Sheikh Ahmad was, according to Rahimmula, deeply concerned with the

---

[33] Rahimmula, "The Patani Fatawa," p. 202.

[34] Azra, *The Origins of Islamic Reformism in Southeast Asia*, p. 126.

[35] Rahimmula, "The Patani Fatawa," p. 202.

[36] See Azra, *The Origins of Islamic Reformism in Southeast Asia*, pp. 124, 126; V. Matheson and M.B. Hooker, "Jawi Literature in Patani: The Maintenance of an Islamic Tradition," *Journal of the Malaysian Branch of the Royal Asiatic Society* 61, 1 (1988).

[37] Rahimmula, "The Patani Fatawa," pp. 194, 258, 313.

[38] Mohammad Redzuan Othman, "The Role of Makka-Educated Malays in the Development of Early Islamic Scholarship and Education in Malaya," *Journal of Islamic Studies* 9, 2 (1998): 148.

preservation of Malay identity, language, and culture in the Patani region, and this motivated him to reprint the works of older scholars, such as Sheikh Daud.[39] Sheikh Ahmad traveled to Jerusalem and then Egypt where, according to Rahimmula, he was the first Malay from Patani to have studied at Al-Azhar University. Upon completing his studies, he moved to Mecca where his family lived. There, he would eventually become one of the leading scholars at Masjid al-Haram.[40] Although Shaykh Daud is a better known scholar, Shaykh Ahmad's role as a mediator of the religious developments of the time in the Middle East through his work as editor, writer, and teacher, in fact surpassed that of his elder relative. Sheikh Ahmad's reputation was such that the famous Dutch scholar of Islam, Snouck Hurgronje, referred to him as a "*savant* of merit."[41]

Sheikh Ahmad's family left Patani before the opening of the Suez Canal in 1869 and subsequent spread of steamers across the Indian Ocean that by the 1890s led to the disappearance of smaller sailing vessels. This revolution in transportation reduced the once arduous trip from Southeast Asia to the Middle East to just two weeks. Improved communication across the Indian Ocean was crucial to Sheikh Ahmad's work. Even before steamers replaced sailboats, scribes had also begun to become obsolete, replaced by printing presses. Although the Egyptian publishing industry emerged as early as the 1820s, it only began publishing *kitab jawi* for the Malay-speaking world in the late 19th century. Among the earliest and most active publishers of Malay books was Mustafa al-Babi al-Halabi. He began work in 1859 in his publishing house near the al-Azhar Mosque where Sheikh Ahmad worked as a proofreader. In 1884, Sheikh Ahmad al-Fatani was appointed chief editor of the newly established Malay section of the Ottoman Press.[42] Sheikh Ahmad also established the Patani 'Ulama Association, which was involved in correcting and publishing religious works written in Malay. Sheikh Ahmad would eventually serve as the Association's chief editor.

---

[39] Rahimmula, "The Patani Fatawa," p. 191.

[40] Ibid., p. 309.

[41] C. Snouck Hurgronje, *Mekka in the Latter Part of the 19th Century: Daily Life, Customs and Learning, The Moslims of the East-Indian-Archipelago*, Slightly rev. 2nd ed. (Leiden: Brill, 1970), p. 286.

[42] See Rahimmula, "The Patani Fatawa," p. 321; Laffan, *Islamic Nationhood and Colonial Indonesia*, p. 25. Mohammad Redzuan Othman also notes that the Al-Maktaba al-Fataniyya Press was established by Sheikh Ahmad in Qashashiyah; see Mohammad Redzuan Othman, "The Role of Makka-Educated Malays in the Development of Early Islamic Scholarship and Education in Malaya," p. 149.

Mohammad Redzuan Othman describes Sheikh Ahmad as "the prolific author of perhaps as many as 160 original and annotated works in both Malay and Arabic. These covered a wide range of subjects in the Islamic sciences as well as medicine, history, and politics. Some are still in print and available to this day, being widely used as religious texts in traditional education."[43] Rahimmula claims that Sheikh Ahmad was the first Malay from Patani to have written religious treatises in Arabic. Edwin Wieringa observes that Sheikh Ahmad's language in his Jawi work entitled *Nur al-Mubin*, was "deeply imbued with Arabic," a characteristic feature of *kitab jawi* through which Arabic ideation entered the Malay lexicon.[44] Nevertheless, most of his writings dealt with the Islamic sciences. Some of his works continue to be used in southern Thailand's *pondok* today.[45] One of the most important of these, *Kitab Al-Fatawa Al-Fataniyyah*, is a 220-page collection of judgments (Ar. *fatwa*) on a range of religious questions posed to him by Southeast Asian Muslims.[46] Such question-and-answer exchanges on contemporary issues were made possible by the greatly increased degree of communication across the Indian Ocean which connected Patani to the center of Islamic scholarship in the Middle East. Rahimmula claims that not only was Sheikh Ahmad the first Mecca-based Malay *'ulama* to have established a didactic genre based on answers to written questions received, but that most of the subjects that were addressed were on issues that the Siamese authorities had begun to interfere with in his homeland. Indeed, Matheson and Hooker note that this 1903 work

---

[43] Mohammad Redzuan Othman, "The Role of Makka-Educated Malays in the Development of Early Islamic Scholarship and Education in Malaya," p. 148. For a summary of his main works, see: Matheson and Hooker, "Jawi Literature in Patani," pp. 50–5.

[44] Edwin Wieringa, "Some Light on Ahmad al-Fatani's Nur al-Mubin," in *Lost Time and Untold Tales from the Malay World*, ed. Jan van der Putten and Mary Kilcline Coby (Singapore: NUS Press, 2009), p. 191. For more on *kitab jawi*, see: Mohammad Nor Bin Ngah, *Kitab Jawi: Islamic Thought of the Malay Muslim Scholars*, v. 33, Research Notes and Discussions Paper (Singapore: Institute of Southeast Asian Studies, 1983); Ismail Hamid, "Kitab Jawi: Intellectualizing Literary Tradition," in *Islamic Civilization in the Malay World*, ed. Mohammad Taib Osman (Kuala Lumpur: Dewan Bahasa dan Pustaka, 1997).

[45] Matheson and Hooker, "Jawi Literature in Patani," pp. 28–30.

[46] See Rahimmula, "The Patani Fatawa"; Matheson and Hooker, "Jawi Literature in Patani," p. 55.

appeared a year after the Siamese abolition of the *shar'iah* system of law in the territory.[47]

The influence of Sheikh Ahmad's publications on Islam was part of the wider impact of religious literature printed in the Middle East on Southeast Asian Islam in the late 19th and early 20th centuries. For example, the Egyptian modernist journal *al-Manar* [*The Lighthouse*] edited by Muhammad Rashid Rida from 1898, inspired *Jawi* publications such as *al-Imam* [*The Leader*] published in Singapore between 1906 and 1908.[48] That the goal of *al-Imam* was the dissemination of the reformist goals of *al-Manar* in the Malay world is demonstrated by the fact that many of its articles were Malay translations of articles from *al-Manar*. *Al-Imam* became the most widely read journal in the Malay-speaking regions of Southeast Asia before the Second World War, with a circulation reaching 5,000 at its height. Following *Al-Imam*'s demise in 1908, a number of modernist publications were produced. One of these was *al-Munir* [*The Illuminating*] published in Padang, West Sumatra, for five years from 1911.

Sheikh Ahmad was a leading scholar in Mecca in his own right and taught at Masjid al-Haram. He was also one of few non-Arab *'ulama* to have been appointed by the Sharif of Mecca to represent the Shafi'ite *madhhab*. One of his most influential students was a Malay from Kelantan, Haji Muhammad Yusuf (1868–1933), better known as Tok Kenali, who studied with Sheikh Ahmad for 17 years. Upon returning to Kelantan in 1908, Tok Kenali became a prominent scholar, a founding member of the Kelantan Religious Council, and editor of its fortnightly journal.[49] Rahimmula notes

---

[47] Matheson and Hooker, "Jawi Literature in Patani," p. 55. Although family and inheritance cases were exempt from Bangkok's replacement of Islamic law with Thai secular law, even in these cases, according to Wan Kadir, "the decision of a Muslim judge was not final until it was agreed upon by the sitting Thai judge. Otherwise, contending parties had the right to appeal to the Thai Superior Court, where the judge was not a Muslim"; see Wan Kadir Che Man, "The Thai Government and Islamic Institutions in the Four Southern Muslim Provinces of Thailand," *Sojourn: Journal of Social Issues in Southeast Asia* 5, 2 (1990): 256.

[48] For more on *Al-Imam*, see: Abu Bakar Hamzah, *Al-Iman: Its Role in Malay Society 1906–1908* (Kuala Lumpur: Pustaka Antara, 1991); Azyumardi Azra, "The Transmission of al-Manar's Reformism to the Malay-Indonesian World: The Cases of *al-Imam* and *al-Munir*," *Studia Islamika* 6, 3 (1999).

[49] Mohammad Redzuan Othman, "The Role of Makka-Educated Malays in the Development of Early Islamic Scholarship and Education in Malaya," p. 151. On Tok Kenali, see Abdullah al-Qari bin Haji Salleh, "Tok Kenali: His Life and Influence," in *Kelantan: Religion, Society, and Politics in a Malay State*, ed. William Roff (Kuala Lumpur: Oxford University Press, 1974).

that Sheikh Ahmad al-Fatani encouraged his students to become informed about politics and local events by reading newspapers, at the time something relatively rare among the *'ulama* of the Haramayn, which suggests the influence of Muhammad Abduh's modernist ideas.[50]

The most important ambassador for Muhammad Abduh's modernist agenda in Patani, however, was Shaykh Muhammad Sulong bin Abdul Kadir bin Muhammad al-Fatani, better known as "Haji Sulong." He was born in 1895 in the village of Lukson, Pattani, and died in mysterious circumstances, widely presumed to have been at the hands of Thai security forces, in 1954.[51] Like Sheikh Ahmad, Haji Sulong's relatives included a number of Patani's creole *'ulama*. The most famous of these was his grandfather, Sheikh Zainal 'Abidin bin Ahmad al-Fatani (Tuan Minal) (1820–1913). Ockey notes that Haji Sulong came from a wealthy family which for generations had sent family members to Mecca. His father, Haji Abdul Qadir bin Muhammad, was wealthy enough to support three wives and to send his eldest son to the best schools. Haji Sulong was born to Haji Abdul Qadir's first wife, Sarifah. He studied at a *pondok* in Krue Se run by Tok Guru Wae Muso, before being sent by his father to study in Mecca in 1907.[52] There he studied at the newly established Ma'ahad Dar al-Ulum, which was well-known among Mecca's Malay-speaking residents, staying in a *wakaf* (boarding house).[53] He did well in his studies and later became a teacher.

That Haji Sulong was able to return to Patani for a brief period during the First World War testifies to the increasing ease and affordability of traversing the India Ocean. In 1922, he married Sabiya, the daughter one of the teachers at Mecca. According to Ockey:

> Along with his status as a teacher came increased wealth and, since his wife was from Mecca, a house for his new family. Haji Sulong thus came to occupy a privileged position at Mecca, and planned to spend his life

---

[50] Rahimmula, "The Patani Fatawa," pp. 259, 344.

[51] On Haji Sulong, see: Liow, *Islam, Education and Reform in Southern Thailand: Tradition and Transformation*, pp. 81–8; Joseph Chinyong Liow, "Religious Education and Reformist Islam in Thailand's Southern Border Provinces: The Roles of Haji Sulong Abdul Kadir and Ismail Lutfi Japakiya," *Journal of Islamic Studies* 20, 3 (2009); Chalermkiat Khunthongpetch, *Haji Sulong Abdul Qadir: A Rebel … or a Hero of the Four Southern Province* (Bangkok: Matichon, 2004); James Ockey, "The Religio-Nationalist Pilgrimage of Haji Sulong Abdulkadir al Fattani," in *Pilgrims, Spectres and World-Reforming* (University of Michigan Student Conference, 2006).

[52] Ockey, "The Religio-Nationalist Pilgrimage of Haji Sulong Abdulkadir al Fattani."

[53] Liow, *Islam, Education and Reform in Southern Thailand*, p. 81.

there among the Jawi community. His marriage to a Meccan gave him a certain status in relations with those from Mecca, and with those from other communities. He was in a position to broker deals, to ease social relations, and consequently to gain considerable respect ... This prestige, and the role of intermediary, allowed many of the scholars who married Meccans entry to the business of providing guides for pilgrims, which was very lucrative financially. [54]

However, after only one year, Sabiya died. The following year — the same year that the Ibn Saud and the Wahhabi finally captured Mecca and Medina — Haji Sulong married Khadijah, the daughter of Haji Ibrahim and sister of Haji Mohammad Nor, who would later serve as the Mufti of Kelantan. Ockey observes that while his first marriage strengthened his network in Mecca, his second reinforced that with the *Jawah* community. This enabled Haji Sulong, upon his return to Patani, to retain and reactivate a strong local Malay identity.[55] Later, back in Mecca, Haji Sulong had begun teaching in the al-Haram Mosque. This was a time of considerable political and religious ferment in the Middle East with the victory of Ibn Saud's forces. It is significant that Haji Sulong was promoted at a time when many Southeast Asian scholars were leaving Mecca due to the political turmoil and gradual enforcement of the religious orthodoxy of the Wahhabis who had supported Ibn Saud.

Following the death of Khadijah and his one-year-old son, Haji Sulong returned to Patani in 1927. Soon after his return, he encountered a religious life that to him resembled the *jahiliyya* of pre-Islamic Arabia. Initially as an itinerant preacher, he became an ambassador for Muhammad Abduh's project of modernisation and reform.[56] Despite strong opposition from the *kaum tua* in 1933, Haji Sulong established the Madrasah Al-Ma'arif Al-Wattaniah, Patani's first modern Islamic school, whose educational model sharply departed from the traditional *pondok* education that the city-state had been famous for. His involvement in modernizing education and politics was informed by the belief that the role of an *'alim* extended beyond the teaching of religion and into the socio-political sphere. Indeed, he is best known for the "seven demands" for greater autonomy for the Malay Muslims that he made to the Thai government in 1947. According to Liow, Haji Sulong

---

[54] Ockey, "The Religio-Nationalist Pilgrimage of Haji Sulong Abdulkadir al Fattani."

[55] Ibid.

[56] Imtiyaz Yusuf, "Islam and Democracy in Thailand: Reforming the Office of the Chularajamontri/Shaikh Al-Islam," *Journal of Islamic Studies* 9, 2 (1998): 286.

possessed an "abiding interest in political and social activism which was to preoccupy him for the rest of his life, and catapulted him to a position of prominence as a leader of southern Thailand's Malay community."[57]

Conclusion

While Sheikh Said and Sheikh Safiuddin al-Abbasi of Pasai were important ambassadors for Islam during Patani's "magical" epoch, Sheikh Daud, his grandnephew Sheikh Ahmad, and Haji Sulong influenced Islam in Patani during the "theological" and "modernist" periods that followed. Similar to such earlier luminaries as Hamzah Fansuri and Nur al-Din al-Raniri, they were members of a religious elite that generated the circulating Islam described above. Although commonly referred to as "Malays," and proudly claimed by the residents of present-day Pattani, Yala, and Narathiwat, I have shown that they were more mobile and multilingual that other Malays of their time. Their families possessed the financial means and personal connections that permitted both the long journey across the Indian Ocean and their long-term relocation to Mecca.

The prominent role of Patani's creole ambassadors suggests that this city-state resembled other Southeast Asian port city-states where peoples, goods, and ideas circulated via the Indian Ocean trade. It was this circulation that created the religious intermediaries who selectively appropriated and mediated religious developments in the Haramayn, and through their writings and their students maintained and indeed deepened Patani's connections to the Middle East across the Indian Ocean.

---

[57] Liow, *Islam, Education and Reform in Southern Thailand*, p. 81.

PART THREE

Alternative Histories of Patani's Decline and Fall

CHAPTER 7

Siam's Conquest of Patani and the End of *Mandala* Relations, 1786–1838

Francis R. Bradley

Established scholarship on the political history of early modern Southeast Asia agrees that political entities were borderless, whether characterized as *mandalas* or "galactic polities."[1] These "states" revolved around charismatic leaders positioned in political centers from which they extended their power as far as their resources would allow. In this system, relations between greater and lesser political centers were a matter of constant contestation and negotiation. The relationship between Siam and Patani from the 16th to the 18th centuries falls into this category. There were periods of peaceful relations when Patani sent tribute to Ayutthaya, but there were also protracted periods of political conflict when Patani's rulers refused to acknowledge Siamese political domination, especially in the period 1634–1694.

Extrapolating upon conflicts between "states" in early modern Southeast Asia, Anthony Reid characterized warfare as a relatively non-lethal affair due to the scarcity of large, stable workforces in the region which compelled rulers to engage in low-casualty warfare in early modern times.[2] Viewed in

---

[1] Stanley Tambiah, "The Galactic Polity: The Structure of Traditional Kingdoms in Southeast Asia," in *Anthropology and the Climate of Opinion*, vol. 293, ed. M. Freed (New York: Annals of the New York Academy of the Sciences, 1977), pp. 69–97; O.W. Wolters, *History, Culture, and Region in Southeast Asian Perspectives*, rev. ed, Southeast Asia Program Publications series (Ithaca, NY: Cornell University Press, 1999).

[2] Anthony Reid, *Europe and Southeast Asia: The Military Balance*, Centre for Southeast Asian Studies Occasional Paper, no. 16, ed. Bob Hering (Townsville: James Cook University of North Queensland, 1982), p. 1; Anthony Reid, *Southeast Asia in the Age of Commerce 1450–1680*, vol. 2: *Expansion and Crisis* (New Haven: Yale University Press, 1993), pp. 219–33.

this way, generals and rulers competed with their enemies over the control of people, rather than land. Whether by near-constant small-scale raiding or in the clashes between great armies, the main goal of any conflict was to increase the labor force of a particular ruler at the expense of an enemy. The weaker party in a conflict often responded with quick flight into a nearby forest or mountainous region where they sought refuge until the soldiers of the invading army had satisfied themselves by carrying off as much loot as they could manage and withdrew back to their capital. Even when fighting occurred, opposing sides often went to great lengths to intimidate their enemies into surrendering, whether by amassing an overwhelming force or by shooting into the air, beating drums, or making other impressive shows of strength, rather than by defeating them through sheer force of arms.[3] At other times, a contest might be decided by man-to-man combat between two opposing generals, the loser's army thereafter submitting to the victor to be taken as captives back to the opposition's royal court and offered to the ruler as war booty. Generals engaged in these sorts of tactics because they could scarcely afford to lose a large number of soldiers when their labor forces were in perpetual shortage.

This chapter seeks to question this view of warfare in Southeast Asia by focusing upon the defeat and destruction of the Patani sultanate in the course of five wars, in 1785–1786, 1789–1791, 1808, 1831–1832, and 1838. No previous study has analyzed these conflicts and their impact on our understanding of warfare in the pre-colonial period. Because the greatest amount of source material exists for the wars of 1785–1786 and 1831–1832, I have chosen to give particular attention to these conflicts. I argue that Siam employed four main tactics to subdue Patani: massacre, slave-raiding, environmental warfare, and the expulsion of refugees to break the power of the Patani sultanate once and for all. The fall of Ayutthaya in 1767 and the escalation of warfare between Siam and Burma throughout the late 18th century not only brought about an end to traditional *mandala* state relations in the period, but also transformed the way in which leaders and armies chose to carry out conflicts between political centers. The fall of Patani heralded the beginning of a new phase in Siam's political power over the lower peninsula. The triumphant extension of the Siamese political authority over the Malay tributaries ultimately coalesced in the signing of the Anglo-Siamese Treaty in 1909 that for the first time formulated a definitive border between Siam and British Malaya.

---

[3] Reid, *Europe and Southeast Asia*, p. 1.

Massacre

The political chaos that enveloped the peninsula and central Siam after the fall of Ayutthaya reached a climax in 1785. After slaughtering a Burmese army lodged at Nakhon Si Thammarat, a Siamese army pushed further south to bring its peninsular tributaries back into obeisance, following Patani's refusal to pay its customary annual tribute or to render supplementary military support to the Siamese authority since the demise of Ayutthaya. In letters to the British governor general of India, Francis Light reported from Penang on the strength of Patani's defences:

> [Pujut, which was Patani's main fort] was deemed impregnable. It was surrounded by Seven thick rows of Bamboes, within the Bamboes an exceeding wide and deep Canal, and within the Canal a Strong Rampart of Earth, on which was mounted a Number of large Cannon. The Area within the Walls Contained all the Inhabitants Cattle and Grain. Their Strength Amounted to near 4,000 Fighting Men.[4]

This was just one of a number of Patani's forts and armies. Despite the impressive fortifications, however, after a year-long siege Patani fell to Siam's armies in November 1786. In the initial aftermath, the Siamese army appears to have carried out a large-scale massacre of the inhabitants of Patani. Light again reported: "The Siamese General is extirpating Pattany. All the men, Children and old women, he orders to be Tied and thrown upon the grounds and there Trampled to Death by Elephants."[5] While Light's understanding of the situation may have been exaggerated, it nevertheless reveals that not all captives were returned to Siam's imperial court. Killing with elephants in this manner was a commonly method of execution in Southeast Asia and was probably reserved for the elites that the Siamese had identified after capture. Nevertheless, the mass execution of the captured Patani people, even if just of the leading *orangkaya*, generals, and principle soldiers, suggests something quite different from Reid's "low casualty" thesis. Massacre appears to have been the method deliberately employed to decisively break the will of any further resistance from Patani and to instill terror into the population.

If we look closely at Light's choice of words, we see that he explicitly excluded any mention of the "young women" who became victims of the

---

[4] Light to Governor General, September 12, 1786, *Straits Settlements Records* 2: 312 (FWC October 9, 1786).
[5] Ibid., p. 281.

invading army. Light's silence is perplexing as we must assume captive young women were treated differently. Given the general brutality evidenced in 1786 and later wars, rape does not seem out of the question, but more likely young women were taken back to Thonburi and Bangkok to be distributed as concubines in a less dramatic form of sexualized violence. As I discuss below, this was commonly the case in later wars between Siam and Patani. What is clear from the report is that the people selected for death in the massacre were determined at least partially by a person's gender. In any case, these acts of selective killing demonstrate that arbitrary annihilation of inhabitants was being deliberately carried out, that leaders of the victorious army were controlling and directing the process of slaying, and that these killings were being carried out long after the Siamese had vanquished the Patani soldiers. Much later, in the 1832 war between Patani and Siam, clearer evidence of the disproportionate killing of men can be seen, supporting the tertiary evidence that something similar occurred in the aftermath of the 1785–1786 war.

By mass killings, expulsion, and capture, Siam dealt Patani society a blow from which it would take many generations to recover. In terms of demographics, the 1786 massacre contributed to other factors that together resulted in a shrinking population. Mid-17th-century estimates of Patani's urban population generally range around 20,000, but other estimates suggest a substantial rural population bringing the total of the Patani *mandala* to perhaps as high as 180,000.[6] By the turn of the 18th century, such numbers were already in decline, and proportionally did not match the high levels of growth in the Chao Phraya delta.[7] Furthermore, Light, in an economic report of the peninsula in 1789, observed simply: "Pattany — destroyed by the Siamese, the inhabitants dispersed." The destruction of the Patani sultanate was thus only accomplished through very bloody warfare.

---

[6] Reid estimates Patani's population to have been 10,000–20,000, but some primary sources indicate a much larger population. Nieuhoff, for example, believed that the city of Patani could muster 10,000 soldiers itself. John Nieuhoff, "Mr. John Nieuhoff's Remarkable Voyages and Travels into Brazil, and the Best Parts of the East-Indies," in *A Collection of Voyages and Travels, some now First Printed from Original Manuscripts*, vol. 2 (London: Printed for Awnsham and John Churchill, at the Black Swan in Pater-Nester-Row, 1704), p. 220.

[7] W.P. Coolhaas, ed., *Generale missiven van gouverneurs-generaal en raden aan Heren XVII der Verenigde Oostindische Compagnie*, vol. 5 ('s-Gravenhage: Martinus Nijhoff, 1960): p. 721; ibid., vol. 7: 98.

Enslavement

While the massacres of Patani's inhabitants in the war's aftermath must have severely weakened it, enslavement played a far more significant role in Patani's subjugation. A large number of the residents of Patani who managed to survive were taken prisoner. Clearly one of the objectives was to depopulate the Patani region as a means of establishing Siamese political dominance once and for all. The number of Patani inhabitants who were taken as prisoners of war is unclear, however many of the captives likely served as slaves in the building of the newly established Siamese political center of Bangkok.[8] Female prisoners were also distributed as concubines to elite men of the capital. As late as 1828, John Crawfurd noted, "Besides the Malays living in their own countries, there are said to be at Bangkok not less than ten thousand, chiefly captives, carried off from Queda and Patani, but especially from the latter."[9]

Siam again captured many slaves during the sacking and looting that followed Patani's defeat in 1832. According to the Christian missionary, Howard Malcolm, who passed through the region at the time:

> The district [of Patani] fell under the displeasure of Siam, and war ensued, which was terminated by the present [General], who, in 1832, laid waste [to] the country, and brought away all the inhabitants he could find. These were distributed to the principal families in Bangkok as slaves, and this fine region now lies almost depopulated and desert.[10]

Malcolm's account is remarkably similar to Light's descriptions of the battle and aftermath of 1785–1786. J.H. Moor, a British trade official, gave a more descriptive account, contemporary to the taking of slaves:

> We are informed by [a] person who accompanied the expedition, that the hordes of Siamese soldiers, or more appropriately armed coolies, which

---

[8] The existence of at least 10,000 "Malay" slaves, mostly from Patani, witnessed by John Crawfurd during his diplomatic mission to Bangkok in 1828 suggests that the Siamese capital was the main destination for most of those enslaved in 1786. Siam's need for a workforce would have been greatest there, especially following the founding of Bangkok. John Crawfurd, *Journal of an Embassy from the Governor-General of India to the Courts of Siam and Cochin China; Exhibiting a View of the Actual State of Those Kingdoms* (London: Henry Colburn, 1828), p. 449.

[9] Ibid.

[10] Howard Malcolm, *Travels in South-Eastern Asia, Embracing Hindustan, Malaya, Siam, and China; with Notices of Numerous Missionary Stations, and a Full Account of the Burman Empire; with Dissertations, Tables, etc.* (Boston: Gould, Kendall, and Lincoln, 1840), p. 106.

were landed at [Songkhla] from the Junks, having proceeded overland
to *Patani*, committed every outrage there. Most of the inhabitants fled
at their approach; but many of them previously set fire to their houses.
Such as were taken, were made prisoners, and to prevent the fugitives
from re-occupying the country, (which is described as having been most
beautiful and in good cultivation) every fruit tree was cut down, and
the country devastated ... Of the captives, the women suffered most
from their brutality, as neither infant youth, nor age were spared. But to
close this ... revolting scene, the captives were thrust by hundreds into
the filthy holds of the junks, which were totally incapable of containing
so many, and in most instances, the wretched beings were obliged to
trample or lay on each other, by which numbers of them perished![11]

The focus of Siam's efforts in the aftermath of the fall of Patani in 1832
appears to have been to depopulate the region and by doing so, defuse
whatever resistance remained. In a separate account, Moor recorded:

About the end of August, the [Patani] Malays being *quiet*, and every-
thing settled to the satisfaction of the [General], he proposed to return
to Bangkok with his principle spoils: *viz.* from four to five thousand
prisoners, or slaves. Those miserable, wretched creatures were forced
on board the small junks and war-boats, and were crowded together as
thickly as they could be stowed, without any room being left for them
to move. When they arrived at Bankok and were landed on the banks
of the river the sight they presented was most miserable, and the stench
of their persons and vessels, dreadful. One fourth were covered with the
small pox. They were all placed or huddled together, in one side of the
building called the British Factory ...[12]

In a more detailed account that Moor sent to the *Singapore Chronicle*
newspaper that appeared in the November 22, 1832 issue, he wrote:

I have seen most of the poor, wretched creatures that have been brought
up from the Malay Coast, and were I even capable of conveying to you,
in a slight degree, the miserable sights I have seen, it would make you
shudder ... The number of Malay slaves brought up here, within the
last six weeks, will amount to between 4,200 and 5,000 souls, consisting
principally of very old women and numbers of young children, and only

---

[11] "Siam," *Singapore Chronicle*, November 22, 1832.

[12] J.H. Moor, *Notices of the Indian Archipelago, and Adjacent Countries; Being
a Collection of Papers Relating to Borneo, Celebes, Bali, Java, Sumatra, Nias, the
Philippine Islands, Sulus, Siam, Cochin China, Malayan Peninsula, & c.* (Singapore,
1837), p. 202.

a very few able-bodied men. Those, I suppose, who were able to run, made their escape, and left the old, sickly and very young to the mercy of the ... Siamese invaders.[13]

Moor likely made the assumption that the men had escaped more easily. As we discussed in our account of earlier conflicts, men were sometimes summarily executed in the aftermath of defeat, leaving the old, the young, and many women to be taken as slaves by the victors. In the wake of Patani's 1832 defeat, much like that of 1786, men again numbered among the vast majority of the dead. Women, children, and old people figured most significantly among those enslaved and forced aboard ships to Bangkok. On the condition of the slaves and how they were divided and distributed to the chief families of Bangkok and elsewhere, Moor wrote:

> Out of compliment, of course, to their *Ally*, the British Indian Government, the poor, wretched, diseased creatures, (and few indeed, were free of disease) were quartered in what the Siamese style, 'the British Factory.' I occupy one side, and the Malays, to the amount of 400 or 500, were confined to the other, until a conveyance could be got to take them up the country, or perhaps until they were given as presents to some of the great men here. They were counted in and out just like so much sheep, and when an order was given in presents to some of the Siamese Chiefs to send off 40 or 50, it did not matter whether they were sick or well; off they must go, the healthy carrying the sick, and in some instances you would see them counting out old men and women, in such a condition, that it was scarcely possible they could have lived, had they been left alone, a single hour. Most of the [Patani] Malays had immense large ulcers about their feet or legs, and the stench from them alone was enough to breed a plague. Besides that, they were all swarming with lice, and covered with the itch and to wind up all, had sore eyes. At night, could you but have seen them — without beds, or mats, or musquito curtains — the sick, the young and the old, all huddled together; and even dead bodies lying amongst them. The children, from sunset to sunrise were continually crying — the poor little wretches must have been nearly eaten up by the musquitoes. Another thing I was obliged to observe, was that no regard was paid to the parental feelings of either the father or mother. I often saw the children taken away from their parents, altho' the father generally seemed quite *callous*, the poor mother used to set up such a howling, tearing her hair, and begging and praying to be allowed to accompany her only child ...[14]

---

[13] "Siam," *Singapore Chronicle*, November 22, 1832.
[14] Ibid.

The taking of slaves in the manner described by Moor — and it is likely that the events of 1786 were not dissimilar to those of 1832 — suggests that political motives were paramount. Enslavement of large numbers of war captives was a deliberate attempt at depopulation — a political act of controlling a distant territory — more than it was a rationalized attempt at bolstering the workforce at the capital. When compared to battle massacres, the taking of slaves appears to have been an even more crucial tactic aimed at breaking the remaining resistance in Patani.

Environmental Warfare

Now let us consider environmental warfare and the effects this had upon the Patani population. A contemporary account of the battle's aftermath may help illustrate the situation in Patani following the fall of the fort at Pujut and the collapse of defenses around the royal palace. James Scott, an official with the English East India Company, wrote of the environmental impact of the wars in the region in 1785:

> If we follow an Army in its Progress, Desolation and Depopulation goes hand in hand. Carrying off every thing of value, Men, Women, and Children included. And Burning what the[y] cannot carry they Render the country they have overrun untenable, on their Retreat those who had Retired to the fastnesses appear ½ of which die or emigrate for want of sustenance, so that one Campaign leaves the country over run a Wild.[15]

Similarly, in the aftermath of the 1832 war, the Siamese forces again appear to have been determined to make the region uninhabitable, destroying Patani's agricultural yield wherever possible. Moor wrote:

> On the [General]'s arriving [in Songkhla], he found the [Patani] Malays had been already dispersed, and he had nothing left to perform, but to plunder the people, to do which, it may be certain, he did not lose so good an opportunity as then presented itself … The [General] … removed his headquarters to *Patani*, and employed his people in plundering in every direction. Not content with the taking of whatever the poor people possessed, they caught every person they could find, young and old, sick and healthy, promiscuously; and not satisfied with capturing the unfortunate inhabitants of *Patani*, *Jella*, and *Jarim*, they

---

[15] Scott to Governor General, October 28, 1785, *Straits Settlements Records* 2: 8 (FWC March 2, 1786).

also carried off all the cattle, and burnt and cut down all the fruit trees that came in their way.[16]

In a similar vein, Malcolm recounted, in reference to the destruction in 1832, that "[Patani] was once the most populous and well-cultivated part of the peninsula …"[17] Agricultural degradation appears to have been common practice by the Siamese army during this period when it retreated from a plundered, depopulated, recently razed city or province. Agricultural destruction could easily have led to far greater casualties than direct combat-related deaths, and remained the most effective means to depopulate a region. Given Moor's credible estimates of 4,000–5,000 captured slaves taken to Bangkok, it could be estimated that as many as 15,000 people, or rather 10–20% of the total population, died or permanently relocated to the neighboring states of Kedah, Kelantan, Perak, and Trengganu as a result of the 1832 conflict, but these numbers only reflect the urban casualties.[18] The rural population was much more numerous and would have been similarly devastated by the effects of the war.

Refugee Experience

The Patani people, who escaped death or capture in 1786, fled by the tens of thousands into the neighboring polities of Kedah, Kelantan, Perak, and Trengganu. They carried food and other mobile possessions on the journey as the Siamese army plundered the city and destroyed their homes. Records of the refugees survive only in Kedah, where British observers nervously noted their presence in reports to their superiors in Calcutta. Having escaped Patani, their troubles were not over. Light wrote:

> The Siamese have conquered Pattany, such of the People as have escaped their Sword, are Perishing in the Forests, The King of Queda being afraid to grant them admittance into any Part of his Country having received from the Siamese General Strict injunctions not to Succour one of them.[19]

---

[16] Moor, *Notices of the Indian Archipelago*, p. 201.

[17] Malcolm, *Travels in South-Eastern Asia*, p. 106.

[18] Nicholas N. Dodge, "Population Estimates for the Malay Peninsula in the Nineteenth Century, with Special Reference to the East Coast States," *Population Studies* 34, 3 (November 1980): 439.

[19] Light to Governor General, November 25, 1786, *Straits Settlements Records* 2: 410 (FWC January 22, 1787).

This report provides further evidence that the Siamese intended to permanently depopulate Patani as part of achieving a complete political victory. Those who fled were preceded by a Siamese messenger who apparently warned the neighboring rulers not to assist the vanquished refugees who were then flooding their borders. With a large Siamese army not far away, the rulers of neighboring polities were fearful of offering asylum to the displaced Patani people. In Kedah, however, it appears that the sultan appealed to the British on their behalf, though the latter never acquiesced to their pleas. Light wrote, "I have received repeated solicitations from the King of Queda to come and Consult with him respecting the Siamese and People of Pattany" — referring to the arrival of the Patani refugees. He continued, "Yesterday the King of Queda sent the Shabander to enquire if I would consent to the People of Pattany settling opposite to Pinang and assist him if attacked by the Siamese."[20] He further elaborated:

> The Laxamana[21] [of Kedah] is desirous I should receive a Thousand of the Pattany People on this Island. This would be highly imprudent while we have a small Force, especially as the Laxamana from the beginning was much averse to our Coming here, and wishes to expel us.[22]

Light's suspicion of the *laksamana*'s motives seems to have been a convenient excuse to ignore the plight of the refugees. The fact that no subsequent report records any British aid indicates that in all likelihood the East India Company was not at that time in a strong enough position to fend off a major Siamese offensive, nor was it willing to take on the potential political risk of offering support to the Patani refugees.

Many more Patani refugees fled into Kelantan and Trengganu where they possessed kinship ties as well as cultural affinities with the local residents.[23] Details of their fate are obscured by the dearth of surviving records. It seems clear, however, that the refugees must have overwhelmed

---

[20] Ibid.

[21] Malay: *laksamana* (admiral or general). Light to Governor General, September 12, 1786, *Straits Settlements Records* 2: 311 (FWC December 13, 1786).

[22] Light to Governor General, November 25, 1786, *Straits Settlements Records* 2: 412 (FWC January 22, 1787).

[23] Evidence exists for entire settlements in Terengganu, for example, that were founded by Patani refugees; Shaharil Talib, "The Port and Polity of Terengganu during the Eighteenth and Nineteenth Centuries: Realizing its Potential," in *The Southeast Asian Port and Polity: Rise and Demise*, ed. J. Kathirithamby-Wells and John Villiers (Singapore: Singapore University Press, 1990), p. 220.

the limited ability of "border" guards to keep them from infiltrating their kingdoms, particularly in rural areas, via which routes many escaped. It is likely that widespread famine resulted amongst the survivors of the massacre, as had taken place in other regions during the same period as a side effect of warfare, which would have further increased the death toll.[24] How many people died as a result of displacement is unclear, but it is probable that it accounted for more deaths than those actually killed in battle. An estimate in the tens of thousands seems within reason if the total population of Patani in 1785 was around 150,000.[25]

Conclusion

Based on the evidence of massacres, enslavement, the practice of environmental warfare, and the harsh reality of the refugee experience, it appears that Patani's subjugation was far more violent and systematically carried out than previously thought.[26] The 1785–1786 and 1831–1832 wars were not small-scale slave raids or diplomatic manicures, but rather a systematic and definitive restructuring of the relations between Siam and Patani. Whereas the *mandala* relationship had always afforded Patani considerable autonomy, as well as the ability to maintain its own traditions of sovereignty, post-1786 Patani existed as a conquered population bereft of a political apparatus by which to orient or constitute itself. Patani's experience from the late 18th to the mid-19th centuries runs counter to prevailing paradigms concerning early modern Southeast Asian warfare.

Rather than characterizing the object of war as gaining land or people, we might be better served by asking: how did conquering armies best eliminate political or economic threats? Rather than incorporating territory,

---

[24] See above for mention of earlier famines in the region in the aftermath of war. Light to Governor General, November 25, 1786, *Straits Settlements Records* 2: 409 (FWC January 22, 1787).

[25] These are rough approximations given 17th-century European estimates and British estimates from the 18th and 19th centuries, many of which have been noted previously.

[26] Kobkua Suwannathat-Pian glosses over this uncomfortable period in her seminal work, characterizing Patani-Siamese political developments in the period as a "failure of tributary relations." Kobkua Suwannathat-Pian, *Thai-Malay Relations: Traditional Intra-Regional Relations from the Seventeenth to the Early Twentieth Centuries*, East Asian Historical Monographs series, ed. Wang Gungwu (Singapore: Oxford University Press, 1988), pp. 159-62.

because of the often vast distances between political centers, low population density, and large stretches of land unfit for human settlement in the pre-modern era, military leaders in Southeast Asia sought to capture people as a means of eliminating resistance. As I have argued in this chapter, war captives did not always make good slaves or were not necessarily intended for the purpose. Rather, *depopulation* was often the goal, especially when a distant territory could not otherwise be feasibly controlled by a visiting garrison or forced political allegiance. This assertion is only further reinforced by the fact that armies regularly carried out destruction of agricultural lands so that for decades afterward conquered regions would not easily accommodate returning refugees. Depopulation and environmental destruction were the tactics employed to control territory, if only to render it uninhabitable or no longer threatening.

For our understanding of the political history in the region, we can see that the demise of the Patani sultanate signified nothing less than a restructuring of the entire system of political relations in the region. The constant process of political negotiation that had existed for much of the previous two centuries between Patani and Siam definitively ended, though not without great resistance and the deaths of tens of thousands of people. By depopulating Patani and shattering the old sultanate into seven principalities, Bangkok set the foundation for the rise of the modern Siamese state apparatus in what is today Thailand's "deep south." Furthermore, the legacy of the wars of 1785–1838 may help explain Patani's sustained resistance to national integration in the 20th and 21st centuries.

CHAPTER 8

A Tin Mine in Need of a History: 19th-Century British Views of the Patani Interior

Philip King

Histories of the Malay Peninsula are histories of its littoral. In contrast to the many excellent accounts of the port polity, the interior of the Malay Peninsula has remained a historical blindspot. Luxury forest products from the interior played a critical role in an Indian Ocean trade of great antiquity and these same resources were critical to processes of local state formation. But unlike the coastal polities, peoples of the interior did not compose elaborate legitimizing genealogies or establish the types of permanent settlement that have provided historians of the littoral with an array of sources. Only in the late 20th century did the colonial state — be it British, Siamese, or indeed Malay — begin to whittle away at the distance that separated the coast from the largely uncharted interior.

The low historical profile of Raman — an interior polity that rose to prominence in the watershed of the Perak-Patani-Muda river systems during the 19th century — can be partially attributed to physical isolation. On the map, the distances separating the interior from the coast were not particularly significant. Yet the mountainous terrain of the interior meant that a downstream court such as Kedah might have a much closer relationship with Aceh than an interior settlement a mere 30 kilometers inland.[1] Raman could never boast Dutch or British maritime trading stations. It was never embroiled

---

[1] James C. Scott, *The Art of Not Being Governed: An Anarchist History of Upland Southeast Asia* (Singapore: NUS Press, 2010), p. 47.

in conflicts with Siamese overlords. It is therefore not surprising that this highland polity is a footnote in Malay and Thai histories of the region.

By contrast, for a sequence of high profile British colonial figures Raman was a pivotal piece of the Peninsula map. It captured the imaginations of John Anderson, John Crawfurd, Hugh Low, J.W. Birch, and W.E. Maxwell. Sir Frank Swettenham's interest in Raman was such that this landlocked polity was eulogized — and perhaps somewhat hyperbolized — as "the scene of his life's labours."[2] This chapter has the modest ambition of introducing Raman to readers. The sources are still comparatively limited, but the preliminary view of the Malay Peninsula from this interior vantage point provides a range of useful insights into the history of the region. Conventional understandings of political history are challenged, agency is restored to previously silent historical actors, and techniques of colonial expansion — particularly the writing of history itself — can be charted in new directions.

The Resource-Rich Interior

Prior to the 19th century, any references to the subject of the Malay Peninsula interior are largely connected to the topic of overland trade. Indigenous histories and merchant reports presented the interior as an uninhabited zone of transit rather than settlement — an ironic view given that existing populations were in fact nomadic and semi-nomadic. It was not until the second half of the 18th century that the growing Chinese demand for tin and gold drew the interior of the Peninsula into closer association with downstream polities and sponsored labor migration to semi-permanent settlements. During this period, labor scarcities were slowly ameliorated by the migration of Chinese miners to various upriver districts on the east coast. By the 1770s, the ports of Patani and Kelantan were drawing several hundred Chinese goldminers every year.[3] In addition to the influx of foreign labor, a series of political disturbances from the second half of the 17th century onward saw increasing numbers of Patani Malays migrating upriver to open up new land in the watershed zone. For those fleeing from war and conscription, the interior was a sanctuary beyond the reach of the coastal courts. Over time, settlements began to take

---

[2] *In Tinland: A Journal of Interesting Mining News* 2, 30 (1907): 304.

[3] Jennifer Cushman and Anthony Milner, "Eighteenth and Nineteenth-Century Chinese Accounts of the Malay Peninsula," *Journal of the Malaysian Branch of the Royal Asiatic Society* 52, 1 (1979): 21–3.

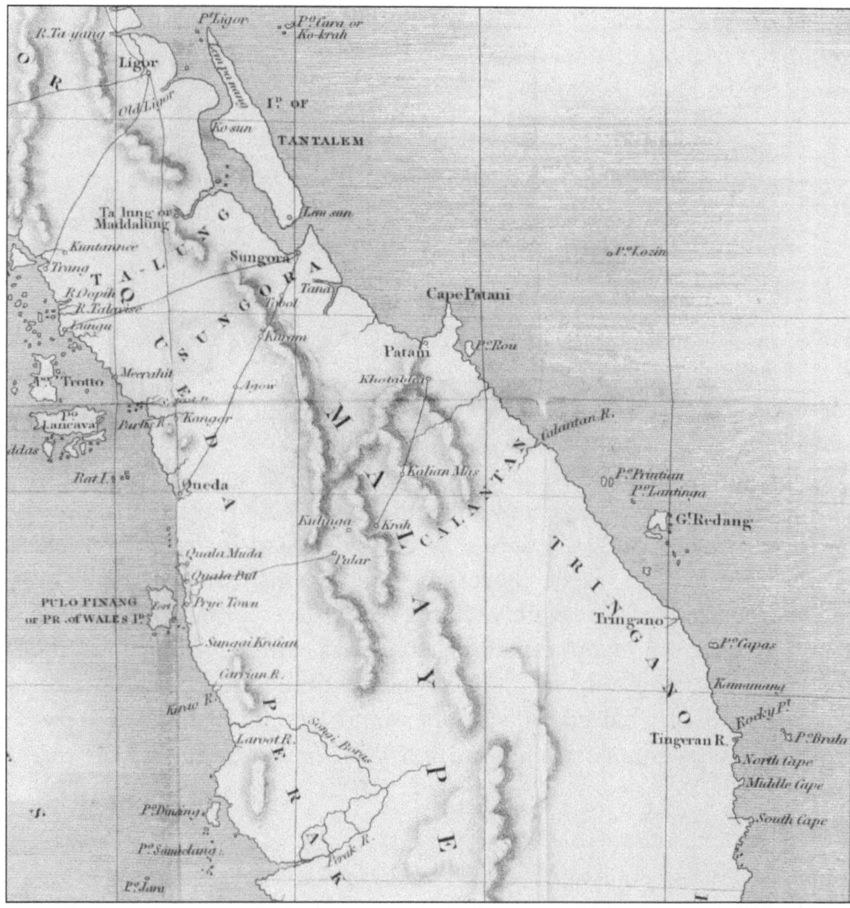

Map 8.1 Excerpt from Crawfurd's 1828 "Map of the Kingdoms of Siam and Cochin China," showing the middle part of the Malay peninsula.

form around rich mineral deposits or river junctions where opportunities for taxation existed.

The development of settlements was prompted by clear political choices as migrants to the upper Patani and Perak rivers engaged in what Lieberman has called the "endemic search for individual patrons who would demand a smaller share of their wealth."[4] This search might see an individual assume any number of positions in relation to downstream or local potentates — or

---

[4] Leiberman cited in Tony Day, *Fluid Iron: State Formation in Southeast Asia* (Honolulu: University of Hawai'i Press, 2002), p. 57.

indeed assume the role of local potentate themselves. In the early 1770s, for example, a Malay of Patani origin, who had come to control the primary tin mines on the Perak side of the watershed,

> informed Sultan Aladdin [of Perak] that he was prepared to relinquish his rights to the mines of Rui and Indah, usurped by Patani during the previous reign, if the Perak ruler would grant him a more imposing title than that of 'Datuk Sri Paduka Raja Muda', which had been bestowed upon him by the Yang di Pertuan of Kedah.[5]

Here was a Patani chief, with a Kedah title, bargaining for a higher feudal rank from the ruler of Perak. This was not a unique scenario. Throughout the watershed, Perak chiefs were ruling on the Patani side of the watershed and Patani chiefs on the Perak side.[6] Alternatively, entirely new patterns of descent could emerge in situations where allegiances to larger downstream political units were abandoned altogether.[7] The chief protagonists in the creation of new political spaces may be understood in terms of Vickers' "Panji-style hero ... in the process of building his own set of alliances, followers and marriages, while building new palaces and wealth."[8] For our Panji-style hero and his followers, there was nothing anomalous about the task of carving out new domains of political authority.[9] Contrary to what British colonial administrators would later refer to as the classic riparian Malay state with its unified *ulu-ilir* (upstream-downstream)

---

[5] Barbara Watson Andaya, *Perak: The Abode of Grace* (Kuala Lumpur: Oxford University Press), pp. 340–1.

[6] M. 1561/68. Office Diary of Hubert Berkeley. Kept Intermittently as District Officer of Upper Perak and Covering from about 1900 to 1908.

[7] The way in which physically isolated communities could develop high degrees of autonomy is discussed by Carl A. Trocki, "Chinese Pioneering in Eighteenth-Century Southeast Asia," in *The Last Stand of Asian Autonomies: Responses to Modernity in the Diverse States of Southeast Asia and Korea, 1750–1900*, ed. Anthony Reid (London: Macmillan, 1997), p. 91.

[8] Adrian Vickers, "The Eighteenth Century in Southeast Asian History," *Asian Studies Review* 18, 1 (1994): 66–7.

[9] Craig J. Reynolds, "A New Look at Old Southeast Asia," *The Journal of Asian Studies* 54, 2 (1995): 429. See also O.W. Wolters, *History, Culture, and Region in Southeast Asian Perspectives* (Singapore: Institute of Southeast Asian Studies, 1982); Chris Baker, "Afterword: Autonomy's Meanings," in *Recalling Local Pasts: Autonomous History in Southeast Asia*, ed. S. Chutintaranond and Chris Baker (Chiang Mai: Silkworm, 2003), pp. 171–6.

segments, indigenous perceptions of political space in the late 18th century suggest polities being seen in terms of constantly changing social networks organized around what we usually translate as palaces. These social networks did not cover all the people within a given geographical area — for example, nomads had a marginal status in relation to them — and people who lived in one area could actually "belong" to another palace in some way. To some degree, these were formations in which there was usually not one single state, but a cluster of courts, related in some way or another, the personnel of which tended to change rapidly from one generation to another.[10]

Raman, the polity that would emerge to control much of the central Malay Peninsula watershed zone by the early 19th century, conformed to such a model. The *istana* or palace of Raman shifted a number of times before finally being established at Kota Bahru in the upper Patani valley in the early 19th century. The economic backbone of the polity was located on the tin-rich Kroh plateau in the upper Perak valley. The commerce of Kroh itself was tied most closely to Kedah on the west coast of the Peninsula. Combined, the various nodes of this polity controlled the headwaters of three major river systems. The hilly terrain and access to three major rivers enabled Raman to circumvent attempts by any single downstream center to subordinate the interior.

The Emergence of Raman

According to standard Thai and Malay(si)an accounts, the emergence of Raman was a unilateral Siamese initiative. Raman is presented as a product of Bangkok's decision to dissolve the ancient polity of Patani in 1810 and replace it with a more pliable confederation of petty states under the supervision of Songkhla.[11] According to this version of events, the creation

---

[10] Vickers, "The Eighteenth Century in Southeast Asian History," p. 67.

[11] Authors using Siamese sources tend to date the break-up of Patani from the failed rebellion of the Patani Rajah Tungku Lamidin in 1791. Tej Bunnag, *The Provincial Administration of Siam, 1892–1915* (Kuala Lumpur: Oxford University Press, 1997), p. 31. A date closer to 1810 would appear to be more accurate, however. Syukri links the division of Patani to the 1808 rebellion of the Rajah Datuk Pangkalan. See Ibrahim Syukri, *History of the Malay Kingdom of Patani*, trans. C. Bailey and J.N. Miksic (Athens, OH: Ohio University Centre for International Studies, 1985), pp. 47–8.

of Raman was achieved by the stroke of a Siamese pen and the weight of its armies. It simply comes into being; a new polity with its capital located some 20 miles upstream from the mouth of the Patani river at Kota Bahru where the first Raja of Raman resided.

This image of Siam as a colonial aggressor that broke up the once great Sultanate of Patani is simplistic.[12] The stirrings of an increasingly independent group of chiefs in the interior had been noticed by both the Perak court and the Dutch as early as 1780. It was in that year that Sultan Alauddin of Perak received a mission from "the so-called King of Patani," a figure that Barbara Watson Andaya has tentatively identified as the chief of the region that would later be known as Raman.[13] In the early 1790s, a certain Mengkong Ras of Legeh (a small polity adjacent to Patani) had led a large contingent of his peoples out of the Patani lowlands to establish new settlements at Tapang and Bendang Niang on the upper reaches of the Perak river.[14] In the Betong valley, a Perak official who was cut off from his nominal downstream rulers oversaw a number of settlements that connected the Patani and Perak sides of the watershed. By opening up new land along the empty river valleys and mobilizing manpower for the collection of tin, men such as Mengkong Ras and Mengkong Jarum of Betong came to exist in a patchwork of autonomous settlements across the watershed.

Precisely how Tuan Loh Teh, the first ruler of Raman, managed to rise to the top of this pile of opportunists is unclear. Oral histories recorded in the early 20th century render him as a figure who "gathered together a body of fighting men and declared himself the independent Raja of the Upper Patani valley"[15] at some time in the first decade of the 19th century. Whether his rise was facilitated by genealogical links to the Patani court is unclear. His alias of Toh Nik suggests as much, for the title Nik was one bestowed upon the offspring of a union between a female royal and a commoner.[16] However, another tradition states that he was a commoner whose descendents adopted humble titles in recognition of their non-royal origins, hence the lineage of the Raman rajas including names such as Tuan

---

[12] Syukri, *History of the Malay Kingdom of Patani*, pp. 49–50.

[13] Barbara Watson Andaya, *Perak: The Abode of Grace*, pp. 340–1.

[14] M. 1561/68. Office Diary of Hubert Berkeley.

[15] W.E. Everitt, "The Rahman Mines at Intan," *The Malayan Historical Journal* 2, 2 (1955): 104.

[16] Syukri, *History of the Malay Kingdom of Patani*, p. 86n69. The word Toh is likewise an abbreviation of Datoh, a Malay honorific held by local rulers and district chiefs.

Kundur (pumpkin), Tuan Jagong (maize) and Tuan Timung (cucumber).[17] Both traditions may have some truth to them, for inconsistencies in different accounts of Tuan Loh Teh's rule admit the possibility of a break in the ruling line in the mid-1830s.

The only point that can be made with any certainty in the absence of further evidence is that by 1808 when Siamese efforts to break up Patani into a number of confederate states commenced, Tuan Loh Teh was already a figure of some influence in the interior. If we follow Bunnag's dictum that during times of crisis, "the natural leader, whom the government had to accept as governor, was usually a military leader,"[18] the Siamese most likely confirmed — rather than inaugurated — the rule of Tuan Loh Teh. He in turn acknowledged Siamese suzerainty over Raman. This is an important distinction. It turns the conventional history of the region on its head. Rather than being a product of Patani's demise, Raman becomes a contributor to the declining fortunes of the downstream court, in much the same way that the downstream court of Perak was greatly weakened by the increasingly independent stance of its own *ulu* chiefs in the last decades of the 18th century. The demise of Patani cannot be solely attributed to Siamese aggression. Upstart Malay polities in the interior played an active role in this drama.

From the Autochthonous to "Classic" State

While Thai and Malay sources have little concern with Raman beyond the date of its establishment, British colonial sources present a very different story. Raman first came to the attention of the British in Penang during the second decade of the 1800s when it was identified as a key node in an ambitious regional tin scheme.[19] John Anderson, the architect of the proposed scheme, lobbied strongly for a commercial treaty between Penang and Raman. He was supported in his efforts by John Crawfurd, who took the Raman issue to Bangkok during his well-documented embassy of 1822. For Penang's merchants, Raman was suspected to possess mineral deposits that rivaled the famed island of Bangka in the Straits of Melaka. The tin scheme

---

[17] W.W. Skeat, "Reminiscences of the Cambridge University Expedition to the North-Eastern Malay States, 1899–1900," *Journal of the Malayan Branch of the Royal Asiatic Society* 28, 4 (1953): 86.

[18] Tej Bunnag, *The Provincial Administration of Siam*, p. 19.

[19] C.D. Cowan, "Governor Bannerman and the Penang Tin Scheme, 1818–1819," *Journal of the Malayan Branch of the Royal Asiatic Society* 23, 1 (1950): 52–83.

was ultimately frustrated by the unwillingness of the East India Company to advance claims over Kedah, a polity that Anderson viewed as the natural downstream complement of Raman. The 1824 Burney Treaty officially doused the first attempt by British merchants to develop a relationship with Raman, for the document formally acknowledged Siamese suzerain rights over Kedah. Interest in Raman faded further as the attention of Penang's merchants and administrators shifted to the tin wealth of nearby Larut in Perak. The grey area at the northern boundary of Perak remained beyond the colonial horizon for almost half a century. Wars between Songkhla and Kedah during the 1830s saw various scorched earth campaigns conducted across the watershed zone.[20] As is typical of highland populations, dispersal replaced settlement in response to these lowland incursions. While relative stability had returned by the late 1840s, British focus remained on more accessible tin resources close to the coast.

British ambivalence toward Raman was replaced by an acute interest following the annexation of Perak in 1874. The annexation committed Britain to a governing role in the Malay Peninsula and opened up a new frontier of British-Siamese rivalry. Contrary to the impression created by a reading of diplomatic cables, there was little to this frontier rivalry that was geo-strategic in nature. The real issue was control of the tin-rich Kroh Plateau. By the 1880s, both parties had surveyors tramping across the watershed to prove their respective claims. Techniques of triangulation measured the space, while the documentation of settlement patterns was conducted to impart political meaning to the resulting map. This meant scripting a history for a region that was a blank spot on existing maps. More accurately, areas such as the Kroh plateau required a British Malayan history to support the expansionist agenda. Yet the epistemology for such a project was still in its infancy. In the end, the history and its epistemology would have to develop in parallel, making liberal use of indigenous legitimizing devices to try and seal up the cracks.

The character of the British push into the watershed during the latter decades of the 19th century differed markedly in its epistemological underpinnings from that of an earlier generation of "merchant scientists"[21]

---

[20] See Cyril Skinner, *Rama III and the Siamese Expedition to Kedah in 1839, The Dispatches of Luang Udomsombat*, trans. C. Skinner (Melbourne: Centre of Southeast Asian Studies, 1993); Syukri, *History of the Malay Kingdom of Patani*, pp. 50–2.
[21] Hendrik J. Maier, *In the Center of Authority: The Malay Hikayat Merong Mahawangsa* (Ithaca, NY: Cornell Southeast Asia Program, 1988).

such as John Anderson and John Crawfurd. The latter had been Company men and avid students of political economy. When they wrote of the interior, they spoke in terms of natural resource potential and the best means of developing trades. They did not write local histories but collected data that could be assembled with reference to the philosophy of Adam Smith to produce a rational system of commerce. Notions of the classic riparian state in which sub-ethnic groupings and a river valley territory were coterminous were yet to become the template for historical analysis. For example, John Anderson considered the Muda river of Kedah as the most rational access point to Raman and the tin-rich Kroh plateau. Nowhere in his musings on the topic of Raman did Anderson suggest that the downstream Perak court possessed an inalienable connection to the Perak river watershed. The rationale was simple: the shallow and turbulent headwaters of the Perak river were largely inaccessible from the downstream reaches. Access was far easier via Kedah.

The establishment of a protectorate over Perak in 1874 prompted a revision of this political economy view of the Peninsula. Political economists such as Anderson had eschewed expensive government in favor of the low overheads of trade treaties. The protectorate, by contrast, demanded government over a defined territory. Had Kedah been the prize of the 1874 treaty, the British would have no doubt picked up where Anderson had left off and demanded Raman's annexation as a natural extension of the state. But in the 1870s, Kedah remained a Siamese dependency, as was Raman. Thus efforts were quickly made to locate the wealthy state of Raman within the confines of the Malay state that had recently contracted itself to British protection. The British set out to write a non-Siamese history of Raman in order that any Siamese claims over the territory could be "disproved by the standards of 'Eastern' custom as well."[22]

J.R. Logan made a critical contribution to a new epistemology of Malay studies in the 1860s when he declared that "Malay Kingdoms are agglomerations of river settlements, and I doubt if a single instance can be found where a river district is politically divided by a river."[23] By the late 1870s, the image of Malay states as river valley kingdoms had developed into a powerful orthodoxy. Despite the presence of so many exceptions to

---

[22] C.O. 8774. Hugh Low to the Colonial Secretary of the Straits Settlements, Singapore.

[23] J.R. Logan, "Notes at Pinang, Kidah, & c," *Journal of the Indian Archipelago and East Asia* 5 (1851): 64.

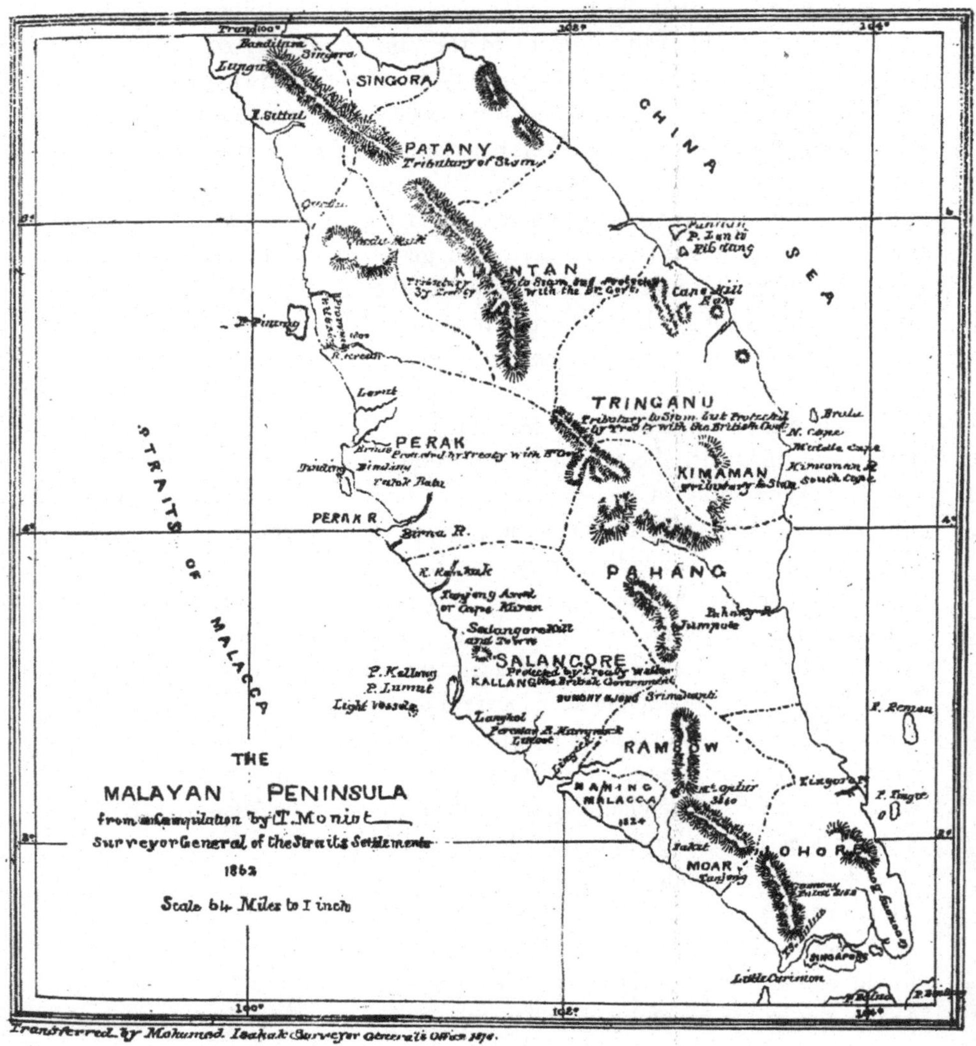

Map 8.2 1862 British map of the Malay peninsula showing approximate boundaries and political status of the various peninsular states, including Patani.

Map 8.3 1878 British map of the Malay peninsula following the establishment of the British protectorate over Perak in 1874, showing the region of Raman and the various mountain chains and river systems.

this "rule," British observers had little interest in testing a category that promised such political gain.[24] The concept of the riparian state presented a neat solution to the ambiguity of indigenous political space. Views of Perak or Patani as river valley states helped colonial scholars to make sense of a complex political situation.[25] According to this schema, Raman — a polity with multiple *ulu* but no *ilir* — was an anomaly that had to be resolved in accordance with the "natural" political schema of the Peninsula.

It is not surprising to find Logan's dictum repeated in George Maxwell's firsthand account of a journey through the watershed zone in 1876. For Maxwell, the logical limits of Perak extended to the headwaters of the Perak river and included the entire watershed of that river and its minor tributaries.[26] A year after he published these thoughts in 1882, the second Resident to Perak, Hugh Low, declared that the Perak river was the natural outlet for the tin of the Kroh plateau and that the rulers of Raman were usurpers whose state made no sense at all.[27] It contained neither a Raman river nor Raman men. For administrators of Low's generation, sub-ethnic distinctions that distinguished between Perak and Patani Malays had begun to take on new meaning. British efforts to advance claims over the tin resources of the Kroh plateau rested on the notion that Patani men belonged in the Patani river basin, while all lands within the Perak river watershed were the natural preserve of Perak Malays. The fact that the Kroh plateau was populated largely by Patani Malays did not — as was the case in indigenous worldviews — create a corresponding political reality in British eyes. This situation was interpreted as proof of an anomaly that the right history could help to rectify.

A kernel of indigenous support for this version of events was already available to the British. The downstream Perak court was only too eager to forward historical claims to the entire watershed zone. Yet, even the most eager British expansionist understood that Raman was far removed in reality from the imaginings of the downstream court. Court chronicles offered little substance for a diplomatic challenge to Siamese claims over

---

[24] See, for example, Jane Drakard, *A Malay Frontier: Unity and Duality in a Sumatran Kingdom* (Ithaca, NY: Cornell Southeast Asia Program, 1990).

[25] J.M. Gullick, *Indigenous Political Systems of Western Malaya* (London: The Athlone Press, 1988).

[26] W.E. Maxwell, "A Journey on Foot to the Patani Frontier," *Journal of the Straits Branch of the Royal Asiatic Society* 9 (1882): 36.

[27] C.O. 8774. Hugh Low to the Colonial Secretary of the Straits Settlements, March 18, 1883.

the watershed. However, the evolution of Logan's opinion into a scholarly maxim by the 1880s offered a degree of scientific credibility to the claims of the Perak court. To demonstrate the soundness of the maxim, efforts to annex the Perak river watershed shifted to the village level where proofs would be sought to confirm the existence of ancient boundaries. Thus it was in the remote watershed itself that the contest for Raman would take place in the late 19th century as local history was written as part of a British imperial agenda. Conventional accounts of Anglo-Siamese rivalries tend to omit the point that metropolitan politicking over the frontier was an effect of local engagements. The case of a Perak claim on the watershed submitted in 1883 provides an excellent example of just how local imperial politics could be.

Mapping Genealogies

In 1883, the British Consul General in Bangkok advanced a land claim on the behalf of the Sultan of Perak that proposed the restoration of territory "occupied" by Raman in the Perak river watershed. The stimulus for the claim was a recently promulgated mining code in the British protectorate. With miners eager to develop tin land outside of the Larut district, the 1879 General Land Code was gazetted as a means to deal with the issue of ancestral land — land that was "owned" by Malay chiefs and could only be mined with the owner's permission and the payment of a royalty fee.[28] For the Perak government, these royalty fees constituted a major disincentive for the expansion of the mining sector and the government revenue that flowed from it. And this revenue was significant. In 1878, tin export duties constituted 70% of the Perak government's revenue.[29] The unwillingness of Chinese miners to open up new country outside of Larut because of high royalty demands by local chiefs provided a strong incentive for the British to strip local chiefs of such privileges.[30] Yet the constraints that ancestral rights placed on the expansion of the tin industry placed colonial administrators in a curious position. On the one hand, the wholesale extinguishment of

---

[28] For details on this legislation, see Wong Lin Ken, *The Malayan Tin Industry to 1914: With Special Reference to the States of Perak, Selangor, Negeri Sembilan and Pahang* (Tucson, AZ: University of Arizona Press, 1965), pp. 54–6.

[29] Philip Loh Fook Seng, *The Malay States 1877–1895: Political Change and Social Policy* (Kuala Lumpur: Oxford University Press, 1969), p. 113.

[30] Royalties typically amounted to around one-third of total tin production.

ancestral title would solve the problem of slow growth in the tin sector and maximize tin receipts. But it also threatened to undermine a key "proof" of territorial ownership. It is also worth noting that British administrators were not entirely adverse to the concept of ancestral rights in principle. As Day has noted, various representatives of "modern" colonial administrations in late 19th-century Southeast Asia were often far from "modern" themselves.[31] Whether it was their aristocratic background or the dependence that they had upon the Malay ruling class in the course of their duties, the pioneers of the revived British forward movement in the 1870s and 1880s were often want to comment upon the "harmony which existed between the values of the English gentleman class and the Malays."[32] It would not be until the turn of the century that the iconoclastic opinions of the commercial planter and miner would gain ascendancy in the Peninsula.[33] Meanwhile, the desires of colonial administrators to increase revenues remained attentive to those aspects of local culture that they identified with. Ruling class rights to land were one such important part of this shared culture.

In seeking a solution to the problem of ancestral land in Perak, the colonial administration opted for a policy of reduction over extinguishment. Over the course of the 1880s, the laborious task of ascertaining individual mine claims within Perak was carried out. Beginning in the Kinta valley, every claimant to mining land (ancestral or otherwise[34]) was requested to demonstrate the validity of their claim by proving a direct line of descent between the original owners and themselves. Where such a direct line could be shown to exist, claimants were granted title to an acre of mining land for every $50 dollars of *usaha* or capital investment that they had put into the mine since it had come into their possession.[35] Where proof was lacking, the

---

[31] Tony Day, "How Modern was Modernity, How Traditional was Tradition in Nineteenth Century Java?", *Review of Malaysian and Indonesian Affairs* 20, 1 (1986): 12.

[32] Hendrik J. Maier, *In the Center of Authority*, p. 53.

[33] Michael Adas, "The Great War and the Decline of the Civilizing Mission," in *Autonomous Histories, Particular Truths: Essays in Honor of John Smail*, ed. L.J. Sears (Madison: Center for Southeast Asian Studies, University of Wisconsin-Madison, 1994).

[34] In addition to ancestral mine claims, regions such as Larut where the domination of Chinese miners had long extinguished any Malay claims over mining land were the subject of land claims that were not based on hereditary links.

[35] Perak 1466/1900: Secretary to the High Commissioner, Federated Malay States. John Anderson, Ancestral claims of the Raja and Raja Muda of Reman to Mines in the Territory Recently Ceded to Perak.

claim reverted to the state who then leased the property to the claimants.[36] General forfeiture legislation provided a means of extinguishing general and ancestral claims for title holders who allowed their claims to remain idle for defined periods of time.[37] This bundle of legislation would be amended in 1885, and once more in 1895 when it was incorporated into the Perak Mining Code. With the burden of proof heavily weighted in favor of the state, the number of ancestral claims within the limits of Perak declined drastically during the 1880s.

The general effectiveness of this genealogy-based policy to stimulate production prompted speculations on whether or not it might be employed as a means of forwarding claims to land beyond the frontier. As Perak Resident J.W. Birch had been informed in 1874, the Perak court harbored vague claims to the mines of the "Patani men" in the remote upper reaches of the Perak river. In 1882, W.E. Maxwell published a series of "native histories" designed to buttress the claim to the entire watershed of the Perak river, the collection of which had been a mandated task during his 1876 expedition into the *ulu*.

On their own, such indigenous histories were not considered entirely reliable sources of data. However, proceedings enacted under the 1879 General Land Code had demonstrated how claims to ancestral lands could be verified by submitting them to a number of tests. As noted above, these tests included being able to supply evidence of direct lines of descent between claimants to ancestral land and proof of the amount of expenditure that petitioners had sunk into the claim. It involved interview processes to establish the credentials of claimants and to verify their identity and that of their descendents. Cadastral surveys were necessary to determine the precise extent of the proposed claim and to ensure that it did not encroach on those of others or land that had been alienated for other purposes. In short, should ancestral claims emerge intact after running this bureaucratic gauntlet, they were legitimate.

Whether it was due to their confidence in such "modern" methods of verification or a misguided belief that the process itself would be enough to intimidate the Siamese, in 1883 the British Consul General in Bangkok forwarded a claim over the entire Perak river watershed on the behalf of the Sultan of Perak. The first stage in verifying the claim took place in

---

[36] W.E. Everitt, *A History of Mining in Perak* (Johore Bahru, 1952), p. 26.
[37] Six months for alienated mining land and, after 1895, two years for ancestral mining land.

March 1883 when Perak Resident Hugh Low set about assembling the "evidence."[38] This evidence took the form of a series of written testimonies.[39] These testimonies were obtained from a variety of individuals: Syed Lam and Syed Samsudin, great-grandsons of a former Seri Adika Raja of Perak; Khoo Eng alias Panjang, a shareholder in the Raman opium farm; Sinneh, a Patani man from Temangoh; Toh Imam Tapa, Penghulu of Pulao Kaman in the Plus district; even Raja Gumbas, younger brother of the then current Raja of Raman and Toh Nang Patani (chief of the Kroh district at that time).

The content of the testimonies roamed across a range of subjects. That of Khoo Eng alias Panjang (a Perak subject) related a tale of his brother's murder at the bidding of Tuan Prang of Krunei, and the Raja of Raman's obstinacy in refusing to investigate the case. That of Syed Lam touched on a similar issue in noting the manner in which the suspected murderer Mohamad Aris was now living as a free man in the Raman country above Jeram Panjang. However, while the subject of criminal jurisdiction would be taken up with great vigor in later years, the majority of the testimonies were concerned with establishing the ancient rights of Perak to the land of the watershed, particularly the mines of Klian Intan and Klian Endah on the Kroh plateau. One example reads as follows:

Syed Samsudin:

I am the great grandson of Toh Lambu, he was the Sadika Raja who governed all the Perak country above the Kuala Temong; this was always the district of the Sadika Raja, I do not remember what Raja's reign it was, I was very young at the time. Toh Lambu died, but I was born before his death, though I don't remember his dying. After him, after Toh Lambu, Toh Tronsoh became Sadika Raja. He was also my moyang (great grandfather). I think I am between fifty and sixty years old, I could hold up my hands in salutation to the Raja when the late Sultan Ali's father was Sultan. It was an uncle of Toh Lambu who opened up the mines of Intan and Endah, he was the son of Toh Lalang and was called Pawang Sering. The mines are called indifferently Klian Intan and Klian Endah. The country was at that time part of Perak, I do not know it of my own knowledge, but I have always heard that it was so for my relations governed it …

---

[38] C.O. 273/120-121. Letter from Frederick Weld to Her Majesty's Agent and Consul in Bangkok, April 14, 1883.

[39] The testimonies are contained in C.O. 8774. Hugh Low to the Colonial Secretary of the Straits Settlements, March 16, 1883.

On the question of ancient boundaries, the testimony of Sinneh, a Patani man who lived at Temengoh in Raman, offered a detailed verbal account of the geography of the Perak river above Temengoh. He would state:

> … there are other rivers falling into the main Perak river from the north before you come to the Batu Priangan which is about the height of a man on the Western bank of the river and opposite it is the place where the 'Poko Kakabu' formerly stood; this is the ancient boundary between Perak and Patani and there are no mountains at this place which it takes 4 days to reach from the Kwala Temengoh. The Perak river comes from the north of the boundary rock and has many streams falling into it but to the north of the boundary stone it flows through territory which always belonged to Patani.

In such a manner, the various testimonies would go on for pages. Each would be signed off with the words

> Set in Malay characters. Taken by the above named ...., before me at Kuala Kangsar this 6 day of March, 1883, Hugh Low, Resident.

For the British, this final clause transformed an assemblage of local stories into credible testimonies. In his preface to the reports, Low argued that the sheer volume of testimonies that he had verified demonstrated that the Sultan of Perak's claim was not only valid by the standards of Western reason, but that it was also reinforced by the "custom of all Eastern states." As an official who was deemed to be an expert in Malay affairs, Low was considered capable of seeing the various reports that he had assembled "in terms of the essence of reality which could be defined by European discourse and European methods of research alone."[40] Having conducted his research in accordance with such methods, by the time Low's numerous accounts had reached the office of the Straits Governor, they had become a voluminous set of documentary proofs.[41] At one point in late 1883 when partaking in a joint-survey commission with Siamese officials, Low actually pointed to his box full of testimonies when discussing the proper course of the boundary with the Siamese survey commissioners. It was as though he expected that the mere sight of them would prove beyond doubt the veracity of the Sultan of Perak's claim.[42]

---

[40] Maier, *In the Center of Authority*, p. 43.

[41] C.O. 273/120-121. Letter from Frederick Weld to Her Majesty's Agent and Consul in Bangkok, April 14, 1883.

[42] C.O. 273/120-121. From H.B.M.'s Resident Perak (Hugh Low) to the Colonial Secretary. Residency Kuala Kangsar, February 18, 1884.

Straits Settlements Governor Frederick Weld greeted Low's evidence with enthusiasm. They proved, he would write in a missive to the British Consul General in Bangkok, that "the true limits of Perak are well known for all practical purposes, and if the principle that all the country of the Perak river basin belongs to Perak be admitted by the Siamese government we obtain all that the Raja of Perak requires [for] we can show to a few yards the ancient boundary."[43] This statement marked the elevation of Logan's observation on Malay riverine political systems into "a principle." An actual survey mission, Weld would go on, was an unnecessary expense at the time considering the weight of proofs supporting the Perak claim. For the moment, it would be sufficient that the Consul General extract from the Siamese a tacit recognition of the validity of the Perak claim.

Such recognition was not forthcoming. On the contrary, the Siamese court took up the offer to conduct a joint survey that would settle the boundary dispute between Perak and Siam. Once again, the issue of political control over the Perak river watershed was returned to the physical points of contention in the watershed itself. To counter the British colonial challenge to its territory, the Siamese court appointed the British surveyor James McCarthy to their party, a decision that demonstrated the Siamese court's understanding of the manner in which "modern" methods of research had become a necessary component of such territorial disputes.

The Siamese response to the land claim of March 1883 was held up for the best part of a year while the Siamese Foreign Minister Prince Devawongse waited on the report of the survey commissioner. When the commissioner's report finally reached the minister, he penned a firm rebuttal of the Sultan of Perak's claim. Devawongse began with a friendly jibe: the "ancient boundaries" proposed by the British as the proper limits of Perak contradicted the boundary marked out on a map printed by their own Government Printing Office in 1880.[44] Following this, Prince Devawongse dismantled the argument that Perak rights to the disputed territory were effectively granted by the terms of treaties that had been signed between Penang and Perak in 1826 and Siam and Britain in 1855. But the most

---

[43] C.O. 273/120-121. Letter from Frederick Weld to Her Majesty's Agent and Consul in Bangkok, April 14, 1883.

[44] C.O. 273/129-130, March 21, 1884. A copy of the Siamese Foreign Minister's Letter to Her Majesty's Agent and Consul General in Bangkok, W.H. Newman, January 24, 1884. Author: Chow Phya Bhanawongse Maha Kosa Thibodi the Phra Klang Minister for Foreign Affairs. Bangkok, January 23, 1884.

significant aspect of the response to the Sultan of Perak's claim would be in regard to the issue of ancestral boundaries themselves. As the Foreign Minister would write:

> Perak is claiming more than 2,300 square miles of territory now under the rule of Siam, some of the villages of which are inhabited by Siamese and others by Siamese Malays, but none by Malays of Perak descent, and which is defined by boundary marks declared by local traditions to have been fixed about three centuries ago, and which so far as His Majesty's Commissioner could learn has never been under the rule of Perak. The important size of the territory now coveted by Perak is such that its transfer would deprive the Rajah of Raman of two thirds of his state and would aggrandize Perak by about a third of its present territory.
>
> The present boundary marks are very clear and appropriate. Chief of them is the mountain Gunong Emas 7000 feet high said to have been agreed on as a boundary in the year 1030 of the Hegera (AD 1651) by Datoh Purapoh of Patani, Datoh Limang of Kedah and Datoh Perala of Perak and the rapids Jagang Panjang or Batu Parala Inyo at the mountain gorge where the Balem river breaks through a chain of mountains and becomes the Perak river.[45]

The Siamese response confronted the British with a set of counter-claims that operated in accordance with the new rules of the game. It was a measured response considering that the Siamese were well aware that Raman's status was most accurately summed up by the axiom of "whoever has the power takes it … Whoever is able to administer, administers."[46] Even Low, in his private correspondences with Weld, had admitted that the occupation of the watershed by the Raja of Raman over the course of the nineteenth century "may be considered to have given some colour of rights to the present possession of the insignificant revenues."[47] But so far as the public dimensions of the dispute were concerned, British discourses of civilization had dismissed the notion of "might is right" as barbaric. Sovereignty was now determined by a curious mixture of ancestral right (that could be traced

---

[45] Ibid.

[46] David Streckfuss, "The Mixed Colonial Legacy in Siam: The Origins of Thai Racialist Thought, 1890–1910," in *Autonomous Histories, Particular Truths: Essays in Honor of John Smail*, ed. L.J. Sears (Madison: Center for Southeast Asian Studies, 1993), p. 133.

[47] C.O. 8774. Hugh Low to the Colonial Secretary of the Straits Settlements, March 16, 1883.

in accordance with modern methodologies) and acknowledgment of certain "timeless" principles regarding the structure of Malay states.

Devawongse responded to the first of these criteria. He simply presented an alternative genealogy that supported Raman's control of the watershed. Whether it could be "proved" was not as important as the fact that it could not be easily disproved. It also engaged the British over the question of distinctions between Perak and Patani Malays, categories that Low and Weld had manipulated to assert the illegitimacy of the Raman "occupation." Here was another example of a Siamese adaptation to a hegemonic discourse that had inscribed local constructions of Malayness with new meanings. Previously, political identities were foremost defined by one's status as a unit of manpower rather than family or group origin. The distinction between Patani and Perak men in the watershed was flexible and had little to do "with where frontiers were imagined to be, or where they were ultimately set."[48] The supposedly unified figure of the "Patani" or "'Perak' Malay" was fractured by more finite territorial jurisdictions and obviated by acts of marriage diplomacy.[49] This is not to say that "Perak" and "Patani" ethnic markers had no significance. The two categories indubitably reflected different cultural traditions that had evolved on opposite sides of the peninsula. But in a manpower deficient zone such as the watershed, ethno-cultural difference was no bar to a common political status. As a state founded by a commoner, populated by migrants, and sandwiched between three neighboring states claiming great historical pedigree, the rulers of Raman governed pragmatically over a heterogeneous population.

Recognizing the manner in which the British claim was predicated upon a distinction between Perak and Patani Malays, the Siamese Foreign Minister parried the move by introducing a third category of "Siamese Malays." The additional remark that no "Malays of Perak descent" were reported to reside within the contested region served to remind Low that certain indigenous principles of political space were not so easily abandoned. It remained the case, as the first Resident to Perak had been informed in 1874, that Patani men controlled the country down to Jeram Panjang because, after years of sporadic conflict over the mines of Klian Intan, they

---

[48] Eric Tagliacozzo, "Ambiguous Commodities, Unstable Frontiers: The Case of Burma, Siam, and Imperial Britain, 1800–1900," *Comparative Studies in Society and History* 46, 2 (2004): 364.

[49] Adrian Vickers, "'Malay Identity': Modernity, Invented Tradition, and Forms of Knowledge," *Review of Malaysian and Indonesian Affairs* 31, 1 (1997): 101.

had "finally got the better of it."[50] The lineages that Low considered as impeccable proof of Perak rights to the watershed zone still had insufficient weight in comparison to a proof of current possession obtained via the more tried and tested means of conquest.

In the end, British recourse to genealogy as part of a push into the interior of the central Malay Peninsula failed to produce the expected result. The complexity of the political map and the cracks created by epistemological incompatibilities saw the 1883 British claim on Raman parried with relative ease by a Siamese court that knew as little about the region as the British themselves. The behavior of local rulers did not help either party: they were accustomed to withholding any definitive statements on their preferred allegiance until such a time as the likely winner of the external debate was beyond all doubt.

*****

With the collapse of the 1883 land claim, British miners would have to wait over two decades to get within striking distance of the Kroh Plateau. Over the course of this intervening period, British expansionists would continually develop their arsenal. Arguments concerning certain "principles" of political space would be joined by powerful discourses of law and order, civilization, and progress. Here too the interior provides a valuable vantage point for the analysis of Anglo-Siamese activity in the region. This vantage point in the remote highland zone of the Malay Peninsula repudiates the idea that the interior was a periphery of little historical consequence. On the contrary, interior zones such as Raman were effects of lowland state-making projects, a topic that has been recently examined in great detail by Scott.[51] When it comes to the subject of Anglo-Siamese rivalries or vassal-overlord tensions in the Malay Peninsula, the interior is a valuable window from which we may critically evaluate processes that have typically been viewed from the port polity or metropole. Along the way, historical blindspots are removed and a new set of agents appears where previously none were assumed to exist.

---

[50] J.W.W. Birch, *The Journals of J.W.W. Birch: First British Resident to Perak, 1874–1875*, ed. P.L. Burns (Kuala Lumpur: Oxford University Press, 1976).
[51] James C. Scott, *The Art of Not Being Governed.*

PART FOUR

The Struggle for Control of Patani and Its History

The Formation of the Islamo-Malay Patanian Nation: Ideological Structuring by Nationalist Historians

Dennis Walker

The Patanian nation formed and evolved over centuries as a group defined by space — a homeland — and by an Islamo-Malay culture that dissolved Arabic elements from the Middle East, the Malay language and Malay customs, and Indic slivers into a new blend. Since the 1970s, the Thai state has further installed the Indicized Thai language into this mix. In "living history," aspects of the past find fulfillment but are conceptually refracted in the modern movements that these re-imagined pasts motivate and sustain. This study will analyze some of the classic works of Patani nationalist historiography, the works of a number of Western scholars who themselves have exercised an influence on current Patanian nationalist thought, as well as the more recent works of Patanian historians writing in Malay and Thai, in both Malaysia and Thailand. It draws also on an emerging, largely uncensored, historical discourse about Patani in Malay and Arabic taking place on numerous internet websites.

In Patanian nationalist historiography, the past is constantly being selected from and restructured by new generations and groups in order to sharpen and feed the nation. Not all Siamese and Patanians have hated each other at all points of their history when the two peoples were forming. But any nationhood can only be defined and delimitated by how a group relates itself to other states and peoples in its region, and also around the globe. History has inculcated into a not inconsiderable number of Patanians a sense that the Buddhist Siamese to their north are their centuries-long "traditional enemy" (*musuh tradisi*). It has led them to build up intellectual conduits to the faraway Sunni Arab Middle East and it provides a sanctuary from which to evade Siamese offensives. Islam and Arabic have been nurtured and institutionalized to differentiate the Patanians sharply from the Siamese. The *jihad* has heartened a national group as it has stood in the face of an aggressive and expanding Siamese state.

Patani's Pre-History and Islamic Foundations

At the core of Patani's early history is its embracement of Islam, yet Patani's pre-Islamic history cannot be ignored. Patani took form from the middle of the 15th century and had become a flourishing international port by its end. Favorably situated between several regions, this coastal sultanate built its prosperity from a Chinese-Javanese-Malayan-Indian trading network which it served as an emporium. The Patanians turned themselves into an active party in their own right in this trade: a Patanian merchant fleet was operating in the east of the archipelago by the end of the century exchanging rice for the spices of the Moluccas. When the profits from those products declined, Patani became a center for Indian merchants of textiles. The sultanate reached its peak as an emporium of global trade during the reign of Queen Hijau (1584–1616). Patani's prosperity was due not just to a temporary conjunction of international trade routes and supply and demand but also to new policies ushered in under the new Queen. The past authoritarianism and exactions of the sultans had largely deterred foreign merchants. Under Hijau, an economic liberalism developed in which international merchants and an indigenous *orang kaya* or "wealthy" class both could flourish. With time, those rich Patanian merchants developed into an oligarchy, and the monarchs sought less input into the management of the trade or income from it. At various times, Patani conveyed trade between Indonesia, China, Japan, Europe, and South Asia. Patani itself, though, produced but limited quantities of pepper, tin, and iron.

In deciphering the abraded Arabic on the earliest gravestones (mostly of royal figures) that have survived in Patani, Kalus has found that most phrases and terms come from the *Qur'an*. They were scrupulously Sunnite in their declarations of tenets, although their selection of Arabic formulas sometimes suggests Sufi mystical gatherings and Sufi prayers to an accessible God (*dhikr*). The tombstones sometimes reveal worried prayers for aid from Allah in military struggles, e.g. "*nasrun minallahi wa fathun qarib. Wa bashshir il-mu'minin*": "aid from Allah and a swift victory: give the glad tidings to the believers" [Q 61:13]. The grave-inscriptions also contain many Malay words. An adaptation of the letters of the *Qur'an* became the national orthography of Malay itself, which would, after a time, equip wide classes among the Patanians to read the *Qur'an* and Arabic, albeit the degree of understanding varied.[1]

From the outset, therefore, Patanian Islam and the Muslim Patanian people had two potentialities. On the one hand, trade pushed the state of Patani to assume a constructive stance toward non-Muslim peoples and their languages. This outlook led to much interaction with trading Thais and resulted in the borrowing of terms from Siamese. In its other aspect, Patanian Islam grew into manhood in a tough region that contained states that could turn into attackers at any minute. Here Islam functioned as an ideology that enabled the Patanians to stand up to attempts to extort money and resources from them, including from the Siamese who long wanted to exercise hegemony over the Peninsula. The Patanians of the 21st century continue to maintain a multicultural-constructive/jihadist-resistant duality.

Modern and postmodern Patanian nationalism has increasingly oriented itself to the Middle East and Islam. However, the progressively more detailed accounts by Western and Thai scholars of Patani's pre-Islamic period could widen imagined margins of past selfhood: that pagan past could give more space for Patanian elites to make quite new decisions about modernizing the nation and negotiating relations with "Buddhists"-"Siamese"-Thais. The historical rediscovery of Patani's precursor, Langkasuka, presents a people much more like the Buddhist Thais than the Patanians are today. Young Patanians who are exploring the old scholastic Islamic books in the Malay language (*kitab*) and issues of nationality, nonetheless, are aware that in antiquity their people shared more Sanskrit-Pali words with the Thais than they do now, given the cumulative influences from Islam. It remains a question whether greater knowledge of such past affinities could help break the cycle of violent conflict that fuels Islamic resistance, and the chauvinist streak among elements in the Thai state. Western scholarship has discovered and diffused many details of Patani's history before the coming of Islam, including pagan Indic religions. In many Arab and Middle Eastern states in the 20th century, pre-Islamic histories and beliefs were crucial for their potential to be used in the service of a re-imagined national identity and to allow modernization more space to expand at the expense of Islam as a total system.

---

[1] Daniel Perret, Amara Srisuchat and Sombun Thanasuk, eds., *Études sur l'histoire du sultanat de Patani* (Paris: Ecole Francaise d'Extreme-Orient, 2004), pp. 228–30, 234–5, 254; Ludvik Kalus, "Inscriptions arabes des cimetieres du Sud-est de la Thailande," in *Études sur l'histoire*, pp. 198, 210, 215, 222.

From the *Hikayat Patani* to Modern Nationalist Historians

The key early source for the construction of a national identity by Patanian scholars and activists is the *Hikayat Patani*, or "Narrative of Patani," believed to have been written down by one or several Malay Muslim authors early in the 18th century. Teeuw and Wyatt, who published the English translation and a commentary in 1970, contrasted the *Hikayat Patani* to the first major Patanian nationalist work, the general history of Patani by "Ibrahim Syukri," *Sejarah Kerajaan Melayu Patani*, printed *circa* 1958. They characterized the author of the section in the *Hikayat Patani* that dealt with Patani's conversion to Islam as a Muslim but "not a zealous apologist for Islam [and not] very critical of the Thais," since he refrained from denouncing other religions. Almost every Patanian nationalist author cites Teeuw and Wyatt's arguments and their data about the history of the homeland. Teeuw and Wyatt argued that the *Hikayat* depicted Siam as showing goodwill to Patani's monarchy-centered governing elite. The main case that Teeuw and Wyatt can cite is the *Hikayat Patani*'s story of King Muzaffar Shah's "first, friendly visit" to the proto-Thai state of Ayutthaya. "Although it was obvious from this story that Muzaffar Shah was not altogether happy about his reception [at the Palace] and had some trouble getting away from Ayutthaya again, it is hard to find a good reason in the story as it is told here for the military expedition against Ayutthaya which Muzaffar Shah begins to prepare immediately upon his return." Teeuw and Wyatt highlight a sentence in the *Hikayat* where the Siamese King (at that time weakened by war with Burma) received Muzaffar with the utmost courtesy when he returned with troops as backing. In a Thai nationalist ideological stand, the two scholars brand Muzaffar Shah's ensuing attack on the Ayutthaya palace as "downright treason."[2]

Teeuw and Wyatt characterized the hegemonic relationship that the proto-Thailand state of Ayutthaya already had with Patani as constructive and benign, rather than as oppression by another nation — as viewed by the Malay side. The relationship as described by Teeuw and Wyatt could lead to modernist Thai citizenship for Patanians, if it were true. But Patanian pro-nationalists living under Thailand in the 21st century often use formalistic decorum in deference to the Thai state in a fashion not unlike that used in the *Hikayat Patani* about the Ayutthaya court — a calm surface

---

[2] A. Teeuw and D.K. Wyatt, eds., *Hikayat Patani: The Story of Patani* (Hague: Martinus Nijhoff, 1970), pp. 62–5.

to veil (but by understatement, or through silence, to state and sharpen) anger and resentment.

Francis Bradley placed the *Hikayat Patani* in the category of "officially-sanctioned" court chronicles penned in such emerging Malay-Islamic polities as Pasai and Aceh in north Sumatra, Kedah on the Malay peninsula, and Banjarmasin on Borneo. These court *hikayats* meant to justify the monarchical-mercantile social hierarchy, its origins and its continued utility to society. Breaking with Teeuw and Wyatt, Bradley also viewed the *Hikayat Patani* as late ideological resistance to an expansionist Siam that could at any time threaten the survival of the Patani court and devastate the country. The court intellectuals had to preserve the vulnerable history, culture and traditions of the sultanate by writing the *Hikayat Patani*. But for Bradley, the *Hikayat Patani* was more than "a political statement" against Thai imperialism. It responded to a long economic and social decline during which bloody struggles for power between individuals and forces at or near the apex of the small polity threatened its survival. The court intellectuals made Patani's golden age a handbook to reverse this fragmentation by re-establishing a moral, monarch-headed polity.[3]

"*Negeri kita*," "our country," and Islam, are rarely verbalized in the *Hikayat Patani*. But Barbara Andaya has traced how in the work's film-flash juxtapositions, sequences of settings, symbols, a huge founding mousedeer which reflects the Divine, recurring statal noises such as cannons and music, and calls to Islamic prayers, compose a solid Islamo-Malay community that monarchs and aristocrats are obligated by God to protect, not just rule.[4] Islamic and national sites — and God — judge barely-veiled corruption, despotism and murders by royal figures. Andaya sees the *Hikayat Patani* as a prototype for a territorial nationality of place and Islam, rather than one of identity delimitated by language.

There are affinities between the way in which the old, long-intoned, *Hikayat Patani* balanced Islam and monarchs, and the stance of the current insurgency toward the two since 2004. The old *Hikayat Patani* noted that not all classical Patanian monarchs were eager to impose Islam. Rulers sometimes had tensions with Islamic clerics, and some monarchs did not respect the sacredness of the physical life of humans in Islam — they

---

[3] Francis R. Bradley, "Moral Order in a Time of Damnation: The Hikayat Patani in Historical Context," *Journal of Southeast Asian Studies* 40, 2 (June 2009): 267–93.

[4] Barbara Andaya, "Gates, Elephants, Cannon and Drums: Symbols and Sounds in Creation of a Patani Identity," in this volume.

committed murder. Yet the *Hikayat Patani* wanted to reform, not abolish, monarchy. The monarchs and nobles must perform their function in an Islamic communitarian system or lose legitimacy. The current jihadists in southern Thailand accept that the sultans of the bygone Sultanate of Patani headed and sometimes managed its greatness. Descendents of that royalty are therefore today in the running to become at least the titular head of state of an independent Patani. Rebel communications appear to envisage that any future royal head of state would not wield great power, that he would be closely supervised by Islamic clerics, and deposable. Neutralizing monarchy would vest most real power in an Arabophone Islamic governing elite that is also, in its turn, to be controlled by some political mechanism that gives agency to wider groups. This is stated with some clarity by the 2004 *Berjihad di-Patani* [*Fighting the Jihad Holy War in Patani*], a document believed to represent the ideology of the insurgent groups.[5]

The *Hikayat Patani*'s discreet hypothetical thinking ruled out any unvarying monarchist ideology. It pivoted around the polity of Patani, as much as the monarchs who headed it. The rulers each had to prove that they were capable of their prescribed functions, as did all its office-bearers. The welfare of the general community of Patanians counted more. It is striking that the *Hikayat Patani*, as old as it is, fits better into the West's later-modern thinking than does the post-1954 nationalist historiography. For the *Hikayat*, the homeland-nation exists, but the monarchs heavily shape outcomes for it in both trade and its self-defense: so it is crucial to sensitize the kings and queens to Islam and its morality. In the nationalist historiography, it is the Nation that wills resistance. Its monarchs only decide ways to defend its sovereignty. The nationalist historians seldom scrutinize the monarchs who only head the Nation, while the pre-modern — semi-monarchist — literary artists and Arabist-legists dissect the conflict between predatory motives and Islamic ethics within royal individuals. By comparison, the post-1945 nationalist historiography sometimes looks simple and stuck in the 1950s with hero-leaders like Sukarno and Nasser.

The *Sejarah Kerajaan Melayu Patani* [*The History of the Malay Kingdom of Patani*], published under the pen-name "Ibrahim Syukri" in 1958 from Kelantan in Malaysia, was the first overview of a recognizably modern type of history written by Patanians. It was fast-moving, stripped-down nationalist mathematics, its clarity and muscular speed fuelled by a hatred

---

[5] See Rohan Gunaratna *et al.*, eds., *Conflict and Terrorism in Southern Thailand* (Singapore: Marshall Cavendish Academic, 2005), pp. 117–45.

of Thailand, whose Buddhists it depicted as the age-old "enemy" (*musuh*) of "the Patanian Malay nation." That animus was only natural. The book was composed in 1954 in the Malayan village of Pasir Putih, to which the British had transferred the many Patanians who had fled over the international border after the Thai state's suppression of village protests and the independence movement following the Second World War. It may have been partly penned by Tengku 'Abdul Jalal Bin al-Marhum Tengku Abdul-Muttalib, one of the Patanian royal strugglers against Thai rule. Prince Muhyiddin and a few others in the exiled GAMPAR[6] independence movement could read English well, and thus could have derived some data about Patani's past from Western scholars. "Syukri's" *Sejarah Kerajaan Melayu Patani* was impressive, too, in terms of scholarship for its time because it carefully drew on a Thai chronicle of Patani published in 1914 (Muhyiddin had once studied in Bangkok). As the old *Hikayat Patani* and the *Sejarah Kerajaan Melayu Patani* had already done, subsequent Patani scholars, such as the Malaysia-based Mohammad Zamberi 'Abdul Malek, also tapped Thai-written sources for their works on Patani's history and culture.[7] The coming Patanian nationalist historians and analysts of local society and cultures will be trilingual or quadrilingual, tapping English-, Malay-, Thai- and Arabic-language sources.

Jory contrasted (a) the *Hikayat Patani*, a monarchist work that focused on courts in the Patanian mercantile state and in its region, to (b) the 1954/1958 "Ibrahim Syukri" work, the main protagonist of which is a people. Now the monarchs and their entourages can at best lead or represent that Nation. The rise of nationalisms in Southeast Asia in the 1920s and 1930s helped Patanian writers shift somewhat from a [Muslim] monarch to a generalized Nation. Jory notes the foundation in the 1940s of the United Malays' National Organization (UMNO) in neighboring Malaya, one stimulus, and Ibrahim Syukri's sense of the 100-million-strong Malay people in the world, a product of the influence of Indonesian nationalism and pan-Malay ideologies.[8] Writing three and a half centuries later, "Syukri"

---

[6] *Gabungan Melayu Patani Raya* — Organization of Greater Malay Patani.

[7] Mohammad Zamberi 'Abdul Malek, *Patani Dalam Tamadun Melayu* (Selangor: Dewan Bahasa dan Pustaka 1994), p. 6, is relying on a Thai chronicle, accessed through C. Skinner in the *JMBRAS* (1983) to trace the detail of Thailand's 1817 division of Patani into seven little much weaker states.

[8] Patrick Jory, "From 'Melayu Patani' to 'Thai Muslim': The Spectre of Ethnic Identity in Southern Thailand," *Southeast Asia Research* 15, 2 (July 2007): 255–79.

recounts the story how in 1603, thousands of Thai troops sailed to Patani to "seize away the independence of the Malays of Patani ... The people of Patani under the leadership of their King came out to resist that attack of the Thais." Monarchs, and royal nobles (like Prince Muhyiddin?) thus retain some importance in the survival of the nation in the "Syukri" vision of Patani's history. The work claimed that the constant struggle on the ground between incoming Siamese and the Malay population ("*orang-orang Melayu*" rather than "Muslims") was the reason behind the Bangkok king's decision to slice Patani up into statelets in 1817.[9]

While "Syukri" presented images of "Malay people" repeatedly engaging the Siamese in large-scale battles, he tended not to use the term *jihad* to describe their motivation. Yet he repeatedly presented images of Islam, the religion of the Patanian Malay people, as being under the protection of the Malay kings who promoted it — for example, in their construction of mosques — since the time of the first installation of its literate legal scholars in the court upon conversion in the 15th century.

Syukri's seminal work still guides Patanian historiography to this day, a full half-century later. Though published in Malaya in 1958, *Sejarah Kerajaan Melayu Patani* has over the decades been a foundation in the ideological formation of Islamic-educated Patanians. The noted recent historian of Patani, Ahmad Fathi al-Fatani, who currently lives and works in Malaysia, has related how his father detested "the schools of Siam." He had made Ahmad study Malay and Arabic in *pondok* Islamic boarding schools before sending him off to Kelantan for his Islamic higher education. Around 1965, his father visited him and handed him a wrapped new copy of the anti-Buddhist perspective-history by "Syukri" before returning to Patani. "Syukri" enabled the 17-year-old al-Fatani to at last understand the role and contribution of Haji Sulong (Sallum), who had disappeared after a meeting with the Thai police in 1954, and about whom he had heard his father and the elders whispering soon after.[10] No adult had ever explained the importance of Haji Sulong to him while he remained in Patani. The fact that his father had waited until he was safely in Malaysia before giving him "Syukri's" nationalist history suggests the importance of the work, and

---

[9] Ibrahim Syukri, *Sejarah Kerajaan Melayu Patani* (Bangi: UKM, 2002), pp. 44, 80–1. On mosque-building under Thai dominance by Sultan Sulayman Sharifuddin (d. 1899), see p. 94.

[10] See Ahmed Fathi al-Fatani, *Pengantar Sejarah Patani* (Kota Bharu: Pustaka Aman Press, 2001), pp. 123–4.

the diligence with which Patanians sought to keep alive their country's history, ancient and modern, in the then fearful atmosphere of Thailand's police state.

Reading the *Sejarah Kerajaan Melayu Patani* has for decades been almost a rite of passage from adolescence to manhood among those Patanians who study *Jawi* (Arabic-script) Malay and Arabic. Its crystal-clear Malay prose, tight argumentation, and sharp portrayal of the enemy, communicate equally to both adolescents and adults. However, for a new generation of Patanian youth taught in Thai in government schools, a Thai translation of "Syukri" was published in 1988 at the Prince of Songkhla University (Pattani Campus) by the Institute of Southeast Asian Maritime States, ensuring the text lives on beyond the confines of its original Malay language.

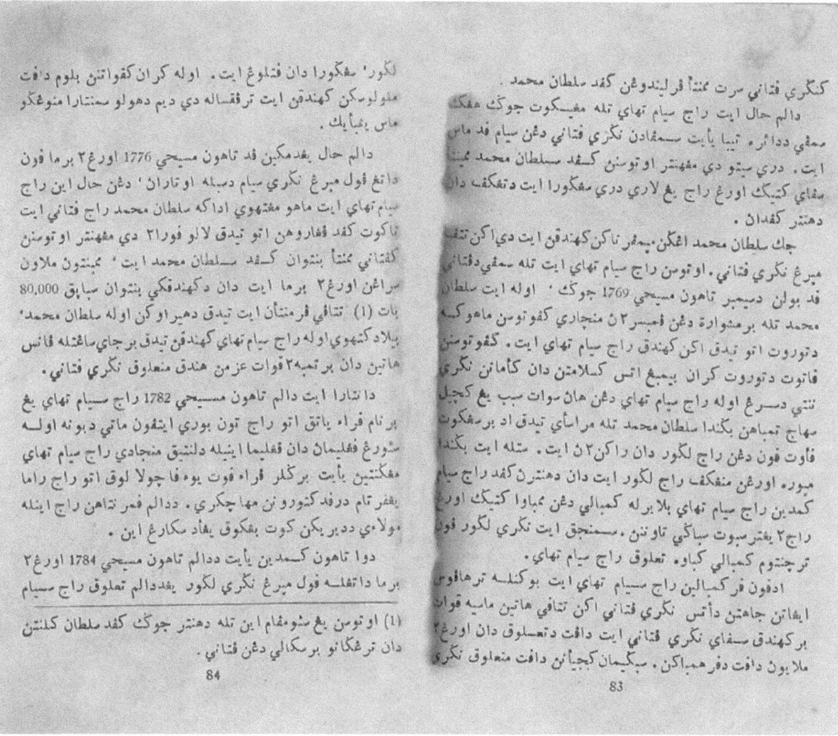

Figure 9.1 From the 1958 edition of Ibrahim Syukri's *Sejarah Kerajaan Melayu Patani*: the Siam-Thai raja, angered by the Sultan of Patani's refusal of a request to help him resist a Burmese attack in 1776, begins to plan Patani's subjugation.

Figure 9.2 Cover of the 1958 *Jawi* edition of Ibrahim Syukri's *Sejarah Kerajaan Melayu Patani*, published by the Majlis Ugama Islam Kelantan in Pasir Puteh, Kelantan.

Ancient Paganism and Modern Definitions of Patani Nationhood

Hinduism and Buddhism have long blurred into each other in the history of Siam/Thailand. The founder of the Chakri dynasty which still reigns today, Rama I (r. 1782–1809), ordered a new translation of the ancient Hindu epic *Ramayana*. Its theme, that society is inherently unequal and requires a divine monarch to check darker-skinned rebels, still inspires cultural products in Thailand that continue to validate the claims to leadership of the Bangkok Chakri kings. Could contemporary Thai high culture which continues to tap into the ancient Sanskrit literature of Hindu India and Buddhism, come to feed in the Bangkok-centered bourgeoisie a pan-Indic bloc to face the pan-Islamic *jihad* bloc now seemingly on the march to dismember southern Thailand? Or could the pre-Islamic tradition come to be seen as the common heritage of both Thai Buddhists and Malays? "Syukri's" *Sejarah Kerajaan Melayu Patani* is a highly ideological nationalist text. Yet even this work is somewhat open and relaxed about the immigration of Indians, Hinduism and even Buddhists — and the polytheistic beliefs they taught — in the earlier history of proto-Patani. The "Ibrahim Syukri" panel appears to have been dispassionate toward the polytheism and idol-packed (*berhala*) temples which those ancient Hindus and Buddhists built in Patani. The "Syukri" committee would have drawn from Indonesian magazines or books on the West's archaeological rediscoveries, but would also have had collaborators who could have located recent scholarly articles in English on the archipelago's pre-Islamic past. British journalist, Barbara Whittingham-Jones, was passionate about Patani and the Patanian people while her comrade Prince Muhyiddin read English well.[11]

A similar acceptance of the aesthetic culture of Patani's long-lost Indic, Hindu and Buddhist past and beliefs is found in Ahmed Fathi al-Fatani's 2001 survey of Patani's history. The growing influence of the Buddhist empire of Srivijaya (7th–13th centuries CE) on Patani "caused [Langkasuka/Patani] to progress" and become the administrative center in the Malay peninsula of that Sumatra-centered empire. This relationship, to which al-Fatani pays tribute, brought from Sumatra the Malay language, Buddhism, navigation and trade, architecture, and music. In one passage, he sounds regretful that "many of these ancient monuments and artefacts were destroyed when the people of Patani came to embrace Islam later. This can make difficult the study of its ancient history." In regard to modern Thai Buddhism, though,

---

[11] Syukri, *Sejarah Kerajaan Melayu Patani*, pp. 16–20.

Fathi assailed dictator Phibun Songkhram, charging that his regime's deculturalization drive against the Patanians included measures to prod them toward converting to Buddhism. Al-Fatani relished the confrontation in 1985 when mass demonstrations by "the *Ummah* of Islam" throughout the South and in Bangkok forced the partly civilian Thai governments to postpone a directive to introduce statues of the Buddha into all government schools. Ahmad al-Fatani exalts a blended Patanian identity that he terms "*penduduk Melayu-Islam*" — "the Malay-Islamic inhabitants" of Patani. He hated the huge faux-gold statues of Buddha that the Bangkok regimes erected near Malay villages to stake Thailand's claim.[12]

Patani's precursor, the kingdom of Langkasuka, takes the pre-Islamic history of the continuous nation as far back as 515 AD — virtually a millennium before Patani's conversion to Islam. This history offers the potential to dilute and relativize the Arabic and Islamic influence in Patanian historiography. Indeed, Pharaonist nationalism in Egypt from 1920 weakened the prescriptiveness of the later Islam and the Arabs for the now-independent Egypt they constructed after the modernist West. That ideological change created space for borrowing more cultural elements from the West. Like Arab and Indonesian nationalisms, "Ibrahim Syukri," "A. Bangnara"/"Patani Forces Research Panel," Ahmad Fathi al-Fatani, and Zamberi all drew on the West's excavations of Patani's ancient pre-Islamic history (Langkasuka) to sketch colorful and sometimes precise and positive pictures of those bygone pagan societies. There is a potential here to reduce the centrality of Islam in Patanian nationalist identity and to rediscover long-gone affinities with the Indicized Buddhist Thais. But the Buddhist element in modern Thai nationalism has highlighted the role of that non-Muslim faith in the motives of the enemy, which the nationalist Patanians have so long sidestepped and fought. For Patanians, this relationship of conflict with Thai Buddhists has led to Islam being regarded as the most coherent core of a national identity built in large part on the idiom of resistance.

In regard to the new Patanian nationalist histories now being penned in Thai, the synthesis-book of Arifin bin Chik, Abdullah La'umen and Suhaymi Isma'il, too, gave a proud account of the precursor "Malay Kingdom of Langkasuka." According to them, the kingdom emerged in 200 AD. The authors were neutral in their coverage of pagan religion. Langkasuka's kings

---

[12] Ahmed Fathi al-Fatani, *Pengantar Sejarah Patani*, pp. 2–8, 13. On the modern struggle against the Buddhists, see pp. 199, 220; for a photograph of one of the huge Buddha statues, and above that another statue commemorating the conquests of Rama I in Pattani province, see p. 220.

were "of Brahmanic Hindu religion." Later, because its Buddhist colleges were so good, many Chinese stayed in Langkasuka until they died. Arifin, La'umen and Suhaymi also highlighted the economic exchanges that linked China and Langkasuka together.[13]

The Coming of Islam and Foreign Muslims in Patanian History

In regard to the conversion of Patani to Islam, Bougas notes from a Malay source, the *Hikayat Raja Langkasuka*, the presence of Arab and Persian merchants as early as the tenth century. However, he downplayed conversion as an informal cumulative process among ordinary people. Instead, Bougas regards Islam as having put down real roots in Southeast Asia only in the 13th and 14th centuries as courts and royal governments began to embrace the faith. Missionaries and teachers from Sumatra induced royalty in Patani, as in other Malay areas, to convert for trivial reasons, such as ailments cured by a propagator, according to most of those court-*hikayats*. But in Bougas' view, Patani's ruling elite also opted for Islam as a shared ideological base that would facilitate trade with harbor principalities in Java, as a rallying-point to keep Ayutthaya at arm's length from Patani, and later to unify Malay rulers to resist expansion by the Portuguese and the Dutch. Patani's rulers selected certain Islamic motifs, such as the doctrine of 'Abbasid Iraq that the Caliph was the "Shadow of God on Earth," that would help them retain some of the despotic power they had relinquished when they gave up their old Indic status as incarnate God Kings of the Universe.[14] Later Islamic legists, such as the renowned Patani scholar Shaykh Dawud al-Fatani (1769–1847), narrowed the scope of the *hadith* that refer to this closeness to the Divine which the monarchs had seized upon to inflate their political claims.

Patani's classical period already had some sense of plural social groupings bound together in the struggle to beat off Siam — inter-class alliances against the great Enemy that form and sustain long-term political nationalities. There also are components in the *Hikayat Patani* that suit an Islamic ideology to direct the conduct and the structure of the state and to help integrate the whole society. This chronicle was deeply religious

---

[13] Arifin bin Chik, 'Abdullah La'umen and Suhaymi Isma'il, *Patani: prawattisat lae kan mueang nai lok melayu* [*Patani: History and Politics in the Malay World*] (Hatyai, Songkla: The Foundation for the Presentation of Islamic Culture in Southern Thailand, 2nd ed. 2009), pp. 31–45.

[14] Wayne A. Bougas, *The Kingdom of Patani between Thai and Malay Mandala* (Selangor: Institut Alam dan Tamadun Melayu, UKM, 1994) pp. 29–31.

and Islamic in its awareness of death, and that individuals and structures that exercise power, and evanescent royal dynasties, are all here on God's sufferance. They will be felled and damned if, in accordance with the dark side in humans, they act against the rights of other Muslims set by Allah.

Post-1945 Patanian nationalist sources repeat the *Hikayat Patani*'s account of Islamization in terms of the conversion of the urban monarch and his royal court, with the order then passing down through all levels of the society. This simplistic semi-myth relates that a Muslim missionary from Pasai, Sumatra, called Shaykh Sa'id, cured a Raja of Patani of a recurring dermatological affliction, in return for a promise by the latter that he would convert to Islam if cured. However, the Raja repeatedly evaded his pledged conversion after several healings by the Shaykh of his recurrent affliction, before finally accepting Islam.[15] The *Hikayat Patani*'s faulting of the king's slowness to convert shows an early ambiguity in Patani about the role of the class of royalty vis-à-vis the local general Muslim community, long before the era of modern nationalisms shifted the focus from monarchs to the nation. Disguised ill-feelings and episodic Byzantine resistance to the kings and aristocracy were to recur in the broad-gauge nationalist movements that have constructed the mini-insurrections since 1945.

The major ideologues of Patanian nationalism have viewed the triumph of Islam in their homeland in different ways, but increasingly came to see the monarchy as only one, later participant in it. Nationalist scholars such as 'Abdullah La'uman (1977)[16] and Mohammad Zamberi 'Abdul Malek (1994)[17] anticipated by more than a decade Daniel Perret (2004), who sees the international trading network in which the Patani entrepôt state took form, rather than the court, as the matrix that Islamized the Patanians. For Perret, Islam spread widely in China under the Mongols who in the 14th century gave Muslims greater trading privileges than other Chinese. Islamized Chinese were also established to the south of Patani on the north coast of Java. Thus, Islamized Chinese on the two margins of the China-Java-Malaya-Middle East trading network could have first conveyed to Patani the Islam that was to become strong by the mid-15th century.[18]

---

[15] Teeuw and Wyatt, *Hikayat Patani*, pp. 221–4.

[16] *Dahulu dan Sekarang* (N.p.: 1977[?]); see footnote 26.

[17] Mohammad Zamberi 'Abdul Malek, *Patani Dalam Tamadun Melayu*.

[18] Daniel Perret, "Tombes musulmanes anciennes et voies possible d'Islamization," in *Études sur l'histoire*, ed. Perret *et al.*, pp. 163–4. Perret tried to document China as a source for the spread of Islam in Patani from similarities of gravestones in Patani and Brunei to earlier ones in Quanzhou: p. 166.

The earliest Patani nationalist history, "Ibrahim Syukri's" *Sejarah Kerajaan Melayu Patani*, follows the sequence of the *Hikayat Patani*: Islam comes to Patani through the conversion of the king. It then passes downward through monarchy-directed institutions to officials and then to the masses. "Syukri" retells the story in the *Hikayat* of how an Arab-descended Sufi missionary from Pasai repeatedly cured the Raja of a rash until the final curing and the final conversion. "From that time, the population of Patani had accepted the religion of Islam which accordingly became their national religion, as it remains to this day." The concern of the *Sejarah Kerajaan Melayu Patani*, in this context is with the nation, of which Islam, though, is a key emblem. "Syukri" had written with some admiration of the civilized Hindus/Buddhists in Langkasuka and Patani in earlier centuries. Yet an anti-Indic tone does come into the work here. Pasai, on Sumatra's coast, was the first area in Southeast Asia in which the whole population embraced Islam. However, in surrounding areas and the hinterland many people still followed "Hinduism" (which for "Syukri" includes Buddhism). Those Hindus were constantly attacking Pasai. Some of Pasai's Muslims therefore moved to other lands for security, hence the "Kampung Pasai" in Patani that brought it Islam.[19] Here the *Sejarah Kerajaan Melayu Patani* could over the long term contribute to a sense among Patanians of the inherent conflict between Islam and Indic religions. Yet he himself rarely mentions Allah or *jihad* in his exuberant accounts of successive battles between Patanians and the (religiously Indic) Thais up to 1909. Still, "Syukri" portrayed the Shaykh from Pasai as motivated solely by his resolve to establish Islam. Thus he refused the rich presents with which the King tried to pay him off for the cures: he wants the soul of the king and his court for Islam. The work depicts their conversion when it comes as complete and swift: the Pasai Shaykh is installed in the palace as an instructor to the King, the royal family and the state's leading figures on the requirements of Islamic law, from where Islam then spreads out among "the masses" ("*rakyat jelata*"). Thus the worship of the Buddhist idols dies out, and Islam and state power become one.[20]

The authors of the *Patani Dahulu dan Sekarang*, who were perhaps Islam-inclined, leftist intellectuals in or near the "pink" Islamic PULO,[21] saw Islam as having spread widely among ordinary Patanians from the tenth

---

[19] Syukri, *Sejarah Kerajaan Melayu Patani*, p. 32.
[20] Ibid., pp. 32–5.
[21] The separatist movement styling itself as the "Patani United Liberation Organisation."

century, and that the conversion of the Palace at the close of the 15th century was a late consequence, or formality. However, the nationalist historian Ahmad Fathi al-Fatani held that Arabs as well as Indians and Chinese were coming for trade to Patani even before Christ. Yet he retains the old story of the repeated curing by the Pasai Sufi preacher of the Raja of Patani as an explanation for the decisive Islamization of Patani.[22] Islamization in the "story" (*cherita*) that al-Fatani recycles from the *Hikayat Patani* remains a superficial choice by one royal individual who did not compare and think through its tenets or creeds, but from which momentous consequences flowed. Fathi did, though, highlight Islam as the rallying-point in culture against the Thais.

Neither the *Hikayat Patani*, the *Sejarah Kerajaan Melayu Patani*, nor Ahmad Fathi al-Fatani who drew upon both works in 2001, sketch a process of the triumph of Islam amid widening pressure from below. But other Patanian nationalist authors saw more to Islamization than a simple order sent downward from a monarch or elite. *Patani Dahulu dan Sekarang* (c. 1977) instead tried to demonstrate "that Islam entered Patani well before the [proto-Thai] state of Sukothai was established after 1219 AD." This red-hot nationalist work stressed that Arab merchants were spreading Islam 300 years before the King's conversion. "Islam had spread among the masses first, and then reached those who governed." The book set the date of the monarch's conversion, after his backslidings, at 1457 AD. According to *Patani Dahulu dan Sekarang*, apart from the monarch's adoption of an Islamic name, and the ending of the eating of pork by the court, Patanians long held on to their established customs. While they stopped worshipping Buddhist idols, animist worship of certain objects continued under his son Muzaffar Shah.[23]

These left-Islamist nationalists who had been active in the 1975–1976 uprising in Pattani city may not have seen the monarchy of the Sultanate

---

[22] Ahmed Fathi al-Fatani, *Pengantar Sejarah Patani*, pp. 3, 12–3.

[23] A. Bangnara (pseudonym), "Patani Forces Research Panel," in *Patani Dahulu dan Sekarang* (N.p.: 1977[?]), pp. 6–8. This work is seen by some Patanian Islamist-nationalists as having been written, edited or supervised by Abdullah La'umen, who in old age was to contribute to the 21st century's new Patani nationalist historiography in Thai, notably *Patani: prawattisat lae kan mueang nai lok melayu* and *Lao khan tamnan tai*. In regard to Arab traders in Islam's classical period specifically, neither G.R. Tibbets (1979) nor Daniel Perret who followed him (2004) found much evidence of visits in Arabic primary sources; Perret, "Tombes musulmanes anciennes," in *Études sur l'histoire*, ed. Perret *et al.*, p. 164.

of Patani as the apex that determined Patanian identity.[24] Mohammad Zamberi 'Abdul Malek in his *Patani Dalam Tamadun Melayu* [*Patani in Malay Civilization*] also saw the conversion of the monarch as a later, albeit decisive, result of the pre-existing spread of Islam among the Patanian population. Malek claimed that Arab merchants descended from Sayyiduna 'Abbas bin 'Abdul Muttalib, an uncle of the Prophet Muhammad, played a major role in propagating Islam in Patani, from which it then spread throughout the region. Malek argued from Malay works of Kelantan that a *shaykh* from Patani came to propagate Islam there around 1150 AD. Yet it was only in the 16th or 17th century that Patani flourished as a center for Islamic scholarship and propagation in the region. Patani's golden age of greatness lasted for only two centuries, the 16th and the 17th. Thereafter, Malek mourned, the increasing influence of the "traditional enemy" Siam, and the Western powers that had seized the south of the Malayan peninsula, caused Patani to gradually decline into unimportance.[25]

Nationalist writers of Zamberi's type argue for the advent of Islam in Patani as far back as they can, to the first formation of Patani and its Malay culture. One motive why they did so was the crucial role they felt Islam had played over centuries as a rallying-point that had enabled the Patanian Malays to resist the ceaseless thrusts south by "the Siamese enemy." Zamberi's 1994 cultural history of Patani opens with little or no attention to the states, history and culture prior to Islam of the Malays who are within the current borders of Thailand. This author only fleetingly referred to the pagan state of Langkasuka. It had been the precursor state to Patani which already covered such areas later brought into Islamic Greater Patani, including Phatthalung, Songkhla, Trengganu and Kelantan. The precursor state of Langkasuka established the international trade on the basis of which its successor state, Patani, flourished. But "the Malay Empire of Langkasuka" had less interest for Zamberi in this book than "the most glorious and majestic Islamic Empire of [Greater] Patani." For Patani, Islam brought a shift from the previous ideology of divine monarchs to that of the human sultan, derived from classical Islam's concept of the Caliph. "The rise of Patani as the leading Malay state clearly followed on from the acceptance

---

[24] It has to be noted, though, that the late 'Abdullah La'uman's brother 'Abdul-'Aziz most vehemently denied to me that he had been a member of PULO or a secessionist.

[25] Mohammad Zamberi 'Abdul Malek, *Patani Dalam Tamadun Melayu* (Selangor: Dewan Bahasa dan Pustaka, 1994), pp. 29–31.

of Islam. When the Raja of Patani Phaya Tu Antara embraced Islam, the Islamic State of Patani Darul Salam ['the Abode of Peace' — one title of the classical Arabs' Baghdad] was born. The advent of Islam also brought many great changes of beliefs, spirituality, concepts, culture, language, education and the socio-political aspects of the governance of Malay society." For Zamberi, Islam's distinction between the *Darul Islam*, or lands governed by Muslims, as against the *Darul Harb*, or areas governed by non-Muslims against which Muslims are obliged by their religion to wage war, is attractive, at least as a rallying-point for resistance against Siam. However, his work does betray some twinges of a dual consciousness. He writes that Islam did not completely obliterate all before it. Islam came from India and Persia as well as from Arabs, and some Indic patterns continued in the Islamic monarchical state.[26] Still, Zamberi in this work only expressed real interest in an Islamic state of Patani. The book may well have contributed elements to a jihadist-Islamist nationalism in Patani itself, although he did not use many Arabic words and expressions in his Malay.

The claims made for the historical duration of "Langkasuka-Patani" in Mohammad Zamberi 'Abdul Malek's *Ummat Islam Patani* could be applied to relativize Islam in Patani's national identity by reference to pagan Langkasuka. However, the understanding of other religions and cultures that preceded Islam is superficial, and the commitment of 'Abdul Malek to Islam as the "national" ideology of resistance to Thailand cannot be overstated. This work was brought out by elements in Malaysia that hoped it would fuel an Islamist militancy that sees the whole range of Muslim countries, not just those of Malay speech, as having to stand together. The book's printer, Abu Muhammad Jawad, with nationalist and pan-Islamic dualism, extolled it as likely "to benefit the sons and daughters of the race ('*bangsa*', i.e., Malay people) who love their religion and their national culture that today are being begrimed by this world that is ultra-modern and complex. For Patani's Malays, may this book serve as an incentive to restore their national honor and rights at present being denied by the international grouping of the infidels."[27]

The 21st century's Thai-medium Patani nationalist histories have followed the earlier Malay works in pushing the conversion back as far as they dare. Arifin bin Chik, Abdullah La'umen and Suhaymi Isma'il (2009) even suggest that, before the King of Patani converted to Islam, some of

---

[26] Zamberi 'Abdul Malek, *Patani Dalam Tamadun Melayu*, pp. 12–5, 17–8, 20.
[27] Ibid., p. xii.

the monarchs of the old Langkasuka had been Muslims as well. Like most Malay-medium nationalists, though, the authors seek to trace longstanding trading and social relationships that alter the tenets of a general population very gradually. They depict an Arab-Langkasuka relationship as having long preceded the court's conversion to Islam. Arabian and Persian merchants were already coming to Langkasuka even when the Arabs/Persians still believed in such diverse religions as Zoroastrianism, Judaism, and Christianity. They set the preaching of Islam in Patani back to 1000. Citing Muslim tombstones in Cambodia dating from the early 1000s, and the dubious *Ta'rikh Fatani*, Arifin, La'umen and Suhaymi depict merchants who came from Cambodia trying to draw the Langkasukans into Islam. From the outset of the decisive switch to Islam, they see tensions between neo-Muslims and Buddhists in Patani because Islam and Buddhism prohibit the foods (pork and beef) that the other eats.[28] In the early 21st century, Patani nationalist intellectuals have achieved an historical vision of their relationship with Arabs and Middle Easterners that — while driven by Islam — now sees them with nuances far beyond the concepts of the old Arabophone scholastics.

Some old narratives of foot-dragging in the Palace about conversion to Islam, coupled with speculation that some ordinary Malays may have been more willing to convert, could feed agendas by factions among secessionist groups to control or end the political role of royalty in Patani nationalist movements. But Isma'il Benjasmith's influential 2008 account of the coming of Islam to Patani depicts the daughter or wife of the King of Patani as the one who has the skin disease. Shaykh Sa'id al-Basisa, a physician and professional missionary of Islam, sets conversion by the king as the condition on which he will heal her. When he does, the King utters "There is no God but Allah," without the resistance or holding back in the *Hikayat Patani* or the *Sejarah Kerajaan Melayu Patani*. Everyone in his kingdom now believes in Islam.[29] There is no sense of a pagan king resisting the establishment of Islam that we get in the *Hikayat Patani* and in some modern Patanian historians who perhaps want to narrow the roles of the royal aristocrat class in nationalism. With Benjasmith, royalty in Patani history makes itself the cutting edge of Islamization in Patani.

---

[28] Arifin, Abdullah La'umen and Suhaymi, *Patani: prawattisat lae kan mueang*, pp. 47–51; Isma'il Benjasmith, "Bot bat tan kan sueksa lae kan muang khong chaik wan ahmad al-fatani (2399–2451)" [The Roles of Shaykh Ahmad al-Fatani (1865–1908 AD) in Education and Politics], MA thesis submitted to Faculty of Islamic Studies, Prince of Songkla University (P), 2008/BE 2551, p. 36.

[29] Isma'il Benjasmith, *Bot bat tan kan sueksa*, p. 39.

Various nationalist ideologies in the West, the Arab world's nationalist revolutions and later its salafist jihadisms, Malaysia and republican Indonesia, as well as Phibun's republican-leaning Thailand, have influenced the shift in Patanian nationalist discourse from the narrow focus on monarchy and the ruling aristocracy to the Patanian people in general. Yet the affirmations of the Patanian nationalists that society had been introduced to Islam before the monarchy's decision to adopt it seem to be more realistic rather than an ideological construct. Moreover, it accords with the viewpoint of the Patanian masses, as distinct from the court writers who exalted the monarchs and modern nationalists. The Patani scholar Bang Lah (2009), an expert in local oral tradition, believes that the king had converted after the local people were already practicing Islam.[30]

Foreign Muslims, including Middle Easterners, later became important actors in Patani. Arabs and other Muslims from the Middle East helped to build up Patani's military strength to withstand the pressure from Siam. The *Hikayat Patani* indicates that (as in Sumatra) a "Rum" (= Turk or Arab) cast the first cannon in Patani, for the first sultan, Isma'il. Arabic became one means of written communication between even Western traders and the Patanians.[31] Thenceforth, there would always be some Arab instructors in Patani's Shafi'i Islamic schools, so that a stratum of Malay clerics was to evolve with a high degree of bilingualism in Arabic and Malay, and who frequently made pilgrimage to, or lived in, the Arab countries.

The Arab-Patanian relationship continues in our postmodern era. Immediately following the outbreak of the uprising in 2004, young Patanian students of Islam and Arabic in the Middle East, aflame with the passion to redeem their faraway homeland, transferred onto the Arabic internet details from the old *Hikayat Patani* (Arabicized into "*al-Akhbar al-Fataniyyah*") and from the modern nationalist historians, about Patani's conversion to Islam and its age of greatness under the four queens. One communication to the world's Arabic-readers gave the story of the *sufi* Shaykh Safiyy al-Din's conversion of the Patani Buddhist *raja* by way of his curing of the ruler's skin affliction, but left out the symbolic or mythological sub-story of the idol-addicted Raja's twice going back on his word, and thus the need for a third healing by the Islamic Shaykh. This 2004 Patanian nationalist presentation to Arabs of the homeland's history looked beyond the stylized depiction of the *Hikayat Patani*, toward "Ibrahim Syukri" and the other modern nationalist

---

[30] Bradley, "Moral Order in a Time of Damnation," p. 271n16.
[31] Bougas, *The Kingdom of Patani*, p. 61.

historians. It stresses the products and entrepôt trade of Patani and global commerce, which drew "the Muslim traders who used to traverse around the world bearing the message of Islam to all the peoples." The conversion is thus more than a local Malay-archipelago matter. Long-term interaction between the indigenous people and Muslim traders from the Middle East has already prepared the thinking of the people when the King and his court convert. The global Muslim traders have left their marks and their descendents in Patani, as they have elsewhere in Southeast Asia.

But what of the disparity between the prominent role played by women in Patani's history and governance, and the fewer such roles of women in Arab and Middle Eastern history? One Arabic discourse by Patanians carried over the internet gives the names of the four queens, and treats them (not their ministers) as the rulers who decreed state policies. This Patanian who had lived for many years in the Middle East presented Queen Hijau as closer to the norms of his Middle Eastern readers when he observed that (although she governed) she did not meet alien men face to face, instead ruling on their requests from behind a screen/curtain (*hijab*).[32] In any case, Patanian intellectuals have robust self-esteem when interacting with Middle Eastern or South Asian Muslims. They do not modify their conduct when Pakistanis, prodded by their Hanafi school of law in Sunnism, object to their eating shellfish that the Patanians' Shafi'ite law school allows, or when outside, Muslims fault the considerably free mixing between the sexes in the colonies of Patanians who go to study Arabic and Islam in Islamic countries.

Western-based, Southeast Asian and Thai historians have tended to view Patanian *jihad* and the leadership that Islamic clerics provided for it in two contrasting ways: (i) as a new pattern that took shape in the later 20th century, and particularly after 2004, with salafist or Wahhabite Arabs as the catalyst; or (ii) as having taken form during the destruction of the Patanian monarchical state by the Thais in 1785–1840. Following the eclipse of the political elite, leadership shifted *somewhat* from royal nobility to Arabophone clerics, some of whom were themselves of royal blood. Patanian nationalist historians have increasingly woven the Islamic *'ulama'* into the golden age monarchy. They depict the Malay sultans and kings as intent on conserving

---

[32] "Fatani: Qissatu Sha'bin Muslimin Yujahidu min Ajli Dinihi wa Ardih" [Patani: The Story of a Muslim People That is Fighting in Jihad for Its Religion and Its Land], published online at *Dunya al-Watan Forum* on May 2, 2004, and still appearing on many Arabic Islamic websites in 2012; originally printed in the Kuwayti Islamic magazine *al-Balagh*.

the *'ulama'* as a protective framework for Patanian society and identity. Arifin bin Chik, Abdullah La'umen and Suhaymi Isma'il write that before Siam and Holland attacked Patani together in 1634, Queen Ungu (r. 1624–1635) feared that if war broke out the *'ulama'* might be captured and killed so that no one would be left to transmit the religion. On the Queen's orders, the cleric Wan Husayn led the *'ulama'* with their families into the mountains of Talok Manok where they built a village and constructed a mosque. As Wan Husayn did not have the tools, nails, stone or bricks to build a foreign-style conventional mosque, he made it from wood; Talok Manok thus became the earliest example of a distinct Patanian style of mosque architecture. Arifin, La'umen and Suhaymi Isma'il weave this cluster of motifs — the monarchs and the *'ulama'* (Islam) in united resistance to Thailand, and a distinctly local aestheticism that retains its originality even as it taps the Middle East — into the political aims of such clerical scholars as the Shaykh Wan Ahmad Zayn al-Fatani (1865–1908). Their book states that Wan Ahmad had a blood connection to the long-departed Wan Husayn: Wan Ahmad was a scion of an extended family that had promoted Islam in politics and society, and had built and operated *pondok* Islamic schools for decades.[33]

In Patani, images of the past are political and military weapons akin to physical arms. As they continue to strive to contain this latest insurgency, the Thai military and intelligence are acutely aware of what strength the Patanian psyche draws from the oneness of Islam with the memory of a glorious Malay past. They must somehow separate or split those two elements of the alloy of Patanian nationality. In one foray in the psychological warfare waged to this end, a forgery posted over the internet assailed Patani's golden-age history as being against Islam. Neither the glorious queens nor their state could have been Muslim because they did not wear the *hijab* and they built a palace bigger than Patani's defining Krue Se mosque. Both the *Hikayat Patani* and the *Sejarah Kerajaan Melayu Patani* recorded the murder by one of those monarchs of two Muslims who disobeyed the order that brass not be taken out of Patani town (since the metal was needed to make weapons to defend the city from the Siamese). In calling themselves "Malay Muslims" the insurgents held themselves apart from non-Malay Muslims such as the Arabs: it was an old Zionist plot to split the Muslims into conflicting nationalities.[34] In this way, the Thai state sought to set the neo-Wahhabis

---

[33] Arifin, La'umen and Suhaymi Isma'il, *Patani: prawattisat lae kan mueang*, p. 254.

[34] See Duncan McCargo, "Patani Militant Leaflets and the Uses of History," in this volume.

and the insurgents at each other's throats. Yet this Thai intelligence author seemed unaware that the rebels closely study the struggles of their fellow Palestinian, 'Iraqi and Afghan "brethren" in *jihad*. They are liable to apply outside lessons at home because the enemy camp in Iraq, Afghanistan, and Patani is seen as one.

Nationalist Attitudes to the West

Patanians have for centuries possessed a sharp awareness of Westerners that is dualistic. As a mercantile state well-placed on international trade routes which were the source of its wealth, Patani in its golden age got to know well the Portuguese, the Dutch, the Spanish and the English as they established their international empires. Wariness about Westerners, the repeated drawing of parallels between modern Western imperial states (plus Zionist Israel) and "Siamese imperialism," were to recur in modern Patanian nationalist ideologies. But there was more often positive interaction between the state of Patani and the Dutch and the British, including the transfer of technologies to the Patanians through those useful foreigners. Post-1945 Patanian nationalists continued to hold some open, dualistic attitudes to various Western states, hoping on the one hand for economic and educational exchanges that the West could provide and which Patani badly needs, while distrusting some white non-Muslims on the other.

While not as yet printing any English words or phrases, *Sejarah Kerajaan Melayu Patani* already drew upon sources in English to flesh out the Westerners who came to Patani in its golden age. "Syukri" allows us to hear their voices in long quotations that he gives only in clear Malay translations. The main focus is on the English East India Company's ship *The Globe* (1611). Western sources underscore the international importance of Patani during its golden age, yet the limited acculturation of Patanians to Westerners in the 1950s still worked against the injection of slivers of English into Malay nationalist texts. Patanian ideologues were to inject English-language quotations through their works only from the 1990s, equipping Patanian youth for a much more radical engagement with America and its discourses.

The *Sejarah Kerajaan Melayu Patani* held the dualistic view that Westerners could either provide crucial aid or cause havoc. In 1603, European traders based in Patani provided guns and cannons to the Patanian war effort to beat back the Siamese. As to their destructive mode, "Syukri" noted the "hatred" that existed between the Portuguese, Dutch and English who competed with one another for trade in the region. In 1618, Dutch ships bombarded two English ships entering Patani's harbor; the cannon fire and explosions terrified the Patanians for five hours.[35] While radical jihadist Islamo-nationalists in Patani can now think of the Crusader West — "Siam" — Israel as one global enemy bloc, at the same time their nationalist literature has long orientated them to recognize diverse political units and conflicting national loyalties that divide Westerners.

For Ahmad Fathi al-Fatani in 2001, the golden age that Patani had enjoyed under its four queens corresponded to the West's expansion of trade with the East. On one hand, by 1538 there were 300 Portuguese residing in Patani for trade. Queen Hijau in 1602 gave permission to the Dutch to establish a trading station. But the Western peoples moving into Patani's region were also colonizers: Portugal occupied Melaka in 1511, Manila fell into the hands of the Spanish in 1571, and Holland conquered what it then called Batavia in 1619. Al-Fatani noted that Holland, during the reign of Queen Ungu, aided the two attacks by Siam upon Patani in 1632–1634 and 1636, both of which the Patanians defeated. Yet Patani's trade with the Dutch, Portuguese, British, and French Europeans brought it profits and prosperity.

Such dualistic relations with European powers in the first centuries of the Sultanate of Patani can *either* nurture within the Patanian nationalist ethos both a constructive openness to some non-Muslim states and their languages, cultures, technologies and economies, *or* confirm a binary, jihadist dichotomy of Crusader Westerners, who with their Siamese, Jewish and Hindu auxiliaries wage a global war against Muslims. As the middle-aged al-Fatani reflected in the beginning of his 2001 book on Patani history, while "the Muslims of Palestine, Kashmir, and now Bosnia undergo the bitterest sufferings, their condition is still better than that of the Muslims in Patani, because those other peoples and countries are still mentioned in international media and forums."[36]

Closer than al-Fatani to the beating heart of Patanian secessionist nationalism at the street level was, *Patani — Adit lae Patjuban* (Thai)/*Patani Dahulu dan Sekarang* (Malay)[37] published in 1977 by the "Patani Forces Research Panel." This book was written in the wake of mass protests in Pattani city in 1975–1976, sparked by an incident of brutality committed by Thai marines which brought onto the streets large numbers of Malay Muslim

---

[35] Syukri, *Sejarah Kerajaan Melayu Patani*, pp. 44–7, 50.
[36] Ahmed Fathi al-Fatani, *Pengantar Sejarah Patani*, pp. xii, 13, 19–20, 22–3, 27.
[37] "Patani: Past and Present."

protesters from a range of classes and diverse regions of the south. European traders in the pre-1800 period are again vividly portrayed in *Patani Dahulu dan Sekarang* from the English writings of Westerners who visited it for profit in its bygone golden age. Western sojourners are vividly presented as part of the pageantry of royal Patani.[38] Western and Thai sources, by filling gaps in the indigenous Malay record and memory, have made the nation's independent golden age much more detailed and compelling to the Patanians who advocate independence — and then to a wider audience.

Episodes from Patani's history which Patanian secessionists post onto the Arabic internet, following the standard Malay histories, similarly highlight the importance of international trade to Patani's classical prosperity. Contemporary Arabic-language discourse on websites thus repeat the tributes to Patani's wealth and affluence noted by contemporary Europeans, which modern Patanian nationalist historians had previously highlighted in earlier Malay and Thai works.[39]

Recent Thai-language-medium historians produced inside Patani itself take a similar stance. For example, Isma'il Benjasmith did not show a great dislike of global trade or suspicion of Westerners. He projected two possibilities: that Westerners could be an economic boon to Patani, and that Westerners could destroy Patani for trade supremacy. The possibility existed of a symbiotic overlap of interests. Benjasmith traced the development of Patani's relations with Holland and England under the fifth monarch, Raja Hijau. Benjasmith portrayed Queen Biru as concerned to develop relations with foreign powers for the long term, rather than a mere trader who must extract great profit from each discrete deal. For example, when the capital of traders who came from England or Holland ran low, she offered them loans so that they would not leave but could continue to trade in Patani.[40] At the same time, there was always the possibility that some Western state might conquer or destroy Patani — the jihadist reading of the West. Benjasmith

---

[38] A. Bangnara, *Patani Dahulu dan Sekarang*, pp. 18–20.

[39] "Fatani: Qissatu Sha'bin Muslimin" transmits the remark of the 18th-century Englishman Alexander Hamilton that Patani city had a male population aged from 16 to 60 of around 150,000 souls, lodged in houses whose successive close-set roofs a cat could traverse continuously with no need to return to earth because the houses were so close-set in the built-up city. This and other quotations from Hamilton had originally come from Ibrahim Syukri's Malay-language *Sejarah Kerajaan Melayu Patani*, pp. 60–1.

[40] Mohammad Zamberi 'Abdul Malek, *Ummat Islam Patani: Sejarah dan Politik*, p. 51.

does depict Holland as coming close to making itself a co-destroyer of Patani when in 1634, in return for the granting of a monopoly over the trade of sandalwood and deerskins in Thailand, it promised to bombard Patani city from the sea while the Thais attacked it from the land. However, the Dutch fleet did not arrive in time for the attack by the Thai army, which was beaten off by doughty Patani.[41]

Benjasmith's 21st-century Thai-language historiography, like Ahmad Fathi al-Fatani in Malay a few years before, thus represents a dualism about foreigners that resonates today, as multiple global states and entities are sucked into the Patani insurgency as never before. Patanians today view relations with Western countries as being able to offer economic and educational benefits but at the same time they harbor deep distrust of Western governments, suspect Western scholars of being possible CIA agents, and imagine both to be enemies of Islam, the Muslims and Patani. Similarly, European traders in the national golden age could turn unscrupulous. If they allied with the expanding Thai state for material benefit, the two together could wreak great harm on Patani. Yet in Benjasmith's retrospective view, those Westerners who considered conquering Patani through violence in order to exploit it, were not motivated by hatred of Muslims *qua* Muslims, *à la* the postmodern jihadist image of Westerners. Patanians are, of course, acutely conscious that Western states can invade Muslim countries, and recognize the close relationship that exists between Thailand and the United States. Some of them believe this relationship has ensured a steady flow of weapons to the Thai security forces even while the United States' government ritually criticizes interventions by the army in Thai politics.

Patani's Gradual Decline

A central trope in the historiography of Patani is its gradual decline and eventual fall. Changes from the 17th century in the routes on which trade was conducted in East and Southeast Asia caused much commerce that had formerly passed through the Patani emporium to bypass it. From 1615, the English and Dutch procured directly from Jambi the pepper that the Patanians had been procuring for them. Increasingly, the Dutch captured the trade of the region using their own strongholds. As the commerce, shipping,

---

[41] Ahmed Fathi al-Fatani, *Pengantar Sejarah Patani*, p. 47; Benjasmith, *Bot bat tan kan sueksa*, pp. 45–6.

and population of Patani shrank, its efforts to defend itself from Siamese attacks consumed much of its remaining resources.[42]

Arifin, La'umen and Suhaymi's 2007/2009 history of Patani, on the cover of which the silver-bright *kris* dagger gleams against the gloom, encompasses the whole timeframe of Patanian nationalist history. In a strict sense, Patani's golden age and sovereignty gradually ended from around the middle of the 17th century when its royal family melded into that of Kelantan. Not only did the Patani monarchs' primacy become spasmodic, but there was increasing migration by the Kelantanese into Patani. This deepening interaction of Patanians with other Malays to their south poses issues for Patanian nationalist thinkers and politicians because it touches on the subject of the delimitation of the nation and of community. Arifin, La'umen and Suhaymi view the period of union with Kelantan as positive, for instance cosmopolitan trade continued despite some decline from the golden age. They too present excerpts of the impressions of Patani by the English captain Alexander Hamilton (c. 1718). Merchants still came from Tonkin, China, Siam and South Asia to do business in a Patani that was safe and peaceful. Hamilton noted the strict respect that Patanians had for their monarchs — respect that lingers, although thinned out over time, within the diverse currents of Patanian nationalism in the 2000s.[43]

Again, this history has contemporary relevance. The era of the Patani monarchs' alliance with, and sometimes their subordination to, the royal establishment of Kelantan can provide historical justification for a modification to the Patanian nationalists' territorial delimitations of their political community. Some Patani nationalists, especially following the bad blood occasioned by Malaysia's cooperation with Thailand in security operations against them from 2000, would like Kelantan to be detached from Malaysia and join an independent Patani in a single state.[44]

The economic decline and political disorder of the 17th and 18th centuries did not put an end to the cosmopolitanism and plurality of languages in Patani. Henceforth, a literature, a class of religious scholars, and networks of Islamic schools, were established which spread a coherent Sunni

---

[42] Perret, "Patani dans les grands reseaux marchands du XVIIe siecle," in *Études sur l'histoire*, ed. Perret *et al.*, pp. 246, 254.

[43] Arifin, La'umen and Suhaymi, *Patani: prawattisat lae kan mueang*, pp. 137–8. On Hamilton's perception that trade was shrinking, see Teeuw and Wyatt, *Hikayat Patani*, p. 20.

[44] Personal communication.

Islamic intellectualism. The widening literacy in Arabic bound the Patanians more and more to the Arab world. Bilingual Sunni Islamic clerics, some of them resident in Arabia, increasingly became the backbone of resistance to incursions from "the traditional enemy": Siam.

The Buddhist Thai "Traditional Enemy" (*Musuh Tradisi*)

Patanian nationalist intellectuals have projected, and continue to project, a binary model of Siamese-Patanian relations. This model sometimes takes on pan-Malay features, for example when highlighting past aid to the Patanians in their struggle against Siam by rulers in what are today Malaysia and Indonesia. Ahmad Fathi al-Fatani (2001) noted that the first attempt by Siam to take Patani came at the height of its trading prosperity under Queen Hijau in 1616. For al-Fatani, the relationship between Siam and Patani would always be "akin to that between a fowl and the fox that wants to eat it." Her successor, Queen Biru, 50 years old when she came to the throne, sought a federation with Sultan 'Abdul Qadir of Kelantan in order to build a large united army to beat off the attacks from Siam which could come at any time. This alliance of "Greater Patani" lasted 131 years, to 1750. Al-Fatani also noted the savage clashes between southward-thrusting Thai forces and the federated Kelantese and Patanians under the succeeding "Kelantan Dynasty." Indeed, after leadership of the union passed to Kelantan, Raja Sakti I carved out an empire stretching up to Phatthalung, well to Patani's north, "as a means to try to hold off the attacks and thrusts of Siam to its south." However, al-Fatani also records the Thai title of "Phra Chao" or "female ruler" taken by Raja Dewi of Kedah when she was appointed ruler of Patani-Kedah in the earlier 17th century.[45]

Patanian intellectuals and their Arab supporters have, however, noted another different category of Muslims who were present in the courts and capitals of the various Thai states and who were active in their economic life. The Sa'udi Muhammad Nasir al-'Abudi wrote that Indian and Arab Muslim traders built influence even in the courts and retinues of the Thai kings, occasionally gaining high positions in the army and as governors as they furthered the interests of the state.[46] Thai officials have experienced centuries of interaction with Muslims, at home and abroad — notably with Iran — which gave them considerable cultural skills in understanding,

---

[45] Ahmed Fathi al-Fatani, *Pengantar Sejarah Patani*, pp. 20–1, 33–5.
[46] Muhammad bin Nasir al-'Abudi, *Fatani aw Janub Thailand: Dirasah wa Mushahadat* (Mecca: Muslim World League c. 1998), pp. 16–7.

utilizing, finessing and controlling them. Colonies of Islam-propagating foreign merchants did create a Muslim community in the Thai capital of Ayutthaya, which the court utilized as one link outward to Muslim India and the Middle East for trade.[47] Perret has speculated that the Muslim community in Ayutthaya, which had been founded as the Siamese capital in 1351, may have taken part in preliminary Islamization of the populations of Patani during its trading activities there.[48]

The pragmatic Thai state has always been aware of points of weakness in its position vis-à-vis a Patani which in religious, cultural and linguistic terms sometimes seemed almost another country. Its policy to make Patani part of Thailand has alternated between the use of, on the one hand, diplomacy, inducements, temporary retreats, indirection, persuasion, cooption of individuals, feints, superficial recognition of difference, and fleeting concessions, and on the other force, pervasive spying, repression and bursts of violence.

All formative golden ages of nations which nationalist ideologues construct anew must have their end, although thenceforth they haunt nationalists who struggle for a successor-state in order to duplicate their glorious bygone sovereignty. As a littoral country, Patani had always been dependent on its international trade, but from the end of the 17th century it had contracted to become a local port as international trade turned to Johor, Aceh and Banten. The shift in international shipping routes, combined with internal instability and the "unrelenting attacks by Siam" in the 18th century reduced Patani to a sleepy agricultural area that had lost its regional influence and erstwhile military strength, Ahmad Fathi al-Fatani lamented.[49] Yet this periodization, common to most nationalisms, misses the triumph of the late construction of a highly literate scholastic Sunni Islam that emerged precisely during the time of the late 18th-century economic contraction and the devastation caused by Siamese invasions. Nourished by the print editions of religious texts that Patanian intellectuals in the Middle East published from there, this scholastic literature supported the evolution of a rock-hard Arabic-Malay literate identity that was to prove tough for successive Thai regimes to wear down or split.

---

[47] M. Ismail Marcinowski, "The Iranian Presence in the Indian Ocean Rim: A Report of a Seventeenth-Century Safavid Embassy to Siam," *Islamic Culture* (April 2003): 59, 70–2.

[48] Perret, "Tombes musulmanes anciennes …," in *'Etudes sur l'histoire*, ed. Perret *et al.*, p. 167.

[49] Ahmed Fathi al-Fatani, *Pengantar Sejarah Patani*, p. 31.

Final Conquest and Absorption of Patani

In 1785, as the recently re-constituted Thai kingdom fought for its life with Burma, a military expedition was sent south to establish Thai garrisons in the Malay sultanates of Patani, Kedah, Kelantan, and Trengganu. Siam thenceforth made attempts to ensure the loyalty of its Malay vassal kings by balancing them with her own governors or commanders. In 1789, Bangkok faced an uprising in Patani that later caused it to change its administrative organization of those Muslim Sultanates. To disintegrate Malay power in 1817, Patani was broken up into seven much smaller principalities or *hua muang*. The rulers of these dependencies were still selected from the descendants of the old *rajas* or sultans, but they now had to be invested by the Thai king in Bangkok, who could withhold their investiture to sap the self-assertion of local Muslim rulers. This breaking up of the former sultanate still figures largely in the memory of Patanian nationalists. In the 1990s, Tengku Ramli Bin Tengku 'Abdullah, President of the Islamic Council in Narathiwat province and one of the descendents of the *raja* of that area, told Muhammad Bin Nasir al-'Abudi of Sa'udi Arabia's World Muslim League that Thailand's fragmentation of indigenous government in Greater Patani had been her most effective technique in bringing the former sultanate under her rule.[50] Yet Thailand's presence would for the rest of that century be confined to thin strips of Patani, and she would take many decades to construct even a semblance of a statal administration there in the 20th century.

Primary British documents collated by Francis Bradley suggest that Siamese armies conducted large-scale massacres, deportations and the systematic starvation of Patani Muslims following the wars of 1786 and 1838 in order to break all will to resist and to depopulate large stretches of the country.[51] After the crushing of a revolt in 1832, Thai forces seized the *rajas* of Ra-Ngae, Saiburi, and the president of the short-lived Raman "republic," together with thousands of their subjects, and transported them to Bangkok where the deportees were made slave laborers to develop the capital city's superstructure. These transfers or resettlements of whole populations also figure as polarizing motifs today in the Patanian nationalists' perceptions of the Thais. Such images, highly subjective, nonetheless are still among the political realities that shape the relations between these two peoples. Yet some Patanian historians make relatively small estimates of the original

---

[50] al-'Abudi, *Fatani aw Janub Thailand*, p. 89.
[51] See Bradley's chapter in this volume.

number of enslaved deportees. Ahmad Fathi al-Fatani estimated the number of Patanians whom Ayutthaya transferred up to Bangkok for slave labor following the 1832 uprising at 4000.[52] Yet in 2009, memories of the deported slave-laborers who "built canals and railroads [*sic*] from Sungai Golok up to Bangkok" fuelled the resolve of former students of the Islam Burapha school (*Ma'had al-Dirasat al-Islamiyyah*) in Muang District, Narathiwat, to "expel the Siamese from Patani." The school had been closed by the Thai authorities in July 2007 because its teachers were allegedly extolling *jihad* in the Arab world, Afghanistan and Patani, and even giving weapons training to those adolescents. Since a significant number of the Thai Muslims in central Thailand today are descendents of the Malays who underwent those deportations, oral memories nourish a pan-Islamic solidarity among some Thai-speaking Muslims with the Patanians to the south.[53]

Yet some Patanian nationalist historians also display a faint double-mindedness that registers historical interactions between Patanian Muslims and Buddhists which go beyond the usual theme of violence and exploitation. Siam long ago routinized relations with Muslim states in South Asia and the Middle East, and Muslims from there entered its elite. Muslims can even be represented as being on the "right side" of the Thai nationalist narrative. Arifin, La'umen and Suhaymi recount the famous story of Khunying Jan, the ("Malay Muslim") widow of the king of Phuket, who after the Burmese capture of that island led the resistance that drove them out. The Thai king Rama I then rewarded her and her sister with high titles. This episode has become a staple of Thai nationalist history thanks to the Thai education system, which has made Thais well-aware of the "patriotic" resistance of the two heroines Khunying Jan and her sister Muk against the Burmese enemy. Few Thais, however, are aware that the two sisters were actually Muslims.

Nevertheless, the Buddhists are not to be trusted. Arifin, La'umen and Suhaymi suggest that the ferocity and unreasonableness of the Thai Buddhists foredoomed any effort by Patanians to build a rational relationship with them. For example, in 1776 when the vassal king of Nakhon Si Thammarat revolted against Siam but was defeated, he fled south toward Patani for refuge. The pursuing Siamese commanders sent a letter to the King of Patani demanding that the fugitive be handed over, to which Patani duly complied. Later, King Taksin asked Sultan Muhammad of Patani for

---

[52] Ahmed Fathi al-Fatani, *Pengantar Sejarah Patani*, p. 65.
[53] Bougas makes the point that the Thai state's deportations of Malay populations for forced labor in part stemmed from the kingdom's sparse population and the consequent demand for manpower; Bougas, *The Kingdom of Patani*, p. 67.

money to help Siam make war on the Burmese, but was refused. Following the Chakri coup against Taksin and his execution, the new king, Rama I, ordered Patani to resume sending the "gold flower" to formalize the Patanians' submission to the Thai state under the new regime. The sultan refused, even though Patani had not fought a war for a long time. For Arifin, La'umen and Suhaymi, Patani's subsequent downfall was partly due to betrayal by a Siamese. Janthong, a Thai Buddhist who was made a minister to advise the sultanate in military affairs, pointed out to the Siamese army the weak points in Patani's defenses. The Siamese proceeded to conquer it in 1786, an event remembered today by Patani nationalists as the sultanate's great historic defeat from which it never recovered.[54]

The Patanian historians do document some Muslim heritage in both the old and modern Thai leaderships, including in 1786. In oral discourse today, some Patanians identify figures who blur the margin between Malayness/Islam and Buddhists in modern history. For example, the Buddhist leader of the New Aspiration Party, General Chavalit Yongchaiyudh, a former Commander of the Armed Forces and Prime Minister from 1996–1997, has an Indonesian wife who speaks the Malay of the south's Muslims; some Patanians even believe that Chavalit's grandfather was a Muslim. As Deputy Prime Minister in the former Thaksin government Chavalit denounced the arrests and "disappearances" of Patanians to the Thai National Assembly on March 18, 2004, based on data confided to him by villagers who trusted him as an avenue of appeal.

Nevertheless, a binary separation and dichotomization of the two nations is much more common. Patanian historians at most points depict Siam as an expansionist state that is too ferocious for any constructive coexistence with it to develop. True, Arifin, La'umen and Suhaymi sometimes betray misgivings that it could have been — and may still be today — courting self-harm for Patanians always to meet Thailand's expansionism with such unmodulated resistance, even when Patani is weak and unequipped. Their general psyche, though, thrills at the rejectionist opposition with which the Islamic Patanian people from Muzaffar Shah onward meets any attempt by Thailand to assert its presence in Patani, even when only symbolic.

Yet the reality of international networks, both economic and political, into which the Kingdom of Patani was plugged do not now, as a national historical memory, usually favor the development of blocist ideas that could

---

[54] See 'Arifin, La'umen and Suhaymi, *Patani: prawattisat lae kan mueang*, pp. 145–50.

dovetail into salafite global jihadism. If truth be told, the Kingdom of Patani benefited more from non-Muslim than Muslim trade. Western and Chinese, as well as Arab, traders were pervasive in the milieu in which Patanian identity evolved. Nevertheless, a bitter sense that Westerners — in particular the Anglophone Western states — maintain close links to Siam/Thailand and are callous about the survival of the Patanians, is manifest in Arifin, La'umen and Suhaymi's account of Siam's conquest and defeat of Patani in the late 18th and early 19th centuries. It was this crucial turning point for Patani that spurred diplomatic efforts by Malay states further south to win the protection of the British against further Thai expansion. This bad triangle between Siamese, Patanians and Westerners is developing and mutating still in our 21st century, so Patanian nationalist thinking goes.

On the place of the British in Patani's history, Arifin, La'umen and Suhaymi address the role of the high-caliber Englishman, Sir Francis Light, who at the fall of Patani governed Penang island at a time when the margin between the British state and England's private enterprise, already well-globalized by then, was blurred.[55] Light had to address the difficult issues of managing the flood of endangered refugees pouring into the neighboring Malay statelets as Siam smashed Patani, and the fears for their own safety on the part of those Malay states that were now tied to his own. Arifin, La'umen and Suhaymi portray Light as having been keenly aware of the extreme desperation and pitiful condition of the surviving refugees. He had mentioned in a letter of September 12, 1786 to General Charles Cornwallis, Britain's Viceroy in India, that the victorious Siamese roped together males, females, old people and children and then had them trampled to death by elephants. The viceroy of Siam in Patani had warned Kedah in August 1786 not to give any sustenance to those refugees (of whom there were 50,000 there alone). Fearful that Siam might attack, on September 24, 1786, the Sultan of Kedah sought British protection, but Sir Francis Light was unwilling to help Kedah perhaps because he himself was apprehensive of the might of Siam, so Arifin, La'umen and Suhaymi speculate. The view of Arifin, La'umen and Suhaymi is that the cold calculation of economic interests and geopolitics that already bound the Thais and the British ruled out the possibility of the latter giving any relief to the threatened refugees from Patani. Well before Rama I smashed Patani in 1785–1786, Light had sold 1,826 reasonably-priced guns

---

[55] Francis Light, founder of Penang Island and its capital Georgetown which became a crucial center of trade and progress in Malaya, was to go on to found Adelaide, the future capital of the state of South Australia.

to Siam, for which the then Siamese king Taksin conferred on him the royal title of Luang Yortawut ("Man of the Best Weapon").[56]

On the fall of Patani in 1786, Arifin, La'umen and Suhaymi do not appear eager to articulate the role of religion — Islam, Buddhism, or Christianity — as motivating the clashes between the Patanian Muslims, and Buddhists and Westerners. The three historians considered Englishmen like Light and those officials who signed the 1909 treaty with Siam as callous and preoccupied with profit and power, but did not represent them as harming Patani Muslims because Islam was their religion. Yet the role of Francis Light and other historical episodes are being seized upon by more radical ideologues, who seek to portray a jihadist division of the world into two warring camps composed of multiple nations: the Anglo-Saxon neo-crusaders-Thailand-India-Israel bloc on the one hand, and the pan-Islamic Patanian-Malay-Arab-Palestinian-Iranian-Indonesian-Muslim South Asia bloc on the other. The educated jihadist youth of the 21st century trace an incremental process that welded Buddhist Siam onto the Judeo-Christian Crusaders camp. The precedence that Light gave to trade with Siam over the lives of the Patanians resonates with Britain's handing Patani over to Siam in 1909's Anglo-Siamese treaty, in the alliance of the Thai state with the English-speaking United States following the Second World War, and in the Thai Buddhists' inter-meshing with America through the globalized economy. This supposed long-evolving Buddhist-Christian-Jewish bloc that fights Patani has reached a new stage with the military aid that America, along with its fellow Anglo-Saxon states, a range of European states, and Israel and India, provide to assist Thailand's efforts to crush the Islamic insurgency. It is no coincidence, a Patanian student youth reflected to me, that the main library at Prince of Songkhla University in Pattani city is named "the John F. Kennedy Library." The Siamese are migrating to the United States where Zionists propagate Zen Buddhism in America and the West, and even to Bangkok. The Americans, both Christians and Jews, and the Siamese long ago became one family of brothers (*ber-adek*). In

---

[56] Arifin, La'umen and Suhaymi, *Patani: prawattisat lae kan mueang*, pp. 151–3. 'Arifin, La'umen and Suhaymi in fact understated the extent of Francis Light's collaboration with the Siamese. As a sea captain, he had once warned them of an imminent assault by the Burmese on Phuket Island. The three nationalist historians also did not note actions by Light that affected the sovereignty of Malay rulers. By 1791, the Sultan of Kedah found his revenues were being drained by the growing prosperity of Penang. He built up a fort at Prye from where he could attack Light's administration but Light captured it on April 12, 1791 in a preemptive strike.

this apocalyptic view of their modern predicament, the Anglo-Saxon and Christian Crusaderist states, Buddhist Thailand, Israel and Hindu India constitute the tight-knit enemy bloc that the Patanians and their allies now have to defeat. From this point of departure, homegrown Patanian nationalist thought can now head off toward the international jihadism of al-Qa'idah and Nusantara's Jama'ah Islamiyyah.

Siamese Attempts to Construct Governance: To 1909

Following the siege and destruction of Patani in 1786, Siam attempted to establish enough control on the ground to regularly collect taxes from the hostile population. The Thai state strove to install itself in Patani's internal politics and governance by giving petty kings a stake in the system, whereby their sons or relatives could become their successors if they received the endorsement of Bangkok. Each petty monarch was to be balanced by a Siamese military commander from Songkhla or elsewhere. The nearly equal powers of Muslim rulers and the Buddhist soldier-governor would overlap. Arifin, La'uman and Suhaymi exult the stories of occasions when the very Malay figures which the Thai state appointed to build a presence and control on the ground sabotage its attempts.

For example, one of the appointed rulers, Pangkalan, along with his Malay high officials, had repeated conflicts with the new Siamese officials over Islamic laws and Malay culture. In 1808, King Pangkalan and the people drove the Thai officials — including Pracharat, Siam's governor — out of Patani. Bangkok responded by ordering the king of Nakhon Si Thammarat to send his troops to fight the Patani Malays. After months of fighting, though, they had to withdraw. Subsequently a heavily-armed Siamese force from Bangkok headed by Chaophraya Pulatep Bunnak marched on Patani with naval support. The assault was bravely resisted by King Pangkalan at Yamu town at Krue Se before he was finally killed by the sword of a Siamese soldier — as portrayed by the Patanian nationalist historians. Hot youths may read into Arifin, La'umen and Suhaymi here the lesson that to fight Siamese imperialism is a natural response not just for all Patanians but for all Malays. The three nationalist historians hold King Pangkalan up as an icon-model: "Datuk Pangkalan is a warrior-hero of the Patanian people. The historians of Patani record his name up to the present time."[57]

---

[57] Arifin, La'umen and Suhaymi, *Patani: prawattisat lae kan mueang*, pp. 157–60. A rudiment for this celebration of Pangkalan in Thai had been sketched by Ahmed Fathi al-Fatani in his 2001 *Pengantar Sejarah Patani*, p. 56.

Of these three authors — Arifin, 'Abdallah La'umen and Suhaymi Isma'il — Suhaymi vehemently stated to me in 2010: "I am an academic historian, NOT a nationalist." Yet 'Abdallah La'uman at least had links to pan-Islamic and Arabist issues not highlighted in either of the two 2007 Thai-language histories of Patani to which he contributed. In his youth, he worked at the Thai-language *al-Jihad* magazine of Ibrahim Qurayshi, who wrote a jihadist history of the Crusader Wars ("*Songkhram Kruset*"), which young Patanians continue to devour today. While at that Bangkok-produced magazine, La'uman published Thai articles on the high civilization of Muslim Spain that fell to the pitiless Christians, although his writings on classical Arabs were more often like liberal Islamic apologetics in Egypt and South Asia that took pride in the sciences and Islamic classical culture, rather than in fighting. Like the Arabophone Ahmad Fathi al-Fatani, the very young La'umen was also influenced by Egypt's Muslim Brotherhood with its call for an Islamic state, its preparedness to consider insurrection against the "secular" pan-Arab Nasser to win that state, and even for war against the neo-Crusader West.

Neither Arifin, Abdullah La'uman, nor Suhaymi could understand much Arabic, which the pro-Arab and pro-Iran pan-Islamist youth of Patani cultivate to surf the jihadist websites on the internet. Thai was the language of their formal education. Suhaymi developed his career in Thai statal institutions, earning an MA from the National Institute of Development Administration. By 2008, he was teaching religion in the sociology section of the Yala Technical College. Suhaymi's rivals whisper that his circle was involved in organizing demonstrations in Yala and Pattani City when President Bush ordered the invasion of Iraq. Suhaymi retorts that he only met the pro-Arab, pan-Islamic activists once or twice at social gatherings. These historians live in literary Thai, and write their history of Patani to reconcile all Thais in an intellectual climate that has seen a loosening-up of the former constraints on the public discussion of Patani's history. While they are writers from Patani who try to represent its concerns and vital interests, they are considerably removed from the views of the hot-headed young Arabophone graduates of the *pondok*, *madrasah*, or of al-Azhar who view Saddam Husayn and Bin Laden as heroes.

Patanian nationalist historians who have recently written in Thai are as liable as the Malay-language historians, on whose works they have drawn, to dichotomize Patani's history into the golden age under the sultanate, and the era of decline amid tightening Thai control that followed Thailand's dividing-up of Patani into the seven statelets (*hua muang*). But the trio, Arifin bin Chik, Abdullah La'umen and Suhaymi Isma'il, accurately capture the picture of ongoing resistance from the subordinated petty monarchies that now had to be cultural and religious in approach, rather than by armed violence. Tuan Sulong, appointed ruler of the shrunken "Pattani" statelet, was a nephew of its previous King, Pangkalan, the *icon*-hero who had fought to his death against the Thais. Tuan Sulong took a close interest in Islamic matters and tried to repair the Krue Se mosque and the symbolic ancient Pintu Gerbang mosque which had been damaged in the war. Sulong believed that Krue Se in the past had been the center of Patani and the Malays in Southeast Asia and where many had once come to trade. The Krue Se mosque had been a center for the diffusion of Islamic culture out over the whole of Southeast Asia. The Shaykh Dawud al-Fatani spent most of his life in the Arabian peninsula, writing, but Arifin, Abdullah La'umen and Suhaymi Isma'il imply that King Sulong was the patron who got him started. For them, al-Shaykh Dawud was an author of works that promoted Islam and won him greater fame than anybody else.[58] The reduction of indigenous power by overwhelmingly superior Thai garrisons had led royal families of Patani to widen their promotion of Islam in order to build legitimacy and veiled soft power as a core for a later restored sovereignty. This motif of the ruler repeatedly fostering and protecting mosques, and the fame of Patani's religious scholars, identifies nationalist historians like Arifin, La'umen and Suhaymi Isma'il as reasonably "Islamist" in their definition of Patanian sovereign nationality.

The role that Britain assumed in the early 20th century was in line with a centuries-long history of influential Western powers in Patani, and the duality with which its Muslims regarded those outsiders. There has been apprehension among Patanian Muslims about the possibility that Western states could expand into Patani and come to control or administer it. While rule by any non-Muslims is unpalatable to Islam, and some Patanians over the centuries have indeed opposed the Portuguese, the Dutch and the British (and now, America), others have preferred a presence and degree of control by Westerners to the southward thrust of "the more violent and threatening Thai Buddhist state." For example, the pink-Islamic 1977 work, *Patani Dahulu dan Sekarang*, without much comment excerpted written appeals that Patani's last sultan, Tunku 'Abdul Qadir Qamarud-Din, sent to Sir Frank Swettenham in Singapore in 1901 appealing to the British to expel the Siamese oppressors from the south and save his people from "destruction."[59] Similarly, Patanian secessionist forces headed by the émigré Patanian prince

---

[58] Ibid., pp. 165–6.
[59] *Patani Dahulu dan Sekarang*, pp. 42–3.

Muhyiddin after the Second World War tried to coax the British into taking Patani away from Thailand and integrating it with the Malaya they still administered as it headed for independence.

This review of the Patanian nationalists' version of the history of Patani up to Britain's recognition of the Thai state's sovereignty over it in 1909, has given attention to the ongoing tensions and intermittent outbursts of bloody fighting between the precursor-states of modern Thailand and the Malay Muslim people of Patani. Yet the latter today is to some extent culturally affiliating itself with the Thai people. In comparison to Western and Thai Buddhist historians, Patanian authors have underrated the ancient affinities and connections of their people to the Buddhist Thais, and the regular economic interactions that have been lucrative to both parties. Nevertheless, the emphasis in much nationalist historiography is on political conflict and war between the two evolving peoples. Islam, though in some ways initially lax in Patani's royal courts, was there as a rallying-point for resistance, along with the Malay language (transcribed in the *Qur'an*'s Arabic letters as *Jawi*), to help Patanians further differentiate themselves from what was being constructed as their defining enemy (*musuh*) in history — Siam.

The Consolidation of Islam in Patani's Identity

Although the Patani kingdom lost its prosperity and population after the golden age of the four queens, it was by no means a backwater of the world of Islam but indeed, now became one of its intellectual centers in Southeast Asia. This would never be an easy people for Thai regimes, even the later ones with the multiple instruments of modern government at their disposal, to deculturize and "Thaify." The crushing of the royal state of Patani only speeded up the production of Arabic-script intellectual works on Islam by Patanians from the strategic depth of the Middle East. With that print-learning coming in on the steamers, Islamic clerics in Patani waxed as defenders of Patanian Muslim identity.

Islamic mysticism or Sufism (*tasawwuf*) has centuries-old roots in Patani. It too entailed close interaction with Arabs and Arabic, as did the adoption of the Sunni *shari'ah* law and Baghdad's old theological learning that could open into rational arguments for Islam from the ancient Greeks.[60] Patani's *tasawwuf* mysticism was very much drawn from a literate Sunni

---

[60] Virginia Matheson and M.B. Hooker, "Jawi Literature in Patani: The Maintenance of a Tradition," *Journal of the Malaysian Branch of the Royal Asiatic Society* 61, 1 (1988).

orthodox Islam in the Middle East. It moved the emphasis from the "unity of existence" ideas of Ibn 'Arabi toward Abu Hamid al-Ghazzali's sober *tasawwuf* that desired the implementation of Sunni religious law. Patani has always had the Islamic cultural grit to defend against attacking non-Muslims. The Patanian al-Shaykh Dawud al-Fatani's *fiqh* works of the late 18th and early 19th centuries made resistance against attacking polytheists mandatory. A Patani intellectual told me in 2006 that this legist's *fatwas* defining the Thais as "idol-worshipping infidels" who had to be expelled with *jihad*, were still taught in the Islamic *pondok* from which he graduated in the 1980s. No Patanian Islamic scholar has ever issued a counter-*fatwa* to annul that one, he smiled.[61]

Benjasmith's account of the Shaykh Dawud takes us into the modern Middle East sanctuary of the Patanians, where pan-Islamists and pan-Arabs come to improve their Arabic. Benjasmith in his biography notes that the Shaykh Ahmad Bin Wan Zayn Bin Wan Mustafa al-Fatani (1856–1908) was of Hadrami extraction and some Arabic was spoken in his childhood home in Patani. It was he who, from the Ottoman Empire and Egypt, arranged to have the Shaykh Dawud's Malay books printed and sent by steamer back to Patani for fear that Islam might be dying out there. Shaykh Ahmad knew the Sharif Husayn who led the Hijazi uprising against the Turks in the First World War. Benjasmith speculated that Shaykh Ahmad had already tried to get the Ottoman Sultan 'Abdul Hamid, through Britain, to oppose the consolidation of the thin and shaky Thai state in Malay areas. But did Benjasmith have an integrationist streak? In his 2007 work, he did not regret that Queen Kuning agreed to send the flowers of gold again to the king of Ayutthaya, and that Patani and Siam then put that blood-letting behind them.[62]

By 1909, the point at which the imposition of a still very thin and shaky Thai rule was internationally recognized, the Patanian Muslims had built an integrated historical and cultural personality. The sense of a delimited Patani homeland, sovereign before the coming of the Thais, is linked to a strong loyalty to literate Malay conceived of as a sacred Islamic language, the auxiliary language of Arabic which is the channel outward to classical Islam, and a modern Middle Eastern history of Arab nationalism and *jihad*. Malay

---

[61] True, in some *pondok*, such a *fatwa* of Dawud is unknown.

[62] Benjasmith, *Bot bat tan kan sueksa lae kan muang khong chaik wan ahmad al-fatani*, pp. 191–7, interview August 9, 2010/28 Sha'ban 1431AH, and his photographic exhibition at the Festival of Education in Southern Thailand, Yala City, August 8–9, 2010.

translations of Arabic legal and Sufi works in *Jawi* script gave the high Islam from the Middle East a wide audience among ordinary Malays. True, there remains a simple or diluted folk-Islam in Patani, but it is overlapped by literate formulations of Shafi'i Islam derived from the Arabs. The porous folk-Islam and magic, and the similarly porous literate scholastic Islam, blur into each other — much to the concern of the neo-Wahhabis.

Senior Thai administrators themselves concede that this imagined sultanate is an objective factor in mass politics in Patani which stymies the best efforts of Bangkok to master the "Deep South." In August 2009, Thaworn Senniam, Deputy Interior Minister in charge of a burst of development projects in the south, had to concede that human beings are not swayed by individual material interests alone. For this reason, in his view, returning the south to "normal" would take at least 20 years. He encouraged people to come up with projects they wanted. For example, one group of traditional fishermen had asked the government to fund their artificial reef projects to provide them with a habitat for marine life and to provide them with fishing gear. Yet, he reflected, "it is a tough job to change local people's minds and attitudes about the history of the Malay peninsula and Siam" (the former name of Thailand).[63] The *Saudara* ("Brotherhood") students at Prince of Songkhla University take these history books back home to their villages in Narathiwat in the holidays. Teenagers at the grassroots, too, now read or hear these historical accounts. The two editions of Arifin, La'umen and Suhaymi's thick history (in the Thai language) sold out quickly. Some tertiary youth deduce from those sufferings and losses in Patani's torturous history that the way out is the *jihad* for independence — "*kemerdekaan.*" Even taxi-drivers in Patani's growing towns who mostly speak Thai know this Malay term.

Conclusion

This overview of the historiography of the formation and struggles of the Patanian people over the centuries highlights historical motifs which resonate to the present day. Islam cumulatively diffused across a range of classes as the defining frame of the state and of the nation. The Patanian mercantile state declined, the population thinned, but the religion has always maintained its incremental growth as a high intellectual system sustained by a burgeoning network of religious boarding schools or *pondok*. Those schools diffused their religious instruction and Malay works which drew upon Arabic learning

---

[63] *Bangkok Post*, August 8, 2009.

out among peasant masses in the villages. Islam has provided a culture and ideology that link different classes and functional groups, often in resistance to the Thai state, despite the gradual integration of the Patanians into that state via language and even some aspects of Thai intellectual culture. The past sovereignty and greatness of Patani under its sultans and queens, made so solid in a range of Malay and Thai historical works, fills today's Patanian youth with a soaring confidence that they too can soon wrest back that independence which is evoked by the extremists as inherent to their nationality. The delay in the coming of independence is only a manifestation of the wisdom (*hikmah*) of Allah to test the belief, endurance and patience of Patani's Islamic Malays.

Young internet warriors argue the Patanians must take pride in the fact that they were "the last Malays to be colonized in this archipelago. When the Portuguese established themselves in Melaka and Indonesia in 1511, Patani continued to enjoy its independence." It was only conquered in a qualified way in 1786, which made the Thais only one player among several. Patani underwent real colonization only with the Anglo-Siamese treaty of 1909. "The Patanians are truly a formidable people of prowess and might," as one Malay-language posting on a blog site proclaimed.[64] The post-1980 nationalist historiography published from Malaysia feeds the current insurgency in Patani with a super-optimism about the future of Patani. It can also, however, at the same time feed a fear of the West in a globalized Islamist paradigm that dichotomizes Western and Islamic countries into two warring blocs. While Patani's past greatness through trade is stressed, this globalized IT-jihadist view does not want even economic interaction with Westerners, the infidel world bloc of which Thailand is one member:

> Rise up brothers and sisters! Expel Siam! Patani is not the property of Siam or Thailand, but of the Malay people. They are descended from a skilled voyaging race that flourished before the advent of the Portuguese, Dutch and English imperialists in our Malay Nusantara Archipelago. All those foreign nations are betrayers who envied the successes of the Malay Race in carrying out trading ventures and buying and selling with the Arab People of the Islam religion in our Archipelago. They are fearful that Islam would cause all the triumphs of the Archipelago-wide Malay race to make it an international superpower in coming times …

The classical history of Patani is drawn upon to provide guidelines about how to vanquish the Siamese occupiers. In one of several victorious wars, Patani

---

[64] Post by "Hasan" at http://www.patanibook.blogspot.com, May 5, 2008, 4:23 am.

had conquered all of Thailand up to its capital with Muzaffar Shah's attack on the royal palace at Ayutthaya. They skillfully constructed great cannons. "We certainly have the capacity to vanquish them again now." Before the conquest, the Patanian Muslims had been more advanced than the Siamese, but under the corrupt governments of Thailand they went backward in all fields. The glorious achievements of the earlier Patani sultanate now motivate nationalist Patanians to make Malay once again the formal language of administration, law and the judiciary, science and technology in the border provinces of southern Thailand. To return the Malay language, its literature and *Jawi* script, and the history it recorded to their former glory in Patani would end the current threat to Patani's survival.

We see in such Islamo-nationalist visions how the glorious trading past of the sultanate and its "commercial ethic" validate the aspirations of a newly forming Muslim bourgeoisie which seeks to achieve modern commercial livelihoods, build roles in globalization, and fill the apparatus of a new state. Malaysia has won international respect as a possible model country for the global *ummat* of Islam. Since that country had been built by Malays, it is possible that an independent Patani would duly become even more advanced.[65]

In their sense of a wider ethno-linguistic "Nusantara" region that extends far beyond the Patani homeland, of past trading links and a literate language that binds the peoples of this archipelago together, of a national language under threat from colonial occupation, and of encounters and sometimes conflict with global religions, civilizations and economies, 21st-century Patanian internet nationalism reveals old Sukarnoist and pan-Arab DNA. Classical Arabic, too, had been endangered by the use of a colonial language in the Egypt of 1952 as well as in the French Algeria of 1954. Nasser's Egypt, Boumadyan's Algeria, and nationalist pre-1965 Indonesia all imposed a reinvented national book-language at break-neck speed. Sukarno's linguistic and territorial nationalism had a pan-Malay Nusantara extension, while President Gamal 'Abd al-Nasser's pan-Arab regime (1952–1970) sometimes read a Crusading, religious dimension into Western and Israeli attacks.

For centuries, global trade led the Patanians to engage with a range of languages and cultures, most of them non-Muslim. The Patanians have always been a small people situated on converging fault-lines between highly

---

[65] *Patanikini* [*Our Patani*] at http://patanikini.wordpress.com/2007/08/22/patani-merayu-kapada-bangsa-sendiri/, September 6, 2007, 7:30 am.

disparate Indic-Buddhist, Arabo-Islamic and Malay, and modern Western civilizations. The Patanians formed as a globalized people at a key point of an Islam-mediated international trading system that connected North Africa, the Middle East, South Asia, Southeast Asia, China and Japan. The plurality of languages and cultures in Patani was further elaborated by the development of Islamic formal education which traditionally alternated between bursts of Arabic and explanatory Malay. Then, from the close of the Second World War, literate Islamic Patanians progressively sharpened their comprehension of Western intellectual culture and its medium, the English language. With time, even the "Buddhist" language of the Thais would penetrate the Muslim population in Patani — not excluding the institutions of Islam. But the late modern and post-modern era have also provided new channels for Arabic and the Arabs to surge into the psyche of the Patanians. The ever more diverse languages in Patani have caused mutations in perceptions of a continuous national history, including in Islamic ideologies of resistance.

This small Malay-Muslim people in southern Thailand could on its own only have managed a thin recreation of Patani's earlier era of greatness and its pre-Islamic past. However, the modern academic institutions of Malaysia have trained some Patanian scholars and students in modern, Western historical methodologies, and have then acted in aggregate as a huge publishing house of nationalist Patanian historiography. An ideologically structured historical literature is a precondition for nationalist independence movements to succeed.

When allowances are made for constraints on the ground — political, of course, but also the limited number of academic institutions until recently in southern Thailand — Patanian intellectuals have successfully transmitted from academics linked to the West and even Thai Buddhist scholars, vivid details about the early mercantile greatness of Patani but also its pre-Islamic history. And now something much more like modernity's standard literate nationalisms is taking form in southern Thailand. However, we live in a postmodern world of which Thailand is a dynamic unit. There are opportunities here for Muslims who can shake off particularistic nationalisms. The secessionists have to hammer out a compromise deal with the Thai state in which their links to the Arabs, Malaysians and Indonesians via their specialized language and cultural skills, could bring profit for both Patanians and for Thailand's expanding capitalism. Malay Patanians and Thais could make good money together in ASEAN and the Arab World. That may be the best way forward to peace for both parties.

CHAPTER 10

Historical Identity, Nation, and History-Writing: The Malay Muslims of Southern Thailand, 1940s–1980s

Kobkua Suwannathat-Pian

Evidently it was the recalcitrance and rebelliousness of Patani that led King Rama I (1782–1809) to break the sultanate up into seven political units, called *hua muang* or principalities.[1] The main aim was to weaken the resources which had enabled Patani to repeatedly defy Bangkok's authority. These Seven Principalities — Tani, Jaring/Yaring, Legeh/Ra-ngae, Saiburi, Raman, Yala and Nongchik — were separate political units with individual Malay rulers appointed by Bangkok. These Malay rulers were given the status of frontier provincial governors answerable to the governor of Songkhla, then Bangkok's viceroy for the lower southern region. In retrospect, it is clear that with the 1809 disintegration of the old sultanate, Patani had lost not only its

---

[1] On the history of relations between the Sultanate of Patani and Siam, see Kobkua Suwannathat-Pian, *Thai-Malay Relations: Traditional Intra-Regional Relations from the Seventeenth to the Early Twentieth Centuries* (Singapore: Oxford University Press, 1988), and "Historical and Contemporary Conditions of Muslim Thais," in *Muslims' Rights in non-Muslim Majority Countries*, ed. Abdul Monir Yaacob and Zainal Azam Abdul Rahman (Kuala Lumpur: Institute of Islamic Understanding Malaysia, 2002), pp. 1–28; Surin Pitsuwan, "Islam and Malay Nationalism: A Case Study of the Malay Muslims of South Thailand," PhD thesis, Harvard University, 1982; Ibrahim Syukri, *Sejarah Kerajaan Melayu Patani* [*The History of the Malay Kingdom of Patani*], trans. Connor Bailey and John Miksic (Columbus: Ohio University Press, 1985); Omar Farouk, "The Muslims of Thailand," in *Islamika: Esei-Esei Sempena Abad ke Limabelas*

prathetsarat or tributary status but also its geo-political body. Since then, the Sultanate of Patani no longer appeared in geo-political maps of Southeast Asia. By the mid-19th century, relations between Bangkok and the Seven Principalities entered into an era of peaceful coexistence. Yet Bangkok, as a

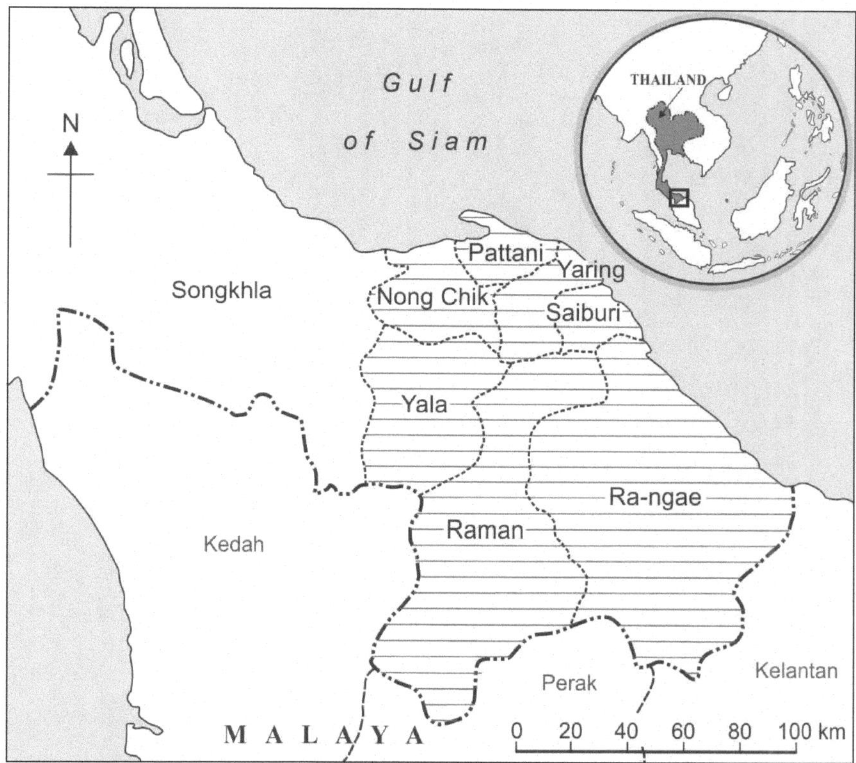

Map 10.1 Map showing the division of the former Sultanate of Patani into seven principalities (*hua muang*) in the early 19th century.

Hijrah, ed. Lupti Ibrahim (Kuala Lumpur: Sarjana Enterprise, 1981); A.D.W. Forbes, ed., *The Muslims of Thailand, Vol. 2*, *Politics of the Malay-speaking South* (Bihar: Centre for Southeast Asian Studies, 1989); Wan Kadir Che Man, "The Demise of the Patani (Pattani) Sultanate: A Preliminary Enquiry," in *National Past: National History and National Historiography in Brunei, Indonesia, Thailand, Singapore, the Philippines and Vietnam*, ed. Putu Davies (Brunei Darussalam: Department of History, UBD, 1996); Rattiya Salleh, "Patani Darussalam (Melayu-Islam Patani)," in *Rat pattani nai 'sivichai'* [*The Patani Polity within the Srivijaya Empire*], ed. Sujit Wongthes (Bangkok: Matichon, 2004) and Nik Anuar Nik Mahmud, *Sejarah Perjuangan Melayu Patani 1785–1954* [*A History of the Struggle of the Patani Malays, 1785–1954*] (Bangi: Penerbit Universiti Kebangsaan Malaysia, 1999).

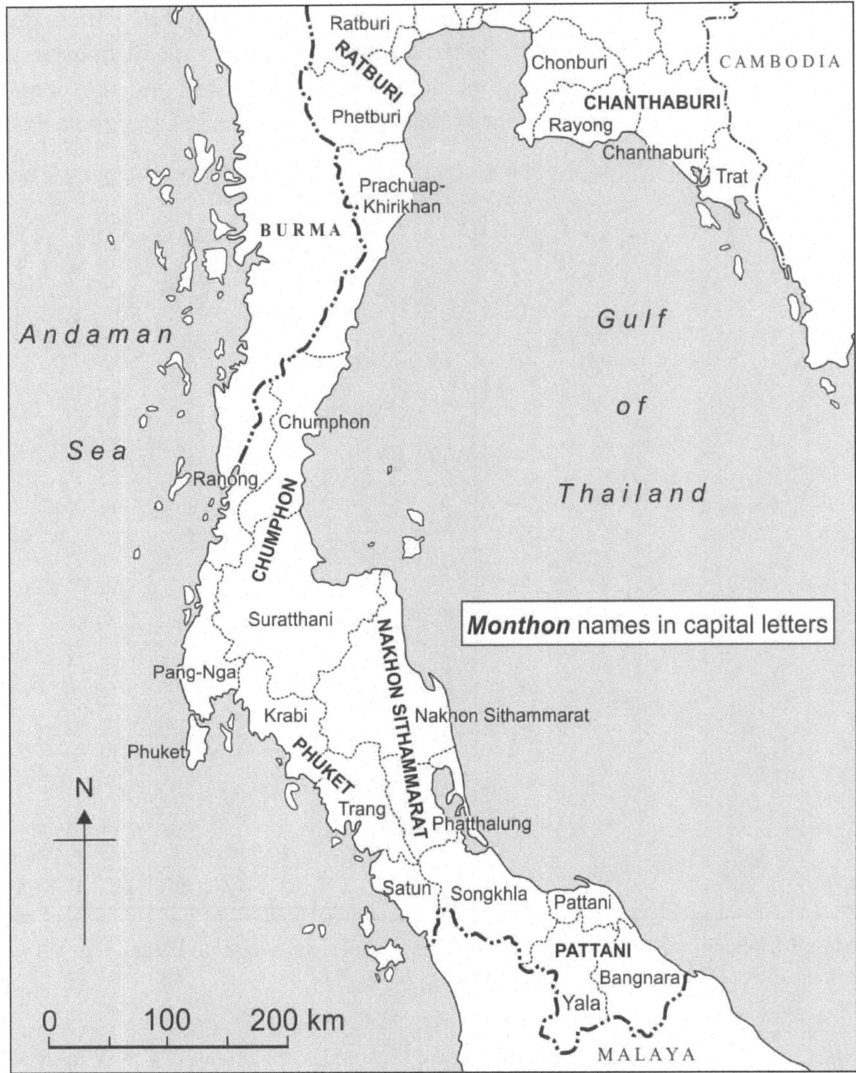

Map 10.2 1915 map showing the new *monthon* (administrative divisions) of southern Siam, including the *monthon* of Pattani.

result of ever-increasing pressure from the Western colonial powers, began to implement a comprehensive restructure of its provincial administration in the Seven Principalities at the beginning of the 20th century. The objective of the provincial administrative reform was to transform Siam from a feudal and traditionally fragmented kingdom into a modern unified state with the authority of Bangkok effectively prevailing over all Siamese territories.

The politico-administrative development of the years 1896–1907 is without doubt the key historical cause of the modern socio-political conflict between the Thai central government and the Malay Muslim leadership in southern Thailand. The 1896–1902 restructure of the Seven Principalities transformed these semi-tributary polities into integral, inner provinces of the kingdom with the *raja*/ruler-governors losing what remained of their executive and administrative powers as well as their rulership status. Three rulers, Tani, Sai and Legeh (Ra-ngae), found the new administrative order especially unacceptable. Under the leadership of Tengku Abdul Kadir, the newly-appointed ruler of Tani, the three rulers sought the intervention of Great Britain through the British colonial regime in Malaya to release them from the political clutches of Bangkok. Such intervention, however, never materialized. The 1901–1902 uprising of the *jet huamuang* was swiftly and firmly put down with the arrest of the ruler of Tani who was kept under house arrest in Phitsanulok, while his accomplices suffered the loss of their positions.[2] The Seven Principalities became officially an integral part of Siam by the Royal Decree of 1901/R.S. 120. In spite of sporadic local disturbances, Bangkok was able to follow up its plan to incorporate the Seven Principalities within the kingdom proper with little difficulty. Between 1905 and 1906, all the remaining attributes of a frontier province were abolished and in 1907 the Principalities were reorganized into three *monthon* ("administrative spheres") of Pattani (Tani, Yaring and Nongchik), Yala (Yala and Raman) and Bang-Nara (Sai and Legeh). Finally, after the 1932 Revolution and the abolition of the *monthon* system, the three *monthon* re-emerged as provinces. The provinces of Pattani, Yala and Narathiwat now formed an inalienable part of the geo-body, to borrow Thongchai's terminology, of the Thai kingdom.[3]

The incorporation of the Patani territory did not, however, succeed in changing the socio-cultural and historical identity of the Malay Muslim inhabitants of Patani. Since the beginning of the 20th century, the Malay Muslims of the three provinces were well aware of their close historical ties, their shared socio-political experiences, and their Islamic brotherhood. Evidently they were alive to the fact that they were of different historical

---

[2] Tej Bunnag, *Khabot R.S. 121* [*The 1902 Uprisings*] (Bangkok: Project for the Social Sciences and Humanities Textbooks, 1981); Kobkua, *Thai-Malay Relations*, pp. 176–82.

[3] Thongchai Winichakul, *Siam Mapped: A History of the Geo-Body of a Nation* (Honolulu: University of Hawai'i Press, 1994).

and socio-cultural molds to their compatriots in other parts of Thailand.[4] The consciousness of a Malay Muslim identity made efforts on the part of Bangkok to "modernize" the Deep South a challenging exercise. The Malay Muslims' apprehension of the Thai state's designs to dilute their historical and socio-cultural identity led to increasing mistrust and suspicion of Bangkok. Even before the enforcement of the nationalist assimilation policy during and after the Second World War, this historically rooted identity contributed, maybe as much as the Thai authorities' insensitivity and abuses of power, toward the unhappy and hostile relations between the Thai government and Malay Muslims.

From Bangkok's perspective, the Siamese leadership's legitimacy in incorporating the former Sultanate of Patani into the kingdom proper was based on the principle of conquest through war, which made Patani "a Siamese property, a gain from war a long time ago."[5] The principle of conquest by war was an accepted practice before and during the colonial era. Great Britain, the dominant colonial power on the Malay Peninsula, not only concurred with the action taken by Bangkok but also provided protection for Siamese claims over Patani through the signing of the Anglo-Siamese Secret Treaty of 1897.[6] In fact, Great Britain appeared ready to apply such principles to secure the former Patani provinces from Bangkok following the end of the Second World War and make the old Patani a spoil of the British war victory, a state within the British Federation of Malaya. Only strong objections by its great and powerful war ally, the United States, prevented London from realizing Britain's postwar ambition.

---

[4] These differences have been well documented by one of the leaders of the separatist movements, Wan Kadir Che Man, who argues for the separation of Patani (together with Satun) from Thailand based on the following perceived differences: (i) ethnicity (Malay and Thai); (ii) religion (Islam and Buddhism); (iii) history (the Patani sultanate and the Siamese kingdom); and (iv) language (Malay and Thai); see Wan Kadir Che Man, "The Problem of Patani Malays in South Thailand: Neither Assimilation Nor Separation," in *Nork niyam khwam pen thai. Thai-Patani: muea rao mai at yu ruam lae baeng yaek jak kan dai* [*Outside the Definition of Thainess. Thai-Patani: Neither Assimilation nor Separation*], ed., trans. Prinya Nuanpian (Songkhla: Institute of Peace Studies, University of Prince of Songkhla, 2008), p. 20.

[5] R. 5, M.2.22 Ng., vol. 2, Memorandum of the Conversation between Prince Devawong, Lord Salisbury and Philip Currie on the Raman Border Dispute, July 1887, in Devawong to Chulalongkorn, August 9, 1887.

[6] Thamsook Numnonda, "The Anglo-Siamese Secret Convention of 1897," *Journal of the Siam Society* 53, 1 (January 1965): 45–60.

Up to the end of the Second World War, the status of the three southern provinces of Pattani, Yala and Narathiwat, and Bangkok's authority and legitimacy over them had never seriously been an international issue. Nonetheless, awareness of their socio-historical identity had often inspired the Thai Malay Muslim leaders in the three provinces to demonstrate their unhappiness with Bangkok's rule. This unhappiness came in the form of disturbances which at times broke out into armed conflict with the central and provincial authority, for example, the 1923 uprising against the Compulsory Education Act of 1921.

The assimilation policy which was applied vigorously by the Phibun government during the Second World War added socio-political fuel to the fire of Malay Muslim discontent. It led to an escalation of hostility and mistrust among the Thai Malay Muslims against Bangkok. After the Second World War, Thai Malay Muslim leaders took full advantage of the weakened postwar political status of Bangkok in the international arena and the latter's uncertain political and territorial future. They were able to mobilize world opinion to support their plight and to attract great sympathy for their struggle to be liberated from Thai rule. As stated above, Great Britain, in particular, seriously entertained their desire to become a part of British Malaya. The 1945–1948 years represented the height of the Thai Malay Muslims' anti-Bangkok campaign. Simultaneously conducted both in and outside of southern Thailand, the campaign successfully applied pressure on the Thai government to concede at least to the substance of their demands against the unjust, oppressive and often incompetent nature of Bangkok's administration over the Thai Malay Muslims.

The year 1945 in fact marked the beginning of the new chapter in the Thai Malay Muslim struggle against Bangkok. Between 1945 and the 1980s, the Malay Muslim desire to be masters of their own community took myriad forms and objectives, ranging from autonomy under the conservative leadership of the traditional rulers, to inclusion as a state within the Federation of Malaya, and finally to an independent Patani.

Often referred to as "bandits," "terrorists," and later as "separatists" by the Thai authorities, the postwar Malay Muslim leaders and organizations are now no longer bound by the socio-political tradition of their predecessors. They have taken their fight to the international community, especially to the universal Muslim brotherhood. More sophisticated in their understanding of and ability to adjust to the changing world, the new Malay Muslim leaders have proved themselves capable of mobilizing both international and domestic resources and support, covert and overt, for the cause of their people. They have become a political thorn in the administrative flesh of the Thai government.

Fundamental Differences and Historical Identity

Buried deep in the long-drawn-out conflict and violence was the legacy of strong suspicion and mistrust entertained by both the Thai authorities and the Thai Malay Muslim community against each other. Such suspicion was largely a result of mutual socio-cultural ignorance and bigotry. To the Thai authorities in Bangkok, the Thai Malay Muslims' insistence on maintaining their socio-cultural and ethnic identity as Malay and Muslim in the era when loyalty and patriotism to the homogeneous nation were the premium requirements of good and responsible citizens, served as ample evidence of Malay disloyalty to the country of their birth. Conversely, the Malay Muslims of the former Sultanate of Patani were deeply suspicious of Bangkok and its policy of modernization of the south and assimilation of the Malay Muslims into the national socio-cultural and economic mainstream. To most Malay Muslim leaders, the real aim of such policies was the erasure of their socio-cultural and ethnic identity. As a result, they objected strongly to the official use of the term "Thai Muslims" employed to identify their community and individual Malay Muslims. Malay Muslim leaders vigorously stated that they were not ethnically Thais who happened to be Muslims but Malays who embraced the Islamic faith as an essential part of their socio-cultural identity.[7] Therefore, any novelty introduced by Bangkok into the region would more often than not be interpreted by the Malay Muslim nationalists as yet another covert attempt to dilute or even wipe out their Malay Muslim identity. Such efforts thus had to be opposed with the utmost vigor. The widespread disturbances following the implementation of the 1921 Compulsory Education Act provides clear evidence of the depth of such suspicions.[8]

It did not take much to realize that as long as Bangkok insisted upon homogeneous citizenship based on the socio-ethnic identity of the majority community, namely the Thai Buddhists — as it did actively during the war years and only slightly less actively throughout the rule of the military

---

[7] Wan Kadir Che Man, "The Problem of Patani Malays in Southern Thailand: Neither Assimilation Nor Separation," pp. 19–25. See also the argument put forward by Haji Sulong in his seven-point demand to the Thamrongnawaswat government in 1947.

[8] For an analysis of such mutual suspicions, see Astri Suhkre, "The Thai Muslim Border Provinces: Some National Security Aspect," in *Studies of Contemporary Thailand*, ed. Robert Ho and E.C. Chapman (Canberra: Research School of Pacific Studies, Australia National University, 1973), pp. 296–311.

— and the Malay Muslims held firm to their historical and cultural identity, there could be no mutually acceptable solution to the conflict between the Bangkok-Thais and the Malay Muslims.

Historically and socio-culturally, the Muslims of southern Thailand are mostly of Malay ethnicity who follow the Sunni sect. The overwhelming majority of Thai citizens are Thais and Buddhists of the Theravada sect.[9] These fundamental differences have not, however, proved to be insurmountable to peaceful coexistence and meaningful ties between compatriots. Muslims — of Malay and other ethnicities — live in peace and harmony with their Thai Buddhist compatriots in all other parts of Thailand. Indeed, the Malay Muslims of the southern provinces of Satun and Songkhla have also managed to live in relative peace and harmony with their Thai Buddhist neighbours.[10] It seems that it is only the Malay Muslim leadership from the former Sultanate of Patani which has long harbored feelings of hostility toward the Thai authorities. History helps explain the reasons for such tenacity in defense of Malay Muslim identity in this region. The Sultanate of Patani had long been a sovereign polity and was regarded as a cradle of Malay and Islamic civilization in Southeast Asia until the closing years of the 18th century. Such a glorious past could not but shape an inherent legacy of identity, socio-cultural pride and the ardent desire to maintain this legacy. For the Thai Malay Muslims of the former Sultanate of Patani, it appears that the preservation of Islam and their socio-cultural Malay identity are the central issues in their relations with the Thai state. This implies that to achieve a resolution, at the very least Bangkok would have to embrace liberal and progressive policies that would respect the historical identity of the Malay Muslims, encourage and trust Malay Muslim participation in the administration of the south, and undertake the comprehensive socioeconomic development of both the resources and manpower of the region for the benefit of the local community.

Yet such liberal and progressive approaches were not forthcoming until the 1980s. Bangkok's administration of the southern provinces was based mainly on the national security requirements of the Cold War era and showed little regard for the socio-cultural sensitivities of the people of the

---

[9] Thai Buddhists form over 80% of the total population of Thailand while the Thai Chinese make up 10%, and the Muslims form about 4%.

[10] See Kobkua Suwannathat-Pian, "National Identity, the 'Sam-Sams' of Satun and the Thai Malay Muslims," in *Thai South and Malay North, Ethnic Interactions on a Plural Peninsula*, ed. Michael J. Montesano and Patrick Jory (Singapore: NUS Press, 2008), pp. 155–72.

region. The results were disheartening. Apart from the deep-rooted negative sentiments among the Malay Muslims toward Bangkok, economically the south remained underdeveloped and impoverished under the incompetent rule of Thai officials who knew little and cared less about the local customs and socio-cultural habits of the people they governed. Administratively, therefore, there existed a widening gap between the rulers and the ruled, resentful of the authorities' abuses of power and oppressive government. By the beginning of the 1960s, the unhappiness and discontent of the Malay Muslim leaders had reached a peak.

The Separatist Leadership's Concepts of a Nation-State

The immediate postwar years marked the emergence of the new Thai Malay Muslim leadership in southern Thailand. This new leadership was distinguished from the old one by its different socio-political stand and objectives. The traditional elite looked upon the ex-Ruler — Governor Abdul Kadir of the Pattani Principality — or his heirs as their legitimate leaders, and opposed the incorporation of the Patani sultanate as an integral part of the Thai kingdom. Its main objective was to revive the old sultanate and to restore Abdul Kadir or his heir as its rightful ruler. Failing that, they would accept as a minimal requirement an autonomous Patani under a ruler of their own choice. The new Malay Muslim elite of the postwar years was not so beholden to the political interests of the traditional elite. Though it varied in socio-political ideology and the political system it desired be adopted for the three provinces, it shared a common definite goal: an independent, sovereign Patani, completely severed from the Kingdom of Thailand. Although the original purpose was to liberate the old Patani from the unjust and oppressive rule of Bangkok and make it a sovereign, modern nation, as the struggle continued its fundamental purpose likewise underwent a significant change. It has become evident that the new Patani nation is not limited to the restoration of the territories which once formed the limits of the geo-body of the old sultanate. The new modern and independent Patani would embrace also the Songkhla corridor and Satun province — territories that had not formed part of the old Sultanate of Patani.

It is appropriate to focus our attention on the new leadership of the Thai Malay Muslims and their plans for the Malay Muslims in southern Thailand. The socio-cultural shock suffered during the war years under Premier Phibun's comprehensive policy of nation-building and the modernization of the Thai kingdom aroused political awareness and ethnic pride among the young generation of Patani Malays, especially those who had

had an opportunity to experience the rise of nationalism in other parts of the Muslim world. The postwar Malay Muslim leadership can roughly be classified into two main streams: the old school of conservative nationalists and the modern school of progressive nationalists.

The first group of leaders consisted of the immediate postwar traditional figures such as Tengku Mahmud Mahyuddin (Muhyiddin), the youngest son of the last Patani ruler, Tengku Abdul Kadir; Haji Sulong Abdul Kadir/Tuan Guru Haji Muhamad Salom Patani; Tengku Abdul Jalal/Adul Na Saiburi, and his elder brother Tengku Petra of the royal house of Saiburi.[11] The aim of the conservative Patani nationalists was to achieve a socio-political separation from Thailand by becoming a part of British Malaya. Scrutiny of their background and association well explains their attachment to the restoration of the power of the old ruling elite, whether by reviving the Sultanate of Patani or by setting up a democratic form of government under the leadership of the old ruling house of Patani.[12] Tengku Mahmud Mahyuddin was without question the recognized supreme leader of this group, which still saw the success or failure of their efforts to liberate the homeland in the context of traditional *realpolitik*.[13] It accepted the fact

---

[11] Haji Sulong's name as given on the cover page of his *Gugusan Cahaya Keselamatan*, sealed and issued by Haji Muhamad Amin bin Haji Muhamad Salom Patani, 1958, is Muhamad Salom Patani.

[12] For details of their struggle for the independence and sovereignty of Patani, see Nik Anuar Nik Mahmud, ed., *The Malay Unrest in South Thailand: An Issue in Malayan-Thai Border Relations* (Bangi: Institut Alam dan Tamadun Melayu, UKM, 1994); for a good description of Haji Sulong, see Chalermkiat Khunthongphet, *Haji sulong abdul kadir — kabot rue wiraburut haeng si jangwat phak tai* [*Haji Sulong Abdul Kadir — Rebel or Hero of the Four Southern Provinces?*] (Bangkok: Matichon, Silpawatthanatham, 2004); Surin, "Islam and Malay Nationalism"; and Wan Kadir Che Man, "Conflict and Conflict Resolution: Malay Muslim Liberation Movements in Thailand," Paper presented at the Conference on "Conflict and Conflict Resolution in the Muslim World," International Islamic University Malaysia/IIUM Kuala Lumpur, February 18–19, 2004; and *Muslim Separatism: The Moros of Southern Philippines and the Malays of Southern Thailand* (Singapore: Oxford University Press, 1990); Nantawan Haemindra, "The Problems of the Thai-Muslims in the Four Southern Provinces of Thailand, (Part One)," *Journal of Southeast Asian Studies* 2, 2 (September 1976), and "The Problems of the Thai-Muslims in the Four Southern Provinces of Thailand (Part Two)," *Journal of Southeast Asian Studies* 8, 1 (March 1977).

[13] The fact that Thailand ended the war as a defeated nation gave rise to an expectation among the Malay Muslim leaders, both in Kelantan and in southern Thailand, that Great Britain would annex the three former Patani provinces and Satun to British Malaya as "a reasonable penalty for Siam's attitude during the war."

of Malay Muslim political and military weaknesses *vis-à-vis* Bangkok, and thus regarded as essential the help and support of a great power, in this case Great Britain, to pressure Bangkok to agree to the liberation of Patani and its eventual future as a part of the independent Federation of Malaya. These leaders could not yet visualize the success of an armed struggle given the superior military strength of Bangkok. It was likely that they viewed such a struggle as suicidal rather than heroic given the international politics of the day. Naturally, once Great Britain's expected support was not forthcoming, the movement, together with its leader, Tengku Mahyuddin, became discredited.[14] The whole situation became unredeemable for the conservative Malay Muslim leadership. In January 1949, Bangkok signed an Anglo-Thai Agreement with Great Britain resulting in their cooperation in safeguarding the Thai-Federation of Malaya borders. It was obvious by then that Britain would never agree to any move that might accommodate the wishes of the Thai Malay Muslims to join their Muslim brothers in Malaya. The security of British Malaya was their prime concern. With the British change of heart, the struggle of the old school nationalists of the Thai Malay Muslims came to a sad end.

The second group of postwar leaders was made up of men from a quite different socio-political background. Most of them came from the common stock of Patani Malays. They were well-educated and exposed to developments in the Muslim world, especially the Middle East. They took up the struggle for the liberation of Patani not simply as an historical obligation to the motherland but rather as a fulfillment of their political ideology. Perhaps because of the fragmented nature of the progressive nationalist leadership, both Bangkok and the world at large seem to have given little credit to their struggle until recently.

Of these mushrooming and frequently splintering movements the first, the *Barisan Nasional Pembebasan Patani* (BNPP), or the National Liberation Front of Patani, was set up in 1959, surprisingly by the conservative nationalists with Tengku Abdul Jalal as leader. The BNPP offered a clear and definite

---

Also, British interests in Southeast Asia — rice, trade and the defense of its colonial possessions — made such an annexation likely. Bangkok believed that Great Britain's designs on southern Thailand were further driven by the valuable deposits of tin in the south.

[14] See CO 717/156 Extract from the *Pan-Malayan Review of Political and Security Intelligence*, no. 3 of 1949, February 2, 1949; CO 717/156 A.M. Palliser to O.H. Morris, Co, March 10, 1949; Cp 717/156 H. Gurney to Arthur Creech-Jones, June 29, 1949 and O.S. Morrison to Sir A. Abraham, July 29, 1949.

manifesto. Its aim was to obtain independence for Patani. The movement was equipped with a military wing, thus clearly signaling its willingness to take up arms to achieve its objective. In spite of a fresh and impressive start, the movement soon fell prey to personality clashes. A dispute between the conservative and the progressive elements within the movement eventually led to a split in 1963. In 1980, the BNPP changed its name to *Barisan Islam Pembebasan Patani*/BIPP, the Islamic Liberation Front of Patani, to more accurately reflect its socio-political philosophy.

The *Barisan Revolusi Nasional* (BRN), or the National Revolutionary Front, a BNPP splinter group under the leadership of Ustaz Karim Hassan, declared its ultimate objective to be similar to the BIPP — namely an independent, sovereign Patani. The difference was in the ideology and strategy adopted to achieve the objective. The BRN leadership embraced the concept of Islamic socialism and worked toward the establishment of an Islamic socialist republic of Patani, while the BIPP adhered to a more orthodox Islam and the goal of setting up of a democratic Islamic state of Patani. The BRN declared its intention to employ guerrilla warfare tactics as the primary means of achieving its political aim. To achieve that goal, the BRN concentrated on recruiting members from students from the *pondok* schools within the three provinces of the former Patani sultanate. It was reported that by 1968 the BRN had been able to set up a military wing ready to engage in guerrilla activities against the Thai authorities. Yet in spite of its impressive growth within a short period, the BRN failed to obtain the cooperation and understanding of the BIPP because of ideological differences. It was clear that the 1963 split was deep-rooted and severely affected the ability of the Patani separatists to cooperate in the interests of their ultimate goal: an independent and sovereign Patani.

It was in such an unpromising political environment that the *Pertubuhan Pembebasan Patani Bersatu*/Patani United Liberation Organization (PULO) emerged in 1968 with Kabir Abdul Rahman, alias Tengku Bira Kotanila, as leader. PULO's main aim was to establish a democratic, secular state called "Patani Raya," consisting of the former provinces of Patani, Songkhla and Satun.[15] Like the BIPP and BRN, PULO declared its willingness to engage in an armed struggle to achieve its objectives. The India-educated Tengku Bira, and his present successor, Lukman bin Sima, were effective in making use of their international Muslim networks. PULO received support from Muslims of their generation especially in the Arabic

---

[15] See PULO website at http://www.pulo.org/.

world, Malaysia and Pakistan. PULO was successful in projecting itself — and was regarded internationally — as the face and spokesman of the Thai Malay Muslims who wished to be free of Bangkok rule and to live in their own sovereign state.

With three separatist movements declaring the adoption of armed struggle — read terrorism, banditry, sabotage, *jihad* and martyrdom — as a means of achieving their political objectives, the years between 1968–1975 recorded the highest number of violent incidents, acts of destruction and casualties suffered by the three parties involved: Thai officials, the innocent public, and the separatists. In response to the new wave of violence, the Thai government adopted a dual-pronged strategy: the use of military force to counter the separatist violence, and a policy of integration and liberal socio-administrative measures to win over the Thai Malay Muslim masses from the separatists. By the 1980s, it appeared that the strategy had enabled Bangkok to gain ground in its campaign to win the hearts and minds of the Muslim south.[16]

It is important to be aware of the fact that the struggle of the separatist movements to free themselves from the rule of Bangkok, and the latter's

---

[16] Such positive developments put pressure on the separatists to intensify their struggle against Bangkok. The 1980s saw further fragmentation among the separatist movements: (1) the BIPP split into a splinter group under ex-BIPP Vice-President Wahyuddin Mohammad, forming a new movement named *Gerakan Mujahidin Patani* (GMP); (2) later a GMP leader, Abdul Rahman Putih, Cikgu Mae Anta, left GMP to set up a new movement, *Gerakan Mujahidin Islam Patani* (GMIP); (3) PULO split into the "old PULO" (PULO Bira) led by Tengku Bira with its headquarters in Syria, and the "new PULO" (PULO Kris) under Abdul Rahman Betong as leader; (4) in 1988 the new PULO split into the splinter group, PULO 88, under Harun Museng's leadership (it was only in 2005 that the two PULO were reunited); and (5) the BRN split into two new movements, namely the United Front BRN and the Congress BRN. Amidst the continuing fragmentation of the separatist leadership, there was a move to consolidate and halt such self-destruction. In October 1991, BIPP, BRN Congress, New PULO (PULO Kris) and GMP agreed to form an umbrella body called *Barisan Bersatu Kemerdekaan Patani* (BERSATU) with Dr. Mahadhir Daud, Chairman of BIPP, as Chairman of this new body. BERSATU's official prime purpose was: (1) to take the four southern provinces of Pattani, Yala, Narathiwat, and Satun out of Thailand and form a new and sovereign nation based on Islam and democracy (either as a republic or monarchy), or if the prime objective failed; (2) to set up an autonomous state without outside interference, or if that also failed; (3) to fight for the maintenance of Malay Muslim identity; see Wan Kadir Che Man, "Conflict and Conflict Resolution: Malay Muslim Liberation Movements in Thailand."

desire to uphold and defend the southern provinces as an integral part of the Thai kingdom, were propelled by a mutual desire to achieve the status of, or to defend, a *nation-state*. The progressive Thai Malay Muslim leadership's conception of a nation-state involved a Malay Muslim nation that excluded those who did not share the historical experiences based on the ethnic and socio-cultural identity of the Malay Muslim community.[17] For the Bangkok authorities, since the 1980s the Thai nation-state embraced a multiracial and multiethnic society whose common Thai identity was based not on a narrowly-defined definition of Thai ethnicity, culture, and Buddhism, as it had been in the postwar era, but on being a good citizen whose loyalty to the nation was unquestionable. The conflict between the Thai government in Bangkok and the Malay Muslims in southern Thailand embraced mutual but different desires: the one to strengthen and to defend, and the other to build, respective nation-states. For the majority of the Thai Malay Muslims, the conflict involved a choice between these two different "imagined" communities.

Nation-Building and History-Writing

Postwar, decolonized Southeast Asia witnessed attempts on the part of political leaders to build, strengthen and defend their new nations. Thailand was no different though it could not claim to be a new nation in the same way as Indonesia, Malaysia or the Philippines. King Chulalongkorn and his successors had been successful in turning a traditional and fragmented kingdom into a modern state under the centralized rule of the Chakri monarchs. By the time of the Second World War, Siam was regarded by great and small powers alike to be at least a modernizing nation on par with the "civilized" colonies of the Western powers, with its citizens composed of the majority Thai and the minority communities of immigrant Chinese, Indians, Khmers, Mons, indigenous Malays, Lao and the hill tribes as its main minority communities.[18] It was only with the burning ambition of a crusader that led Premier Phibun to attempt to create a homogenous community

---

[17] The idea of establishing such a nation-state as a Muslim homeland is very much alive today; see "Gaining an Insight into the Terrorists," *Bangkok Post*, August 30, 2004.
[18] It was clear that the concept of a Thai nation prior to the Second World War paid little premium to the concept of "Thai-ness" as an inherent element of a Thai citizen. After 1932, a number Malay Muslims, including Tengku Abdul Jalal, became Members of Parliament and actively participated in the affairs of the nation. See CO 717/156, The Malays of Siam, Paper, FO Research Department, March 20, 1948, Secret. During the 1930s, Bangkok continued to demonstrate its sensitivity

based on Thai identity and Buddhism. Phibun's policy of assimilation caused considerable resentment among his multiracial compatriots, most notably the Thai Malay Muslims of the south.[19] The damage created by this has been enormous and long-lasting, especially in terms of the desire of the Patani nationalists to detach the Deep South and form a Patani nation-state.

The desire on the part of the postwar Thai leadership during the threatening Cold War years to defend and strengthen the security of the Thai nation-state against physical and ideological subversion, sabotage or direct attacks, is the principal reason why Bangkok was hypersensitive, especially since the 1950s, to what it perceived to be a threat to Thailand's existence as a united, integral and sovereign nation.[20] Thai citizens were expected to

---

toward the Muslims in the south. For instance, the Minister of the Interior, Luang Chawengsak-songkram, urged the government to approve a proposed budget by the governor of Narathiwat to help complete a *masjid* in the Bangnara market area, Muang District of Narathiwat, on the grounds that Muslims in Narathiwat had shown their commitment as citizens of the nation. See SR 0201.78/5, Minister of the Interior to the Chief Secretary to the government, September 14, 1939.

[19] On Phibun's wartime socio-cultural policy and the responses, see Thamsook Numnonda, *Thailand and the Japanese Presence 1941–1945* (Singapore: Institute of Southeast Asian Studies, 1977).

[20] To be fair, Bangkok put in place a number of liberal measures to improve the administration and conditions in the south. The measures included Bangkok's acceptance in 1947 of the request for Malay to be taught in government schools in the four provinces; the setting up of a radio station to broadcast in Malay; and the Royal decree of 1945 on the Royal Patronage of Islam setting up the Islamic Council of Thailand, the Provincial Islamic Committees and the Masjid/Surau Committees allowing the local Muslims to manage their own affairs. Bangkok also made a point of bringing in the role of royal patronage which effectively depicted compassion, concern and great efforts to bring about the uplifting of the life of the Thai Malay Muslim subjects. The weakness was, of course, the implementation, especially once the Cold War mentality set in among Thai leaders in Bangkok and the Thai public in general. See SR 0201. 78/7, Ministry of Interior to Prime Minister, January 4, 1946, Urgent-Secret; Yoneo Ishii, "The Thai Muslims and the Royal Patronage of Religion," Paper presented at the 13th IAHA Conference, University of Hong Kong, June 24–26, 1991. On Bangkok's sensitivity to perceived threats to Thailand's national security, see, for example, (2) SR 0201. 92/36 Luang Ratanaphanit, Thai Consul-General, Singapore to Minister of Foreign Affairs, October 31, 1947 on Barbara Whittingham-Jones' article on southern Thailand published in the *Straits Times*, October 30, 1947. The file also contains newspaper cuttings on the subject of the Thai Malay Muslims and Bangkok's unjust and corrupt rule in the region between 1947 and 1948, and the security of Thailand within the Cold War context, as viewed from the perspective of Singapore, London, and Moscow.

support the policies and administrative measures taken by the government without question. There was no room for meaningful discussion of legitimate differences. As far as the Thai government was concerned, such luxuries could not be entertained for fear that they would give the enemy the means to sabotage and destroy the nation. The Thai Malay Muslims thus had little chance to persuade Bangkok to see its failings and to take steps to remedy its unjust and oppressive policies and actions. The very demand that the Malay Muslims, though citizens of Thailand, were different from the Thai majority and thus were entitled to certain considerations, was regarded as a move to sabotage, if not break up, the Thai nation-state. To Bangkok, most Malay Muslim leaders were troublemakers who were bent on discrediting the Bangkok authorities and pushing their own selfish agenda.

The ability of the Patani separatists, especially during 1945–1946, to attract international attention to their plight, forced Bangkok to undertake a damage-control campaign and to put on record the Thai version of Patani history. It was from this period onward that history was employed to justify and legitimize the claims and counter-claims between the Patani nationalist-separatists and the Thai state. History became one of the most important tools used by both Bangkok and the Patani separatists to win support and/or to educate — or indoctrinate — the public. The "history" written from the immediate postwar era roughly up to the end of the 1970s falls into two diametrically opposed viewpoints: that of Bangkok and that of the Patani nationalist-separatists.

From the perspective of the Thai authorities, this history began with the old Patani sultanate as a traditional tributary state of Siam. The cause of the continuing conflict between Bangkok and Patani was Patani's own doing, as the sultanate increasingly proved to be an unreliable tributary. Bangkok was repeatedly compelled to dispatch its military forces to bring law and order back to this strategically important frontier area of the kingdom. By the closing years of the reign of King Rama I, the founder of Bangkok as the capital of Siam, the territory of Patani belonged to the Thai kingdom based on the time-honored principle of conquest by war. Since then, the fragmented sultanate legitimately formed a part of the traditional Siamese kingdom until 1902 when it was incorporated into the kingdom proper, forming an integral part of Siam's geo-body. The integration of the former Patani sultanate as a part of Siamese territory was done with the acquiescence of Great Britain, the predominant power in the Malay peninsula at the time. In its subsequent attempts to modernize and build a modern Thai nation-state, Bangkok under the "democratic" rule of the People's Party, adopted the then popular principle of assimilation to create a unified Thai state with all its citizens exhibiting a common identity based on the socio-cultural norms of the Thai majority. This policy of assimilation remained the dominant approach in Bangkok's administration of the Muslim south until the end of the Cold War. Yet even during this period of assimilation, there were efforts at nation-building that would afford minority communities in Thailand — the Thai Malay Muslims especially — the legitimate rights and privileges of citizenship enjoyed by the majority Thai community.[21]

Patani's history from the Thai/Bangkok perspective stresses the legitimacy of Thai claims over the three provinces of Pattani, Yala and Narathiwat as an integral and inalienable part of the Thai kingdom. The central government regarded the inhabitants of these provinces as Thai citizens with the same rights, responsibilities, and privileges as enjoyed by other Thai citizens regardless of ethnicity and religion. These claims established, the "official" history of Patani would proceed to admit, either subtly or openly, the shortcomings of its policies and the implementation of these policies as well as the fact that the authorities involved often failed to convince the Thai Malay Muslims of their altruistic desire to work toward the well-being of the Malay Muslims.[22] The immediate postwar years saw a series of responses to the legitimate international scrutiny of Thailand's administration of Malay Muslims in southern Thailand. Strong and active international concern for the plight of the Malay Muslims under the high-handed, oppressive and incompetent administration earned Thailand harmful publicity which, if not swiftly and positively handled, could have led to the loss of the three ex-Patani provinces. The history records that Bangkok accommodated the demands, from Great Britain in particular, to reform and reconstruct its policy and administration of the south to meet the aspirations of the nationalist leaders of the Thai Malay Muslims.

---

[21] Most attempts to liberalize Bangkok's policy toward Thailand's Malay Muslims were dictated by, or were responses to, political changes at the international level. Most reforms were short-lived or failed during the implementation stage, mainly because of inconsistency and/or the lack of political will on the part of the government and officials involved. See Premier Phibun's letter to British Ambassador Thompson, enclosed in FO 371/69999, Thompson to FO, November 4, 1948. Thompson was much impressed by the efforts made by the Thai government, stating that these measures "are indeed admirable," in their desire to improve the lives of the Malay Muslims in the south.

[22] See, for example, Prime Minister Phibun's letter to British Ambassador Thompson, FO371/69998, Thompson to FO, November 4, 1948 and CO 717/56 The Malays of Siam, Paper, FO Research Department, December 20, 1948. Secret.

The onset of the Cold War after 1949 and increasing concerns in British Malaya over the communist threat led to a decisively favorable situation, as far as Bangkok was concerned. Malaya's need for Bangkok's close and continuing cooperation automatically meant an end to British support for and patronage of the conservative nationalists and their struggle to achieve a separation of Patani from Thailand. In August 1957, British Malaya gained independence without the three provinces of Pattani, Yala and Narathiwat forming a part of this Malay-majority independent nation, thus denying the aspirations of the conservative nationalists.[23] For these nationalists under the leadership of Tengku Mahmud Mahyuddin, without the support or patronage of a big power such as Great Britain, a struggle carried out by the Malays in southern Thailand "would be bound to fail and would only worsen the position of the Malays in South Thailand."[24]

The period between the 1950s and the end of the 1970s marked a shift in the official history of the south. The genre of such histories remained nationalistic in tone and nuance, and they aimed for the success of the building of the Thai nation-state as visualized by Bangkok.[25] However, the Thai authorities appeared to have learned a valuable lesson from the problems caused by the former total assimilation policy. Bangkok seemed to accept the fact that a strong, united Thai nation-state could not be built purely on the basis of the common cultural identity of the Thai majority. Thai citizenship should not require individuals to embrace the identity of the Thai majority and relinquish their own ethno-religious identity. The common identity of Thai citizenship should be based on only selective elements of the majority community, the most important of which were the Thai language

---

[23] Konthi Suphamongkol, *Kan-Withesobai khong Thai B.E. 2483–2495* [*Thai Foreign Policy, 1940–1952*] (Bangkok: Post Publishing Ltd., 1993), Chapter 29; Nik Anuar, *The Malay Unrest in South Thailand*, pp. 77–8.

[24] Tengku Mahmud Mahayiddin's stand was reported by W.F. Churchill, British Adviser to the state of Kelantan, quoted in Nik Anuar, *The Malay Unrest in South Thailand*, p. 86.

[25] As the Cold War in Southeast Asia intensified with the escalation of the second Vietnam War in the 1960s, the task of building and strengthening the Thai nation-state had become urgent for the Thai government. As a front-line state, Bangkok was conscious of the need of a united and strong Thai nation to defend itself against communist attack and ideological subversion; see Chaiwat Satha-anand, ed., *Phaendin chintanakan: rath lae kan kae panha khwam runraeng nai phak tai* [*Imagined Land: The State and Solutions to the Problem of Violence in Southern Thailand*] (Bangkok: Matichon, 2008).

and an unquestionable loyalty to the nation. Respect and recognition had to be accorded to local socio-cultural practices.[26] Thai citizens must be allowed to preserve their indigenous identity without prejudicing their loyalty to the nation of their birth. The Thai-nation state was now no longer officially conceived of as a homogenous society but a multi-faceted nation of diverse socio-cultural characteristics, made up of citizens bound together by unquestioned love of the land of their birth and shared socio-cultural values. For Bangkok, those who still could not accept such a basis for a common identity and the obligations it entailed, and who preferred Malaya as their homeland, would be allowed to leave the Thai territory. Under no circumstances would Bangkok allow the former Patani to be separated from the Thai geo-body.[27]

It was evident to the government that education held the key to the success of this common identity. Education became the principal means to wean the majority of Malay Muslims from Bangkok's opponents, the "bandit movements for the secession of south Thailand."[28] Education was seen as the key to reduce socio-cultural differences, and to wash away all negatively-preconceived ideas entertained by the Thai Buddhists and the Malay Muslims of each other. Education would also raise the socioeconomic status of the Malay Muslims and eventually bring about the participation of the Malay Muslims in the mainstream affairs of the nation. Historical works of the period reflect the need on the part of the authorities to understand Malay Muslim grievances against the Thai authorities without being judgmental.[29]

---

[26] MTH 020/2.15/14 (39) Memo of Ministry of the Interior answering questions of M.P. Lieut-Captain Charubutr Ruangsuwan on the implementation of the Government Policy as tabled in the House of Representatives, April 1952.

[27] (3) SR 0201.61/6 Phraya Ratnaphakdi to Director-General, State Affairs Dept., October 16, 1957; and Memo on Actions taken for the Reform of the Administration of the Four Southern Provinces by 1955.

[28] In this psychological war for the hearts and minds of the Thai Malay Muslims from the 1950s to the 1970s, Bangkok consistently rejected the claims of the Thai Malay nationalist-led movement that they had an honorable intention to liberate their Malay Muslim compatriots from the unjust and oppressive rule of "foreigners." During this period, the separatists were labeled "bandits," "terrorists" or 'rebels'. See, for example, Col. Kampanat Jintawiroj, *Bandit Movements for the Secession of Southern Thailand* (Bangkok: Pho-sam-ton Publications, 1973).

[29] See "Phu-seu-khao," "A Letter from Southern Thailand," 1966; Khajadphai Burutphat, *Thai Muslims*, 1976; Nantawan, "The Problems of the Thai Muslims in the Four Southern Provinces of Thailand (Part 1)," and "The Problems of the Thai Muslims in the Four Southern Provinces of Thailand (Part 2)"; Uthai Dulyakasem,

The objective was to find solutions to these grievances and convince the majority of the Thai Malay Muslims that their political destiny was with Thailand through the process of national integration.

The relatively stable political atmosphere of the period gives credit to the claim that the liberal approach to the problem in southern Thailand brought significant dividends to Bangkok and aided its psychological campaign to wean the majority of the Malay Muslims from the lure of separatist ideology and movements. Malay Muslims in southern Thailand seem to have accepted a certain degree of socio-cultural compromise. The clearest indicator was the increasing number of young Malay Muslims in state schools learning the Thai language and modern academic subjects and acclimatizing themselves to the mainstream socio-cultural atmosphere while preserving their Malay Muslim heritage.

From the Patani nationalist-separatist perspective, the failure of the conservative nationalists in the 1940s to separate the former Patani sultanate from the Thai geo-body to form a part of the independent Federation of Malaya resulted in a dramatic decline in the influence of the traditionalist-nationalist leaders. The movement for the liberation of Patani appeared to be in disarray. The majority of the Malay Muslims seemed willing to give Bangkok another chance to prove its sincerity in the administrative and socioeconomic reform of the south for the betterment of the Thai Malay Muslim community. Temporarily, Bangkok had won the political and psychological struggle. Then the unexpected happened. Bangkok watched first with little concern, later with increasing perplexity and annoyance, and finally with a determination to suppress, the emergence of new separatist movements under new or reformed leaderships with the clear objective of liberating not only Patani but also Satun and Songkhla, the two southern provinces that historically lay outside the territorial limits of Patani, from Thailand's jurisdiction and geo-body. The closing years of the 1950s marked the beginning of a new round of struggle by separatist movements motivated by new political ideologies as well as by a sense of their socio-religious duty. The "History" of Patani in particular and of the Thai Malay Muslims in general, underwent a spectacular revision.

The immediate postwar period saw the first efforts by Haji Sulong Abdul Kadir, a renowned religious leader, to put right the historical record

---

"Education and Ethnic Nationalism: A Study of the Muslim Malays in Southern Siam," PhD diss., Stanford University, 1981; Patya Saihoo, "Social Organization of an Inland Malay Village Community Southern Thailand," D.Phil thesis, Oxford University, 1974.

of Patani. His *Gugusan Chahaya Keselamatan* [*The Light of Peace*] explained the personal reasons that compelled him to demand from Bangkok an autonomous rule for Patani.[30] These reasons later formed the basis of Sulong's famous seven-point demand in 1947 to the Thamrongnawaswat government.[31] Basically, the objective of the Haji Sulong-led movement was to demand that Bangkok recognize and respect the Malay Muslim identity of its citizens in southern Thailand. The demand was, in retrospect, ill-timed. Any positive sign that the Bangkok government might entertain the demand soon evaporated amidst the intensified political struggle at the national level. The situation was made more complicated by the development of the Cold War and the increasing fear of communism in Southeast Asia in general, and in Thailand in particular.[32] Haji Sulong and his followers became the casualties of the nationalistic, conservative and anti-communist policies of Bangkok. At the time, these policies received the total support and cooperation of Great Britain and its anti-communist allies. In the prevailing atmosphere of fear for Thailand's national security, expressions of a desire for autonomy could only court serious trouble. To Bangkok, Haji Sulong's actions could be interpreted as disloyalty to the nation on the part of those who wanted to assert a "non-Thai" socio-cultural heritage. There was in fact no psychological room for "unity in diversity" in the minds of the Thai leadership of the 1950s and 1960s. More importantly, there was no third international alternative during this period for the Patani conservative nationalists to seek refuge, assistance and moral support for their cause.

---

[30] Haji Sulong bin Haji Abdul Kadir/Tuan Guru Haji Muhamad Salom Patani, *Gugusan Cahaya Keselamatan* (Pattani, 1958).

[31] The seven-point demands were: (i) that the four provinces of Pattani, Yala, Narathiwat, and Satun form an autonomous unit under Patani Malay administration; (ii) that Malay be a learning and teaching language of primary education in the Malay autonomous area; (iii) that revenue accrued within the area be strictly used for the benefits of the area; (iv) that 80% of all officials in the autonomous Patani region must be Malay Muslims; (v) that both Thai and Malay be recognized as official languages of the area; (vi) that the Islamic Provincial Committee administer Islamic affairs with the approval of the High Commissioner; and (vii) that the *syariah* court be separated from the provincial civil and criminal courts. See Chalermkiat Khunthongphet, *Haji Sulong Abdul Kadir*, p. 22.

[32] An example of a positive response on the part of the Bangkok authorities was Pridi's advocacy of a Swiss-type federalism and cultural autonomy for the Malay ethnic minority group within the Thai nation. See Surin, "Islam and Malay Nationalism," pp. 146–51.

Not surprisingly, the 1950s was a relatively quiet and peaceful time for the Deep South.[33]

During this period, Patani nationalists resorted to writing history as a means of keeping alive the memory of the Thai Malay Muslims' glorious past, heritage, and destined future. In 1949, they found a strong historical voice in "Ibrahim Syukri." An apparent well-educated Patani Malay Muslim adopting the pen-name of Ibrahim Syukri wrote his *Sejarah Kerajaan Melayu Patani*, in which he emphasized the Malay identity of the Muslims living within the territory of the former Patani sultanate, and urged them to be forever proud of their identity and heritage.[34] The work became a classic text for the new leadership of Patani separatists who often quoted it as evidence of their righteous struggle for a sovereign Patani. The most outstanding achievement of the book is arguably Ibrahim Syukri's introduction of politico-historical terminology when discussing southern Thailand. The long forgotten spatial body of the old sultanate was effectively resurrected by Ibrahim's use of the term "Patani." It was no longer to be confused with the official Thai term for the administrative province of "Pattani" which, as far as Ibrahim was concerned, represented only the truncated part of the realm of the old sultanate. "Patani" (spelled with one "t") thus served as a potent political symbol for all Malay Muslim separatists in their efforts to achieve their political ideal — an independent motherland. The term suggested a

---

[33] Conversely, the period may also have brought home to the Malay Muslim leaders the realization of the failure of their scheme to establish a Malay Muslim autonomous region within the Thai kingdom. This may have strengthened the calls for armed struggle for a separate and independent Patani among these young leaders; see Wan Abdul Kadir Che Man, "Conflict and Conflict Resolution: Malay Muslim Liberation Movements in Thailand," Paper presented at the Conference on "Conflict and Conflict Resolution in the Muslim World," International Islamic Universiti Malaysia, Kuala Lumpur, February 18–19, 2004.

[34] Ibrahim Syukri, *Sejarah Kerajaan Melayu Patani* [*History of the Malay Kingdom of Patani*] (Kota Bharu, Kelantan: Majlis Ugama Islam Press, 1958). The book was first published in 1949, apparently with the aim of establishing as *a priori* historical fact that Patani was an independent and sovereign kingdom long before it was forced to submit to the Siamese *mandala* as a tributary state. Written from a Patani nationalistic perspective, the book, though in Malay, was banned by both the Bangkok and Kuala Lumpur authorities. Bangkok regarded it as subversive propaganda that threatened the unity of the Thai nation-state, while Kuala Lumpur was evidently bound to act against the publication in order to maintain good relations with Thailand; see Davisakd Puaksom, "Of Lesser Brilliance: Patani Historiography in Contention," in *Thai South and Malay North*, ed. Montesano and Jory, pp. 71–88.

socio-political demarcation between the Thai Buddhists represented by the Bangkok rule and the Malay Muslims of the south represented by Malays who devoted their lives to the revival of an independent Patani state. From the 1960s onward, the term "Patani" and what it has come to represent has slowly but effectively gained ground, both among the Malay Muslims themselves and those interested in southern Thailand. By the 1990s, "Patani" had been sanctified as the politically correct term when reference was made to the homeland of the Malay Muslims in southern Thailand.

Since the emergence of the politically-loaded term "Patani," more terminology that reinforces an awareness of the cultural and political identity of the Thai Malay Muslim community has increasingly come into use. Such terms have tended to emphasize the differences between the Malay Muslim community of the southern border provinces and the Thai mainstream. As the international and domestic political environments underwent a fundamental transformation at the end of the 1980s with the end of the Cold War, public attitudes toward Thailand's Malay Muslims, especially among the academics, have also undergone significant change. The official terms, "Thai Muslims," "terrorists," and "bandits" used since the Cold War era now seem confined mainly to the realms of Thai officialdom. Among the academics and informed public, these terms, if employed at all, are interpreted as representing the biased viewpoint of those who support the authorities. In their place, various politically-correct terms have come into existence: instead of "Thai Muslims," the terms "Malay Muslims," "Malay-speaking people," "Thai Malay Muslims," or simply "Malays of southern Thailand" have been widely adopted. For "terrorists" and "bandits," the terms "separatists," "Patani nationalists" or "Malay nationalists" are now employed.

Ibrahim Syukri brilliantly succeeded in employing history not only to halt the decline of the Malay Muslims' imagined nation known as "Patani" but also to preserve the memory of this lost territory and to implant it forever in the minds of subsequent generations of Malay Muslims in southern Thailand. Moreover, *Sejarah Kerajaan Melayu Patani* appears to have helped set in place an historiographical trend that eventually had an impact even on the Thai authorities. The book played a significant role in the process by which informed Thais and non-Thais since the 1960s have become aware of and are obliged to show respect for the basic rights of a minority ethnic community within the context of the Thai nation-state. The historical perspective presented by Ibrahim Syukri has gradually been reflected in the writing of the history of Patani since the 1970s. This achievement may appear minor in the contemporary world where recognition and respect for ethnic and cultural difference are now loudly acclaimed, yet in the context of Bangkok-Malay Muslim relations, the acceptance represented a very considerable step forward toward reaching a solution to this century-old conflict.

History and the Search for a "Solution"

A brief survey of the prominent historical works written by Thai Buddhist, Malay Muslim, and Western scholars during the transition period of the 1960s–1980s on the history of the region, the social and cultural values and way of life of the local population, their political and administrative grievances against the Thai authorities and the economic backwardness of the Malay Muslims, shows that the main focus was to identify the root-causes of the conflict and to offer ways and means to remedy or diminish them.[35] In general, the works display sympathy for Bangkok and accept the legitimacy of its task of national integration. The general impression favored the ongoing process of nation-building which had clearly shifted emphasis from assimilation to a more culturally accommodating form of integration. In essence, the shift acknowledged the legitimate claims of the minority community citizens — in this case, the Thai Malay Muslims — to preserve and practice their way of life and to enjoy their share of the benefits of citizenship of the Thai nation.

As the armed struggle intensified in the 1970s, the study and writing of the history of the Malay Muslims, in contrast, became more comprehensive, balanced, and academic in nature.[36] Most scholars and the informed public appeared convinced that violence was not the answer to the problems in southern Thailand. Most also came to the conclusion that the conflict could

---

[35] These include Astri Suhrke, "The Thai Muslim Border Provinces: Some National Security Aspects," in *Studies of Contemporary Thailand*, ed. Robert Ho and E.C. Chapman (Canberra: Research School of Pacific Studies, Australian National University, 1973), "Irredentism Contained: The Malay Muslim Case," *Journal of Contemporary Politics* 7, 2 (1975), and "Loyalists and Separatists: The Muslims in Southern Thailand," *Asian Survey* 17, 3 (1977); Arong Suthasasna, *Panha khwam khat yaeng nai si jangwat phak tai* [*The Problem of the Conflict in the Four Southern Provinces*] (Bangkok: Phithakpracha, 1976); Kasem Rangsiyokrit, "Itthipon khong sasana islam tor kan-jat kan pokkhrong jangwat chai daen phak tai" [The Influence of Islam on the Administration of the Border Provinces in Southern Thailand], MA thesis, Thammasat University, 1976; see also works cited in footnote 29.

[36] It is generally agreed that the height of the separatist movements' armed struggle was between 1968 and 1975; see Wan Kadir Che Man, "Conflict and Conflict Resolution."

only be resolved by having a clear understanding of its root causes and a flexible and compromising approach from both the Bangkok authorities and the separatist movements. The 1980s witnessed a rich production of academic works, not only by Thai and Malay Muslim scholars but also by leading international Southeast Asian scholars, on the Thai Malay Muslims, their history, their troubled relations with Bangkok, the contemporary armed struggle, and the role of Muslims from a national perspective.[37] The most outstanding work of the period to date remains that of Surin Pitsuwan.[38] The work, written with deep compassion and sympathy for the Malay Muslims,

---

[37] These include Chaiwat Satha-anand, *Islam and Violence: A Case Study of Violent Events in the Four Southern Provinces, Thailand, 1976–1981* (Florida: University of South Florida, Department of Religious Studies, 1987); and "Pattani in the 1980s: Academic Literature and Political Stories," in *Muslim Social Science in ASEAN*, ed. Omar Farouk Bajunid (Kuala Lumpur: Yayasan Penataran Ilmu, 1994); Chavivun Prachuabmoh, "The Role of Women in Maintaining Ethnic Identity and Boundaries: A Case of Thai Muslims (Malay-Speaking Group) in Southern Thailand," PhD diss., Department of Anthropology, University of Hawai'i, 1980; Andrew D.W. Forbes, ed., *The Muslims of Thailand, Vol. I: Historical and Cultural Studies* (Bihar: Centre for Southeast Asian Studies, 1988); and *The Muslims of Thailand, Vol. II: The Politics of the Malay-Speaking South* (Bihar: Centre for Southeast Asian Studies, 1989); Omar Farouk Bajunid, "The Political Integration of the Thai Islam," PhD thesis, University of Kent at Canterbury, 1980; "The Origins and Evolution of Malay Muslim Ethnic Nationalism in Southern Thailand," in *Islam and Society in Southeast Asia*, ed. Taufik Abdullah and Sharon Siddique (Singapore: Institute of Southeast Asian Studies, 1984); "The Historical and Transnational Dimensions of Malay Muslim Separatism in Southern Thailand," in *Armed Separatism in Southeast Asia*, ed. Lim Joo Jock and S. Vani (Singapore: Institute of Southeast Asian Studies, 1984); Raymond Scupin, "Islamic Reformism in Thailand," *Journal of Siam Society* 68, 2 (1980); Seni Mudmarn, "Language Use and Loyalty among the Muslim Malays of Southern Thailand," PhD diss., The State University of New York, 1988; and "Social Science Research in Thailand: The Case of the Muslim Minority," in *Muslim Social Science in ASEAN*, ed. Omar Farouk Bajunid; Wan Kadir Che Man, *Muslim Separatism: The Moros of Southern Philippines and the Malays of Southern Thailand* (Singapore: Oxford University Press, 1990); and "Muslim Elites and Politics in Southern Thailand"; Uthai Dulyakasem, "Muslim Malay Separatism in Southern Thailand: Factors Underlying the Political Revolt," in *Armed Separatism in Southeast Asia*, ed. Lim and Vani; Astri Suhrke, "The Thai Muslims: Some Aspects of Minority Integration," *Pacific Affairs* 43 (1980); and Kobkua Suwannathat-Pian, *Thai–Malay Relations*.

[38] Surin, "Islam and Malay Nationalism." Surin is currently Secretary-General of the Association of Southeast Asian Nations. A Thai Malay Muslim academic turned politician, Surin was a popular MP of the Democrat Party in the 1990s, representing a constituency in Nakhon Si Thammarat, a province in the upper part of the southern

is a comprehensive and academically balanced study of the Malay Muslim community, its socio-political ambitions, its long sufferings under unjust and unsympathetic authorities, its legitimate claims as an ethnic minority community, and a keen awareness of the administrative constraints facing Bangkok as well as the latter's genuine though often ineffective efforts to meet the aspirations of its Thai Malay Muslim citizens.

The history of Patani written in the 1980s, whether by Malay Muslim scholars or "outsiders," tended to come to a similar conclusion, namely that it was futile to expect Bangkok to agree to a separate and independent Patani. It is also clear that these works disapproved of the harsh measures meted out by the security forces. If Bangkok wished to silence the separatists, it would have to change its longstanding strategy based on the use of superior military force and abandon its lingering desire for national assimilation. Bangkok also needed to win over the silent majority of Thai Malay Muslims through enlightened administration and sensible economic policies toward the south. A significant step to achieving this would be for Bangkok to respect and trust the Thai Malay Muslims and to appreciate their different identity. In other words, in order to win this war for the nation-state, Bangkok has no other realistic alternative but to embrace the principle of unity in diversity as a basis for the contemporary Thai nation-state.

Conclusion

The writing of the history of Patani since the 1940s has been dictated by the ever-increasing political awareness on the part of the Thai Malay Muslims on the one hand, and the determination of Bangkok to transform Thailand into a modern nation-state based on Thai characteristics on the other. Historical facts are never neutral, yet in the case of the history of Patani between the 1940s and 1970s, they became blatantly and unashamedly politicized to serve the political agendas of the interested parties: the Bangkok authorities and the Patani nationalists. It is undeniable that history has always played a role in furthering the political interests of the victors. To a degree, what we witness in the writing of Patani history in our time, particularly looking through Bangkok's prism of history, is nothing new. A survey of historical works written between the 1940s and the 1980s clearly

---

region where Malay Muslims form a sizable and significant minority. He also served as Thai Foreign Minister during the Chuan Leekphai premiership in the 1990s. Surin represents at the same time the liberal face of Thai government policy and the moderate face of the country's Malay Muslims.

shows that there are Patani histories of various "declensions," namely the Bangkok versions, the Patani nationalist versions, and the academic versions. These histories might as well be records of different socio-political territories since they seem to disagree on most important phases of Patani's historical development. Yet these divergent histories have managed to coexist and to play their differing roles as "proven truths" supporting certain socio-political objectives, hoping to eventually succeed in winning over a large and devoted audience. This surely represents something new. Never before have contradicting versions of history been allowed to coexist and challenge the history of the victors. That the different narratives are now allowed to compete for public attention virtually on the same platform can be seen as a positive development in history-writing in Thailand. One might even go further in Patani's case and claim that the contradicting histories of Patani have been the main reason for the emergence of an historically more balanced and proven factual analysis of the story of the Thai Malay Muslims in Patani, as clearly displayed since the 1980s.

CHAPTER 11

Locating Traditional, Islamic, and Modern Historiography in Patani-*Jawi* Identity

Iik Arifin Mansurnoor

The contents of the book, *The History of the Malay Kingdom of Patani*, deeply influenced my emotions and sentiments as a son of Patani. I was then 17 years old.

—Ahmad Fathi al-Fatani[1]

Modern historiography is a novel genre of recounting the past in Thailand's restive southern region. It is instructive, therefore, to examine how this new genre relates to the older genres of historiography which were formerly dominant in the south: traditional and Islamic historiography. How has each genre developed and been perceived by their authors and their intended audience? This chapter will examine some of the most influential works of historiography about the former Sultanate of Patani composed in *Jawi*-Malay and widely circulated among Patani *Jawi* readers.[2] Based on an examination of the layering of different genres of Patani historiography, it is possible to outline the major elements and the transformative stages in the shaping of Patani identity. Despite the fact that prior to the 20th century, Islam had become the religion of most of Patani's inhabitants, including its rulers, it

---

[1] Ahmad Fathi al-Fatani, *Pengantar Sejarah Patani: Negeri Setanjung Bunga* [*Introduction to Patani History: The Bulletwood Flower-Shaped Land*] (Kota Bharu: Pustaka Aman Press, 2001; Alor Setar: Pustaka Darussalam, 1994), p. 123.
[2] I use the term *Jawi* here to refer both to the Malay language transcribed in the Arabic script, as well as, more generally, Southeast Asian Muslims.

had yet to develop as a political marker of identity in the way that language and customs had done. Nevertheless, according to Surin Pitsuwan, the rise of the "question of ethnicity" in Patani that was oriented toward Muslim politics and resistance to Siamese and modern Thai authority, can be attributed to emerging nationalism in the 20th century. He ascribes the surfacing of this "problem of ethnicity" to a "collective reaction" to Siamese administrative reforms led by the former Sultan 'Abdul Kadir Kamarudin in 1903 and again in 1922.[3] Notwithstanding Surin's assertion of the importance of this historical period to the formation of Patani ethnic identity, Islam also emerged as a strong, new marker of independence following the abolition of the sultanate, when Patani's paramount political symbol, the sultan, had been made irrelevant to the political process.

Traditional, Islamic, and Modern Historiographies of Patani

The best-known example of traditional historiography of Patani is the *Hikayat Patani*. The *Hikayat Patani* can be identified as an example of traditional Malay historiography because of its close identification with an existing genre of Malay literature. With its focus on the state — the sultan, the elite, customs and ceremonies — the *Hikayat Patani* bears the mark of palace culture centered on the ruler with all the paraphernalia associated with the throne. As the account of events stops by the late 17th century when the state degenerated, a nostalgic thrust could have been the trigger for the work's composition or recension. Despite such nostalgia, it is undeniable that by the 17th century the Patani ruler was the buttress and landmark of Patani's historical identity. Since Teeuw and Wyatt have clearly shown the merits and weaknesses of this work,[4] here I generally refer to their characterization of the *Hikayat Patani* as a guide to this discussion.

What we understand in this chapter as Islamic historiography is not reducible to the historiographical genre that was developed by Tabari (d. 923) and those after him. This genre is best represented in Malay historiography by Raja Ali Haji of Johor-Riau (d. 1873). Although Patani scholars are known to have composed Islamic works of quantity and quality, the historical literature that we have today is very limited. This is not surprising since

---

[3] Surin Pitsuwan, *Islam and Malay Nationalism: A Case Study of the Malay Muslims of Southern Thailand* (Bangkok: Thai Khadi Research Institute, Thammasat University, 1985), p. 51.

[4] A. Teeuw and David K. Wyatt, eds., *Hikayat Patani: The Story of Patani* (The Hague: Martinus Nijhoff, 1970).

Muslim scholars in the Malay world largely opted out of writing the "difficult and enigmatic subject of history."[5] However, there does exist a little-known Patani historical text that bears traits of this genre, known as the *Tarikh Fatani*. The *Tarikh Fatani* was written in Arabic by Shaykh Faqih `Ali ibn Muhammad ibn Safiyuddin, at the order of the Sultan of Patani. The date of its composition is uncertain. According to the author or his later editors, in composing the treatise the Shaykh depended on the following sources: information from a Buddhist chronicler from Ligor who was eventually granted residence by the sultan in Yala; Patani rulers through their own accounts; Shaykh Safiyuddin's personal notes in Arabic; and a scholar from Bogor in Java who knew Javanese terms well. The present text derives from a version that was translated from Arabic into Malay sometime before the middle of the nineteenth century by the prolific Patani scholar residing in Mecca, Shaykh Daud ibn `Abdullah al Fatani.[6]

The *Tarikh Fatani* represents a Patani Malay view of ancient Patani before the arrival of Islam. Why was this necessary? The introductory pages of the text suggest that the author regarded it as essential to contrast the two periods of Patani history. Indeed, in a sense it is a representation of Patani's past in order for it to function as a reference point from which to compare the later Islamic period: between light and darkness; between Islam and the *jahiliya*. Its importance also lies in the fact that it was written and circulated among religious scholars (*ulama*). However, since history, including the history of Islam in the region, as a subject did not attract much attention in the religious circles, the *Tarikh Fatani* never occupied an important reference even among Muslims.

Shaykh Faqih's *Tarikh Fatani* displays an important difference to the *Hikayat Patani* in its emphasis on society, consisting of the people and culture

---

[5] Iik A. Mansurnoor. "Historiography and Religious Reform in Brunei during the Period 1912–1959," *Studia Islamika* 2, 2 (1995): 77–113; Donald E. Brown, *Hierarchy, History and Human Nature: The Social Origins of Social Consciousness* (Tucson, AZ: The University of Arizona Press, 1988).

[6] The main text of the *Tārīkh Faṭāni* [*History of Patani*] referred to in this chapter is a copy written by Sha`rani bin Haji `Abdullah Ahmad bin Haji `Abd al-Ra'uf Jeringa, dated 1968. The text, comprising 23 pages, was republished in its original handwritten *Jawi* and given an introduction by Haji Wan Muhammad Ṣaghir `Abdullah; see *Tārīkh Faṭāni* (Kuala Lumpur: Khazanah Fathaniyah, 2002). I also refer to a transliterated version of the *Tarikh Fatani* by Mohd. Shaghir Abdullah, *Khazanah Karya Pusaka Asia Tenggara* [*Treasures of Invaluable Works in Southeast Asia*], Vol. I (Kuala Lumpur: Khazanah Fathaniyah, 1991), pp. 149–60. Mohd. Shaghir's suggestion that the text was written before 1500 has no strong basis anywhere in the text.

of old Patani. The nucleus of the story may have belonged to an earlier period, even though the changing environment in the 19th century which saw the declining power of the Patani state might have had some semblance with that earlier period of state formation in Patani. A further interesting feature of the *Tarikh Fatani* is its representation of cordial relations and trust between Malay Muslims and Buddhists, which suggests that the text was composed at a time when relations between the Muslims (Malays) and Buddhists were relatively warm and mutually beneficial. The *Tarikh Fatani* of Ibn Safiyuddin even maintains that the Patani Muslims had the same origin as local Buddhists (Buddhist Malays).[7] Patani's close relations with the Buddhist Srivijaya kingdom, however, brought it into intensive contacts with the Arabs and Persians who had established a flourishing trading network in the region. Consequently, when the Straits of Melaka came increasingly under the influence of Muslim traders, Patani also began to experience religious change. Conversion to Islam of the Malays created friction in Patani, especially with the Buddhist Malays (*Melayu Buddha*), however, it did not lead to any serious outbreak of fighting or war.[8]

The most famous example of modern historiography is the *Sejarah Kerajaan Melayu Patani*, or *History of the Malay Kingdom of Patani* by Ibrahim Syukri. Ibrahim Syukri's work emerged as a crucial bridge for the Patanis to move to the era of the nation-state. As far as Patani is concerned, it retains the best of the past and seizes onto relevant new ideas to help the Patanis deal with the reality and new opportunities in a national, regional and global context. The Malaysian editors of the *Sejarah Kerajaan Melayu Patani* claim that the work was very influential among the Patanis and became a major source for later historians of Patani.[9] Ibrahim Syukri uses a diverse range of sources in order to present a history of Patani that could be meaningful for the reconstruction of Patani. The thinking and discourse developed in Ibrahim's book appears to have come from among the leading Patanis who left their villages around the time of the Pacific War as refugees and moved to Kelantan.[10]

---

[7] *Tarikh Fatani* (Kuala Lumpur: Khazanah Fathaniyah, 2002), pp. 4–5.

[8] Ibid., pp. 13–4.

[9] See "Foreword," in Ibrahim Syukri, *Sejarah Kerajaan Melayu Patani* [*History of the Malay Kingdom of Patani*], ed. Hasrom bin Haron and Mohd. Zamberi A. Malek (Bangi: National University of Malaysia Press, 2002), p. 9.

[10] Passages quoted from W.R. Roff (1968) by Hasrom bin Haron and Mohd. Zamberi A. Malek, "Foreword," Ibrahim Syukri, *Sejarah Kerajaan Melayu Patani* (2002), p. 10.

The *Sejarah Kerajaan Melayu Patani* was written as a protest against Thailand's aggressive policy of national integration, which the authors considered unjust and humiliating.[11] As a polemic, it is markedly different from the prevailing style of local writing. Its potential to foment a national awakening among the local population not surprisingly led to its ban both in Thailand and Malaysia. Indeed, for these governments the ban was effective, temporarily at least, in sidelining the Patani issue and halting the spread of what could be termed a Patani version of national history. The publication and re-publication of the *Sejarah* were clearly designed to have a cultural impact. Even the new publisher could not fail to emulate this motto: "to promote Patani history among the younger generation of Malays in Patani and beyond."[12] For Ibrahim Syukri, the book was a response to the prevailing mode of political discourse and reflected conditions as they existed in Patani at the time. It was, above all, a hope, if not a call for, a different future: "It is especially hoped that this book will become an eternal legacy (*pusaka yang kekal*) for succeeding generations …"[13]

Who was the intended audience of Ibrahim Syukri's *Sejarah Kerajaan Melayu Patani*? Wyatt claims that "Because the *Sejarah* was published in Malay using the Jawi script, it is clear that its author intended it only for a local audience …"[14] As early as 1985, David Wyatt warned his colleagues not to ignore the potential impact of a new emerging force of "amateur local and regional historians."[15] In commenting on Ibrahim Syukri's work, Wyatt suggested that it belonged to a genre of writing which responded to the centralization drive launched by the new nation-state.[16] For Wyatt, "At various points in this long history, the people of Patani have felt impelled to recall and make known its history …"[17] The past plays an important role among the population of Patani. It continues to inspire and act as a reference point for Patani Malays in navigating changing political environments and challenges.

The nationalistic ardor of the *Sejarah Kerajaan Melayu Patani* has been sustained in numerous more recent works of modern historiography

---

[11] Ibid., p. 9.

[12] Ibid., p. 11.

[13] Ibrahim Syukri, *History of the Malay Kingdom of Patani*, trans. Conner Bailey and John N. Miksic (Athens, OH: Ohio University Press, 1985), p. 2.

[14] Ibid., p. x.

[15] Ibid., pp. vii–viii.

[16] Ibid., p. viii.

[17] Ibid., pp. ix–x.

composed mostly across the modern-day border in neighboring Malaysia, but which are well-known to Patani intellectuals. Among the most prominent such authors are A. Bangnara, Ahmad Fathi al Fatani, Mohd. Zamberi A. Malek, and Nik Anuar Nik Mahmud, who, in different tones, utilize the past to construct a foundation for a more hopeful future for Patani. Such a "presentist regime of historicity" (to use Hartog's terms, as elaborated by Berger and Lorenz), which has become increasingly popular since the end of the Second World War, means that the nation-state is no longer the central custodian of "history-memory," because its definition of the "national history memory" is "rivalled and contested in the name of partial, sectoral or particular memories (groups, associations, enterprises, communities, which all wish to be recognized as legitimate, equally legitimate, or even more legitimate)."[18] Despite their weaknesses and flaws, such alternative histories must be seen not in terms of their presentism but for the "other neglected representations" that they offer.

I shall now proceed to show how these various genres of Patani historiography deal with different themes in Patani's history, which have become embedded in contemporary conceptions of Patani-*Jawi* identity.

On the Origins of the Patani Kingdom and Dynasties

If earlier works in *Jawi* such as the *Tarikh Fatani* and *Hikayat Patani* consider the local population in Patani to share common origins and maintain identity markers within that unity, the later *Jawi* works insist on the importance of Islam and Malayness as key identity markers. However, all agree on the centrality of the Malay sultan. Patani is presented as existing in an aura of political power, economic prosperity and religious harmony.

Whatever the ethnic name and identity of the Patanis, the *Tarikh Fatani* shows that they had a common ethnic origin in the area. Before the coming of Islam, they experienced and shared the same religions: traditional ancestral beliefs, Hinduism and then Buddhism. The division between the *melayu Budha* and *melayu Islam* formed an important mark of distinction but never separated them in their land and in their loyalty to the sovereign.[19] At the peak of its power, the older kingdom of Langkasuka had a port city in Patani (albeit not necessarily the present one). Langkasuka

---

[18] Stefan Berger and Chris Lorenz, eds., *The Contested Nation* (London: Palgrave Macmillan, 2008), pp. 19–20.
[19] *Tarikh Fatani* (2002), p. 14.

held territories from Ligor and Singora (Songkhla) in the north to Kedah in the south. Later, the Patani ruler inherited and took control of the former territories of Langkasuka. The old Patani kingdom became involved in a conflict between Srivijaya and Java, 500 years after its foundation in 750 CE (around 1250), supporting the former. When both agreed to peace and prosperity, Patani also came under the influence of both powers. Indeed, Patani regained its glory because of the Javanese Sailendra kingdom's protection.[20]

The origin of Patani is discussed at length by the author(s) of the *Sejarah Kerajaan Melayu Patani*. This may be summarized as follows: the area was originally inhabited by pre-Malay and Thai races such as the Sakai, Semang and the Mon until the eight century, when the Malay kingdom of Srivijaya based on Sumatra took political control of the Malay peninsula and "the whole of Malaya was subject to the Srivijaya kingdom."[21] The Thais came to the area as a result of their migration from southwest China and their success in building a strong polity, Sukhothai, toward the end of the 13th century.[22] Srivijaya's influence and power from the eighth to the 14th centuries led to the foundation of major Buddhist temples and monuments as well as Buddha statues throughout the length of the peninsula. The emergence of Majapahit and Sukhothai ended Srivijaya's power over the Peninsula resulting in its division into an upper part dominated by the Thai and the lower part subject to Majapahit. However, the decline of Majapahit by the 15th century and the emergence of new Muslim polities paved the way for the formation of various local Malay states on the peninsula. Kedah was one of the first polities to be visited by Arab, Persian and Indian Muslims. By the ninth century, Kedah had shown an acceptance of Islam. The Melaka ruler followed in 1403. Some Siamese also adopted Islam and were known as Sam-sam.[23]

Although the Malays succeeded in founding such states as Kedah, Melaka, and Temasik, Patani and other surrounding territories continued to be dominated by the native Siamese (*Siam Asli*). The Malays were under the sovereignty of states to the north, including Ligor (Nakhon Sri Thammarat). The local ruler in Patani, Raja Seri Wangsa, resided in "Kota Mahligai" or Perawan in the interior. With the coming of more Malays to settle near the

---

[20] Ibid., pp. 15–7.
[21] *Serajah Kerajaan Melayu Patani* (1985), p. 7.
[22] Ibid., p. 22.
[23] Ibid., pp. 27–8.

coastal region, Kota Mahligai failed to compete as foreign trade became the domain of emerging coastal fishing and trading villages.[24]

By contrast, for A. Bangnara the emphasis in his depiction of Patani's origins is on the importance of Islam and Patani's glorious past. The Patanis were the first Southeast Asians to endorse Islam, even though their rulers only embraced it in the 15th century. More specifically, the outward policy adopted by the Patani sultans attracted contemporary international trading ships and merchants to invest and trade in the Patani capital. Various stories and accounts of old Langkasuka, the predecessor of the Patani sultanate, are cited. In regard to religion, initially people held to local beliefs and animism before the arrival of Brahmanism in around 200 CE. Later, when Srivijaya expanded to the area, Buddhism also spread using Malay as the lingua franca. Langkasuka declined and vanished after the 15th century. To show that Siam had no contact with the south, A. Bangnara points out that there is no record of Langkasuka in the Siamese accounts, while Patani was known and recorded in the Nakhon Sri Thammarat chronicle.[25] Patani had developed into an entrepôt since ancient times. Patani in fact is claimed to be older than Melaka. Islam also came to Patani earlier than to Melaka, in 1150 CE, however, its *raja* accepted Islam only in the mid-15th century. Even then, only the drinking of alcohol and the worship of idols were forbidden. Under its third ruler, Sultan Mansur, Patani developed into a prosperous port, visited by Western and Eastern merchants. Patani thus emerged as an important cultural center from an early period. Several factors worked to protect Patani from foreign domination: economic and political stability, active foreign relations, the acceptance of Islam, the establishment of extensive networks in trade, and solidarity in spirit.

According to Nik Anuar Nik Mahmud, following the downfall of Melaka in 1511[26] Patani lost an important ally but it also benefited from the coming of more Muslim traders to its ports. These factors contributed

---

[24] *Serajah Kerajaan Melayu Patani* (2002), pp. 29–35. Indeed, one of these coastal villages, "Patani," has its origins in the name of a respected fisherman, "Pak Tani." The village enjoyed a strategic location for fishing and settlement as it is located in a gulf, protected by an inlet and crossed by a river. The growing port town attracted foreign traders and migrants.

[25] A. Bangnara, *Patani Dahulu dan Sekarang* [*Patani: Then and Now*], trans. A. Patani and A. Jala (Patani: Penyelidikan Angkatan al-Fatani, 1397/1977), pp. 1–4.

[26] Nik Anuar Nik Mahmud, *Sejarah Perjuangan Melayu Patani* [*History of the Patani Malay Liberation Movement*] (Bangi: National University of Malaysia Press, 2000), pp. 13–9.

to its strength and influence. In the face of the southern advance of the Thai states of first Sukhothai then Ayutthaya, Patani was never an exclusive part of these kingdoms. Rather, Patani maintained relations with them depending on the changing political and military environment, thus oscillating between the status of vassal and independent state.

For Mohd. Zamberi A. Malek, as the older Malay states from Tambralinga to Songkhla were defeated and eliminated by the emerging power of Ayutthaya, Patani became the symbol of Malay glory.[27] Its downfall was mainly caused by disunity and the weakening spirit of religion and ideology among the Malays. Even before the 16th century, Islam had played an important role in buttressing Malay identity and bringing them pride and glory as Muslim Malays. Phatthalung came under Muslim rule during the reign of Sultan Sulaiman and his tomb is still honored today. Singora and Ligor at one time or another also came under Muslim Malay rule. This was true until the time of Ayutthaya's downfall in 1767. Patani's glory followed its acceptance of Islam by the Patani ruler Phaya Tu Antara. Islam transformed Patani's belief, culture, language, education, governance and society, but Patani continued to maintain a balance between Islamic influence and earlier layers of tradition and system.[28]

On Patani's Relations with Siam and Malay States

All our Patani *Jawi* sources maintain that Patani had emerged as an independent polity before the coming of the Western powers to the region. This identification with an independent polity — the *Jawi*/Malay Muslim sultanate — forms an important element in strengthening and even transforming a political identity *vis-à-vis* the newly formed modern nation-states in the region. If Islam emerged as the most important element in Patani-*Jawi* identity after 1902, the sultanate was the key element in pre-20th-century Patani-*Jawi* identity.

---

[27] Mohd. Zamberi A. Malek, *Patani dalam Tamadun Melayu* [*Patani in Malay Civilization*] (Kuala Lumpur: Dewan Bahasa dan Pustaka, 1994), Chapter 2.

[28] By the 16th century, Patani had emerged as the most powerful Malay state. Its importance lay with its strategic trading position attracting merchants from the east and west. Its economic prosperity was due to the brilliant policy of the rulers. Patani sultans represented the landmark of glorious Malay statecraft. Its economic prosperity buttressed the dignified culture of Patani, especially in the scientific and linguistic fields. For Mohd. Zamberi, therefore, Patani developed as an advanced and important state (1994: Chapter 2).

The *Tarikh Fatani*, like other Patani works, presents the old Patani kingdom as a regionally oriented polity. It succeeded in winning acceptance from various centers and participated in cooperation and exchange. For example, the Patani kingdom became involved in the conflict between Srivijaya and the Javanese Sailendra kingdom around 1250, supporting the former. Following the takeover of power by Srivijaya's prince around 750 CE, Langkasuka's capital was at Ligor. Kedah and Patani thus came under Ligor from 800 CE. The Khmers also came under its domination following a major defeat. Ligor and Java were in conflict with the ruler of Srivijaya as the latter sent more missions to the region. It appears that the *Tarikh Fatani* considers this period as a watershed for the increasing autonomy of Patani as a separate polity.[29]

The *Hikayat Patani* projects Patani's rulers as outward-looking and open-minded. For example, the text relates how Sultan Muzaffar Shah personally went to Ayutthaya in order to expand Patani's relations with other regional powers. The sultan is depicted as addressing his prime minister: "'What would you say if We went to Ayudhya, for the king is no stranger to Us, and after all, two countries are better than one.' All the ministers replied respectfully: 'Hail my Lord, what You say is perfectly true, it would add to Your Majesty's greatness in the eyes of all foreign countries.'"[30]

In a similar manner, the *Sejarah Kerajaan Melayu Patani* insists that the Patani rulers were peace-loving and willing to extend the hand of co-operation, as shown, for example, by the visit paid by Sultan Muzaffar Shah to Ayutthaya in the 16th century.[31] Sultan Muzaffar Shah went to Ayutthaya but was not warmly welcomed. He returned in deep disappointment, even though he had been awarded Pegu and Khmer slaves/war captives by the Ayutthayan king. These Buddhist slaves were given freedom to practice their religion. However, following the attack on Ayutthaya by the Burmans of the Toungoo kingdom, after consultation, the Patani ruler decided to mobilize his forces to avenge the early humiliation he had suffered at Ayutthaya and joined the Burman onslaught.

For A. Bangnara, relations between the Patani region and the major Thai states since Sukhothai were never fixed.[32] These states were characteristic of what Oliver Wolters called "*mandala*" polities — circles of free

---

[29] See *Tarikh Fatani* (2002), pp. 15–6.
[30] *Hikayat Patani: The Story of Patani*, p. 155.
[31] *Sejarah Kerajaan Melayu Patani* (2002), pp. 37–8.
[32] Bangnara, *Patani: Dahulu dan Sekarang*, pp. 10–1.

states.[33] Since the extent of Sukhothai's territories on the southern peninsula remains debatable, it is unfair to claim the finality of any version based mainly on non-contemporary sources. The true extent of King Ramkhamhaeng's territories therefore must be carefully defined. The same applies to Ayutthaya's supposed expansion to include control over Melaka, which the book claims had not been definitively shown. Bangnara devotes a lengthy discussion to relations between Patani and Ayutthaya. Sultan Muzaffar initiated peaceful coexistence with Ayutthaya as demonstrated by his visit, even though he was not formally and properly welcomed by the Ayutthaya ruler. Later, during the Burmese sacking of Ayutthaya in 1563, Sultan Muzaffar had led a force of 200 boats to occupy the palace at Ayutthaya. The capital city, however, was soon retaken by Ayutthaya's forces. Interestingly, Bangnara provides only a very brief description of these events.[34] The era of Patani's queens is discussed thoroughly by Bangnara. Since no male prince or descendant could be found, Patani was for the next few years ruled by queens. Raja Hijau began her rule in 1584 (d. 1616). Under her, a new waterway was dug and trade prospered as foreign merchants came in larger numbers, especially the Portuguese and the Dutch. In 1603, Ayutthaya launched an expedition against Patani but it was repelled with the help of foreign gun suppliers. Indeed, Ayutthaya itself later also purchased cannons from Patani. For Bangnara, the sending of tribute to Ayutthaya is often misinterpreted. On the part of the sender, the tribute simply represented a wish to strengthen friendly relations between the two sides. However, the recipient considers the presenter as being willing to submit to his sovereignty. He uses the example of the tributary relationship between Ayutthaya and China: the present or tribute submitted by the Ayutthayan king to the China court was considered by Beijing to represent the submission of Ayutthaya to China. However, tribute did not represent the submission of an occupied country to the master. It was a show of friendship.

Similarly, Nik Anuar argues that in its long history, Patani as a regional power had options to establish relations with regional powers and neighboring states in "multi-centric circles." Patani thus opted for the arrangement that served it best.[35] In the face of advances by Sukhothai and Ayutthaya, Patani was never an exclusive part or colony of these kingdoms.

---

[33] See Oliver Wolters, *History, Culture, and Region in Southeast Asian Perspectives* (Ithaca, NY: Southeast Asia Program, Cornell University, 1999).

[34] Ibid., pp. 15–8.

[35] Nik Anuar, *Sejarah Perjuangan Melayu Patani*, pp. 18–23.

Rather, Patani maintained loose relations depending on the changing political and military environments — oscillating between acting as a vassal and an independent state. However, internal divisions and elite rivalry, common features of contemporary Malay politics, led to Patani's decline and forced its ruler Raja Kuning (1635–1688) to send tribute to Ayutthaya in return for the Thai title, *Phra Chao*. In the early 18th century, Patani witnessed the rise to power of the Kelantan dynasty. Basing his account on the *Hikayat Patani*, Nik Anuar explains the Thai incursion into Patani. He identifies the last ruler of this dynasty as Along Yunus, who was murdered by his own older brother, the *bendahara* Dato Pangkalan. Around the mid-18th century continuing political instability led to the decline of trade as foreign merchants left to trade at other regional ports. In the wake of the Thai revival after the expulsion of Burmese forces from Ayutthaya and the coming to power of the Chakri dynasty (Patani and its allies in the south had taken advantage of the wars to declare their independence), in 1785, Patani's ruler Sultan Muhammad and his troops were defeated. 4,000 Patanis were brought as war captives to Bangkok. The Chakri ruler then appointed Tengku Lamidin as Patani's ruler. In 1791, he led a rebellion against the central Thai government's troops in the southern towns, but the rebellion was soon suppressed. Datuk Pangkalan was then appointed by the Chakri to the throne of Patani. In 1808, Patani once again rebelled against the central government but was defeated. In the wake of all these rebellions, Patani was divided into seven divisions, each led by a *raja* under the supervision of the Songkhla governor. This reorganization led to the demise of the great Patani Malay kingdom. The reorganization was obviously designed to weaken Patani's resistance. The new policy introduced among other things: a new code of death penalty for those who rebelled against the central government; the appointment of a Siamese ruler of one of the seven divisions as an agent of Bangkok to report on the other rulers; and the resettlement of Siamese to the south.

Mohd. Zamberi locates Patani in a regional geopolitical structure linking the Thai kingdom of Ayutthaya and the Malay states of the peninsula. He argues that Patani's role was to provide peace for its southern neighbors by acting as a buffer polity between the Thai state and Patani's Malay neighbors. This was due primarily to Patani's sacrifices and resilience in facing Siam's unceasing challenges.[36] By the 16th century, Patani had emerged as the most powerful Malay state on the peninsula. Its importance lay with its

---

[36] Zamberi, *Patani dalam Tamadun Melayu*, pp. 13–8.

strategic trading position which enabled it to attract merchants from both the East and the West. More specifically, Patani's greatness depended on its system of defenses and the security of its capital which inspired awe among its rivals. The legendary Malay hero Hang Tuah is quoted as having praised Patani's impregnable defenses. Its three great cannons were renowned. Patani was not only a center of power and trade but was also well-known as a part of a crucial network for Islamization. It became a melting pot for many Muslim nationalities, encouraging further exchange between Muslim states. Patani thus emerged as a great capital. Indeed, Patani was able to mount a formidable army which was crucial in defending its independence from its traditional enemy, Siam, which had been waiting for an opportunity to strike. Later, the imposition of Siamese vassalage over the Malay states was made possible because of military threats and the manipulation of local conflict. Thus, Patani as a Malay Muslim state had long acted as a buffer against the threat of this traditional enemy, protecting other Malay states and preserving their independence and sovereignty in order to implement Islamic government. Patani's defenses were seriously tested when Ayutthaya launched major attacks on May 11, 1634, in the wake of the Queen's criticism of the Ayutthaya king. But the attacks were successfully repelled. From that time onward, Patani became the target of the Siamese rulers' vengeance. Its strong defenses clearly made Patani an influential state in the region. Patani's territories expanded to Trengganu, Kelantan, Patani, Songkhla and Phatthalung — as the earlier kingdom of Langkasuka had once done. Patani's strength came from its new style of governing which was suited to the contemporary context. When faced with impending attacks by Ayutthaya, Patani rallied support from its allies Johor and Pahang which had a common interest in defending themselves from the same northern threat. Even though the attacks were staved off, the Thais never ceased to seek Patani's annihilation. The fact remains, however, that for centuries Ayutthaya had failed to conquer Patani.

On War and Diplomacy

Later Patani writers have been enthusiastic in attesting to Patani's victories and resilience in the face of defeat and humiliation.

The author of the *Hikayat Patani* provides us with numerous accounts of Patani's combination of diplomacy and war in dealing with external powers. This can be seen clearly in the two initiatives taken by Sultan Muzaffar Shah *vis-à-vis* 16th-century Ayutthaya. We are told that the sultan first paid homage to the Ayutthayan king, who did not show great interest, despite providing hospitality and personal comforts for the Patani ruler.[37] The author of the *Hikayat Patani* recounts another episode of a military expedition against Ayutthaya without clearly defining the reasons for the undertaking. Only the sultan's previous visit and the humiliation he underwent can be taken as a clue to the decision to launch the expedition. Owing to the strength and greatness of Ayutthaya, it is not surprising to find that the expedition was disguised as a diplomatic mission. Indeed, the sultan was warmly welcomed on his second visit to Ayutthaya.[38] Interestingly, the *Hikayat Patani* gives us some frank descriptions, rare in the Malay historiography, about the defeat suffered by the Patani forces in Ayutthaya.[39] The reigns of Patani's queens are presented as mixing both defensive warfare and diplomacy. For example, during Ayutthaya's attacks on Patani during Raja Hijau's reign, victory for Patani was achieved through the use of deceptions designed to upset Ayutthaya's logistics and food stocks. Under Raja Ungu, more aggressive diplomacy toward Ayutthaya was undertaken. Interestingly, Patani's later rulers are represented as having neglected diplomacy.[40]

Ibrahim Syukri's *Sejarah Kerajaan Melayu Patani* shows that Patani succeeded in attracting foreign traders to its ports, including the Europeans after the 16th century, which led to prosperity and progress. However, Patani failed to win Ayutthaya's permanent cooperation, as can be seen in attacks and counterattacks by both sides.[41]

A. Bangnara also emphasizes the importance of war and confrontation with Siam, as can be seen from the campaign launched by Sultan Muzaffar to resistance movements led by local leaders.[42]

According to Zamberi, by the early 17th century, Patani had emerged as a great capital. Indeed, Patani was able to mount a formidable army which was crucial in defending its independence from its traditional enemy who was constantly waiting for an opportunity to strike.[43] Nevertheless, Patani eventually submitted to its enemy to the north. In 1786, following almost a year of incessant attacks which destroyed Patani's defenses, the city was sacked by its avenging enemy. Many Patanis met their deaths

---

[37] *Hikayat Patani: The Story of Patani*, pp. 155, 157.

[38] Ibid., p. 158.

[39] Ibid., pp. 160–1.

[40] Ibid., pp. 166–7, 181–3.

[41] See *Sejarah Kerajaan Melayu Patani* (1985), pp. 35–61.

[42] Bangnara, *Patani: Dahulu dan Sekarang*, pp. 13–8.

[43] Zamberi, *Patani dalam Tamadun Melayu*, pp. 16–9.

or suffered extreme hardship. Even though Patani experienced death and starvation, its commitment to the struggle for independence never died. Indeed, from 1789, for the next three years the Patanis (*orang Patani*) under Tengku Lamidin launched a rebellion but to no avail. Vigorous resistance was revived again in 1808 under Datuk Pangkalan, who also eventually met his death. In response to the continuing resistance among the Patanis, the Bangkok regime eventually adopted a divide-and-rule policy by splitting the sultanate up into separate districts. Yet as late as 1832, the Malays from Patani, Kelantan, Terengganu, and Kedah came together in a revolt against Bangkok's interference. Despite early advances, they were once again defeated by the mighty Bangkok forces. Bangkok then applied a strict policy of control. Patani's fate as a buffer state was sealed in the early 20th century when Patani, without the approval of its people, became the only Malay state to come under the direct control of Bangkok.

On Patani's Decline and Defeat

The end of Patani's founding dynasty toward the end of the 17th century occupies an important place in Patani's decline. Attempts at finding a solution were initiated but to no avail. Indeed, during the reign of the last queen, Raja Kuning, initiatives to follow a more open policy, including more active diplomacy toward Ayutthaya, were launched. During Patani's golden days, it was easier to identify Patani with the state, its rulers and/or achievements. But after its defeat and devastation in the late 18th century, Patani must have looked for an identity. For Patani historians, successive defeats since the late 18th century did not stop the resistance of the Patani people against the central Thai government. In fact, diverse resistance movements and rebellions were constantly launched. For some, the 1832 rebellion is a watershed in the open warfare launched by the Patanis.

The signs of Patani's decline are expressed by the *Hikayat Patani* in terms of a moral crisis and overspending. The embarrassing love affairs which involved the Queen's husband were merely the tip of an iceberg of a deeper crisis in the palace. More specifically, the fact that the Queen had to resort to the use of her own private purse to fund state affairs is also an indication of the state's bankrupt finances. The emergence of new trading centers in Johor-Riau, Manila and Melaka-Batavia, seriously undermined Patani's trading role.[44] Political crises and infighting followed the death of Raja Kuning. A

---

[44] *Hikayat Patani: The Story of Patani*, pp. 185–6.

new dynasty came to power, reflecting the changing geopolitical constellation and shaky political arrangements. This was a period dominated by what is popularly known as the Kelantan rulers.[45]

For Ibrahim Syukri's *Sejarah Kerajaan Melayu Patani*, Patani's decline and defeat came from a complex mix of internal and external factors. A lack of leadership since the end of the founding dynasty was the major reason for the diplomatic failures and military catastrophes in 1786, 1791 and 1832. Yet, the heroic resistance of the Patani Malays is given great prominence in this representation of Patani's fate.[46]

The decline and defeat of Patani in the second half of the 18th century, according to Bangnara, was due to political instability, economic decline and the emergence of the newly-installed Chakri dynasty in Bangkok. Like other modern Patani historians, Bangnara gives special attention to the leaders and people of Patani who worked together and repeatedly launched resistance movements.[47] For Mohd. Zamberi, despite the defeat and the end of the independent sultanate, Patani showed its resilience in reviving its cultural strength and accommodating itself to the challenging new political environment.[48]

For Ahmad Fathi, the great defeat of 1786 was due not to a lack of capability for war, but to mistaken strategies, since Patani had been free from foreign attack for the previous half-century. He argues that unpreparedness for war and neglect of its defenses was the cause of a major strategic blunder. Also, the death of Patani's last queen, Kuning, in the mid-17th century had led to internal instability as rival claimants fought for the throne. No less than 11 claimants were deposed, murdered or killed. Following its defeat in 1785, Patani mounted several failed rebellions until Bangkok decided to install non-Patani rulers in power in 1816.[49]

Unlike Nik Anuar, Ahmad Fathi argues that the major battles fought in 1832 were decisive for the future of Patani. His view of the importance of these battles for Patani is based on what he calls "traditional accounts" and "popular lore" among the Patanis, who refer to these events as a life-or-death struggle to repel "the enemy of the country of Patani" (*musuh*

---

[45] Ibid., pp. 185–201.

[46] *Sejarah Kerajaan Melayu Patani* (1985), pp. 39–62.

[47] See Bangnara, *Patani: Dahulu dan Sekarang*, pp. 29–42, 49–62.

[48] See Zamberi, *Patani dalam Tamadun Melayu*, pp. 18–9, and Mohd. Zamberi A. Malek, *Umat Islam Patani: Sejarah dan Politik* [*The Patani Islamic Community: History and Politics*] (Shah Alam: Hizbi, 1993), pp. 130–44.

[49] Ahmad Fathi, *Pengantar Sejarah Patani*, pp. 48–51.

Patani). Cooperation between different Malay states, especially between Patani and Kedah, is regarded by the Patanis as not only a crucial moment in determining their own future, but also a significant marker in their perception of the external threat from Bangkok to all the regional — read Malay — polities.[50] By contrast, Nik Anuar, who relied heavily on British sources, does not give even a note to the 1832 war. For Nik Anuar, the major resistance in the post-1786 defeat was that led by Tengku Lamidin and Datuk Pangkalan in 1791 and 1808, respectively. These rebellions led to a major restructure of the administration of Patani into seven smaller territorial divisions. Interestingly, Nik Anuar does not mention the major battles led by Kedah and Patani leaders against Bangkok. However, he does refer to the Siamese invasion of Kedah in 1821 and the Burney Treaty of 1826 between the British and the Bangkok governments. Internally, the now divided Patani state was governed by Bangkok-appointed Malay officials under the supervision of the Songkhla commissioner or governor. From 1842 Patani proper was assigned to a Kelantan aristocrat, Tuan Besar. His descendants occupied the seat of the Patani sultanate until Bangkok ended the system in 1902. For Nik Anuar, the decision by Rama III to appoint local elites as his officials in the now divided Patani lessened the central government's interference in local affairs and led to a degree of stability and security for the next half century.[51]

For Ahmad Fathi, the defeat in 1832 was a catastrophe for Patani. Based on local tradition, he points to the failure of the production of staple crops, the exodus of a large part of the population from Patani, and starvation, as the result of the devastating war. "After the 1832 war, no major battle took place between Patani and Bangkok (Siam). Any resistance movement that took place after 1832 was no more than local unrest that had little repercussion for Patani."[52] For Ahmad Fathi, the weak local response was due mainly to the increasing control of the central government over local affairs, including over the territorial divisions of Patani, appointments of outsiders to local administration, and Bangkok's administrative centralization of the south mediated by the supervision of a High Commissioner in Songkhla. He also considers the role of the British as having been crucial to determining Patani's fate, especially from the beginning of the 20th century. In his view, Patani was sacrificed for British

---

[50] Ibid., pp. 62, 64.

[51] Nik Anuar, *Sejarah Perjuangan Melayu Patani*, pp. 22–3.

[52] Ahmad Fathi, *Pengantar Sejarah Patani*, p. 66.

larger regional interests when the 1909 treaty was signed between the British and the Bangkok government.[53]

On Centralization and Resistance

The formal end of the Patani sultanate at the beginning of the 20th century has been taken very seriously by modern Patani historians and writers. Despite or because of the fact of Ibrahim Syukri's nationalist leanings in the *Sejarah Kerajaan Melayu Patani*, it is evident that the disappearance of the sultanate forced Patani to empower itself by invigorating cultural and religious identity.[54] Bangnara uses highly evocative expressions when discussing this period of Patani history, for example, Bangkok's "policy of oppression and cleansing." Such emotionally charged passages are certain to have influenced the thinking of many Patani *Jawis*.[55] For Zamberi, the process of administrative centralization launched by the government in Bangkok since the beginning of the 20th century never failed, almost by default, to provoke resistance and opposition among the Patanis.[56]

According to Ahmad Fathi, the dawn of the 20th century did not provide a new opportunity for freedom in Patani, as the Patanis lost their own rulers, the sultans, who were replaced by Thai bureaucrats. He contrasted the political failure in Patani with the emergence of new generations of nationalist movements in other Southeast Asian countries striving for independence.[57] Ahmad Fathi maintains that the loss of the key cultural and political symbol of the sultan seriously eroded Patani identity. Without the sultan, Patani became a mere territorial entity of no local significance within the Siamese state: "The sun had already set in Patani: it is too painful to long for tomorrow's dawn." Moreover, he contrasted the praise customarily given to King Chulalongkorn in keeping Siam's independence and territories and modernizing the kingdom from the late 19th century, with the loss of the sultan's throne in Patani. Indeed, the abolition of the Patani sultanate in 1902 gave Bangkok increased bargaining power *vis-à-vis* the British to retain Patani as an integral part of its territory during the negotiation for the 1909 Anglo-Siamese agreement.

---

[53] Ibid., pp. 67–72.

[54] *Sejarah Kerajaan Melayu Patani* (1985), pp. 63–77.

[55] Bangnara, *Patani: Dahulu dan Sekarang*, pp. 49–62.

[56] Zamberi, *Umat Islam Patani*, pp. 130–44.

[57] Ahmad Fathi, *Pengantar Sejarah Patani*, pp. 72–4.

Ahmad Fathi does not, however, mention any violent reaction to the dismissal of the sultan in 1902. Even the oft-mentioned Nasa unrest in the south in 1922, in protest against the implementation of the new national education policy by Bangkok, only receives a passing remark in his account. Indirectly he alludes to the changing mood of the Malay "awakening" in neighboring British Malaya, where organization among the Malays had weakened as British development programs won the day. The fact that in July 1923 the Siamese king issued an amendment to the education policy with the aim of soothing Muslim religious sensitivities, demonstrates, for Ahmad Fathi, that the Patanis had been unfairly treated.[58] Cultural and social pressures on Patani through the state's education policy intensified, however, with the introduction of the Thai *Rattaniyom*, or "Cultural Directives," in 1939. The euphoria for democratic reform in Thailand following the 1932 *coup d'état* against the absolute monarchy soon came to an end when it became clear that the people's representatives in the National Assembly were powerless to convey the wishes of the voters, especially in the case of the Patanis in the south. For Ahmad Fathi, the new Thai nationalism campaigns worsened the prospects for cultural survival, not to mention autonomy, of minorities in modern Thailand. The Thai state's new assimilationist policy on which the *Rattaniyom* were based gave no hope for the Patanis to expect a major change in the direction of increased political participation. A different path had to be sought. Indeed, the initial participation of the Patanis in and expectation from the new democratic regime shifted to a more confrontational stand after 1939. This confrontation took place not in terms of armed resistance but through diplomatic maneuvering, in particular by the Patani religious leader, Haji Sulong. Haji Sulong is credited with formulating the famous seven-point memorandum of self-rule presented to the Thai government. Interestingly, Ahmad Fathi argues that there was no immediate protest or negative reaction to the Thai *Rattaniyom* in Patani until the proposal to establish a council dealing with questions of Islamic law in Patani (*al-Hay'at al-Tanfidhiya lil-Ahkam al-Shar`iya*) sometime in 1939. Haji Sulong was elected chairman of the new council. Its major decision in 1943 to form a local religious court led by religious scholars was a specific response by the Patanis to the Thai *Rattaniyom*. According to the proposal, three religious scholars, including Haji Sulong, were appointed to administer family issues among Muslims in Patani according to Islamic law.[59]

---

[58] Ibid., pp. 77–8.
[59] Ibid., pp. 84–6.

For Nik Anuar, the period of Patani's awakening following the end of the Pacific War produced two prominent figures: one, an aristocrat, Tengku Muhyiddin and the other, a religious leader, Haji Sulong. If Haji Sulong consolidated local resilience through modern forms of religious instruction and organization, the Tengku led a movement to attain freedom for his countrymen through negotiation with the British. Sulong represented a grassroots movement while the Tengku launched diplomatic maneuverings outside Patani. Yet according to Nik Anuar, the result was the same. Tengku Muhyiddin's diplomatic efforts and demands were sidelined by more pressing British interests in Southeast Asia. On the other hand, Haji Sulong eventually faced the hard reality of politics in postwar Thailand. In 1954, he disappeared, presumed murdered, after having earlier been released from three years' imprisonment.[60]

On Patani's Heroes and Resilient Patriotism

Modern Patani historiography provides discursive tools to reformulate events, places and figures in Patani's past as national symbols that contribute to contemporary Patani identity. Such a use of the past is particularly prominent in Ahmad Fathi's *Pengantar Sejarah Patani*.

For example, the history of Patani is elided with that of the great maritime empire of Srivijaya which controlled much of the Malay peninsula and Sumatra. Patani developed into an important regional center in the wake of Srivijaya's territorial expansion in the eighth century. Patani eventually came under the influence Srivijaya's *mandala* — or political, religious and cultural circle. It endorsed Mahayana Buddhism which facilitated the wider use of Srivijaya's Malay lingua franca, leading to the formation of a locally-based, Srivijaya-oriented elite and ruling class. It was around this time that the actual polity called Patani emerged.

Another meaningful symbol for Patanis today is perhaps its greatest ruler, Sultan Muzaffar Shah. He is represented by Ahmad Fathi as the true builder of the Patani polity as shown by his determination to establish stability and facilitate trade through an outward orientation. His diplomatic stance toward Ayutthaya can be seen as open and directed toward expanding economic and trading opportunities. His decision to take advantage of the crisis that beset Ayutthaya in the second half of the 16th century can be viewed in this context. His military campaigns against Ayutthaya, where on

---

[60] Nik Anuar, *Sejarah Perjuangan Melayu Patani*, Chapters 4 and 5.

one occasion he attacked and occupied the royal palace, indeed, place him among the greatest of heroes of the Patani *Jawis*.

Patani's famous queens, Raja Hijau, Raja Biru, and Raja Ungu, also feature prominently as contemporary symbols. Patani's queens emerged as leaders of nation-building. Indeed, under their reign, Patani experienced its golden age of prosperity, enjoying expansive trade and emerging as an influential political center in the region.

Not least among the most potent symbols of Patani in the work of Ahmad Fathi are the political figures who are reconstituted as resistance leaders: Tengku Lamidin, Datuk Pangkalan and Tengku Sulung. The subject of resistance to the Siamese advance and centralization has occupied a major part of such historiography. For Ahmad Fathi, the events of 1832 are considered the act of resistance *par excellence*, as they reflect the heroic actions and wider solidarity among the Patani people to defend Patani's right to self-rule.

Patani's last sultan, ʿAbdul Kadir Kamaruddin, is considered by many Patanis as a modern Patani statesman who used the modern means of diplomacy to protect his power and his people. Although he did not achieve anything but imprisonment and exile, he initiated a new way of defending Patani.[61] His determination to maintain his status and Patani's right to self-rule has inspired many Patanis who continue to respect the ideal of the Malay sultanate as important and indispensable to Patani identity.

For Ahmad Fathi, the career of Haji Sulong represents another crucial episode in Patani's endeavor to achieve self-rule. If the 1932 Revolution and overthrow of the absolute monarchy in Bangkok inspired new hope for winning an ear in the Thai capital through open political representation, events after 1939 brought only disappointment and despair. Political representation meant nothing, as shown by the oppressive policy of the Phibun government toward minorities, including the Patanis. Sulong won popular recognition for his religious knowledge and his dedication to the Patani people. According to Ahmad Fathi, following the abolition of the administrative enactment on Islamic family law in 1943, Sulong formed a local organization to take over the matter. He thus grew close to ordinary Patanis through his handling of family issues and legal cases among the Patani Muslims. Such an undertaking is not a novelty among Muslim scholars; however, he did it by means of a modern form of social and political organization. With such influence, not surprisingly, he had the courage to

---

[61] Ahmad Fathi, *Pengantar Sejarah Patani*, pp. 71–2.

initiate a political movement in 1947 that led to the submission of the seven-point proposal for Patani autonomy.

Conclusion

Successive genres of Patani *Jawi* historiography — traditional, Islamic, and modern — which are widely read among the Patani intellectual community, have thus left their mark on contemporary Patani identity. First of all, long before the arrival of Islam, the Patanis had identified themselves as Patani Austronesians who lived independently of Thai control and without any association with or subjection to a major kingdom, i.e., a Patani Austronesian identity without a crown. The acceptance of Islam by a Patani ruler, contemporary with the Sultanate of Melaka, led to the foundation of the Patani *Jawi* sultanate. The sultan thus became the upholder of religion and state. He was the pivot of state, religion and society. This lasted until the formal abolition of the sultanate by the Bangkok regime in 1902. The crisis created by the end of the symbolic head of the Patani polity (even if the real power of the Patani sultan had ended over a century earlier) paved the way not only for the emergence of the Patani *Jawi* nation, but also for an *ulama*-oriented solidarity. The intensification of Thai nationalism after 1939, concomitant with the rise of nationalism in Southeast Asia during and after the Second World War, stimulated the search for a new political formula including autonomy, under the aegis of modern political movements but with continuing reference to Islam. Following the end of the Patani sultanate incorporation within the reorganized and centralized Thai state became the political fate for the Patanis, but a steadfast defense of religious and cultural autonomy was necessary for the *umma*-oriented Islamic community.

CHAPTER 12

Patani Militant Leaflets and the Uses of History[1]

Duncan McCargo

Matters in history are the source of the consequences in the present.[2]

Since January 2004, the southern Thai provinces of Pattani, Yala and Narathiwat have experienced serious political violence that has claimed the lives of around 7,000 people.[3] Opinion about the causes of the violence remains divided, but most scholars agree that the majority of major incidents have been orchestrated by local militant groups. These groups seek to legitimate their actions with reference to "separatist" ideologies emphasizing

---

[1] The research presented here was funded by the Economic and Social Research Council, grant number RES-000-22-1344. Research assistance for this chapter was provided by Saronee Duerae and Kaneeworn Opetagon. Many thanks are due to Srisompob Jitpiromsri and his colleagues at Prince of Songkhla University, Pattani, for hosting my fieldwork from September 2005 to September 2006. I gratefully acknowledge further support provided during my time at the Asia Research Institute, National University of Singapore (2006–2007), where two earlier presentations of material in the paper were given. My thanks go to Anthony Reid and Michael Laffan for inviting me to speak on this topic.

[2] Leaflet 18. On April 24, 2005 at 9pm, two teenage boys on a grayish-black Honda Wave motorcycle threw these leaflets in front of Nong-rad health center, Yaring, Pattani.

[3] For recent studies of the Southern situation, see Marc Askew, "Thailand's Intractable Southern War: Policy, Insurgency and Discourse," *Contemporary Southeast Asia* 30, 2 (2008): 186–214, Chaiwat Satha-Anand, ed., *Imagined Land: The State and Southern Violence in Thailand* (Fuchu: ILCAA, Tokyo University of Foreign Languages, 2009); Chaiwat Satha-Anand, *Khwamrunræng kap kanchatkan "khwamching": Pattani nai*

Malay historical and cultural oppression at the hands of the Thai state, and by invoking the idea that Islam has been suppressed and abused by Thailand.[4] Because no group has claimed formal responsibility for the violence, hard evidence about the explanations used to invoke these sources of historical and religious legitimacy is difficult to come by. However, some indications of the themes of the radical discourse underpinning the violence may be found in the anonymous leaflets widely distributed in the Southern border provinces, which may originate with militants or their sympathizers.

The use of anonymous leaflets (*baipliw*) has an honorable tradition in Bangkok and central Thai politics, an ideal medium given the constraints on information imposed by monarchical and military regimes. For decades, they were commonly distributed in the vicinity of the Sanam Luang. Paul Handley cites examples of the royal family using such leaflets in their own internal feuds.[5] This tradition is related to the practice of using pen-names, and the prevalence of anonymous newspaper columns.[6] Leaflets have been an important element in the Southern conflict for decades, and have become especially salient given the escalation of the conflict since late 2001, which did not penetrate popular consciousness until January 2004. The proliferation of leaflets contributes to a general sense that the violence is decentralized, "a network without a core" and lacks conventional leadership. This form of decentralized communication is an indirect way of laying claim to attacks and linking them to an unidentified and unnamed struggle. The use of leaflets by militants creates a sense of proximity (since their distribution is highly localized) and fear.

----

rop krug sattawat [*Violence and Managing the Truth: Pattani in the Last Half Century*] (Bangkok: Thammasat University Press, 2008); and Duncan McCargo, *Tearing Apart the Land: Islam and Legitimacy in Southern Thailand* (Ithaca, NY: Cornell University Press 2008), and *Mapping National Anxieties: Thailand's Southern Conflict* (Copenhagen: NIAS Press, 2012).

[4] For a classic statement of such positions, see Ibrahim Syukri, *History of the Malay Kingdom of Patani*, trans. Conner Bailey and John Miskic (Chiang Mai: Silkworm, 2005). The question of how far Bangkok ever really controlled Patani is explored in Davisakd Puaksom, "Of a Lesser Brilliance: Patani Historiography in Contention," in *Thai South and Malay North: Ethnic Interactions on the Plural Peninsula*, ed. Michael J. Montesano and Patrick Jory (Singapore: NUS Press, 2008), pp. 71–88.

[5] Paul Handley, *The King Never Smiles* (New Haven: Yale University Press, 2006).

[6] The classic study of these newspaper columns during their heyday in the sixth reign is Matthew Copeland, "Contested Nationalism and the 1932 Overthrow of the Absolute Monarchy in Siam," Unpublished PhD thesis, Australian National University, 1993.

The use of anonymous notices and leaflets to fuel insurgencies and violent conflicts is by no means confined to Thailand. Much the same applies to the recent violence in the Malukus, where Nils Bubandt has argued that anonymous pamphlets functioned as what he terms "hardcopy rumors." Locating these pamphlets within an Indonesian tradition of *surat kaleng* (can letters),[7] also known as "dark leaflets" (*selebaran gelap*) or "circular letters" (*surat edaran*), Bubant argues:

> Can letters are a subgenre of Indonesian political instigation, the centrality and complexity of which have so far been ignored. Although political 'black letters' and leaflets may start their lives as instruments of propaganda, their politics is not exhausted by rational choice or resource mobilization theory. Their unclear origins and the persistent obscurity about whether they are revelations of hidden plans or planted fakes make them part of both political discourse and practice. This paper has argued that can letters are best analyzed as 'hardcopy' rumors that have the affectivity of rumor and both the authoritative and contested nature of writing. I have further suggested that it is in the interplay between political authority and political contestation that the hardcopy rumors need to be analyzed.[8]

The anonymous leaflets circulated in Patani blended the Thai *baipliw* tradition with the Malay *surat kaleng*, though with a sinister twist reminiscent of similar communication techniques used in Afghanistan. The distribution of so-called "night letters" by the Taliban has been extensively discussed in media reports.[9] Thomas Johnson's academic analysis of Taliban night letters identifies six major themes: an appeal to past Afghan struggles against "foreign invaders"; the battle between the Taliban and the Karzai regime as a "cosmic conflict" between good and evil; the enemies of the Taliban are crusaders seeking to undermine Islam; martyrdom is celebrated as a powerful weapon; fighting enemies involves saving honor; and supporting the enemy is prohibited and may result in death.[10] While the themes of martyrdom and honor are little found in the Patani leaflets, the other "night letter" themes

---

[7] Nils Bubant, "Rumors, Pamphlets and the Politics of Paranoia in Indonesia," *Journal of Asian Studies* 67, 3 (August 2008): 790.

[8] Ibid., p. 811.

[9] See, for example, Declan Walsh, "Night Letters from the Taliban Threaten Afghan Democracy," *The Guardian*, September 19, 2004; and Thomas A. Johnson, "The Taliban Insurgency and an Analysis of Shabnamah (Night Letters)," *Small Wars and Insurgencies* 18, 3 (September 2007): 317–44.

[10] Johnson, "The Taliban Insurgency," p. 339.

have striking parallels in their southern Thai counterparts, especially the first theme about historical struggles, and the last theme about not aiding the enemy.

Sources of the Leaflets — Official, Personal, Public

In a research paper on leaflets commissioned by the National Reconciliation Commission, Saronee Duerae claimed that people are scared to circulate leaflets and so, often destroy them or hand them in to officials.[11] He refers to leaflets ironically as "the worst form of media, just because they are too good." Peddlers are regular sources of rumors and stories based on leaflets, which are often exaggerated. Teashops and mosques are the main places where contents are discussed in public, while women commonly discuss the leaflets at home. Leaflets form one element in the climate of fear and rumor that pervades much conversation in the South. People will be given hints or advice about the likely future location of bombs or other attacks, advice that may be based on genuine information from the militant movement, or entirely false.[12] On the basis of those rumors, people may avoid certain locations at certain times, leaving popular areas or restaurants surprisingly quiet.

This chapter draws on a collection of copies of around 120 leaflets, mainly dating from 2004 to 2006, which I gathered from a range of sources, primarily during major fieldwork in Patani between September 2005 and September 2006.[13] Many of the leaflets disseminated are in Thai, while a few are in Jawi script. Certain leaflets use some elements of *romi* (romanized Malay). Sometimes scripts are not what they appear: Thai is sometimes used to transliterate Patani Malay, and occasionally Jawi is even used to transliterate Thai. The writers and readers of the scripts are in a linguistic twilight zone between Thai and Malay, and often seem semi-literate in both languages. Simply deciphering the leaflets is often technically challenging,

---

[11] สะรอนี ดือแระ, ความเห็นของคนท้องถิ่นต่อสถานการณ์ความรุนแรงภาคใต้: ศึกษาจากใบปลิว ข้อเขียนข้างอาคาร สื่อท้องถิ่น [Saronee Duerae, *Perceptions of Local People Concerning the Southern Violence: A Study from Leaflets, Graffiti, and Local Media*] (Bangkok: National Reconciliation Commission, 2006), pp. 21–6.

[12] See Michael K. Connors, "Another Country: Reflections on the Politics and Culture of the Muslim South," in *Divided Over Thaksin: Thailand's Coup and Problematic Transition*, ed. John Funston (Singapore: Institute of Southeast Asian Studies, 2009), p. 121.

[13] Numbers used to refer to leaflets in the footnotes are those I assigned to the collection in my possession.

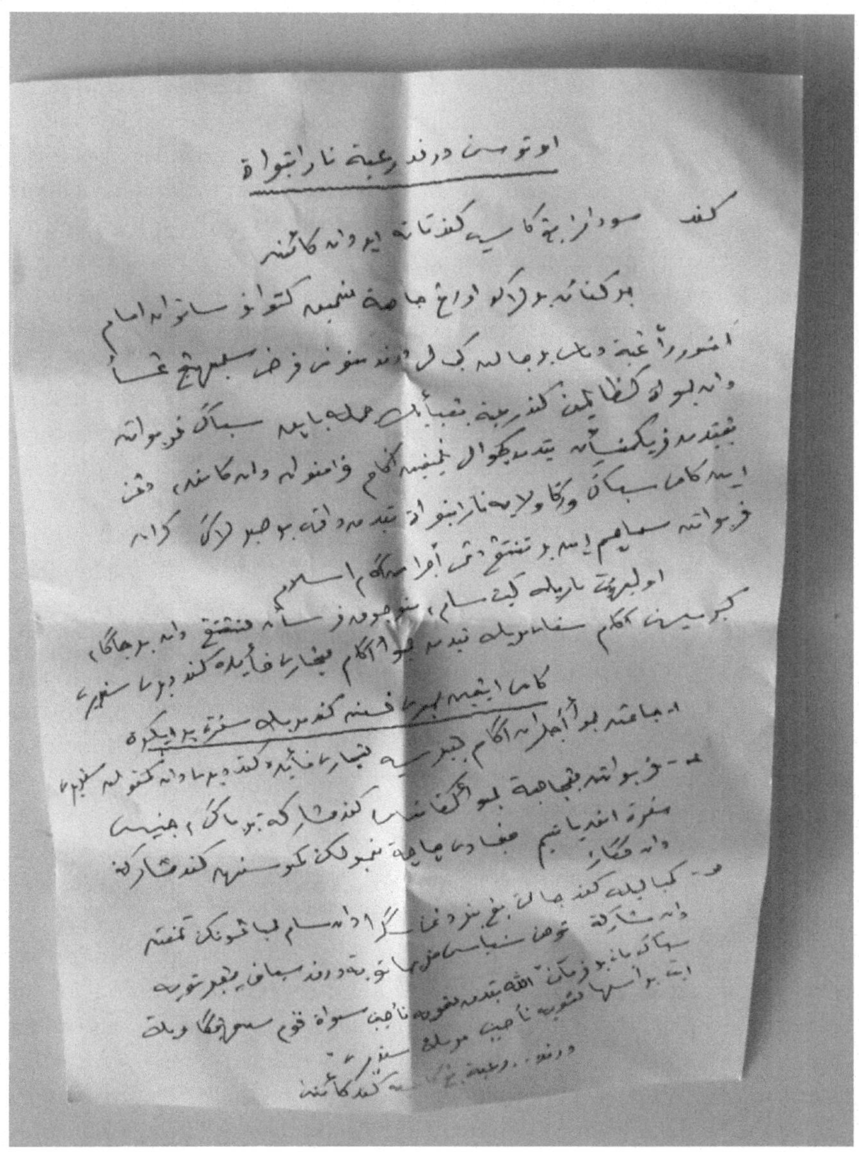

Figure 12.1 Militant leaflet in *Jawi* script found in Jo Airong district, Narathiwat province, 2005.

let alone producing a robust translation. For some leaflets, the main impact is apparently visual and psychological, notably those using cartoons or cut-and-pasted images from newspapers. Other leaflets contain elaborate texts and very sophisticated messages.

Leaflets may be classified into different groups. The most common are warning leaflets, usually issued in advance of incidents, urging people to desist from acting as spies, working with the state in posts such as village headman, or offering services such as selling goods or teaching in government schools. Another genre of warning leaflets are post-incident leaflets, highlighting the significance of events that have already occurred to increase a sense of fear and deliver specific messages. Most warning leaflets are short and to the point. A second group — the main focus of this chapter — might be termed militant propaganda leaflets. Themes of these leaflets include the work of the security forces, sexual abuses by military, injustice, abuses by the Thaksin government, and historical and religious grievances. It is striking that these leaflets are almost entirely regional or domestic in content, though there are occasional references to the United States or to international issues.

Some leaflets are clearly not issued by militants, but are "counter-militant" documents. These include what might be termed "Muslim anti-militant leaflets." These purport to be from fellow-Muslims who are disgusted by the actions of the militants. Many of these are presumably faked by people working for or aligned with the Thai state. Another category are "Buddhist-originated leaflets." Some of these try to enflame anti-Muslim sentiments among Buddhists, and may be distributed either by hard-line Buddhists, or by people with militant sympathies trying to provoke a deterioration of community relations. A final category of leaflets are simply highly satirical. Many of these are quite bizarre, and like other categories of leaflets offer an outlet for individual creativity, testifying to the conditions of social and moral confusion generated by the conflict.

Distinguishing between a "genuine" leaflet and a "fake" leaflet becomes extremely difficult in the polarized and contested conditions of the Southern conflict. But some leaflets are much less plausible than others. Some of the warning notes and many of the anti-militant leaflets seem rather unconvincing. Most of the latter were probably produced by government officials as "psy-ops" ploys to discredit the movement. Some are apparently faked by people sympathetic to the authorities to generate resentment and confusion, such as leaflets urging people to close their shops on Thursdays or Saturdays (when the militants' demand only concerned Fridays). Those leaflets suggesting a significant degree of Islamic knowledge, citing medieval authorities with some confidence, and so reflecting good educational backgrounds, seemed most likely to be genuine. The use of Jawi script or romanized Malay added to their credibility.

The militant (or quasi-militant) leaflets support messy and uncomfortable readings of the violence, and cannot readily be reduced to a simple master narrative. They reflect confusion and ambiguity, mixing themes of Malay or Patani nationalism and Islam. The major concerns articulated are framed in terms of land and other grievances, however, rather than explicitly religious complaints. References in the leaflets were largely domestic: their main themes were focused on greater Patani and its relations with the Thai state. There was little evidence for a globalized view of the world, and few attempted to link the conflict with wider Muslim struggles. One leaflet mentioned the CIA, another Iraq, another the Jews, and one included an image of then US president George W. Bush. But overall they reflected an intensely parochial world view. They contained quite regular reference to issues of history; and numerous references to Islam and to terms such as *munafik* and *kafir*. In these leaflets, Islamic references outnumbered the conventional "separatist" references to Malay history and identity roughly five to three.

Five leaflets, here designated leaflets A, B, C, D and E, are translated below.[14] They have been selected because they pay the greatest attention to historical questions. The first four are typical of the anonymous genre, while E is not really an anonymous leaflet; it first appeared on the internet, and includes an email address for feedback. Leaflets D and E are not militant leaflets. Leaflet D adopts the format of a militant leaflet but the content suggests that it has actually been faked by someone on the Thai side of the conflict. Leaflet E is critical of the violence used by the militant movement and has a propagandist, implicitly pro-Thai tone, though it also reflects some rather confused historical and religious understandings that resonate with militant discourse.

Underlying the discourse of the leaflets are several key issues and questions, including: the glorious history of Patani as a center of Malay culture and Islamic learning; the extent to which Patani was ever an "independent" state; the significance of Patani's tradition of Queenly rule; the extent to which Patani could be considered an Islamic state; the colonization of Patani by Siam/Thailand; the exploitation of Patani labor by the Siamese; the suppression and murder of Patani leaders such as Haji Sulong; and

---

[14] Leaflets A–D have been translated in full, but Leaflet E was so long that I have edited out one section.

especially parallels between historical events and recent actions by the Thaksin government, such as the bloody Krue Se and Tak Bai incidents. The clear aim of leaflets A–C is to assert such parallels. History here is a weapon of war, to be appropriated, often quite opportunistically, for an immediate political purpose.

Militant Leaflets: A, B, and C

Leaflet A

Warning — Guidance[15]

The Patani State Mujahidin Warriors have declared war on the aggressive Siamese Empire. There will be no withdrawal by professional revolutionaries like us. Our lives are given to this cause to attain freedom for the Patani state. Over the last more than 200 years we have experienced the greatest possible oppression, our people are ignorant, under-educated and poor. The natural resources in the area are utilized to feed the capital (Bangkok). Does anyone know or understand the pain and suffering that we are going through? Do [they] even know the feeling of being the slaves? What, then, can demonstrate the commitment of *akidah* and our own *iman*-ness?

We are making a plea to all Malay Muslims, rich, poor, no matter who you are, including state officials, soldiers, policemen or those in various businesses. Please know that even if you don't want to help us directly, Patani *Mujahidin* Warriors please remain neutral. Don't become servants, ears and eyes, spies, or running dogs for the imperialistic Siamese. Thaksin is actually the Pharaoh of Southeast Asia.

- In the time of *Nabi* Musa, Pharaoh has said Musa was the destroyer and betrayer of God, which is impossible except for me. I know all things.[16]
- In the present time Thaksin has declared that whoever shall fight against the Thai government has no religion and has distorted both religion and history.

However, we Patani Malay Muslims know what's going on. We can judge right from wrong. Only those whose hearts have been sealed shut by Allah have become slaves or the running dogs for Pharaoh Thaksin.

---

[15] Leaflet 77. Fax sheet dated November 17, 1997 (clearly wrong). The second page of this leaflet is exactly the same as the second page of Leaflet 18 — apparently recycling some of the same text.

[16] Meaning here is obscure.

Those people have unintentionally become *munafiks*, for they fear their enemies as much as they fear Allah. To make matters even worse, someone who calls himself a Muslim leader of this country has stated at the 38th Leaders' Meeting in Saudi Arabia, that *Mujahidin* Patani State Warriors have killed innocent, guiltless people.[17]

[page 2]

We proclaim this statement to the entire peaceful Islamic world. What we are doing is taking back what belongs to us. We are declaring war with *kafir* Siam who took away our human rights and the sovereignty of Patani state. We want to reclaim our once glorious land of Barokat. Our lives are in the hands of Allah, not *kafir* Thaksin, unlike those who serve as the ears and eyes of the government. It should be made known to the underdogs of Thaksin not to waste their time trying to locate our warriors. We are out there to find you instead, no matter where you are. You will begin to understand the suffering we have to go through.

The Patani Mujahidin fighters
Rise and fall.
We will never give up, not even once.
Iman still keeps us going.
The obstacle that is
If we stay
We will stay with completeness

Good Luck
From P.H.M.

Commentary

A number of leaflets end with the sign-off "P.H.M." The discourse of the leaflet stresses the longstanding conflict between Malay Muslims in Patani and "*kafir* Siam." Major themes include a rejection of Thaksin's claim that those fighting for Patani separatism have distorted religion and history; and a complaint that self-proclaimed Thai Muslim leaders seemed to echo a similar view. The authors of the leaflet seek to undercut Thai state attempts to monopolize discussions about the nature of Patani history, and appeal for sympathy even from moderate Malay Muslims whom they recognize will not give any direct support for the separatist cause.

---

[17] This seems to refer to a statement at the OIC by a prominent Thai Muslim, but I have not been able to trace the exact reference.

Leaflet B

The History that the Malay People Have Never Forgotten[18]

The southern border provinces were once the Patani state, which had its own religion, language, culture, and tradition. There is no reason to hide this fact any longer, because there are many historical documents to prove that Patani was an independent state.

- In 1785 (BE 2328) Patani became a protectorate of the Thai state for the first time.
- In 1789 (BE 2332) Patani became a protectorate of the Thai state for the second time. The name of the country was still Siam at that time. After having incorporated territory from Lan Chang (Laos), Lanna (the North) and part of Cambodia in 1902 (BE 2445), the Thai state enacted a law which included the Patani state as part of the indivisible Thai state, and then changed the name of the country from Siam to Thailand, which it remains today.

The pains that are embedded in the hearts of the Malay people from past to present include:

- Who else dug the San Saeb canal, if not the prisoners of war from Patani?[19]
- Who else burnt down the Krue Se mosque, if not the *kafir* Thai government?
- How many Patani *ulamas* have disappeared without any trace for their *kubors*?[20] Who else could have done that other than the *kafir* Thai government?
- Who killed Hayi Sulong, if not the *kafir* Thai government?
- From past to present, how many innocent people have been killed, 'disappeared,' arrested, and become scapegoats? Who is the one behind it, if not the *kafir* Thai government?
- Lawyer Somchai Neelaphaijit was abducted and killed by evil people. Who ordered the murder, if not the *kafir* Thai government?

---

[18] Leaflet 99.

[19] Similar grievances are commonly expressed by Cambodians. According to the Cambodian Chronicles, 10,000 Cambodian prisoners were taken to Bangkok in 1791 for an earlier canal construction project. See Khin Sok, *Le Cambodge entre le Siam et le Viêtnam (de 1775 à 1860)* (Paris: École Française d'Extrême-Orient, 1991), p. 55. I am very grateful to Trudy Jacobsen for calling my attention to this source.

[20] Trans. "graves."

- Who was behind the Krue Se incident, where around a hundred lives were lost, if not the *kafir* Thai government cooperating with the CIA?

The Tak Bai case:

- The *kafir* government must know where they have kept more than a hundred corpses of innocent Malay people.
- Who ordered the killing of 78 lives of the innocent Malays, if not the *kafir* Thai government?
- Who arrested more than a thousand innocent Malays and accused them of being terrorists, if not the *kafir* Thai government?

'This is not an exaggeration. It's the reality of the Southern border provinces'

What's happening to Patani Malays these days?

[*text box*] Those who know refuse to speak out. They are telling lies to the people and the international community. They trade religion for money and positions.

[*Accompanied by several small pictures at the foot of the page. These are not hand-drawn but seem to be a composite of graphics. One of Thaksin, another of a Muslim with his mouth covered by a dollar bill, another of a headscarf wearing student (caption 'nakrian'), a Thai-looking teacher, and a man with a gun which he is pointing at villagers (caption 'chaoban'). The man whose mouth is covered is being imagined by the student and the villagers, while the teacher is holding a string attached to the man's nose — like a string to control a buffalo*]

A Cry from the People

Commentary

Leaflet B is quite systematic about cataloguing historical grievances against the Siamese state and relating them to the much more recent actions of the Thaksin government. The leaflet makes specific reference to a series of Thai blunders which form the basis of Malay Muslim rejection of Bangkok's rule. The pictures satirize the behavior of the Malay Muslim elite who are accused of colluding with Thai rule and suppressing their identities, bought by "money and positions." Other than the use of the word "*kafir*," there is no obvious Islamic dimension to a set of complaints concerning the appropriation of territory and the use of state violence.

Leaflet C

The Filthy Policies of Imperialistic Siam[21]

1. In 1785, Patani state became the protectorate of imperialistic Siam. Tens of thousands of Malays were killed. The town was burned all the way from Krue Se to the T-Junction Palace.
2. Thousands of Patani Malays became prisoners of war. They were tortured and brutally treated like animals by being chained up together with rattan cords at their heels and having to walk barefoot for thousands of kilometers to become enslaved in the capital city (Bangkok).
3. They forced the Patani-Malay prisoners of war to dig a canal with their bare hands for about ten kilometers around the capital city, until their hands were soaked with blood, and blood came out of their eyes.[22] This is the origin and legend of the present day San Saeb canal.
4. Many Patani Malays were killed in the Dusongor incident. In that same year, there was more killing at Baan Blue Klasamoh, where houses and rice-barns were burned down.
5. In the year 1975, the world was shocked by the news that several Patani Malays were treated like animals by being stuffed into red barrels and burned alive.
6. There were killings of innocent Patani Malays; many of them died and disappeared on 28 April 2004 at Krue Se mosque.
7. Thousands of innocent Patani Malays died and disappeared in the Tak Bai incident. This unprecedented incident shocked the world.
8. Four innocent people were seriously injured in the bombings at the Ma-be village co-operative in Yaha.
9. The shooting of three innocent *pondok* students, who lived in the rented house number 29/23, on the way to Kubor Kubangitae in Pattani. They tried to blame the incident on an internal conflict, a claim which was completely untrue.

It can be determined that both incidents above prove the intention of the *kafir* occupiers to commit genocide against the innocent Malays.

This is only a part of what we want to reveal for the people to learn about the cruelty of the megalomaniac *kafir* Siam. We would like to make a plea to our beloved Patani people to realize that *kafir* Siam the oppressor is actually unreliable, tricky, deceitful, using two faces twenty four hours a day, and cunning in tempting Malay people to fall into

---

[21] Leaflet 102.

[22] This is an idiomatic expression in Thai rather than a literal statement.

their traps and forget about who they really are. They are trying to find a way to wipe out the entire Malay ethnic group using both gentle and aggressive methods.

We! are the warriors to protect the Patani state and to liberate Patani Malays from Allah's tests. We will not flinch, no matter how harsh are the torments the *kafir* occupier inflicts upon us. We will stand firm for the highest goal and the independence of Patani until our deaths!

Warning for those who are at risk:

To all those people involved with the 4,500 baht scheme,[23] including volunteers, various informants, village police, and all those loyal running dogs of *kafir*, please know that you actually are of Malay blood, Malay nationality and the Muslim religion just like us. You are not at all enemies of the Patani *Mujahidin* warriors. However!, if you give cooperation and support to the *kafir* Siam, the aggressors of the Patani state's sovereignty, it is though you are intentionally declaring war on the warriors of Patani state as well.

For this reason, we hope you know which way to choose to keep you and your property safe in this *dunia* and on *Arkiroh* day?

May Allah open up your hearts and guide you and our beloved Malay Muslim people of Patani to the just path.

Amine, With Love and Care

Commentary

This leaflet is divided in the three sections: a numbered list of specific historical grievances, a highly emotive elaboration of those grievances, and a warning to those reading the leaflet not to cooperate with the Thai state. Several of the historical grievances echo those of other leaflets (such as Patani being made a protectorate in 1785, the use of Malay labor to build the Saen Saeb canal, the Dusongnyor episode, and the Krue Se incident), while points 8 and 9 refer to much smaller and more localized events that would have been familiar to people where the leaflets were distributed. An explicit political message includes the demand for Patani independence.

---

[23] This was a job creation scheme operated by the Thaksin government, which paid unemployed local young people 4,500 baht a month to work for the public sector or in voluntary projects.

Questionable Leaflets: D and E

Leaflet D

The Disorder in the Southern Region of Thailand[24]

Assalam Maulaikum my beloved Muslim brothers and sisters.

When did that disorder happen?

First, we have to look at the history.

In the period of Field-Marshal Pho Pibulsongkram, he had his police buddy, Police General Phao Sriyanont, the director general of the Police Department. His famous slogan is 'under the sunlight, there's nothing that the Thai police officers cannot do.' They were responsible for the disappearance of Haji Sulong Tohmeena after the court filed the order to release him. It marked the origin of the separatist movements in the Southern region.

Under Prime Minister M.R. Kukrit Pramoj (B.E. 2518) 1975, an incident occurred when the marines killed five students, one survived at Baan Koktor, Saiburi. It was the cause of a massive demonstration at Benjamarachuthit School Pattani. On the second day of the protest, the security sector of that time threw a bomb into the crowd of protestors. Many people died from the incident.

In the period of Prime Minister Chatchai Chunawan, there was a protest at the Krue Se mosque. The reason was because, being an historical site, the mosque should not be used for a place to pray. Many core protesters who are *tohkhru*[25] were arrested.

The period of Prime Minister Chuan Leekpai:

Several schools were burned down simultaneously. Mr. Chuan shifted the responsibility to the Interior Minister. A *tohkhru* from Jana district was arrested. He was accused of setting off a bomb at the Hat Yai railway station, which caused many deaths. Also, there was a policy to provide each school, including the ones in three provinces, a Buddha image for worshipping. This policy upset Muslim people a great deal.

The time of Thaksin's government
Massacre at Tak Bai and Krue Se

Who ordered the killing? Who did they listen to? Who did it affect? Don't forget that before the disorder, the three southern border provinces,

---

[24] Leaflet 127, found in August 2006.
[25] Islamic teachers.

allegedly a religious territory, was full of influential people, hit men, drugs, illegal goods, outlawed businesses such as gambling houses and prostitution.

The strange thing is that Mr. Palakorn Suwannarat, *Pa* Prem's good boy, as the director of SBPAC ignored the problems. He didn't care about what happened. It's because he benefited from the situation. It's normal, when the Director of the SBPAC was dismissed and Mr. Palakorn got to be a Privy Councillor, that he would try to make people believe that the unrest was a result from canceling the SBPAC.

At the Krue Se incident, Gen. Pallop didn't obey the command from Gen. Chavalit not to shoot at the people in the mosque. Instead, he took the order from Gen. Prem, the statesman, as his former commander. This resulted in bloodshed and resentment towards state authority until today.

In the case of the Tak Bai incident, how does the government benefit from that incident besides affecting the stability of Muslim brothers and sisters and the world community? Why didn't the soldiers follow orders from the government? Instead, they listened to Gen. Surayuth, another one of Prem's children (ex-commander of the ???), who ordered the shooting at the protestors and the maltreatment of the protestors (piling them up in trucks). On their way to the Inkhayuth camp, hundreds of them got suffocated and died in agony.

Some evil soldiers tried to create disorderly incidents by shooting innocent people and blaming it on the government. They take orders from the big guy (Palakorn). They even built a spacious building in the Inkhayuth camp, Pattani, as their headquarters. The constant guest is Gen. Prem, who would come to supervise the mission.

Gen. Prem didn't want Gen. Sonthi to become Army Commander, because Gen. Sonthi is Muslim. Gen. Prem doesn't like Muslim people. He spoke at CS Hotel once that he didn't want the people in the three provinces to use Malay as the official language. It's not a mistake at all that the government appointed Gen. Sonthi, with absolute power, to take care of the situation in the south. He really knows about the *Luk Pa*[26] movement to create incidents in the area.

Why did all these violent incidents occur frequently during Thaksin's government? Even so that it seems like the chaos in the south just

---

[26] The "*Luk Pa*" movement means a movement orchestrated by the "sons of *Pa*," i.e., subordinates, protégés and supporters of Prem Tinsulanond, former army commander, prime minister and now president of the Privy Council.

started during Thaksin's government. Many people try to conclude that Thaksin is the cause of all the problems in the south and Thailand just like all the Luk Pa movement — the movement of Gen. Prem, Gen. Surayuth, and Mr. Palakorn — wanted people to believe. The reason is because Gen. Prem himself wanted to become the prime minister. He's the reason Article 7, a royal-appointed prime minister, was proposed. This also caused trouble in our country, especially in our three southern border provinces.

May peace be with our Muslim brothers and sisters
Wassalam

Commentary

Leaflet D is very focused on the post-1945 period, and especially on the history of the past couple of decades. The leaflet takes issue with those who single out Thaksin for criticism over the escalation of the conflict in 2004, and broadens out the complaints to include former premier Chuan Leekpai, and three current members of the Privy Council. Superficially, the message drawn from recent history is that whoever is in charge in Bangkok, Malay Muslims will suffer. But the sub-text of the leaflet is to shift responsibility from pro-Thaksin forces and toward those associated with the military and the monarchy. Despite the rather tokenistic references to "our Muslim brothers and sisters" at the beginning and end of the leaflet, this appears in fact to be a "fake" document designed to advance a particular perspective on the Thai side.

Leaflet E (shortened version)

An Open Leaflet, First Published on the Internet[27]

A Message to my bothers and sisters who love peace

(greetings in Malay)

Allumduliah. All the prayers go to only Allah. We pray to thee. We ask thee for help. We ask thee for guidance. We ask thee for forgiveness. We would like to return to thee. May Allah grant the blessing of peace to the prophet Muhammad (*sol*) and his lineage and also the righteous *Sohaba*.

---

[27] Leaflet 124.

Currently, the area of the three southern border provinces is on fire. People are dying. Killings and destruction are everywhere, all the time. Even though the causes and those responsible for the incidents vary, the most important cause are the people who called themselves Muslims. They believe in Islamic principles given by Allah — their God. They follow the teachings of the divine angels. However, in many cases, in the past they chose to follow the orders from the Sultan and rulers of Patani, or the servants of the court, who hoped to bring back an immoral government (*solem*) for the sake of their own dynasties. But because of their incompetent rule in the past, they had to deceive their own people to fight, citing religious causes. It's concerning to us, the descendants of Patani.

We have been fooled about the glorious history of Pattani that was ruled by Muslim principles. In fact, the city was ruled by selfish Sultans, *Tuanku*, and their greedy relatives. They built the Sapphire Palace (*Istananilum*) that was bigger than the Krue Se mosque. During various periods of time, over many generations, Patani was ruled by women such as Queen Hiyao, Queen Biru, and Queen Kuning. What rights did these ladies claim to rule the land? Was it because they were knowledgeable in Islamic principles? That's definitely impossible. They themselves did not even wear the *hiyab*, which is a fundamental standard for every female Muslim to uphold: it's considered *haram* should any female Muslim not do so. This was one clear example; we hardly need ask about other issues such as:

a) Did those women use Islamic laws to judge cases?
b) Was there evidence suggesting the support of high-level Islam experts in their administration?

It should be enough to conclude that those Queens were not Islamic leaders. Undoubtedly, female leaders are discouraged and unacceptable in Islam. Therefore, how could these ladies become the leaders of Patani Muslims? Can any religious expert prove that the governments of those Queens were Islamic ones? Even the rulers continuously broke the rules and committed sins (not wearing *hiyab*) themselves. One example illustrating their immoral and arbitrary rule was the story of two Muslims who did not obey their orders that brass should not be taken out of Patani town. When they got caught, the Queens gave orders to kill them and dump their bodies in the ocean. Is this an example of Islam? We can find more detail about this from the *History of the Malay Kingdom of Patani* by Ibrahim Syukri, translated by Mahattama Saki Jaeha and Associate Professor Dolmanaj Baka. The document was edited and published by the Institute of Southeast Asian Maritime Studies, PSU, Pattani, 1998.

The verdict was clearly against the teachings of Islam. No matter how serious the offences are, we always give respect to dead bodies, not dump them in the ocean. It's a serious sin for Muslim people to do that. The prophet *Nabi* Muhammad (*sol*) commanded Muslim people to stand up to pay respect for a non-Muslim dead body that was being carried past. As mentioned in the *hadis soyia* report of Bukoree, the prophet *Nabi* (*sol*) said,

> When you see that dead bodies are being carried past your way, stand up and give them respect until they go past your sight or the bodies are placed down on the ground. One day, a body was carried past them and Nabi (*sol*) stood up to pay respect to the body. Someone said to him, 'That body belongs to a Jew.' The prophet answered, 'Is it not of a human being?'

This is real Islam. We have to give respect even to corpses. How did Queen Hiyao (Hijau) of Patani treat those Muslim dead bodies? Dump them into the ocean? We can see something of that sort happened today — the beheadings and getting rid of the bodies. Considering the above *Hadith*, this is really degrading the image of Islam. As a matter of fact, we learn from this story that the Queen judged the case by herself without any *Alim* or *Kordee* present at the judgment. She ordered the execution right away. In fact, in Islamic law, did the offence deserve such a punishment? We will not cite any verse of the Koran, but will give the example of the prophet Muhammad (*sol*), who taught us that, "Anyone being tested by mortal judgment, treat them justly, even in the way you look at them, point at them, or sitting — from *al-Daraqutni Ali: al-Sunan 1966: Medina: Sharikat al- Tiba'ah al-Fanniyah al-mutahidah.* This is the history of Islam that came from the Islamic prophets, which emphasize upholding justice, even with seating or using eye contact. We must remain unbiased. Let's compare this to Patani's leaders in the old days and the insurgents these days. On what grounds are they making judgments about life and death?

There are many stories recounting the immorality of Patani's leaders. One of the great blasphemies people believe until today is that the Siamese government enslaved Patani people and chained them at the ankles with rattan straps. We never stop to think about this. Have we asked any physicians about this? How could humans walk in that condition? If the Achilles tendon was torn, what would be the condition of that person? We have been telling this lie from generation to generation. If we look closely at this, what would it be like just to walk on foot, without any binding, from Pattani to Bangkok? They fabricated the story to cause us to despise Siam. The *Koran Suroh Almadiah* 8 stated, 'And don't let hatred towards any particular group become a crime that prevents all of you from treating them justly.'

This message is written in the hope of warning all of you to come back to Islam, and not become the tools of the insurgents, whose aim is the greatness of the Malay race, not Islam's. They look down upon Muslims in other parts of the world. They only praise and make demands for the 'Melayu,' and want to call themselves Malay Muslims. This is clearly a Zionist plot, the enemies of Islam. Zionists are trying to undermine the strength of Islam by getting Muslims to pride themselves on their ethnicity. It's like what they did to Muslim empires in the past, using the idea of nationalism (*aksohbiya*) of the Arab people who were fighting with the Turks, while the Zionist British were watching. The British wanted the Muslim empire to fall apart into fractions. Until today, this evil plot still has an influence among the Malay people that were once ruled by the British people. Those people have left the seeds of nationalism and ethnic chauvinism. Since the Ayutthaya period, while Muslim people are progressing to become important political figures or state officials, the trend of 'Malayism' is used to limit Muslim influence in Thailand. They created violence so that most people in the country despise Islam and distrust Muslims. It leads to suppression of the Muslims and the control of Islam, *pondok*, and religious schools, which fits perfectly with the Zionists' plan. More detail will be added later. *Insa-allah.*

[*passage edited out*]

Finally, we pray that Allah (*sorbor*) will open the hearts and minds of those with bad intentions who cause harm to others to repent in the Islamic way. Help them to feel contrite and forgive the sins that they have committed on the face of the land and to mankind. May Allah receive those who have repented and provide them with solutions with thy mercy. 'We all come from thee, and we all return back to thee.'

Wabillahidoafigwalhidayawasalammulaikum

The Alumni Association of Students in Thailand, Malaysia, and Indonesia (*suemannunyongmalayu*)

Please forward this along. Should you have any questions, please contact us via Email: patani_babusalam@muslimthai.com.

Commentary

This lengthy leaflet sets out to employ Islamic references and learning in conjunction with academic scholarship to challenge popular Malay Muslim understandings of their history — such as the idea that Patani used to be an Islamic state, or that Malay forced laborers had to march to Bangkok wearing rattan straps. The leaflet seeks to de-legitimize the militant movement by questioning the Islamic credentials of the leadership and arguing that its actions are un-Islamic. The leaflet appears to have been created by someone sympathetic to the government position, either a pro-government Muslim or a Buddhist who is well-versed in Islamic teachings and Malay history. It strongly resembles a piece of state propaganda, possibly assembled by military intelligence officers.

Conclusion

A brief review of some anonymous leaflets circulated in Thailand's southern border provinces illustrates the way in which these documents seek to use alternative readings of history for propaganda purposes. Leaflets A, B and C use carefully constructed lists and catalogues that aim to create parallels between the past oppression of Patani by Siam, and the government's handling of incidents since 2004. The primary purpose of the leaflets is to fuel resentment against the security forces, the government and the Thai state. Leaflets D and E are of rather murky origin, but appear to have been created by people close to or sympathetic to the state. Leaflet D promotes a "Thaksinist" view of the conflict, directing criticism toward the Democrats and those aligned with General Prem Tinsulanond and the palace. Leaflet E engages in an elaborate attempt to discredit Patani nationalist readings of history and so to de-legitimate militant violence. Taken together, the five leaflets illustrate the potential of events which occurred as much as four centuries ago to be actively deployed by different sides in a complex and extremely violent civil conflict in Southern Thailand.

The widespread distribution of such leaflets illustrates the salience of local understandings of "autonomous histories" that subvert the master-narratives of the Thai state; and the attempts of the state to counter those autonomous histories through appropriating similar strategies of subversion and manipulation.[28] Johnson's conclusions concerning the Taliban night letters are highly relevant to a reading of Patani history:

---

[28] For a discussion of such views of Southeast Asian history, associated with the work of John Smail and applied in Thailand by historians such as Nidhi Eoseewong and Thongchai Winichakul, see Chris Baker's "Afterword," in Nidhi Eoseewong, *Pen and Sail: Literature and History in Early Bangkok* (Chiang Mai: Silkworm, 2005), and Thongchai Winichakul, "Writing at the Interstices: Southeast Asian Historians and Post-National Histories in Southeast Asia," in *New Terrains in Southeast Asian History*, Ohio University Research in International Studies, Southeast Asia Series, number 107, ed. Abu Talib Ahmad and Tan Liok Ee (Athens, OH and Singapore: Ohio University Press and Singapore University Press, 2003), pp. 3–39.

The risk of losing tribal independence to 'infidels and puppets of the West' outweighs the possibility of improving tribal social welfare or increasing economic opportunities that would probably be gained by accepting state authority. Any concession in tribal independence should exceed any compensation offered in return for submission to state authority. Kabul as well as the US and its coalition partners have failed miserably to understand this.[29]

Like their equivalents in Afghanistan, anonymous militant leaflets in Patani invoke historical narratives of resistance that aim to de-legitimize the Thai state. Their primary aim is to celebrate independence, to foster an "imagined land" of Malay Muslims, and to reject all forms of Thai state intervention in the region. On the use of anonymous leaflets in the Malukus, Bubant writes:

> Introducing clear intentions, rational motives, and clearheaded plans into murky political violence may analytically be a valuable contribution to an understanding of the structural determinants behind a conspiratorial political struggle. Such an analysis fails, however, to show how obscurity is not only cultivated but also takes on a momentum of its own that ends up enveloping most, and not just a few, actors.[30]

Much the same applies to the dissemination of such anonymous leaflets in Patani. While these materials can be analyzed systematically and located within a logical framework, this can only be achieved by doing further violence to the murkiness and ambiguity at the core of the conflict, and the manifold confusions surrounding the contested historiography that they both reflect and construct.

This chapter has shown how the contested historiography of Patani is mobilized by the militants as part of a political agenda, which remains otherwise largely unstated. Militant groups operating in the region have failed openly to claim responsibility for their actions or to explain either their critiques of the Thai state, or their goals in opposing state power. History has formed a significant theme of the militants' political ideology, at least as expressed in anonymous leaflets distributed in the conflict zone. Multiple narratives of Patani's history are to be found in these leaflets, which reflect the ambiguities underpinning the violence, and the fact that none of the parties to the conflict is able to impose its readings unchallenged — politically, militarily or historically.

---

[29] Johnson, "The Taliban Insurgency," p. 341.
[30] Bubant, "Rumors, Pamphlets and the Politics of Paranoia in Indonesia," p. 813.

Bibliography

'Abd al-Rahmân al-Jabartî. *'Ajâ'ib al-âthâr fî al-tarâjim wa al-akhbar*, ed. Hasan Muhammad *et al*, vol. 1. Cairo, 1957–1958.

Abdullah al-Qari bin Haji Salleh. "Tok Kenali: His Life and Influence." In *Kelantan: Religion, Society, and Politics in a Malay State*, ed. William Roff. Kuala Lumpur: Oxford University Press, 1974, pp. 87–100.

Abû al-Fallâh b. 'Abd al-Hayy Ibn al-'Imâd. *Shadharât al-Dhahab fî Akhbâ man Dhahab*, 8 vols. Cairo: al-Baghdâdî, Hadiyyat al-'Ârifîn, I.

Abu Bakar Hamzah. *Al-Iman: Its Role in Malay Society 1906–1908*. Kuala Lumpur: Pustaka Antara, 1991.

Adas, Michael. "The Great War and the Decline of the Civilizing Mission." In *Autonomous Histories, Particular Truths: Essays in Honor of John Smail*, ed. L.J. Sears. Madison: Center for Southeast Asian Studies, University of Wisconsin-Madison, 1994.

Ahmad, A. Samad, ed. *Hikayat Amir Hamah*. Kuala Lumpur: Dewan Bahasa dan Pustaka, 1987.

Ahmad Fathy al-Fatani. *Pengantar Sejarah Patani* [Introduction to Patani History]. Kota Bharu: Pustaka Aman Press, 2001.

Ahmad Fathi al-Fatani, *Pengantar Sejarah Patani: Negeri Setanjung Bunga* [Introduction to Patani History: The Bulletwood Flower-Shaped Land]. Alor Setar: Pustaka Darussalam, 1994.

______. *Ulama Besar dari Patani* [Great Islamic Scholars of Patani]. Bangi: Universiti Kebangsaan Malaysia Press, 2002.

Ahmad, Kassim, ed. *Hikayat Hang Tuah*. Kuala Lumpur: Dewan Bahasa dan Pustaka, 1975.

Ahmad Omar Chapakia. *Politik Thai dan Masyarakat Islam di Selatan Thailand* [Thai Politics and Islamic Society in Southern Thailand]. Alor Setar: Pustaka Darussalam, 2000.

Al-Attas, Syed Muhammad Naguib. "New Light on the Life of Hamzah Fansuri." *Journal of the Malaysian Branch of the Royal Asiatic Society* 40 (1967): 42–51.

______. *Preliminary Statement on a General Theory of the Islamisation of the Malay-Indonesian Archipelago*. Kuala Lumpur: Dewan Bahasa dan Pustaka, 1969.

______. *The Mysticism of Hamzah Fansuri*. Kuala Lumpur: University of Malaya Press, 1970.

______. *Islam dalam Sejarah dan Kebudayaan Melayu* [Islam in Malay History and Culture]. Kuala Lumpur: UKM Press, 1972.

Al-Fatânî. *Furû' al-Masâ'il wa Usûl al-Masâ'il*, MS., Jakarta, National Library, Ml.

`Ali bin Muhammad bin Safiyuddin, Shaykh Faqih. *Tarikh Fatani*. Handwritten manuscript. N.d.

Ali, Daud. "Connected Histories? Regional Historiography and Theories of Cultural Contact between Early South and Southeast Asia." In *Islamic Connections: Muslim Societies in Southand Southeast Asia*, ed. R. Michael Feener and Terenjit Sevea. Singapore: Institute of Southeast Asian Studies, 2009, pp. 1–24.

Allen, Graham. *Intertextuality*. London and New York: Routledge, 2000.

Amir Sutarga, *et al. Katalogus Koleksi Naskah Melayu Museum Pusat* [Catalogue of the Collection of Malay Manuscripts in the National Museum]. Jakarta: Departemen P&K, 1972.

Amporn Marddent. "From Adek to Mo'ji: Identities of Southern Thai People and Social Realities." In *Knowledge and Conflict Resolution: The Crisis of the Border Region of Southern Thailand*, ed. Utai Dulyakasem and Lertchai Sirichai. Nakhon Si Thammarat: School of Liberal Arts, Walailak University, 2005, pp. 269–338.

Andaya, Barbara Watson. *Perak: The Abode of Grace: A Study of an Eighteenth Century Malay State*. Kuala Lumpur: Oxford University Press, 1979.

______. "Gates, Elephants, Cannon and Drums: Symbols and Sounds in Creation of a Patani Identity." Proceedings of International Conference, The Phantasm in Southern Thailand: Historical Writings on Patani and the Islamic World, December 11–13, 2009, Bangkok, pp. 257–76.

Andaya, Leonard. *The Kingdom of Johor, 1641–1728*. Kuala Lumpur: Oxford University Press, 1975.

Appadurai, Arjun. ed. *The Social Life of Things: Commodities in Cultural Perspective*. Cambridge: Cambridge University Press, 1988.

Arifin bin Chik, Abdullah La'umen and Suhaymi Isma'il. *Patani: prawattisat lae kan mueang nai lok melayu* [Patani: History and Politics in the Malay World], 2nd ed. Hatyai, Songkhla: The Foundation for the Presentation of Islamic Culture in Southern Thailand, 2009.

Arifin Mansurnoor, Iik. "Radicalization of Islamic Discourse among Muslims in Southeast Asia: A Historical Interpretation." *Kultur: The Indonesian Journal for Muslim Cultures* 3, 1 (2003).

Arong Suthasasna. *Panha khwam khad yaeng nai si jangwat phak tai* [The Problem of the Conflict in the Four Southern Provinces]. Bangkok: Phithakpracha, 1976.

Askew, Marc. "Conspiracy, Politics, and a Disorderly Border: The Struggle to Comprehend Insurgency in Thailand's Deep South." In *Policy Studies* 29. Washington DC: East-West Center Washington, 2007.

______. "Thailand's Intractable Southern War: Policy, Insurgency and Discourse." *Contemporary Southeast Asia* 30, 2 (2008): 186–214.

Askew, Marc, and Erik Cohen. "Pilgrimage and Prostitution: Contrasting Modes of Border Tourism in Lower South Thailand." *Tourism Recreation Research* 29, 2 (2004): 89–104.

Azra, Azyumardi. "The Rise and Decline of the Minangkabau Surau." Unpublished MA thesis, Columbia University, 1988.

________. *Jaringan Ulama Timur Tengah dan Kepulauan Nusantara Abad XVII dan XVIII* [Networks of Middle Eastern Islamic Scholars in the Southeast Asian Archipelago in the Seventeenth and Eighteenth Centuries]. Bandung: Mizan, 1995.

________. "The Transmission of al-Manar's Reformism to the Malay-Indonesian World: The Cases of *al-Imam* and *al-Munir*." *Studia Islamika* 6, 3 (1999): 75–97.

________. *The Origins of Islamic Reformism in Southeast Asia: Networks of Middle Eastern 'Ulama' in the Seventeenth and Eighteenth Centuries*. Honolulu: University of Hawai'i Press, 2004.

"Bahrun". *Yihad si thao: khrai sang khrai liang fai tai* [Grey Jihad: Who Started and Who is Stoking the Southern Fire]. Bangkok: Sarika, 2005.

Bajunid, Omar Farouk. "Islam, Nationalism, and the State." In *Dynamic Diversity in Southern Thailand*, ed. Wattana Sugunnasil. Pattani: Prince of Songkla University, 2005, pp. 1–19.

Baker, Chris. "Afterword: Autonomy's Meanings." In *Recalling Local Pasts: Autonomous History in Southeast Asia*, ed. S. Chutintaranond and Chris Baker. Chiang Mai: Silkworm, 2003.

________. "Afterword." In Nidhi Eoseewong, *Pen and Sail: Literature and History in Early Bangkok*. Chiang Mai: Silkworm, 2005.

Bangnara. A. *Patani Dahulu dan Sekarang* [Patani Then and Now], trans. A. Patani and A. Jala. Patani: Penyelidikan Angkatan al-Fatani, 1397/1977.

Barmé, Scot. *Luang Wichit Wathakan and the Creation of a Thai Identity*. Singapore: Institute of Southeast Asian Studies, 1993.

Barnard, Timothy P., ed. *Contesting Malayness: Malay Identity across Boundaries*. Singapore: Singapore University Press, 2004.

Becker, Judith. "Percussive Patterns in the Music of Mainland Southeast Asia." *Ethnomusicology* 12, 2 (May 1968): 173–91.

Berger Stefan, and Chris Lorenz, eds. *The Contested Nation*. London: Palgrave Macmillan, 2008.

Benjasmith, Isma'il. "Bot bat tan kan sueksa lae kan mueang khong Chaik Wan Ahmad al-Fatani (2399–2451)" [The Roles of Shaykh Ahmad al-Fatani (1865–1908 AD) in Education and Politics], MA thesis submitted to the Faculty of Islamic Studies, Prince of Songkhla University (P), 2008/BE 2551.

Birch, J.W.W. *The Journals of J. W. W. Birch: First British Resident to Perak, 1874–1875*, ed. P.L. Burns. Kuala Lumpur: Oxford University Press, 1976.

Blussé, Leonard. "Inpo, Chinese Merchant in Pattani: A Study in Early Dutch-Chinese Relations." Proceedings of the Seventh IAHA Conference, held in Bangkok, August 22–26, 1977. Bangkok: Chulalongkorn University, 1978. Vol. I.

Bonura, Jr., Carlo. "Location and the Dilemmas of Muslim Political Community in Southern Thailand." Paper presented at the First Inter-Dialogue Conference on Southern Thailand, Pattani, Thailand, June 13–15, 2002.

Bougas, Wayne A. "Patani in the Beginning of the XVIIth Century." *Archipel* 39 (1990): 113–38.

______. *The Kingdom of Patani: Between Thai and Malay Mandalas*. Bangi: Institute of the Malay World and Civilization, University Kebangsaan Malaysia, 1994.

______. "The Early History of Sai." In *Études sur l'histoire du sultanat de Patani, Études thématiques*, ed. Daniel Perret, Amara Srisuchat, and Sombun Thanasuk. Paris: École française d'Extrême-Orient, 2004, pp. 259–80.

Bradley, Francis R. "Piracy, Smuggling, and Trade in the Rise of Patani, 1490–1600." *Journal of the Siam Society* 96 (2008): 27–50.

______. "When Patani became Pattani: The End of the Mandala State, 1785–1838." Paper presented at the The Phantasm in Southern Thailand: Historical Writings on Patani and the Islamic World, Chulalongkorn University, December 11–12, 2009.

______. "Moral Order in a Time of Damnation: The Hikayat Patani in Historical Context." *Journal of Southeast Asian Studies* 40, 2 (June 2009): 267–94.

______. "The Social Dynamics of Islamic Revivalism in Southeast Asia: The Rise of the Patani School, 1785–1909." Madison, WI: University of Wisconsin-Madison, 2010.

Braginsky, Vladimir I. "Towards the Biography of Hamzah Fansuri. When Did Hamzah Live? Data from His Poems and Early European Accounts." *Archipel* 57, 2 (1999): 135–75.

Brakel, Lobe. "The Birth Place of Hamza Pansuri." *Journal of the Malaysian Branch of the Royal Asiatic Society* 42 (1969): 206–12.

Brennan, James R. "Lowering the Sultan's Flag: Sovereignty and Decolonization in Coastal Kenya." *Comparative Studies in Society and History* 50, 4 (2008): 831–61.

Brockelmann, Carl. *Geschichte Der Arabischen Litteratur* (GAL) (1937–1947), II. Leiden: E.J. Brill, 1996.

Brown, Donald E. Hierarchy, *History and Human Nature: The Social Origins of Social Consciousness*. Tucson, AZ: The University of Arizona Press, 1988.

Bubalo, Anthony, and Greg Fealy. *Between the Global and the Local: Islamism, the Middle East, and Indonesia*, Analysis Paper Number 9. Washington DC: The Saban Center for Middle East Policy, the Brookings Institution, 2005.

Bunnag, Tej. *The Provincial Administration of Siam, 1892–1915*. Kuala Lumpur: Oxford University Press, 1997.

Burney, Henry. *The Burney Papers*, 2 vols. Farnborough: Gregg International, 1971.

Chaiwat Satha-Anand. *Islam and Violence: A Case Study of Violent Events in the Four Southern Provinces, Thailand, 1976–1981*. Tampa, FL: University of South Florida, Department of Religious Studies, 1987.

______. "Pattani in the 1980s: Academic Literature as Political Stories." In *Knowledge and Conflict Resolution: The Crisis of the Border Region of Southern Thailand*, ed. Uthai Dulyakasem and Lertchai Sirichai. Nakhon Si Thammarat: School of Liberal Arts, Walailak University, 2005 (previously published in *Sojourn* 7, 1 [1992]: 1–38), pp. 211–67.

______. "Pattani in the 1980s: Academic Literature and Political Stories." In *Muslim Social Science in ASEAN*, ed. Omar Farouk Bajunid. Kuala Lumpur: Yayasan Penataran Ilmu, 1994.

______. *Khwamrunræng kap kanchatkan "khwamching": Pattani nai rop krug sattawat* [Violence and Managing the Truth: Pattani in the Last Half Century]. Bangkok: Thammasat University Press, 2008.

______, ed. *Phaendin chintanakan: rat lae kan kae panha kwam runraeng nai phak tai* [Imagined Land: The State and Solutions to the Problem of Violence in Southern Thailand]. Bangkok, Matichon Publications, BE 2551/ 2008.

______, ed. *Imagined Land: The State and Southern Violence in Thailand*. Fuchu: ILCAA, Tokyo University of Foreign Languages, 2009.

Chalermkiat Khumthongphat. *Kabot reu wiraburut haeng si jangwat phak tai* [Haji Sulong Abdul Kadir — Rebel or Hero of the Four Southern Provinces?]. Sinlpawatthanatham special edition. Bangkok: Mathichon Publishers, 2547/2004.

Chaloem Yongbunkoet, trans. "Muang Thai nai chotmaihet Chin" [Thailand in Chinese Records]. *Sinlapkorn* 7, 2 (July 1963): 50–65.

Chang Tseng-hsin. *Maritime Activities on the Southeast Coast of China in the Latter Part of the Ming Dynasty*. Taipei: China Committee for Publication Aid and Prize Awards, 1988.

Chapman, E.C. ed. *Studies of Contemporary Thailand*. Canberra: Research School of Pacific Studies, Australian National University, 1973.

Charnvit Kasetsiri. "Siam to Thailand — A Historian's View." *Bangkok Post*, June 23, 2009.

Chavivun Prachuabmoh. "The Role of Women in Maintaining Ethnic Identity and Boundaries: A Case of Thai Muslims (Malay-Speaking Group) in Southern Thailand." Ph.D. diss., Department of Anthropology, University of Hawai'i, 1980.

Che Man, Wan Kadir. "Muslim Elites and Politics in Southern Thailand." Masters thesis, Universiti Sains Malaysia, 1983.

______. "The Thai Government and Islamic Institutions in the Four Southern Muslim Provinces of Thailand." *Sojourn: Journal of Social Issues in Southeast Asia*, 5, II (1990): 255–82.

______. *Muslim Separatism: The Moros of Southern Philippines and the Malays of Southern Thailand*. Singapore: Oxford University Press, 1990.

______. "The Demise of the Patani (Pattani) Sultanate: A Preliminary Enquiry." In *National Past: National History and National Historiography in Brunei, Indonesia, Thailand, Singapore, the Philippines and Vietnam*, ed. Putu Davies. Brunei Darussalam: Department of History, University of Brunei Darussalam, 1996.

______. "Conflict and Conflict Resolution: Malay Muslim Liberation Movements in Thailand." Paper presented at the Conference on Conflict and Conflict Resolution in the Muslim World, International Islamic University of Malaysia, Kuala Lumpur, February 18–19, 2004.

______. "Panha khong patani lae thai: muea rao mai-art yu ruam lae baeng-yaek jak kan dai" [The Problem of the Patani Malays in Southern Thailand: Neither

Assimilation nor Separation]. In *Nork niyam khwam pen Thai. Thai-Patani: muea rao mai at yu ruam lae baeng yaek jak kan dai* [Outside the Definition of Thainess. Thai-Patani: Neither Assimilation Nor Separation], ed., trans. Prinya Nuanpian. Songkhla: Institute of Peace Studies, Prince of Songkhla University, 2008/BE 2551, pp. 19–25.

Christie, Clive J. *A Modern History of Southeast Asia: Decolonization, Nationalism and Separatism.* London: Tauris Academic Studies, 1996.

Chulan, Raja *Misa Melayu.* Kuala Lumpur: Pustaka Antara, 1968; reprint of 1919 edition.

C.O. 273/120-121. From H.B.M.'s Resident Perak (Hugh Low) to the Colonial Secretary. Residency Kuala Kangsar, February 18, 1884.

C.O. 273/120-121. Letter from Frederick Weld to Her Majesty's Agent and Consul in Bangkok, April 14, 1883.

C.O. 273/129-130, March 21, 1884. A copy of the Siamese Foreign Minister's Letter to Her Majesty's Agent and Consul General in Bangkok, W.H. Newman, January 24, 1884. Author: Chow Phya Bhanawongse Maha Kosa Thibodi, the Phra Klang Minister for Foreign Affairs. Bangkok, January 23, 1884.

C.O. 8774. Hugh Low to the Colonial Secretary of the Straits Settlements, March 18, 1883.

C.O. 8774. Hugh Low to the Colonial Secretary of the Straits Settlements, March 16, 1883.

CO 717/156. A.M. Palliser to O.H. Morris, Co, March 10, 1949.

CO 717/156 Extract from the *Pan-Malayan Review* of Political and Security Intelligence, no. 3 of 1949, February 2, 1949.

CO 717/156. The Malays of Siam, Paper, FO Research Department, 20 March 1948, Secret.

Colenbrander, H.T., ed. *Dagh-Register gehouden int Casteel Batavia vant passerende daer ter plaetse als over geheel Nederlandts-India Anno 1641–1642.* The Hague: Nijhoff, 1900.

Connors, Michael K. "Another Country: Reflections on the Politics and Culture of the Muslim South." In *Divided over Thaksin: Thailand's Coup and Problematic Transition*, ed. John Funston. Singapore: Institute of Southeast Asian Studies, 2009, pp. 110–23.

Copeland, Matthew. "Contested Nationalism and the 1932 Overthrow of the Absolute Monarchy in Siam." Unpublished PhD thesis, Australian National University, 1993.

Copland, Ian. "The Limits of Hegemony: Elite Responses to Nineteenth-Century Imperial and Missionary Acculturation Strategies in India." *Comparative Studies in Society and History* 49, 3 (2007): 637–65.

Cortesao, Armando, and Avelino Teixeira da Mota. *Portugaliae monumenta cartographica.* Lisbon, 1960-1962.

Cowan, C.D. "Governor Bannerman and the Penang Tin Scheme, 1818–1819." *Journal of the Malayan Branch of the Royal Asiatic Society* 23, 1 (1950): 52–83.

Cp 717/156 H. Gurney to Arthur Creech-Jones, June 29, 1949 and O.S. Morrison to Sir A. Abraham, July 29, 1949.

Crawfurd, John. *Journal of an Embassy from the Governor-General of India to the Courts of Siam and Cochin China; Exhibiting a View of the Actual State of Those Kingdoms.* London: Henry Colburn, 1828.

Cushman, Jennifer, and Anthony Milner. "Eighteenth and Nineteenth-Century Chinese Accounts of the Malay Peninsula." *Journal of the Malaysian Branch of the Royal Asiatic Society* 52, 1 (1979): 1–56.

Cushman, Richard, trans. and David K. Wyatt, ed. *The Royal Chronicles of Ayutthaya.* Bangkok: The Siam Society, 2000.

Davenport, William H. "Two Kinds of Value in the Eastern Solomon Islands." In *The Social Life of Things: Commodities in Cultural Perspective*, ed. Arjun Appadurai. Cambridge: Cambridge University Press, 1988.

Davisakd Puaksom. "Of a Lesser Brilliance: Patani Historiography in Contention." In *Thai South and Malay North, Ethnic Interaction on a Plural Peninsula*, ed. Michael J. Montesano and Patrick Jory. Singapore: NUS Press, 2008, pp. 71–90.

Day, Tony. "How Modern was Modernity, How Traditional was Tradition in Nineteenth Century Java?" *Review of Malaysian and Indonesian Affairs* 20, 1 (1986): 1–37.

______. *Fluid Iron: State Formation in Southeast Asia.* Honolulu: University of Hawai'i Press, 2002.

de Barros, João. *Da Asia.* Lisbon: Regia Officina, 1563; reprinted 1973. III.

de Graaf, H.J. and Th. G. Th. Pigeaud. *De eerste Moslimse vorstendommen op Java: studien over de staatkundige geschiedenis van de 15e en 16de eeuw.* Verhandelingen, KITLV, 69. 's-Gravenhage: M. Nijhoff, 1974.

Dodge, Nicholas N. "Population Estimates for the Malay Peninsula in the Nineteenth Century, with Special Reference to the East Coast States." *Population Studies* 34, 3 (November 1980).

Dome Kraipakorn. "Historical Discourse on the Decline and Fall of Patani." Proceedings of the International Conference: The Phantasm in Southern Thailand Historical Writings on Patani and the Islamic World, Chulalongkorn University, Bangkok, December 11–12, 2009, v. 1, pp. 468–80.

Dorairajoo, Saroja D. "From Mecca to Yala: Negotiating Islam in Present-Day Southern Thailand." Paper presented at the Symposium on Islam in Southeast Asia and China: Regional Faithlines and Faultlines in the Global Ummah, November 28–December 1, 2002, City University of Hong Kong.

______. "Violence in the South of Thailand." *Inter-Asia Cultural Studies* 5, 3 (2004): 465–71.

Douglas, F.W. "The Penang Cannon Si Rambai." *Journal of the Malayan Branch of the Royal Asiatic Society* 21 (1948): 117–8.

Dowsey-Magog, P. "Popular Culture and Traditional Performance: Conflicts and Challenges in Contemporary Nang Talung." In *Dynamic Diversity in South Thailand*, ed. Wattana Sungannasil. Chiangmai: Silkworm Books, 2005, pp. 109–52.

Drakard, Jane. *A Malay Frontier: Unity and Duality in a Sumatran Kingdom.* Ithaca, NY: Cornell Southeast Asia Program, 1990.

Enoki Kazuo. "The Liang chih-kung-t'u." In *Memoirs of the Research Department of the Toyo Bunko* 42 (1984): 75–138.

Everitt, W.E. *A History of Mining in Perak*. Johore Bahru: 1952.

______. "The Rahman Mines at Intan." *The Malayan Historical Journal* 2, 2 (1955).

Farrington, Anthony and Dhiravat na Pombejra. *The English Factory in Siam 1612–1685*. London: British Library, 2007, II: 104, 112–3.

"Fatani: Qissatu Sha'bin Muslimin Yujahidu min Ajli Dinihi wa Ardih" [Patani: The Story of a Muslim People that is Fighting the Jihad for its Religion and Land]. Published online May 2, 2004.

Feener, R. Michael. "Hybridity and the 'Hadhrami Diaspora' in the Indian Ocean Muslim Networks." *Asian Journal of Social Science* 32, 3 (2004).

______. "Introduction: Issues and Ideologies in the Study of Regional Muslim Cultures." In *Islamic Connections: Muslim Societies in South and Southeast Asia*, ed. R. Michael Feener and Terenjit Sevea. Singapore: Institute of Southeast Asian Studies, 2009, pp. xiii–xxiii.

Feener, R. Michael, and Terenjit Sevea, eds. *Islamic Connections: Muslim Societies in South and Southeast Asia*. Singapore: Institute of Southeast Asian Studies, 2009.

Floor, Willem. "The Iranian Navy in the Gulf during the Eighteenth Century." *Iranian Studies* 20, 1 (1987): 31–53.

FO 371/69999. Thompson to FO, November 4, 1948.

Forbes, Andrew D.W. "Southern Arabia and the Islamization of the Central Indian Ocean Archipelagoes." *Archipel* 21 (1981): 55–92.

______, ed. *The Muslims of Thailand. Vol. 1: Historical and Cultural Studies*. Gaya, India: Centre for South East Asian Studies, 1988.

______, ed. *The Muslims of Thailand. Vol. 2: Politics of the Malay-Speaking South*. Bihar: Centre for Southeast Asian Studies, 1989.

Franke, Wolfgang. "A Chinese Tombstone Found in Pattani." *Nan-yang Xue-bao* 39 (1984): 61–2.

Franke, Wolfgang *et al. Chinese Epigraphic Materials in Thailand*. Taipei: Shin Wen Fung, 1988.

Fraser, Thomas M., Jr. *Fishermen of South Thailand: The Malay Villagers*. New York: Holt, Rinehart and Winston, 1966.

Freitag, Ulrike, and W.G. Clarence-Smith. *Hadhrami Traders, Scholars, and Statesmen in the Indian Ocean, 1750s–1960s*, Social, Economic, and Political Studies of the Middle East and Asia, v. 57. Leiden: New York: Brill, 1997.

"Gaining an Insight into the Terrorists." *Bangkok Post*, August 30, 2004.

Gell, Alfred. *Art and Agency: An Anthropological Theory*. Oxford: Oxford University Press, 1998.

Gibson-Hill, C.A. "Notes on the Old Cannon Found in Malaya and Known to Have Been of Dutch Origin." *Journal of the Malayan Branch of the Royal Asiatic Society* 26, 1 (1953): 145–71.

Gothom Arya. "Local Patriotism and the Need for Sound Language and Education Policies in the Southern Border Provinces." In *Understanding Conflict and Approaching Peace in Southern Thailand*, ed. Imtiyaz Yusuf and Lars Peter Schmidt. Bangkok: Konrad Adenauer Stiftung, 2006, pp. 17–51.

Gray, Paul, and Lucy Ridout. *Rough Guide to Thailand's Beaches and Islands*. London: Rough Guides, 2001.

Groeneveldt, W.P. "Notes on the Malay Archipelago and Malacca from Chinese Sources." *Verhandelingen van het Bataviaasch Genootschap van Kunsten en Wetenschappen (VBG)* 39 (1880).

Gullick, J.M. *Indigenous Political Systems of Western Malaya*. London: The Athlone Press, 1988.

Gunaratna Rohan *et al.*, eds. *Conflict and Terrorism in Southern Thailand*. Singapore: Marshall Cavendish Academic, 2005.

Gupta, S.K. *Elephant in Indian Art and Mythology*. New Delhi: Abhinav, 1983.

Hadi, Amirul. *Islam and State in Sumatra: A Study of Seventeenth-Century Aceh*. Leiden and Boston: Brill, 2004.

Hamid, Ismail. "Kitab Jawi: Intellectualizing Literary Tradition." In *Islamic Civilization in the Malay World*, ed. Mohammad Taib Osman. Kuala Lumpur: Dewan Bahasa dan Pustaka, 1997, pp. 197–244.

Hamidong, Abdul Latif. "Institusi Pondok Dalam Tradisi Budaya Ilmu." *Kertas kerja Persidangan Antarabangsa Mengenai Tamadun Melayu* [Proceedings from the International Conference on Malay Civilisation]. Anjuran Kementerian Kebudayaan, Belia dan Sukan, Kuala Lumpur, Malaysia, November 11–13, 1986.

Hamka. *Ayahku* [My Father]. Jakarta: Umminda, 1992.

Handley, Paul. *The King Never Smiles*. New Haven: Yale 2006.

Haron Daud. *Sejarah Melayu*. Kuala Lumpur: Dewan Bahasa dan Pustaka, 1989.

Harun, Ramli and Tjut Rahma M.A. Gani, eds. *Adat Aceh*. Jakarta: Departemen Pendidikan dan Kebudayaan, Proyek Penerbitan Buku Sastra Indonesia dan Daerah, 1985.

Hasan, A.A.H. "The Development of Islamic Education in Kelantan." In *Tamaddun Islam di Malaysia* [Islamic Civilisation in Malaysia], ed. Khoo Kay Kim. Kuala Lumpur: Persatuan Sejarah Malaysia, 1980.

Hasjmi, A. "Pendidikan Islam di Aceh dalam Perjalanan Sejarah [Islamic Education in Aceh in Travel History]." *Sinar Darussalam* 63 (1975): 9–18.

______. *Sejarah Kebudayaan Islam di Indonesia* [Islamic Cultural History in Indonesia]. Jakarta: Bulan Bintang, 1990.

Hikayat Patani: The Story of Patani, ed., trans. A. Teeuw and D.K. Wyatt. The Hague: Nijhoff, 1970.

Hill, A.H. "Hikayat Raja-Raja Pasai." *Journal of the Malaysian Branch, Royal Asiatic Society* 33, 2 (1960): 1–215.

Hirth Friedrich and W.W. Rockhill. *Chau Ju-Kua; His Work on the Chinese and Arab Trade in the Twelfth and Thirteenth Centuries, entitled Chu-fan-chï*. St. Petersburg: Imperial Academy of Sciences, 1911.

Holt, John Clifford. *Spirits of the Place: Buddhism and Lao Religious Culture*. Honolulu: University of Hawai'i Press, 2009.

Hooker, M.B. *Islamic Law in South-East Asia*. Singapore: Oxford University Press, 1984.

Hsü Yün-ch'iao. *Bei-da-nian shi* 北大年史 [A History of Patani]. Singapore, 1946.

Hughes, David W. "No Nonsense: The Logic and Power of Acoustic-Iconic Mnemonic Systems." *British Journal of Ethnomusicology* 9, 2 (2000): 93–120.

Hurgronje, Snouck. *Mekka in the Latter Part of the Nineteenth Century*. Leiden: Brill, 1970.

Hutchinson, E.W. *1688: Revolution in Siam. The Memoir of Father de Blèze, S.J.* Hong Kong: Hong Kong University Press, 1968.

Ibrahem Narongraksakhet. "Pondoks and Their Roles in Preserving Muslim Identity in Southern Border Provinces of Thailand." In *Knowledge and Conflict Resolution: The Crisis of the Border Region of Southern Thailand*, ed. Utai Dulyakasem and Lertchai Sirichai. Nakhon Si Thammarat: School of Liberal Arts, Walailak University, 2005, pp. 67–128.

Ibrahim Syukri. *Sejarah Kerajaan Melayu Patani* [History of the Malay Kingdom of Patani]. Kota Bharu, Kelantan: Majlis Ugama Islam Press, 1958.

______. *History of the Malay Kingdom of Patani*, trans. C. Bailey and J.N. Miksic. Athens, OH: Ohio University Centre for International Studies, 1985.

______. *Sejarah Kerajaan Melayu Patani* [History of the Malay Kingdom of Patani], ed. Hasrom bin Haron and Mohd. Zamberi A. Malek. Bangi: National University of Malaysia Press, 2002.

______. *History of the Malay Kingdom of Patani*, trans. Conner Bailey and John N. Miksic. Athens, OH: Ohio University Press, 1985 (re-published Chiang Mai: Silkworm Books, 2005).

Ibn Battûta. *Travels in Asia and Africa 1325–1354*. London: Routledge and Kegan Paul, 1983.

Ibrohim Chukri. *Prawatisat anajak melayu patani* [History of the Malay Kingdom of Patani]. Chiang Mai: Silkworm, 2006.

Iik A. Mansurnoor. "Historiography and Religious Reform in Brunei during the Period 1912–1959." *Studia Islamika* 2, 2 (1995): 77–113.

______. "Intellectual Networking among Muslims Scholars in Southeast Asia: With Special Reference to Patani Works on Society, Coexistence and External Relations." *Islamic Quarterly* 48, 3 (2005): 37–58.

______. "Muslims in Modern Southeast Asia: Radicalism in Historical Perspectives." *Taiwan Journal of Southeast Asian Studies* 2, 2 (2006): 3–54.

______. "Revivalism and Radicalism in Southeast Asian Islam: A Pattern or an Anomaly?" *New Zealand Journal of Southeast Asian Studies* 11, 1 (2009): 222–62.

Ijzerman, J.W. "Hollandsche Prenten al Handelsartikel te Patani in 1602." *Koninkiljk Instituut voor de Taal-, Land- en Volkenkunde van Nederlandsch-Indië . Gedenkschrift uitgegeven ter gelegenheid van het 75-jarig bestaan op 4 Juni 1926*. The Hague: Koninklijk Instituut, 1926.

______, ed. *De Reis om de wereld van Olivier van Noort 1598–1601*. The Hague: Nijhoff for Linschoten-Vereniging, 1926.

Imtiyaz Yusuf. "Ethnoreligious and Political Dimensions of the Southern Thailand Conflict." In *Islam and Politics: Renewal and Resistance in the Muslim World*, ed. Amit Pandya and Ellen Laipson. Washington, DC: The Henry L. Stimson Center, 2009, pp. 43–55, 118–20.

In Tinland: A Journal of Interesting Mining News 2, 30 (1907).

International Crisis Group. "Southern Thailand: Insurgency, Not Jihad." International Crisis Group, Asia Report No. 98, Brussels, May 18, 2005.

Ishii, Yoneo. "The Thai Muslims and the Royal Patronage of Religion." Paper presented at the 13th IAHA Conference, University of Hong Kong, June 24–26, 1991.

______, ed. *The Junk Trade from Southeast Asia, Translations from the Tosen Fusetsu-gaki 1674–1723*. Singapore: Institute of Southeast Asian Studies, 1998.

______. "A Note on Pattani recorded in late 17th and Early 18th Century Japanese Documents." In *Études sur l'histoire du sultanat de Patani*, Études thématiques, ed. Daniel Perret, Amara Srisuchat, and Sumbun Thanasuk. Paris: École française d'Extrême-Orient, 2004, pp. 255–7.

Isma'il Benjasmith. "Bot bat tan kan sueksa lae kan muang khong chaik wan ahmad al-fatani (2399–2451)" [The Roles of Shaykh Ahmad al-Fatani (1865–1908 AD) in Education and Politics]. MA thesis submitted to Faculty of Islamic Studies, Prince of Songkhla University, 2008.

Ito, Takeshi. "The World of the *Adat Aceh*: A Historical Study of the Sultanate of Aceh." Unpublished thesis, Australian National University, 1984.

Jacq-Hergoualc'h, M. *The Malay Peninsula: Crossroads of the Maritime Silk Road (100 BC–1300 AD)*, trans. Victoria Hobson. Leiden: Brill, 2002.

Jairazbhoy, Nazir A. "A Preliminary Survey of the Oboe in India." *Ethnomusicology* 14, 3 (September 1970): 375–88.

______. "The South Asian Double-Reed Aerophone Reconsidered." *Ethnomusicology* 24, 1 (January 1980): 147–56.

Johns, A.H. "Sufism in Southeast Asia: Reflections and Reconsiderations." *Journal of Southeast Asian Studies* 26, 1 (1995): 169–83.

Jones, Russell. "Ten Conversion Myths from Indonesia." In *Conversion to Islam*, ed. Nehemiah Levtzion. New York and London: Holmes and Meier, 1979, pp. 129–58.

Jory, Patrick. "Political Decentralisation and the Resurgence of Regional Identities in Thailand." *Australian Journal of Social Issues*, Special Issue: National and Cultural Identities, 34 4 (November 1999): 337–52.

______. "Luang Pho Thuat as a Thai Cultural Hero: Popular Religion in the Integration of Patani." In *A Plural Peninsula: Historical Interactions among the Thai, Malays, Chinese and Others*. Workshop Proceedings, Walailak University, Nakhon Sri Thammarat, February 5–7, 2004, pp. 27–38.

______. "From 'Patani Melayu' to 'Thai Muslim.'" *ISIM Review* 18 (Autumn 2006): 42–3.

______. "From 'Melayu Patani' to 'Thai Muslim': The Spectre of Ethnic Identity in Southern Thailand." *Southeast Asia Research* 15, 2 (July 2007): 255–79.

______. "Historiography in Thailand since 1945." In *The Oxford History of Historical Writing, Vol. 5*, ed. Daniel Woolf and Axel Schneider. Oxford: Oxford University Press, 2011, pp. 539–58.

"Journael van Roelof Roelofsz." In *De Vierde Schipvaart der Nederlanders naar Oost-Indië onder Jacob Wilkens van Neck (1599–1604)*, vol. I, ed. H.A. van Foreest and A. de Booy. The Hague: Nijoff for Linschoten-Vereeniging, 1980.

Kalus, Ludvik. "Inscriptions arabes des cimetieres du Sud-est de la Thailande." In *Etudes sur l'histoire du sultanat de Patani*, ed. Daniel Perret, Amara Srisuchat and Sombun Thanasuk. Paris: École Francaise d'Extreme-Orient, 2004.

Kampanat Jintawiroj, Col. *Bandit Movements for the Secession of South Thailand.* Bangkok: Pho-sam-ton Publications, 1973/BE 2517.

Kantathi Suphamongkol. *Kanwithesobai khong thai B.E. 2483–2495* [Thai Foreign Policy, 1940–1952]. Bangkok: Post Publishing Ltd., 1993.

Kasem Rangsiyokrit. "Ithipon khong Sasana Islam tor kan-judkanpokkhrong changwat chaidaen Phak-tai." [Influence of Islam on the Administration of the Border Provinces in Southern Thailand]. MA thesis, Thammasat University, 1976.

Kersten, Carool. "The Predicament of Thailand's Southern Muslims." *The American Journal of Islamic Social Sciences* 21, 4 (2004): 1–30.

———. "Islam, Cultural Hybridity and Cosmopolitanism: New Muslim Intellectuals on Globalization." *The Journal of International Studies* 1, 1 (2009): 89–113.

Keyes, Charles F. "Cultural Diversity and National Identity in Thailand." In *Government Policies and Ethnic Relations in Asia and the Pacific*, ed. Michael Brown and Sumit Ganguly. Cambridge, MA: MIT Press, 1997, pp. 197–231.

Khajatphai Burutphat. *Thai Muslims*. Bangkok: Phrae Phitthaya, 1976.

Khin Sok. *Le Cambodge entre le Siam et le Viêtnam (de 1775 à 1860)*. Paris: École Française d'Extrême-Orient, 1991.

Kobata, Atsushi and Mitsugu Matsuda. *Ryukyuan Relations with Korea and the South Sea Countries: An Annotated Translation of Documents in the Rekidai Hoan.* Privately printed, 1969.

Kobkua Suwannathat-Pian. *Thai-Malay Relations, Traditional Intra-Regional Relations from the Seventeenth to the Early Twentieth Centuries*. Singapore: Oxford University Press, 1988.

———. *Thailand's Durable Premier: Phibun Through Three Decades, 1932–1957*. Kuala Lumpur: Oxford University Press, 1995.

———. "Thai Wartime Leadership Reconsidered: Phibun and Pridi." *Journal of Southeast Asian Studies* 27 (1996).

———. "Thailand: Historical and Contemporary Conditions of Muslim Thais." In *Muslims' Rights in Non-Muslim Majority Countries*, ed. Abdul Monir Yaacob and Zainal Azam Abdul Rahman. Kuala Lumpur: Institute of Islamic Understanding Malaysia, 2002, pp. 1–27.

———. "National Identity, the 'Sam-Sams' of Satun and the Thai Malay Muslims." In *Thai South and Malay North, Ethnic Interactions on a Plural Peninsula*, ed. Michael J. Montesano and Patrick Jory. Singapore: NUS Press, 2008, pp. 155–72.

Kodesh, Neil. "History from the Healer's Shrine: Genre, Historical Imagination, and Early Ganda History." *Comparative Studies in Society and History* 49, 3 (2007): 527–52.

Kraus, Werner. "Islam in Thailand: Notes on the History of Muslim Provinces Thai Islamic Modernism and the Separatist Movement in the South." *Journal of Muslim Minority Affairs* 5, 2 (1984): 410–25.

Laffan, Michael F. *Islamic Nationhood and Colonial Indonesia: The Umma below the Winds*. London: Routledge, 2003.

______. "Finding Java: Muslim Nomenclature of Insular SEA from Śrîvijaya to Snouck Hurgronje. WP 52." Singapore: Asia Research Institute, 2005.

Le Roux, Pierre. "Bedé kaba' ou les derniers canons de Patani." *Bulletin de l'École Française d'Extrême Orient* 85, 1 (1998): 125–62.

______. "To Be or Not to Be … the Cultural Identity of the Jawi." *Asian Folklore Studies* 57 (1999): 223–55.

Li Dao-gang. *Tai-guo gu-dai shi-di cong-kao* [泰國古代史地叢考]. 北京: 中華書局, 2000.

Light to Governor General, November 25, 1786, Straits Settlements Records 2: 410 (FWC January 22, 1787).

Light to Governor General, September 12, 1786, Straits Settlements Records 2: 312 (FWC October 9, 1786).

Light to Governor General, September 12, 1786, Straits Settlements Records 2: 311 (FWC December 13, 1786).

Liow, Joseph Chinyong. *Islam, Education and Reform in Southern Thailand: Tradition and Transformation*. Singapore: Institute of Southeast Asian Studies, 2009.

______. "Religious Education and Reformist Islam in Thailand's Southern Border Provinces: The Roles of Haji Sulong Abdul Kadir and Ismail Lutfi Japakiya." *Journal of Islamic Studies* 20, 3 (2009): 1–30.

______. "Religious Education and Reformist Islam in Thailand's Southern Border Provinces: The Roles of Haji Sulong Abdul Kadir and Ismail Lutfi Japakiya." *Journal of Islamic Studies* 21, 1 (2010): 29–58.

Logan, J.R. "Notes at Pinang, Kidah, & c." *Journal of the Indian Archipelago and East Asia* 5 (1851): 53–65.

Loh Fook Seng, Philip. *The Malay States 1877–1895: Political Change and Social Policy*. Kuala Lumpur: Oxford University Press, 1969.

Lombard, Denys, ed. *Le "Spraek ende Woord-Boek" de Frederick de Houtman*. Paris: École Française d'Extrême-Orient, 1970.

Lorenz, Chris. "Representations of Identity: Ethnicity, Race, Class, Gender and Religion." In *The Contested Nation*, ed. Stefan Berger and Chris Lorenz. London: Palgrave Macmillan, 2008, pp. 24–59.

Madmarn, Hasan. "Traditional Muslim Institutions in Southern Thailand." PhD thesis, University of Utah, Salt Lake City, 1990.

______. *The Pondok and Madrasah in Patani*. Bangi: Penerbit Universiti Kebangsaan Malaysia, 1990; 1999; 2001.

Maier, Hendrik J. *In the Center of Authority: The Malay Hikayat Merong Mahawangsa*. Ithaca, NY: Cornell Southeast Asia Program, 1988.

Maktabat al-Qudsî, 1350–1351/1930–1931, VIII.

Malcolm, Howard. *Travels in South-Eastern Asia, Embracing Hindustan, Malaya, Siam, and China; with Notices of Numerous Missionary Stations, and a Full Account of the Burman Empire; with Dissertations, Tables, etc.* Boston: Gould, Kendall, and Lincoln, 1840.

Marcinowski, M. Ismail. "The Iranian Presence in the Indian Ocean Rim: A Report of a Seventeenth-Century Safavid Embassy to Siam." *Islamic Culture* (April 2003): 56–98.

______. "Selected Historical Facets of the Presence of Shi'ism in Southeast Asia." *The Muslim World* 99, 2 (2009): 381–416.

Matheson, Virginia, and M.B. Hooker. "Jawi Literature in Patani: The Maintenance of a Tradition." *Journal of the Malaysian Branch of the Royal Asiatic Society* 61, 1 (1988): 1–86.

Maxwell, W.E. "A Journey on Foot to the Patani Frontier." *Journal of the Straits Branch of the Royal Asiatic Society* 9 (June 1882): 1–68.

______. "The History of Perak from Native Sources." In *A History of Perak*, ed. R.O. Winstedt and R.J. Wilkinson. Kuala Lumpur: Malaysian Branch of the Royal Asiatic Society, 1974.

McCargo, Duncan. *Tearing Apart the Land: Islam and Legitimacy in Southern Thailand.* Ithaca, NY: Cornell University Press 2008.

______. "Patani Militant Leaflets and the Uses of History." Proceedings of International Conference: The Phantasm in Southern Thailand: Historical Writings on Patani and the Islamic World, Bangkok, December 11–13, 2009, pp. 173–5.

______. "Southern Thai Politics: A Preliminary Overview." In *Dynamic Diversity in Southern Thailand*, ed. Wattana Sugunnasil. Pattani: Prince of Songkhla University, Pattani Campus, 2005, pp. 21–36.

Mees, C.A., ed., trans. *Hikayat Pelanduk Jinaka*. Santpoort: C.A. Mees, 1929.

Mills, J.V.G. "Chinese Navigators in Insulinde about 1500." *Archipel* 18 (1979): 69–93.

Milner, Anthony. *Kerajaan: Malay Political Culture on the Eve of Colonial Rule.* Tucson, AZ: University of Arizona Press, for the Association of Asian Studies, 1982.

Ming Shen-zong Shi-lu 明神宗實錄 [The Veritable Records of the Wan-li Reign]. 1630, juan 99.4a.

Mobini-Kesheh, Natalie. *The Hadrami Awakening: Community and Identity in the Netherlands East Indies, 1900–1942*. Ithaca, NY: Cornell University Southeast Asia Program Publications, 1999.

Mohammad Nor Bin Ngah. *Kitab Jawi: Islamic Thought of the Malay Muslim Scholars.* Vol. 33, Research Notes and Discussions Paper. Singapore: Institute of Southeast Asian Studies, 1983.

Mohammad Redzuan Othman. "The Role of Makka-Educated Malays in the Development of Early Islamic Scholarship and Education in Malaya." *Journal of Islamic Studies* 9, 2 (1998).

Mohd. Saleh bin Haji Awang, Dato' Haji. *Haji di Semenanjung Malaysia: Sejarah dan Perkembangannya Sejak Tahun 1300–1405H (1896–1985)* [The Haj in Peninsular Malaysia: History and Progress from 1896 to1985]. Kuala Terengganu: Syarikat Percetakan Yayasan Islam Terengganu Sdn. Bhd., 1986.

Mohd. Sarem Haji Mustajab. "Gerakan Islah Islamiyah di Tanah Melayu 1906–1948" [The Islamic Reform Movement in Malaya, 1906–1948] In *Sejarah dan*

Proses Pembangunan [History and the Development Process]. Kuala Lumpur: Persatuan Sejarah Malaysia, 1979.

Mohd Yusoff Hashim. *Pensejarahan Melayu Nusantara* [Malay Historiography in Southeast Asia]. Kuala Lumpur: Teks Publishing, 1988.

Mohd. Zamberi 'Abdul Malek. *Ummat Islam Patani: Sejarah dan Politik* [The Patani Islamic Umma: History and Politics]. Selangor: Hizbi, 1993.

———. *Patani Dalam Tamadun Melayu* [Patani in Malay Civilisation]. Selangor: Dewan Bahasa dan Pustaka, 1994.

———. *Pensejarahan Patani* [Patani Historiography]. Kuala Lumpur: Penerbit Universiti Malaya, 2006.

Montesano, Michael J. and Patrick Jory, eds. *Thai South and Malay North: Ethnic Interactions on a Plural Peninsula*. Singapore: NUS Press, 2008.

Moreland, W., ed. *Peter Floris, His Voyage to the East Indies in the Globe, 1611–1615*. Hakluyt Society series II, vol. 74. London, 1934.

Moor, J.H. *Notices of the Indian Archipelago, and Adjacent Countries; Being a Collection of Papers Relating to Borneo, Celebes, Bali, Java, Sumatra, Nias, the Philippine Islands, Sulus, Siam, Cochin China, Malayan Peninsula, & c.* Singapore, 1837.

MTH 020/2.15/14 (39) Memo of Ministry of the Interior answering questions of M.P. Lieut-Captain Charubutr Ruangsuwan on the implementation of the Government Policy as tabled in the House of Representatives, April 1952.

Muhammad Khalîl al-Murâdî. *Silk al-Durar fi a'yân al-qarn al-thânî 'ashar*, Vol. 3–4. Baghdad, 1302/1883–1884.

Muhammad Yusoff Hashim. *Malay Historiography*. Kuala Lumpur: Teks Publishing, 1988.

Mus, Paul. *Cultes indiens et indigenes au Champa, l'Inde vue de l'Est*. Hanoi, Imprimerie de l'Extrême Orient, 1934. Translated by Ian Mabbett and David Chandler, *India Seen from the East*. Monash Papers on Southeast Asia, Clayton, Victoria, 1975.

Nanthawan Haemindra. "The Problems of the Thai Muslims in the Four Southern Provinces of Thailand, Part 1." *Journal of Southeast Asian Studies* 7, 2 (1976): 197–225.

———. "The Problems of the Thai-Muslims in Four Southern Provinces of Thailand." *Journal of Southeast Asian Studies* 8, 1, pt. 2 (1977): 85–105.

Nasir al-'Abudi, Muhammad bin. *Fatani aw Janub Thailand: Dirasah wa Mushahadat*. Mecca: Muslim World League, 1998.

National Archives of Thailand, Ministry of Foreign Affairs 43.2/82. "Ngob ngern kha chai jai nai kan dulae nak rian thai nai saudi arabia B.E. 2505–B.E. 2509" [Budget for Expenditure in Organizing Thai Students in Saudi Arabia, 1966–1966].

National Archives of Thailand, Ministry of Foreign Affairs 43.31/4. "Kan khuapkhum nakrian thai nai prathet saudi arabia, B.E.2502–B.E.2505" [Control of Thai Students in Saudi Arabia, 1959–1962].

National Archives of Thailand, Ministry of Foreign Affairs 94.4/1. "Kan jat kan hai chao thai islam doenthang pai prakorp sasanakit na makka, B.E.2504" [Arranging Thai Muslims to Take the Pilgrimage Trip to Mecca, 1961].

National Archives of Thailand, Ministry of Interior 3.1.4.19/52. "Kan chuai luea thai islam pai prakorp sasanakit na mueang mecca, Dec 21, B.E. 2498–Aug. 11, B.E. 2503" [Assistance for Thai Muslims Going to Perform the Pilgrimage in Mecca, December 21–August 11, 1955–1960].

National Reconciliation Commission. *Raingan khanakammakan itsara phuea khwam-samanachan haengchat ao chana khwamrunraeng duai phalang samanachan* [Report of the National Reconciliation Commission: Besting Violence Through the Power of Reconciliation]. Bangkok: National Reconciliation Commission, Office of the Cabinet Secretary, 2006.

Needham, J., Wang Ling and Lu Gwei-Djen. *Science and Civilisation in China*, vol. 4, part III, "Civil Engineering and Nautics." Cambridge: Cambridge University Press, 1971.

Netolitzky, Almut. *Das Ling-wai tai-ta von Chou Chu-fei: e. Landeskunde Sudchinas aus d. 12. Jh. / von Almut Netolitsky*. Wiesbaden: Steiner, 1977.

Ngah, Mohd. Nor bin. *Kitab Jawi: Islamic Thought of the Malay Muslim Scholars.* Singapore: Institute of Southeast Asian Studies, 1983.

Nik Anuar Nik Mahmud, ed. *The Malay Unrest in South Thailand: An Issue in Malayan-Thai Border Relations.* Bangi: Institut Alam dan Tamadun Melayu, UKM, 1994.

———. *Sejarah Perjuangan Melayu Patani 1785–1954* [A History of the Patani Malay Struggle 1785–1954]. Bangi: Penerbit Universiti Kebangsaan Malaysia, 1999.

———. *Sejarah Perjuangan Melayu Patani.* Bangi: National University of Malaysia Press, 2000.

Nora, Pierre. "Between Memory and History: *Les Lieux de Mémoire.*" *Representations* 26, Special Issue: Memory and Counter-Memory (Spring 1989): 7–24.

Nordin Hussin. "A Critical Review of the Early History Textbooks in Malaysian Secondary Schools." *Indonesia and the Malay World* 36, 106 (2008): 451–61.

Nugent, Paul. "Putting the History Back into Ethnicity: Enslavement, Religion, and Cultural Brokerage in the Construction of Mandinka/Jola and Ewe/Agotime Identities in West Africa, c.1650–1930." *Comparative Studies in Society and History* 50, 4 (2008): 920–48.

Numan Hayimasae. "Hj Sulong Abdul Kadir (1895–1954): Perjuangan dan Sumbangan. Beliau Kepada Masyarakat Melayu Patani" [Hj Sulong Abdul Kadir (1895–1954): Struggle and Contribution to the Patani Malays]. MSc. diss., Universiti Sains Malaysia, 2002.

Ockey, James. "The Religio-Nationalist Pilgrimage of Haji Sulong Abdulkadir al Fattani." In *Pilgrims, Spectres and World-Reforming.* University of Michigan Student Conference, 2006.

Omar Farouk Bajunid. "The Political Integration of the Thai Islam." PhD diss., University of Kent at Canterbury, 1980.

———. "The Muslims of Thailand." In *Islamika: Esei-Esei Sempena Abad ke Limabelas Hijrah* [Islamika: Essays on the Fifteenth Century of Hijra], ed. Lupti Ibrahim. Kuala Lumpur: Sarjana Enterprise, 1981.

———. "The Origins and Evolution of Malay Muslim Ethnic Nationalism in Southern Thailand." In *Islam and Society in Southeast Asia*, ed. Taufik Abdullah and Sharon Siddique. Singapore: Institute of Southeast Asian Studies, 1984, pp. 250–81.

______. "The Historical and Transnational Dimensions of Malay Muslim Separatism in Southern Thailand." In *Armed Separatism in Southeast Asia*, ed. Lim Joo Jock and Vani S. Singapore: Institute of Southeast Asian Studies, 1986, pp. 234–57.

______, ed. *Muslim Social Science in ASEAN*. Kuala Lumpur: Yayasan Penataran Ilmu, 1994.

Panoraporn Anurugsa. "Political Integration Policy in Thailand: The Case of the Malay Muslim Minority." PhD thesis, The University of Texas at Austin, 1984.

Panuti H.M. Sudjiman, ed. *Adat Raja-Raja Melayu* [Customs of the Malay Kings]. Jakarta: Penerbit Universitas Indonesia, 1983.

Patya Saihoo. "Social Organization of an Inland Malay Village Community Southern Thailand." D.Phil thesis, Oxford University, 1974.

Perak 1466/1900: Secretary to the High Commissioner, Federated Malay States. John Anderson, Ancestral Claims of the Raja and Raja Muda of Reman to Mines in the Territory Recently Ceded to Perak.

Perret, Daniel. "Patani dans les grands réseaux marchands du XVIIe siècle." In *Etudes sur l'histoire du sultanat de Patani*, ed. Daniel Perret, Amara Srisuchat, and Sombun Thanasuk. Paris: École française d'Extrême-Orient, 2004, pp. 223–54.

______. "Réflexions sur l'émergence du sultanat de Patani." In *Études sur l'histoire du sultanat de Patani*, Études thématiques, ed. Daniel Perret, Amara Srisuchat, and Sumbun Thanasuk. Paris: École française d'Extrême-Orient, 2004, pp. 17–36.

Perret, Daniel, Amnat Sombatyanuchit and Siriporn Limwijitwong. "Sites fortifiés du cours inférieur due fleuve Pattani." In *Etudes sur l'histoire du sultanat de Patani*, ed. Daniel Perret, Amnat Sombatyanuchit and Siriporn Limwijitwong. Paris: École française d'Extrême-Orient, 2004, pp. 79–115.

Prime Minister Phibun's letter to British Ambassador Thompson, FO371/ 69998, Thompson to FO, November 4, 1948 and CO 717/56 The Malays of Siam, paper, FO Research Department, December 20, 1948. Secret.

Prinya Nuanpian, ed. *Nok niyam khwan pen thai. Thai-Patani: muea rao mai at yu ruam lae baeng yaek jak kan dai* [Outside the Definition of Thainess. Thailand-Patani: When We Can Neither Live Together Nor Separate]. Songkhla: Sun thale sap sueksa, 2008.

R. 5, M.2.22 Ng., vol. 2, Memorandum of the Conversation between Prince Devawong, Lord Salisbury and Philip Currie on the Raman Border Dispute, July 1887, in Devawong to Chulalongkorn, August 9, 1887.

Rahimmula, Perayot. "The Pattani Fatawa: A Case Study of the Kitab Al-Fatawa Al-Fataniyyah of Shaykh Ahmed Bin Muhamad Zain Bin Mustafa Al-Fatani." PhD diss., University of Kent, 1990.

Rahman, Fazlur. *Islam*, 2nd ed. Chicago: University of Chicago Press, 1979.

Rath, Richard Cullen. *How Early America Sounded*. Ithaca, NY and London: Cornell University Press, 2003.

Rattiya, Salleh. "Patani Darussalam (Melayu-Islam Patani)." In *Rat pattani nai* 'sivichai' [The Patani Polity within the Srivijaya Empire], ed. Sujit Wongthes. Bangkok: Matichon Publications, 2547/2004.

Reid, Anthony. *Europe and Southeast Asia: The Military Balance*, Centre for Southeast Asian Studies Occasional Paper, no. 16, ed. Bob Hering. Townsville: James Cook University of North Queensland, 1982.

______. *Southeast Asia in the Age of Commerce c.1450–1680*, 2 Vols. New Haven: Yale University Press, 1988–1993.

______. *An Indonesian Frontier: Acehnese and Other Histories of Sumatra*. Singapore: NUS Press, 2005.

______. "A Plural Peninsula." In *Thai South and Malay North: Ethnic Interactions on a Plural Peninsula*, ed. Michael J. Montesano and Patrick Jory. Singapore: NUS Press, 2008, pp. 25–38.

Reynolds, Frank and Mani. *Three Worlds According to King Ruang: A Thai Buddhist Chronology*. Berkeley: Asian Humanities Press, 1982.

Reynolds, Craig J. "A New Look at Old Southeast Asia." *The Journal of Asian Studies* 54, 2 (1995): 419–46.

Riddell, Peter G. "Breaking the Hamzah Fansuri Barrier: Other Literary Windows into Sumatran Islam in the Late Sixteenth Century CE." *Indonesia and the Malay World* 32, 93 (2004): 125–40.

______. "Sharia-Mindedness in the Malay World and the Indian Connection: The Contributions of Nur al-Din al-Raniri and Nik Abdul Aziz bin Haji Nik Mat." In *Islamic Connections: Muslim Societies in South and Southeast Asia*, ed. R. Michael Feener and Terenjit Sevea. Singapore: Institute of Southeast Asian Studies, 2009, pp. 175–94.

Rockhill, W.W. "Notes on the Relations and Trade of China with the Eastern Archipelago and the Coasts of the Indian Ocean during the Fourteenth Century." *T'oung Pao* 15 (1914): 419–47 and 16 (1915): 61–159, 236–71, 374–92, 435–67, 604–26.

Roff, William R. "Kaum Muda-Kaum Tua: Innovation and Reaction amongst the Malay." In *Reading on Islam in Southeast Asia*, ed. Ahmad Ibrahim *et al.* Singapore: Institute of Southeast Asian Studies, 1985.

______. "Patterns of Islamization in Malaysia, 1890s–1990s: Exemplars, Institutions, and Vectors." *Journal of Islamic Studies* 9, 2 (1998): 210–28.

Roseman, Marina. *Healing Sounds from the Malaysian Rainforest: Temiar Music and Medicine*. Berkeley: University of California Press, 1991.

Rungrawee Chalermsripinyorat. "Recruiting Militants in Southern Thailand." Asia Report No. 170, June 22, 2009. Bangkok/Brussels: International Crisis Group, 2009. Available at http://www.icg.com [accessed June 22, 2009].

Sang Phattananothai. "The Envoy from Langkasuka." *Muang Boran Journal* 8, 2 (April–July 1982).

Saronee Duerae. "Khwam hen khong khon thong thin to sathanakan khwam run raeng phak tai: sueksa jak bai pliw kho khian khang akhan sue thong thin" [Perception of Local People about the Violence in Southern Thailand: A Study of Leaflets, Graffiti and Local Media]. Bangkok: National Reconciliation Council, 2006, pp. 21–6.

Sastri, K.A. Nilakanta. *South Indian Influences in the Far East*. Bombay: Hind Kitab Ltd, 1949.

Schrieke, B. *Indonesian Sociological Studies*, Part 2. The Hague and Bandung: W. van Hoeve, 1957.

Scott, James C. *The Art of Not Being Governed: An Anarchist History of Upland Southeast Asia*. New Haven: Yale University Press, 2009; Singapore: NUS Press, 2010.

Scott to Governor General, October 28, 1785, Straits Settlements Records 2: 8 (FWC March 2, 1786).

Scupin, Raymond. "Islamic Reformism in Thailand." *Journal of Siam Society* 68, 2 (1980).

Sd. Sidin Ahmad Ishak and Mohammad Redzuan Othman. *The Malays in the Middle East*. Kuala Lumpur: Universiti Malaya Press, 2000.

Seni Mudmarn. "Language Use and Loyalty among the Muslim Malays of Southern Thailand." PhD diss., The State University of New York, 1988.

______. "Social Science Research in Thailand: The Case of the Muslim Minority." In *Muslim Social Science in ASEAN*, ed. Omar Farouk Bajunid. Kuala Lumpur: Yayasan Penataran Ilmu, 1994, pp. 21–75.

Seymour Sewell, C.A. "Notes on Some Old Siamese Guns." *Journal of the Siam Society* 15, 1 (1922): 1–43.

Shaghir Abdullah, Wan Mohd. *Sufi dan Wali Allah* [Sufis and Allah's Guardians]. Kota Bharu: Pustaka Aman Press, 1985.

______. *Syeikh Daud bin Abdullah al-Fatani: Ulama dan Pengarang Terulung Asia Tenggara* [Sheikh Daud bin Abdullah al-Fatani: Leading Scholar and Author in Southeast Asia]. Kuala Lumpur: Hizbi, 1990.

______. *Khazanah Karya Pusaka Asia Tenggara* [Treasures of Invaluable Works in Southeast Asia], Vol. I. Kuala Lumpur: Khazanah Fathaniyah, 1991.

Shaharil Talib. "The Port and Polity of Terengganu during the Eighteenth and Nineteenth Centuries: Realizing Its Potential." In *The Southeast Asian Port and Polity: Rise and Demise*, ed. J. Kathirithamby-Wells and John Villiers. Singapore: Singapore University Press, 1990.

Shamsul, Amri Baharuddin. "Islam Embedded: Religion and Plurality in Southeast Asia as a Mirror for Europe." *Asia Europe Journal* 3 (2005): 159–78.

Shaykh Faqih `Ali bin Muhammad bin Safiyuddin. *Tarikh Fatani* (handwritten text).

Shellabear, W.G. *Sejarah Melayu*. Kuala Lumpur: Fajar Bakti Sdn. Bhd., 1979.

"Siam." *Singapore Chronicle*, November 22, 1832.

Siddîq b. Hasan al-Qannûjî. *Abjad al-'Ulûm*, 3 vols. Beirut: Dâr al-Kutub al-'Ilmiyyah, n.d., III, pp. 222–3.

Skeat, W.W. "Reminiscences of the Cambridge University Expedition to the North-Eastern Malay States, 1899–1900." *Journal of the Malayan Branch of the Royal Asiatic Society* 28, 4 (1953): 9–147.

______. *Malay Magic*. Reprint of 1900 edition. New York: Dover, 1967.

Skinner, Cyril. *Rama III and the Siamese Expedition to Kedah in 1839: The Dispatches of Luang Udomsombat*, trans. C. Skinner. Melbourne: Centre of Southeast Asian Studies, 1993.

So, Kwan Wai. *Japanese Piracy in Ming China during the 16th Century*. East Lansing, MI: Michigan State University Press, 1975.

Soonthornpasuch, Suthep. "Islamic Identity in Chiengmai City: A Historical and Structural Comparison of Two Communities." PhD thesis, University of California, Berkeley, 1977.

SR 0201. 78/7. Ministry of the Interior to the Prime Minister, January 4, 1946, Urgent- Secret.

SR 0201. 92/36. Luang Ratanaphanit, Thai Consul-General, Singapore to Minister of Foreign Affairs, October 31, 1947.

SR 0201.61/6. Phraya Ratnaphakdi to Director-General, State Affairs Dept., October 16, 1957; and Memo on Actions taken for the Reform of the Administration of the Four Southern Provinces by 1955.

SR 0201.78/5. Minister of the Interior to the Chief Secretary to the Government, September 14, 1939.

Srisakr Vallibhotama [with police Major-General Jamrun, 'Abdullah Alomen and Udom Patthanawong]. *Lao khan tamnan tai* [Recounting Legends of the South]. Bangkok: Lek Prapai 2007.

Streckfuss, David. "The Mixed Colonial Legacy in Siam: The Origins of Thai Racialist Thought, 1890–1910." In *Autonomous Histories, Particular Truths: Essays in Honor of John Smail*, ed. L.J. Sears. Madison, WI: University of Wisconsin Press, pp. 123–53.

Su Ji-qing in Wang Da-yuan. *Dao-yi zhi-lue jiao shi*, annotated by Su Ji-qing. Beijing: Zhong-hua shu-ju, 1981, pp. 181–4.

Subhatra Bhumiprabhas. "Prostitution in Thailand — An Historical Perspective: Journal of a 17th-Century Austrian Merchant Offers a Lopsided View of Siam's Lewd Ladies." *The Nation* (Bangkok), July 22, 2007.

Suhkre, Astri. "The Thai Muslim Border Provinces: Some National Security Aspects." In *Studies of Contemporary Thailand*, ed. Robert Ho and E.C. Chapman. Canberra: Research School of Pacific Studies, Australia National University, 1973, pp. 296–311.

______. "Irredentism Contained: The Malay Muslim Case." *Journal of Contemporary Politics* 7, 2 (1975): 187–204.

______. "Loyalists and Separatists: The Muslims in Southern Thailand." *Asian Survey* 17, 3 (1977): 237–50.

______. "The Thai Muslims: Some Aspects of Minority Integration." *Pacific Affairs* 43 (1980): 531–47.

Sulong, Abdul Ramae. "Botbat khong tok khru: korani sueksa hayi wan idris bin wan ali" [Role of the Tok Gurus: A Case Study of Haji Wan Idris bin Haji Wan Ali). MA Thesis, Prince of Songkhla University, 2000.

Sulong, Haji Muhammad, Tuan Guru. *Gugusan Cahaya Keselamatan*, ed. Al-Haj Muhammad Amin ibn al-Marhum al-Haj Muhammad Sulung. Pattani: Private Publication, 1377 H/2501 B/1958 CE.

Sumio Fukami. "San-fo-qi, Srivijaya, and the Historiography of Insular Southeast Asia." In *Commerce et navigation en Asie du Sud-Est (XIVe–XIXe siècle)*, ed. Nguyễn Thế Anh and Yoshiaki Ishizawa. Paris: L'Harmattan, 1999, pp. 31–45.

Surin Pitsuwan. "Islam and Malay Nationalism: A Case Study of the Malay Muslims of South Thailand." PhD thesis, Harvard University, 1982.

______. *Islam and Malay Nationalism: A Case Study of the Malay Muslims of Southern Thailand*. Bangkok: Thai Khadi Research Institute, Thammasat University, 1985.

Syed Mhd. Khairudin Aljunied. "Making Sense of an Evolving Identity: A Survey of Studies on Identity and Identity Formation of Malays in Singapore." *Journal of Muslim Minority Affairs* 26, 3 (2006): 371–82.

______. "The Role of Hadramis in Post-World War Two Singapore: A Reinterpretation." *Immigrants and Minorities* 25, 2 (2007): 163–83.

"Syekh Muhammad Zain bin Faqih Jalaluddin Aceh." In *Perkembangan Ilmu Fiqh*, pp. 62–74.

Tagliacozzo, Eric. "Ambiguous Commodities, Unstable Frontiers: The Case of Burma, Siam, and Imperial Britain, 1800–1900." *Comparative Studies in Society and History* 46, 2 (2004): 354–77.

Tan Ta Sen. *Cheng Ho and Islam in Southeast Asia*. Singapore: Institute of Southeast Asian Studies, 2009.

Tārīkh Fatāni. Kuala Lumpur: Khazanah Fathaniyah, 2002.

Tej Bunnag. *Khabot R.S. 121* [The 1902 Rebellions]. Bangkok: Social Sciences and Humanities Text-Books Project, 1981 (in Thai).

Terpstra, H. *De Factorij der Oostindische Compagnie te Patani*, Verhandelingen van het Koninklijk Instituut voor de Taal-, Land- en Volkenkunde van Nederlandsch-Indië 1. The Hague: Nijhoff, 1938.

"Thailand's Hungry Military — An Update." *New Mandala*, at http://asiapacific. anu.edu.au/newmandala/2010/09/30/thailands-hungry-military-an-update/ [accessed January 12, 2011].

Thamsook Numnonda. "The Anglo-Siamese Secret Convention of 1897." *Journal of the Siam Society* 53, 1 (January 1965): 45–60.

______. *Thailand and the Japanese Presence 1941–1945*. Singapore: Institute of Southeast Asian Studies, 1977.

Thanet Aphornsuvan. "Nation-State and the Muslim Identity in the Southern Unrest and Violence." In *Understanding Conflict and Approching Peace in Southern Thailand*, ed. Imtiyaz Yusuf and Lars Peter Schmidt. Bangkok: Konrad Adenauer Stiftung, 2006, pp. 92–127.

______. "Rebellion in Southern Thailand: Contending Histories." *Policy Studies* 35. Washington, DC: East-West Center Washington, 2007.

"The History of Muslim Women in Southeast Asia and Thailand. Women: Merchants or Prostitutes or Female Aristocrats. Respectable Commoner Women and Aristocratic Women: Women in Muslim Societies: From Trade, Harbors, Markets to Royal Palaces" (in Thai). In *Isteri*, pp. 4–7.

Thongchai Winichakul. *Siam Mapped: A History of the Geo-Body of a Nation*. Honolulu: University of Hawai'i Press, 1994.

______. "Writing at the Interstices: Southeast Asian Historians and Post-National Histories in Southeast Asia." In *New Terrains in Southeast Asian History*. Ohio University Research in International Studies; Southeast Asia Series, number

107, ed. Abu Talib Ahmad and Tan Liok Ee. Athens, OH and Singapore: Ohio University Press and Singapore University Press, 2003, pp. 3–39.

Tibbetts, G.R. *A Study of the Arabic Texts Containing Material on South-East Asia*. Leiden: Brill, 1979.

Toussant, Auguste. *History of the Indian Ocean*. Chicago: University of Chicago Press, 1967.

Trocki, Carl A. "Chinese Pioneering in Eighteenth-Century Southeast Asia." In *The Last Stand of Asian Autonomies: Responses to Modernity in the Diverse States of Southeast Asia and Korea, 1750–1900*, ed. Anthony Reid. Basingstoke: Macmillan, 1997, pp. 83–102.

Tschacher, Torsten. "Circulating Islam: Understanding Convergence and Divergence in the Islamic Traditions of Mabar and Nusantara." In *Islamic Connections: Muslim Societies in South and Southeast Asia*, ed. R. Michael Feener and Terenjit Sevea. Singapore: Islamic Connections: Muslim Societies in South and Southeast Asia, 2009, pp. 48–67.

Ukrist Pathmanand. "Religious Issues in Political Conflict during the Late Thaksin Government." In *Religion and Democracy in Thailand*, ed. Imtiyaz Yusuf and Canan Atilgan. Bangkok: Konrad Adenauer Stiftung, 2008, pp. 80–102.

Uthai Dulyakasem. "Education and Ethnic Nationalism: A Study of the Muslim-Malays in Southern Siam." PhD diss., Stanford University, 1981.

______. "Muslim Malay Separatism in Southern Thailand: Factors Underlying the Political Revolt." In *Armed Separatism in Southeast Asia*, ed. Lim Joo-Jock and Vani S. Singapore: Institute of Southeast Asian Studies, 1984, pp. 217–33.

van Bruinessen, Martin. "Penggunaan kitab fiqh di pesantren Indonesia dan Malaysia" [The Use of Fiqh Textbooks in the Islamic Schools of Indonesia and Malaysia]. *Pesantren* 1, VI (1989): 36–51.

______. "Origins and Development of the Sufi Orders (*tarekat*) in Southeast Asia." *Studia Islamika* (1994): 111–23.

van der Putten, Jan. "Wayang Parsi, Bangsawan and Printing: Commercial Cultural Exchange between South Asia and the Malay World." In *Islamic Connections: Muslim Societies in South and Southeast Asia*, ed. R. Michael Feener and Terenjit Sevea. Singapore: Institute of Southeast Asian Studies, 2009, pp. 86–108.

van Foreest, H.A. and A. de Booy, eds. *De Vierde Schipvaart der Nederlanders naar Oost-Indië onder Jacob Wilkens en Jacob van Neck (1599–1604)*, 2 vols. The Hague: Linschoten Vereeniging, 1980.

van Neck, J. "Journaal." 1604. In *De Vierde Schipvaart der Nederlanders naar Oost-Indië onder Jacob Wilkens van Neck (1599–1604)*, vol. I, ed. H.A. van Foreest and A. de Booy. The Hague: Nijoff for Linschoten-Vereeniging, 1980.

van Warwyck, Wybrandt. "Historische Verhael vande Reyse gedaen inde Oost-Indien, met 15 Schepen voor Reeckeningh van de vereenichde Gheoctroyeerde Oost-Indische Compagnie." 1604. In *Begin ende Voortgangh van de Vereenighde Neederlandtsche Geoctoyeerde Oost-Indische Compagnie*, ed. Isaac Commelin. 1646, reprinted Amsterdam, 1974.

Vella, Walter F. *Chaiyo! King Vajiravudh and the Development of Thai Nationalism*. Honolulu: University Press of Hawai'i, 1978.

Vickers, Adrian. "The Eighteenth Century in Southeast Asian History." *Asian Studies Review* 18, 1 (1994): 61–69.

______. "'Malay Identity': Modernity, Invented Tradition, and Forms of Knowledge." *Review of Malaysian and Indonesian Affairs* 31, 1 (1997): 173–211.

Vickery, Michael. *Society, Economics, and Politics in Pre-Angkor Cambodia: The 7th–8th Centuries.* Tokyo: Toyo Bunko, 1998.

Virunha, Chuleeporn. "Historical Perceptions of Local Identity in the Upper Peninsula." In *Thai South and Malay North: Ethnic Interactions on a Plural Peninsula*, ed. Michael J. Montesano and Patrick Jory. Singapore: NUS Press, 2008.

Voll, John O. "Muhammad Hayyâ al-Sindî and Muhammad ibn Abd al-Wahhab: An Analysis of an Intellectual Group in Eighteenth Century Haramayn." *Bulletin of the School of Oriental and African Studies* 38 (1975): 32–9.

______. "Hadith Scholars and Tariqahs: An Ulama Group in the Eighteenth Century Haramayn and their Impact in the Islamic World." *Journal of Asian and African Studies* 15, 3–4 (1980): 264–73.

Wade, Geoff. "The Ming Shi-lu (Veritable Records of the Ming Dynasty) as a Source for Southeast Asian History, 14th to 17th centuries." PhD diss., University of Hong Kong, 1994, Vol. VII.

______. "From Chaiya to Pahang: The Eastern Seaboard of the Peninsula as Recorded in Classical Chinese Texts." In *Études sur l'histoire du sultanat de Patani*, Études thématiques, ed. Daniel Perret, Amara Srisuchat, and Sumbun Thanasuk. Paris: École française d'Extrême-Orient, 2004, pp. 37–78.

Wang Gungwu. *The Nanhai Trade: The Early History of Chinese Trade in the South China Sea.* Singapore: Times Academic Press Reprint, 1998.

Wang Tai Peng. *The Origins of the Chinese Kongsi.* Petaling Jaya: Pelanduk Publications, 1994.

Wheatley, Paul. *The Golden Khersonese: Studies in the Historical Geography of the Malay Peninsula before A.D. 1500.* Kuala Lumpur: University of Malaya Press, 1961.

Wieringa, Edwin. "Some Light on Ahmad al-Fatani's Nur al-Mubin." In *Lost Time and Untold Tales from the Malay World*, ed. Jan van der Putten and Mary Kilcline Coby. Singapore: NUS Press, 2009, pp. 186–97.

Winstedt, R.O. "Early Muhammadan Missionaries." *JSBRAS* 81 (1920): 5–6.

Winter, Michael. *Society and Religion in Early Ottoman Egypt: Studies in the Writings of 'Abd al-Wahhâb al-Sha'rânî.* New Brunswick: Transaction Books, 1982.

Winzeler, R.L. "The Social Organization of Islam in Kelantan." In *Kelantan: Religion, Society and Politics in a Malay State*, ed. W.R. Roff. Kuala Lumpur: Oxford University Press, 1974, pp. 259–71.

Wolters, O.W. *History, Culture, and Region in Southeast Asian Perspectives.* Singapore: Institute of Southeast Asian Studies, 1982.

Wolters, Oliver. *History, Culture, and Region in Southeast Asian Perspectives.* Ithaca, NY: Southeast Asia Program, Cornell University, 1999.

Wong Lin Ken. *The Malayan Tin Industry to 1914: With Special Reference to the States of Perak, Selangor, Negeri Sembilan and Pahang.* Tucson, AZ: University of Arizona Press, 1965.

Wyatt, David K. "A Thai Version of Newbold's 'Hikayat Patani'." *JMBRAS* 40, 2 (1967): 16–37.

———. *The Crystal Sands: The Chronicles of Nagara Sri Dharrmaraja*. Ithaca, NY: Cornell University Southeast Asia Program, 1975.

———. "Foreword." In Ibrahim Syukri, *History of the Malay Kingdom of Patani*, trans. Conner Bailey and John N. Miksic. Athens, OH: Ohio University Press, 1985 (re-published Chiang Mai: Silkworm Books, 2005), pp. vii–xi.

Xiang Da. *Shun-feng xiang-song*. Beijing: Zhong-hua shu-ju, 1982.

Ying Jia *et al. Cang-wu zong-du jun-men-zhi*. Beijing photolithograph reprint. Beijing: Quan-guo tu-shu-guan wen-xian su-wei fu-zhi zhong-xin, 1991, *juan* 21.52a.

Yusuf, Imtiyaz. "Islam and Democracy in Thailand: Reforming the Office of the Chularajamontri/Shaikh Al-Islam." *Journal of Islamic Studies* 9, 2 (1998): 277–98.

Zhang Xie. *Dong-xi-yang kao*, annotated by Xie Fang. Beijing: Zhong-hua Shu-ju, 1981.

Contributors

Barbara Watson Andaya is Professor of Asian Studies at the University of Hawai'i. She has held positions at the University of Malaya, the Australian National University, the University of Auckland, Universiti Sains Malaysia and the National University of Singapore, and was President of the American Association for Asian Studies, 2005–2006. Her specific area of expertise is the western Malay-Indonesia archipelago on which she has published extensively. Her most recent book is *The Flaming Womb: Repositioning Women in Southeast Asian History, 1500–1800* (2006). Her current project is a history of the localization of Christianity in Southeast Asia, 1511–1900.

Azyumardi Azra is Professor of History and the Director of the Graduate School at Syarif Hidayatullah State Islamic University (UIN), Jakarta, Indonesia. He was a former Rector of the same university for two terms, 1998–2002, and 2002–2006. He has written 21 books and many chapters in internationally published books. Among his latest works are: *Indonesia, Islam and Democracy: Dynamics in a Global Context* (2006); *Islam in the Indonesian World: An Account of Institutional Development* (2007); and as contributing co-editor, *Islam beyond Conflict: Indonesian Islam and Western Political Theory* (2008). Earlier, he published his best-known work, *The Origins on Islamic Reformism in Southeast Asia: Networks of Malay-Indonesian Ulama* (2005). On August 15, 2005, he received the Bintang Mahaputera Utama from Indonesian President Susilo Bambang Yudhoyono for his dedication to Indonesian education.

Francis R. Bradley completed his doctorate in History at the University of Wisconsin-Madison in 2010 with a dissertation entitled, "The Social Dynamics of Islamic Revivalism in Southeast Asia: The Rise of the Patani School, 1785–1909." He has also published his work in *Oxford Islamic Studies Online*, the *Journal of Southeast Asian Studies*, and is nearing completion of a book that analyzes Islamic reform networks linking Southeast Asia and the

Middle East in the 19th century. He currently teaches at the Pratt Institute in Brooklyn, New York.

Numan Hayimasae is a lecturer in the Malay Studies Section, Faculty of Humanities and Social Sciences, Prince of Songkhla University, Pattani, Thailand, and is a license holder of the Panyabhat Pittaya School also in Pattani. He received his MA and PhD in Islamic Civilization and History respectively from Universiti Sains Malaysia. His research interests are Muslim intellectual history, Patani-*Haramayn* intellectual networks, and the history of *madrasah* in Southeast Asia. He is co-author of *New Theories for Islamic Educational Institutions in Southern Thailand: The Unrevealed Truth* (2010, in Thai).

Christopher Joll is a New Zealand anthropologist who has lived and worked in Thailand's Malay-dominated southern provinces for ten years. Since completing his doctorate from the Centre for the Study of the Malay World and Civilization (ATMA) at the National University of Malaysia (UKM) in 2009, he has held visiting research fellowships at Chulalongkorn University and Victoria University of Wellington. He is the author of *Muslim Merit-Making in Thailand's Far-South*. He is currently working on a project concerned with the Ahmadiyyah-Qadariyyah and Ahmadiyyah-Shadhliyya *sufi* orders in central and southern Thailand.

Patrick Jory (editor) is a Senior Lecturer in Southeast Asian History at the University of Queensland. Between 2001 and 2009, he worked as coordinator of the Regional Studies Program at Walailak University in southern Thailand. His research interests are in Thai cultural history and ethnic relations in southern Thailand. He is co-editor of *Thai South and Malay North: Ethnic Interactions on a Plural Peninsula* (2008).

Philip King works at Murdoch University and was awarded his PhD from the University of Wollongong, Australia. He currently serves as the Resident Director of the Australian Consortium for "In-Country" Indonesia Studies. His research interests are Peninsula history and the Indonesian tertiary education sector. His recent publications include "Penang to Songkhla, Penang to Patani: Two Roads, Past and Present," in *Penang and its Region: The Story of an Asian Entrepôt*, ed. Yeoh Seng Guan *et al.* (2009).

Iik A. Mansurnoor is an Associate Professor in History and Deputy Dean of the Faculty of Arts and Social Sciences at the University of Brunei

Darussalam. His research interests focus on Islam, globalization and modern history. He is the author of *Islam in an Indonesian World: Ulama of Madura* (1992), and *Living Islamically in the Periphery: Muslim Discourse, Institution, and Intellectual Traditions in Southeast Asia* (2011).

Duncan McCargo is Professor of Southeast Asian Politics at the University of Leeds, UK. His *Tearing Apart the Land: Islam and Legitimacy in Southern Thailand* (2008) won the inaugural 2009 Bernard Schwartz Book Prize, awarded by the Asia Society. His most recent book is *Mapping National Anxieties: Thailand's Southern Conflict* (2012).

Anthony Reid is a Southeast Asian historian, now again at the Australian National University after serving as founding Director of the Asia Research Institute at the National University of Singapore (2002–2007). His recent books include: *An Indonesian Frontier: Acehnese and Other Histories of Sumatra* (2004); *Imperial Alchemy: Nationalism and Political Identity in Southeast Asia* (2010); and *To Nation by Revolution: Indonesia in the 20th Century* (2011).

Kobkua Suwannathat-Pian was educated in Thailand, England and Malaysia. She is currently Professor of History and a Senior Fellow in the Faculty of Humanities, at the Sultan Idris Universiti of Education (UPSI), Tanjung Malim, Perak, Malaysia. Prior to her present position she taught at various leading universities in Southeast Asia including Chiangmai University, Chulalongkorn University, National University of Malaysia, Gadjah Mada University, and Hong Kong University. She is an acknowledged authority on Thai-Malaysian relations and contemporary Thai socio-politics. Her publications include: *Thai-Malay Relations, Traditional Intra-Regional Relations from the Seventeenth to the Early Twentieth Centuries* (1988); *Kings, Country and Constitutions* (2003); and *Palace, Political Party and Power: A Story of the Socio-Political Development of Malay Kingship* (2011).

Geoff Wade is a historian currently attached to the Nalanda-Sriwijaya Centre (NSC), Institute of Southeast Asian Studies, Singapore, after stints at the University of Hong Kong and the Asia Research Institute, National University of Singapore. He researches Sino-Southeast Asian historical interactions and comparative historiography, and has worked on a range of other related issues including early Islam in Southeast Asia, Chinese expansions over time, Asian commercial networks, Chinese classical textual references to Southeast Asia, Australia's growing engagement with Asia, and the Cold War in Southeast Asia. His online database of Ming Chinese references to Southeast Asia (http://epress.nus.edu.sg/msl/) comprises over 3,000 references in English translation. He has edited *China and Southeast Asia* (2009), a six-volume survey of seminal works on Southeast Asia-China interactions over time. He also contributed a chapter on Islamic expansion in Southeast Asia (800–1500 CE) to the *New Cambridge History of Islam* (2010).

Dennis Walker received his PhD from the Australian National University; his thesis was entitled "Islamic and Pan-Arab Identities and Acculturated Muslim Egyptian Intellectuals 1892–1952." He has taught Arabic and Middle Eastern ideologies in Melbourne University, the Australian National University, and Deakin University. Since 2005, he has been attached as an Adjunct Research Scholar on Southern Thailand to the Monash Asia Institute at Monash University, Australia. He is author of *Islam and the Search for African-American Nationhood: Elijah Muhammad, Louis Farrakhan and the Nation of Islam* (2005).

Index

A. Bangnara, 196, 260, 262, 264–5
'Abd Allâh al-Basrî, 101–2
'Abd al-Mu'mîn, 96
'Abd al-Rahmân al-Batâwî al-Masrî,
 95, 100
'Abd al-Ra'ûf al-Sinkilî, 90
'Abd al-Samad al-Palimbânî, 95
Abû al-Tâhir ibn Ibrâhîm al-Kûrânî, 90
'Abd al-Wahhâb al-Bugisî, 95, 100, 113
Abdul Kadir Kamaruddin, *see* Tengku
 Abdul Kadir Kamaruddin
'Abdul Rahman al-Batawi, 113
Aceh, xx, xxi, 4, 19, 20–2, 35, 47, 90, 95,
 99–100, 112, 116, 134, 139–40, 161,
 189, 213
Adab, 116
Adam Smith, 169
Adat Aceh, 49
Afghanistan, xxv, xxvii
Africa, 63
ahâdith, 91, 93, 94
Ahmad al-Damanhûrî, 101
Ahmad al-Marzûqî, 102, 113
Ahmad al-Qushâsî, 90
Ahmad Fathi al Fatani, xvii, 112, 192,
 195–6, 200, 208, 212–3, 215, 220,
 255, 260, 270, 272, 275
Ahmad Zayn al-'Âbidîn al-Fatânî, 98
'Alâ' al-Dîn al-Bâbilî, 101
al-Ajrumiyah, 117
al-Azhar, 101, 113, 140, 220
al-Barrâwî ('Isâ b. Ahmad b. 'Isâ b.
 Muúammad al-Zubayrî al-Shâfi'î
 al-Qâhirî al-Azharî), 99, 100–1, 113
al-Fatâwâ, 104, 108

al-Ghazâlî, 91, 105, 223
al-Imam, 143
al-Kalâbâdhî, 91
al-Kharidatul Bahaiyah, 117
al-Kharrâz, 91
al-Manar, 143
al-Maqassârî, 95
al-Munir, 143
al-Nawawî, 104
al-Palimbânî, 100, 102, 113
al-Rânîrî, 95
al-Sammânî, 100
al-Sarrâj, 91
al-Sha'rânî, 105
al-Sharqâwî, 101, 113
al-Sinkilî, 95
Ali Banjar, 127
'Alî b. Ishâq al-Fatânî, 98, 100, 113
Amsterdam, 15
Angkor, 5
Anglo-Siamese Secret Treaty (1897),
 232
Anglo-Siamese Treaty (1909), 150, 218,
 225, 272
Anglo-Thai Agreement (1949), 238
Annam (Dai Viet), 67, 69
Arabic, 15, 19, 116, 133, 204, 222, 227
 printing, 117
 religious instruction in, 122–3
Arabs, 63, 89, 90, 131, 197, 200–4, 222
Ari Wongsan, 124
ASEAN, xxviii, 227
'Ashâb al-Jâwîyyîn', 88
Austronesian, 5, 276
Ayudhya, *see* Ayutthaya

Ayutthaya, 6, 13, 16, 36, 39–40, 41, 43,
  51, 68, 84, 129, 133, 149, 188, 197,
  213, 215, 226, 263–5, 267–8, 274
  fall of, 150–1, 223, 263

Bahadur, Sultan, 11, 38–9
Banda, 16, 29
Bangka, 167
Bangkok, xxv
Bang-Nara, xxv, 230–1
Banjarmasin, 189
Banten, 13, 213
Barbara Whittingham-Jones, 195
Barisan Islam Pembebasan Patani
  (BIPP), 239
Barisan Nasional Pembebasan Patani
  (BNPP), 238
Barisan Revolusi Nasional (BRN), 239
Batavia, 67–8, 75, 95
Bay of Bengal, 14
Bendahara, 39, 50
Bengal, 28
Berjihad di-Patani, 190
Betong, 166
Bidâyat al-Hidâyah, 100
Bombay, 119
Bone Sultanate, 99
Borneo, 16, 28, 30, 189
Bosnia, 208
Britain, 107
British, xxiii–xxiv, 16
Brunei, 16, 20, 64
Buddhism, 37, 57n13, 58, 83, 109, 129,
  195–6, 203, 218, 235, 242, 258, 260,
  274
Bughyat al-Ṭullâb al-Murîd Ma'rifat
  al-Aḥkâm bi al-Ṣawâb, 103–4
Burma, 41, 188
Burmese, 39, 41
Burney, 3
Burney Treaty, 168, 271

Cairo, 100, 104, 117, 119
Calcutta, 157
Caliph / Caliphate, 117, 197, 201

Cambodia, xxi, 16, 29, 57n13, 73, 79,
  108, 203
camphor, 29
Candradevi, 5
cannon, 36, 41–5, 67n49, 204, 207, 265,
  267
Chaiya, 55, 73–4
Chakri dynasty, 195, 216, 241, 256
Cham, 5, 9, 32
Champa, 16, 57n13
Chaophraya Pulatep Bunnak, 219
Chao-zhou, 67n49
Chavalit Yongchaiyudh, General, 216
Chinese
  community in Patani, xxiv, 10, 12–5,
    20, 24, 76, 198
  mining in Patani, 162, 173
  "pirates", 7, 69, 75
  religion in Patani, 19, 24
  sources about Patani, xx–xxi, 63–84
  sources about Langkasuka, 53–63
  trade with Patani, 4–17, 20–1, 26,
    29, 68, 83, 186, 200, 211
Chulalongkorn, King, 241, 272
cloves, 17, 29
Cola, xx
Cold War, 235, 242, 244–5, 248, 250
Compulsory Education Act (1921),
  233–4
Congress of Vienna, 3
copper, 14, 29
Cornwallis, General Charles, 217
Coromandel, 14

damask, 29
Damrong Rachanuphap, Prince, xivn1
Datuk Andi Maharajalela, 99
Datuk Buk, 43
Datuk Sirinara, 16, 20
daulat, 43, 52
Dâwûd ibn 'Abd Allâh b. Idrîs al-
  Faṭânî, xviii, xxi, 90, 95–108, 112,
  131, 137, 139–40, 141, 146, 197,
  221, 223, 257
deerskins, 29

dhikr, 92, 186
Dong-xi-yang kao [Account of the Eastern and Western Oceans], 64–6, 83
Dusongnyor incident of 1948, 288–9
Dutch, 11, 15–8, 20–1, 29, 34, 38, 41, 47–8, 68, 71, 83, 197, 207, 210, 221, 265
Dvāravatī, 57

East India Company, 156, 158, 168, 207
Egypt, 93, 101, 125, 141, 143, 226
elephants, 34–5, 37–40, 58, 151
English, 20, 207, 210

Falak, 116
Fath al-Wahhâb, 104
fatwa, xxiv, 142, 223
Faqîh 'Abd al-Manân, 96
Faqîh 'Alî, 99
Fawâ'id al-Irtihâl wa Natâ'ij al-Safar, 89
Fazlur Rahman, 92
female rule, 20–2, 26–7
fiqh, xxiv, 99, 101, 103–4, 106, 116, 223
Floris, Peter, 10, 13–4, 16, 66
France/the French, 107, 208
Francis Light, 151–2, 157–8, 217–8
Frank Swettenham, 162, 221
Fujian, 10, 13, 26n65, 67–9, 73
Funan, 55
Furû' al-Masâ'il wa Usûl al-Masâ'il, 103–4

gajah keramat, 35
GAMPAR (*Gabungan Melayu Patani Raya*), 191
gender, 17, 20–2, 24–6, 205
Ghâyat al-Taqrîb, 103
gold, xxiii, 9, 16, 29, 75, 88
Guang-dong, 67, 75
Gugusan Chahaya Keselamatan, 248
Gujerat, 134
Gujeratis, 13–4, 21
Gulf of Siam, 8, 55

hadith, 100–1, 113, 116, 121, 197
Hadhramaut, 134–5, 137
Hadramis, 134–8
Hâjî 'Abd al-Rahmân, 96,
Haji Abdul Rahman bin Ahmad, 125
Haji Majid Zainuddin, 123
Haji Sulong Abdul Kadir, 123–4, 131, 137, 144–6, 192, 237, 247, 273–4, 275, 283, 286
   seven-point demand, 248n31, 273, 276
Hai-guo wen-jian-lu [Account of Things Heard and Seen in the Maritime Countries], 73, 83
Hai-lu [Account of the Seas], 75
Hai-shang ji-lue [A Short Account of the Seas] (19th Century), 75
Hainan, 64
Hajj, 88, 93, 111, 115–6, 127, 134, 137
halaqah, xxii, 121–2, 126–7
Hamzah Fansuri, 133–4, 146
Hanafi, 120, 205
Hanbali, 120
Hang Tuah, 267
Hanoi, 4
Haramayn, xxi, xxii, 87–8, 90, 93, 94, 100, 102, 108, 110–28, 146
Hidâyat al-Muta'allim wa 'Umdat al-Mu'allim, 103
Hijaz, 88, 92–3, 131, 140
Hikayat Hang Tuah, 34
Hikayat Marong Mahawangsa, 56
Hikayat Patani, xx, xxv, 5, 10, 11, 13–4, 16, 31–2, 34–9, 41, 43, 45–6, 48, 50–2, 66, 73, 96, 111, 131, 188–92, 197–9, 200, 203–4, 206, 256–7, 260, 264, 264, 268–9
Hikayat Raja Langkasuka, 197
Hindu, 37, 109, 197
Hinduism, 195, 199, 260
Hokkien, 15
Holland, 19, 67, 206, 208, 210
Hou-jian-lu, 68
House of Orange-Nassau, 48
Hsü Yun-tsiao, 12, 55, 67n49

hua muang, viii, xxiii, xxv, 214, 220, 228–9, 231
Husayn b. Muḥammad al-Maḥallî, 104

I'anatut Thalibin, 117
Ibirizud Dari fi Maulidis Saiyidi Adnanni, 118
Ibn 'Arabî', 105, 134, 223
Ibn Battûta, 136
Ibn Ḥajar al-Haytamî, 104
Ibn Saud, 120, 126, 145
Ibrâhîm al-Kûrânî, 89–90
Ibrâhîm al-Ra'îs al-Zamzamî al-Makkî, 102, 113
Ibrahim Qurayshi, 220
Ibrahim Syukri, xv, xxiv–xxv, xxvii, 6, 45, 190–3, 195–6, 199, 204, 207, 249–50, 258–9, 268
Idah al-Bâb li Murîd al-Nikâḥ bi al-Sawâb, 104
Ijazah, 122
ijma, 91
Imam Shanhaji, 117
ilmu gajah, 39
India, 16, 93, 58, 83, 90, 202, 213, 219
Indianization, 59–60
Indian Ocean, xxii, 4, 131, 136, 141, 144, 161
indigo, 30
Indonesia, xxv, 87, 93, 204, 225
Indragiri, 29
insurgency, xix
Iran, 212, 218, 220
Iraq, xxvii, 197, 207, 220, 283
iron, 29
Islam, 89–91, 213
   and Patani identity, 186–7, 192, 197, 200–2, 215
   education, 97, 114, 110–28, 227
   in Southeast Asia, 87–90
   mysticism in, 103
   reformism in, 95–6, 103, 109
Islam Burapha School, 215
"Islamic Private Schools", 124
Islamic revival, xviii

Islamic state, 106–7
Isma'il Benjasmith, 203, 209–10, 223
Israel, 208, 218–9, 226
Istanbul, 104, 117, 119

Jakarta, 4
Jambatan Kedi. 36
Jambi, 16, 20, 29, 45, 210
Jâmî' al-Fawâ'id, 103
Japan, 3–4, 20, 29, 64, 73
Japanese, xx, 6, 9–10, 13, 14, 20
Java, 8, 13, 16, 28, 64, 121, 197, 261, 264
   West, 95
   East, 99, 131
Javanese, xx, 10, 13, 16, 20–1, 88, 111
Jawi, xv, xxv, 40, 88–9, 90, 93, 98, 100, 108–9, 115, 118, 142, 143, 186–7, 193, 222, 224, 226, 255, 260, 263, 280, 283
   kitab jawi, 118–9, 141, 187
Jeddah, 123–4
Jerusalem, 96, 111, 141
jihad, xxiv, xxv, xxvii, 106–7, 186, 190, 192, 195, 199, 202, 204–5, 207, 209–10, 215, 217–20, 223–4, 225, 240
John Crawfurd, 153, 163, 167, 169
Johor, 10, 29, 32, 51, 71, 74, 83, 213, 267
   Prince of, 45
Jordan, 126
Jortan, 13
Junayd al-Baghdâdî, 91

kalam, 91, 101
Kalimantan, 108
   South, 95
Kampar, 29
Karen, 4
Kashf al-Ghummah, 105
Kashf al-Kirâm, 100
Kashf al-Lithâm, 104
Kashmir, 208
Kedah, 5, 32, 96, 114, 129, 157–8, 161, 164–5, 169, 189, 212–3, 217, 261, 264, 271
Kedi, 51

330 *Index*

Kelantan, 35, 39, 55, 63, 74, 76, 83, 114,
116, 129, 143, 157–8, 161, 190,
192, 201, 211–3, 259, 267
Dynasty, 72, 211–2, 265, 270
Kemas Fakhr al-Dîn, 95
Kemas Muḥammad b. Aḥmad, 95
keramat, 37
Khek, 5
Khmers, 5, 83, 264
Khunying Jan, 215
Kitab Al-Fatawa Al-Fataniyyah, 142
Kitab Dara-ilul Khairat, 117
Kota Bahru, 165–6
Kota Mahligai, 5–6, 261–2
kota raja, 34
Kroh plateau, 165, 167, 172, 181
Krue Se (Kresik), 12, 23, 67n49, 99,
139, 144, 206, 219, 221, 284–91
Kulliyyah Syar'iyyah, 123

Lan-chang, 64
Langkasuka, xx–xxi, xxiv, xxvii, 6n4,
55–63, 83, 187, 195–7, 199, 201–3,
260–2
Chinese in, 197
Laos, 32
lapis besar, 29
lead, 16, 29
Lebanon, 126
Legeh (Ra-Ngae), 166, 214, 228, 231
Leng Ju Kiang, 8
Liang shu [*History of the Liang
Dynasty*], 55–7
Liang zhi-gong tu [*Illustrated Tributaries
of the Liang*], 58
Libya, 126
Ligor, 29, 70, 72, 257, 261, 263–4, *see
also* Nakhon Si Thammarat
Lim Kor Niaw, *see* Lin Guniang
Lim Toh Khiam *see* Lin Daoqian
Lin Daoqian, 7–8, 10–3, 65, 67–9, 73,
75, 83
Lin Guniang, 7–8, 12
Lukman bin Sima, 239
Luzon, 21, 68, 75

mace, 29
madhhab, 93, 102, 120
madrasah, xxii, 120–7
Madrasah al-Falah, 123, 125
Madrasah al-Islah al-Diniyyah, 124
Madrasah al-Lailiyyah, 123, 125
Madrasah al-Sa'ah (al-Sa'ab), 123
Madrasah al-Sahir al-Mutawassitah,
123
Madrasah Asasiyyah, 123, 125
Madrasah Dar al-Anwar, 124
Madrasah Dar al-Ma'arif al-
Wataniyyah, 123–4 , 145
Madrasah Dar al-'Ulum al-Diniyyah,
122, 125, 127, 144
Madrasah Indonesia, 125
Madrasah Jeddah, 123, 125
Madrasah Khalid Ibn Waleed, 123
Madrasah Madinah, 125
Madrasah Mu'assasah al-Islamiyyah,
125
Madrasah Rahmaniyyah, 123, 125
Madrasah Shaulatiyyah, 122, 125
Ma'had al-Dirasat al-Islamiyyah, 215
Ma'had al-'Ilmi al-Saudi, 125
Makassar, 16
Maktabah Dar al-Ma'rif, 119
Maktabah Fataniyyah, 118
Malabar, 136
Malabari Muslims, 135
Malay, xxi, xxvi, 9, 16, 21
identity, 12, 20–1, 31, 32, 131, 140,
145–6, 283, 289
Islamic works in, 104
language, 14–5, 20, 23, 47, 133–4,
140, 195, 204, 226
Malaysia, 7, 204
Mâlîkî, 93, 120
Malik Ibrâhîm, 99
Maluku, xxvi, 13, 16
*Manhal al-Sâfî fî Bayân Zumar Ahl
al-Sûfî*, 105–6
mandala, xxiii, 129, 149, 152, 159, 264,
274
Manila, 4, 208

Mansur Syah, Sultan, 38, 43, 66
Masjid al-Haram, 114, 116, 119–20, 122, 125–7, 143, 145
Matbaah al-Ahmadiyyah, 119
Matbaah Riawwiyah, 119
Mawlânâ Malik Ibrâhîm, 99, 131
Mecca, 87, 89, 92, 95, 99, 100, 104, 107, 110–3, 115, 117–9, 122, 125, 128, 134, 139–46
Medina, 87, 89, 92, 95, 110, 115, 145
Mediterranean, 92
Melaka, 4, 7–9, 12–3, 16, 21, 28, 35, 45, 74, 76, 79, 83, 130–1, 225, 258, 261, 265
    Sultan of, 46
metalware, 16
Middle East, xxi–xxiv, xxvii, 45, 63, 87, 94, 103, 133, 136–7, 141, 146, 186, 187, 203, 222
    education in, 110–28
Minangkabau, 36, 96, 111, 116
Ming dynasty, 6–10, 13, 17, 67, 69, 75
Ming Shen-zong Shi-lu [The Veritable Records of the Wan-li Reign], 67–8
Ming shi [History of the Ming Dynasty], 73
Minhâj al-'Âbidîn, 105
Minhâj al-Ṯâlibîn, 104
Misa Melayu, 47
Mohammad Zamberi 'Abdul Malek, 191, 196, 198, 202, 260, 263, 265–7, 270, 272
Mongols, 198
monthon, xxv
Morocco, 93, 126
Moros, 128
Mughal India, 45
muẖaddithûn, 91, 94, 113
Muḥammad 'Abd al-Karîm al-Sammânî, 90
Muhammad Abduh, 144
Muhammad Abdul Wahab, 126
Muḥammad al-Sammânî, 98
Muḥammad b. 'Alî al-Shanwânî, 101, 113

Muẖammad Arshad al-Banjârî, 95, 100, 113, 118
Muẖammad As'ad al-Ḥanafî al-Makkî, 102
Muḥammad Ḥayyâ al-Sindî, 90
Muḥammad Muẖyî al-Dîn b. Shihâb al-Dîn, 95
Muḥammad Nafîs al-Banjârî, 95, 100, 113
Muhammad Nasir al-'Abudi, 212–3
Muḥammad Ṣâliẖ b. 'Abd al-Raẖmân al-Faṯânî, 98, 100, 113
Muḥammad Ṯâhir b. 'Alî al-Faṯânî, 98
Muhammad Yasin Haji Isa al-Pandani, 121, 123
Muẖammad Zayn b. Faqîh Jalâl al-Dîn al-Ashî, 99, 140
Muhsin bin Ali Musawwa, 127
Muhyiddin, Prince, 191–2, 195, 222, 237–8, 245, 274
Muniyyat al-Muṣallî, 103, 106
murâqaba, 92
Murtaḏâ al-Zabîdî, 101
murtadd, 107
Muslim Brotherhood, 220
Mustafa al-Babi al-Halabi, 141
Muzaffar Shah, Sultan, 39–40, 43, 51, 96, 188, 200, 216, 226, 264–5, 267, 274

naga, 34
Nāgarakrtāgama, 56
Nagasaki, 69–70, 71–2, 83
Nahj al-Râghibîn fî Sabîl al-Muttaqîn, 103
Nakhon Si Thammarat, 39, 73–4, 151, 215, 219
    Chronicle, 4, 262
Nang Liu-liu, 43, 50
Nang Tani, 43
Narai, King, 41
Narathiwat, xiv, xxv, 31, 213, 215, 224, 231, *see also* Bang-Nara
Nasser, 220, 226

National Reconciliation Commission, 280

Nihâyat al-Muḫtâj, 104

Nik Anuar Nik Mahmud, 260, 262, 270–1, 274

Nobat, xx, 45–51

Nongchik, 228

Nur al-Din al-Raniri, 134, 146

nutmeg, 17, 29

Nuz-hatun Nazhirin, 117

Okinawa, 9

orang kaya, 13, 16, 18, 151, 186

Ottoman Empire, 117, 120, 140–1, 223

Padang, 143

Pahang, 5, 8, 29, 32, 47, 73–4, 79, 267

Palembang, 9, 16, 20, 43, 95

Palestine, 208

Panare, 125

Pangkalan, Datuk, 219, 266, 269, 275

panglima, 13

Pan-pan, 57

Pasai, 96, 111, 131, 189, 198–200

Pasir Putih, 191

Patani

as a term, xxv, 249–50

British relations with, 217–9, 221–2, 231–2, 237–8, 244

Darussalam, 36, 201

division into seven principalities, 160, 165, 192, 214, 220, 228–9, 231, 266, 269, 271

enslavement of residents of, 153–6

fall of (1786), 150–1, 214, 216–7, 219, 225, 266, 268–9, 270, 288

gold mining in, 162, 164

identity, 31, 48–9, 51, 196, 232, 235, 253, 255, 260, 263

Islamic education in, xix, xxv

Islamization of, 197–200, 203, 213

movement to join Federation of Malaya, 233, 237–8, 245

nationalism, 191, 196, 198, 200–5, 208–9, 211–3, 220–1, 225–7, 237–8, 241, 255, 283, 295

population of, 14, 152, 159

queens of, 65–6, 70–2, 83, 186, 204, 208, 265, 268, 275, 283, 293–4

refugees from, 157–9, 191, 217

separatism, 96, 236–41, 243, 247, 253, 277

Sultanate of, xxiii, xxv, 99, 150, 160, 165, 186, 189–90, 200–1, 208, 224, 226, 228–9, 232, 234–5, 237, 243, 255, 263, 272, 275, 276

trade, 90–100, 186–7, 197, 205, 208–9, 262, 268

ulama, xxi, 87–109, 112–28, 137–46, 205–6, 276

warfare involving Siam and, 150–60

1791 revolt of, 165n11, 266, 271

1808 revolt of, 165n11, 219, 221, 266, 269, 271

1832 revolt of, 154, 214, 269–71

1901–02 uprising of, 231

1923 uprising of, 233, 273

Patani — Adit lae Patjuban, see Patani Dahulu dan Sekarang

Patani Dahulu dan Sekarang, 199–200, 208–9, 221

Patani Dalam Tamadun Melayu, 201

Patani 'Ulama Association, 141

Pattani (province), xxv, 31, 220, 231

monthon, 230–1

Pegu, 30, 35, 264

pelanduk, 35–6

Penang, 45, 114, 119, 158, 167, 178

Pengantar Sejarah Patani, 274

penis-bells, 18, 26

pepper, 9, 12, 29–30, 75, 88

Perak, 49, 114, 157, 161, 164–5, 167, 168–9, 172–80

British annexation of, 168

perkakas kerajaan, 41

pesantren, 112

Persia / Persians, 93, 133, 197, 202–3

Pertubuhan Pembebasan Patani Bersatu,
  see PULO
Phatthalung, 29, 201, 212, 263, 267
Phaya Tani, xx, 42–3
Phaya Tu Antara, 130–1, 202, 263
Phetburi, 5
Phibun Songkhram, 196, 204, 233, 236,
  241, 275, 290
Philippines, 64
Phra Pirun, 41
Phuket, 215
Pintu Gajah, xx, 34–7, 52
Pintu Gerbang, 34–5, 221
Pluralism, xx
Pok Doe Ae, 127
Polynesia, 17
pondok, xxi, 97, 99, 108, 111, 119, 140,
  144–5, 192, 206, 223, 239
Pondok Bendang Daya, 140
porcelain, 29
Portuguese, xx, 8–9, 13, 21, 69, 83, 89,
  130, 197, 207–8, 221, 265
Prince Devawongse (or "Devawong"),
  178–80, 232n5
Prince of Songkhla University, 193,
  218, 224
prostitution, 17
PULO (Patani United Liberation
  Organization), 199

Qing-chao tong-dian [General Statutes
  of the Qing Court], 74
Qing Dynasty, 75
Quanzhou, 26

Rahmatullah Ibn Khalil al-'Uthmani,
  122
Raja Hijau, *see* Raja Ijau
Raja Ijau, 1, 20–1, 38, 66, 186, 205,
  208–9, 212, 265, 268, 275
Raja Bima, 38–9
Raja Biru, 42n44, 45, 209, 212, 275
Raja Dewi, 212
Raja Kuning, 73, 223, 266, 269–70
Raja Sakti I, 212

Raja Seri Wangsa, 261
Raja Ungu, 206, 208, 268, 275
Rama I, 215–7, 228, 243
Raman, xxiii, 161–81, 214, 228
  tin mining in, 167–8, 172–6
Ramayana, 195
Ramkhamhaeng, King, 265
Ra-ngae, *see* Legeh
Rangoon, 4
Rashid Rida, 143
ratthaniyom, 273
"red seal" ships, 13
rice, 16, 29
Rifa`iyya (Sufi order), 134
Riyadh, 119, 126
Ryukyu, 9–10, 75

Sabîl al-Muhtadîn, 104
Sai, 63
Saiburi, 63, 214, 228, 237
Sailendra kingdom, 261, 264
salt, 16, 29
Sambas, 116
Samsam, 261
sandalwood, 9, 29
San Jao Lim Kor Niaw, 7
Sanskrit, 32, 195
San-fo-qi, 61
Satun, 31, 235–7, 239, 247
Saudi Arabia, 115, 121, 124–6, 128
Sayyid 'Abd Allâh, 96
Sayyid Abu Bakar Syatha, 117
Sayyid Ja'afar Ibn Ismail al-Barzanji,
  117
Sejarah Kerajaan Melayu Patani, xv, xxv,
  188, 190–5, 199–200, 203, 206–7,
  249–50, 258–61, 264, 268, 270, 272
Sejarah Melayu, 39, 46–7, 111
Sejarah Perjuangan Melayu Patani, xxv
Selangor, 45–6
Seri Negeri, 39–40, 42–3
sembeh, 16
sex, 17–8, 25–6, 43
Shafi'i, 93, 120, 135, 143, 204–5, 224
Shâfî al-Dîn, 96

Shams al-Dîn al-Ramlî, 101, 104
shari'ah, 97, 101, 103–4, 143, 222
Sharif Husayn, 223
Shaulah al-Nisa, 122
Shaykh 'Abd al-Qâdir, 96
Shaykh Aḥmad Muhammad Zayn, *see* Sheikh Ahmad al-Fatani
Shaykh Faqîh Shâfî al-Dîn, 96
Shaykh Gombak, 95
Shaykh Safiyy al-Din, 205
Sheikh Ahmad al-Fatani, 108, 114, 117, 131, 137, 140–2, 206, 223
Sheikh Daud al-Fatani, *see* Dâwûd ibn 'Abd Allâh b. Idrîs al-Faṭânî
Sheikh Safiuddin al-Abbasi, 131, 146
Sheikh Sa'id, of Pasai, 131, 146, 198, 199
Sheikh Zain al 'Abidin (Tuan Minal), 137, 144
Shihāb al-Dīn Ahmad ibn Mājid, 63
Shan, 4
Shaykh Faqih `Ali ibn Muhammad ibn Safiyuddin, 257
Shihâb al-Dîn b. 'Abd Allâh Muḥammad, 95
Shun-feng xiang-song, 76
Siak, 32
Siamese, 16, 19, 23
silk, 14, 16, 29
Singapore, 7, 9, 119, 143, 221
Si Rambai, 45
Si-yi-guan kao, 63–4
slaves, 16, 26, 28–9
Snouck Hurgronje, 89, 107, 117, 141
Somchai Neelaphaijit, 286
Songkhla, 5, 63, 70, 74–5, 83, 165, 168, 201, 228, 247, 261, 263, 266–7
South Asia, 63
South China Sea, 10
Spanish, 207
spices, 9, 13, 16, 88
spirit possession, 19, 24
Śriksetra, 57
Sri Lanang, 111
Sri Vijaya, xxi, 6, 61n26, 83, 195, 258, 261–2, 264, 274

steel, 29
Sudan, 126
Suez Canal, 136, 141
Sufis and Sufism, 88, 91–2, 94, 96, 105, 132–3, 135, 186, 199, 222, 224
Sukhothai, 200, 263, 264–5
Sulaimān bin Ahmad al-Mahrī, 63
Sulaiman Mar'i, 119
Sulawesi, 90, 95
   South, 95, 99
Sultan 'Abdul Hamid, 223
Sultan 'Abdul Qadir, 212
Sulṭân 'Alâ' al-Dîn Maḥmûd Shâh, 99, 140
Sultan Alauddin of Perak, 165
Sultan Ismail Syah Zillulah Fil-'Alam, 131
Sultan Muhammad Safiyudin, 116
Sultan Zainal Abidin III, 115
Sulu, xx, 4
Sumatra, 6, 35, 119, 121, 123, 136, 195, 197–8, 204
   North, 189
   Northwest, 133
   South, 95
   West, 143
Sumbawa, 116
Sungai Kolok, 215
Sunni Islam, xxiv
swords, 16, 29
Syed Abdul Karim Baryar, 127
Syed Muhummad Naquib al-Attas, 111
Syeikh Abdul Kadir bin Abdul Mutthalib al-Mandili, 127
Syeikh Abdullah Ibn Usman Makki, 117
Syeikh Abdul Malik Abdullah, 111
Syeikh Abdur Rauf Ibn Ali al-Fansuri, 118
Syeikh Abdus Shamad al-Falimbani, 118
Syeikh Haji Melayu, 115
Syeikh Hasan bin Ishak, 116
Syeikh Idris, 115

Syeikh Muhammad Amin Bugis, 118
Syeikh Muhammad Ibn Ismail Daud
    al-Fatani, 118
Syeikh Muhammad Nafis Ibn Idris
    al-Banjari, 118
Syeikh Muhammad Nur bin
    Muhammad al-Fatani, 127
Syeikh Muhammad Yasin bin Isa al-
    Pandani, 127
Syeikh Muhammad Zainudin bin
    Muhammad Badawi, 116
Syeikh Muhammad Zayn al-Asyi, 112
Syeikh Muhamad Zaib Ibn Faqih
    Jalaluddin Aceh, 118
Syeikh Naruddin ar-Raniri, 118
Syeikh Nawawi, 118
Syeikh Nik Dir al-Fatani, 114, 121
Syeikh Nik Mat Kechik al-Fatani,
    114–5
Syeikh Daud al-Fatani, *see* Dâwûd ibn
    'Abd Allâh b. Idrîs al-Faṭânî
Syeikh Safiyuddin, 112
Syeikh Sulaiman al-Jazuli, 118
Syeikh Tok Gudang al-Fatani, 121
Syeikh Wan Ahmad bin Muhammad
    Zain al-Fatani, *see* Sheikh Ahmad
    al-Fatani
Syeikh Wan Ali Ibn Abdur Rahman
    Kutan al-Kelantani, 118
Syeikh Wan Daud bin Wan Mustafa
    al-Fatani, 127
Syeikh Wan Musa, 115–6
Syeikh Zainuddin, 116
Syria, 126

Tafsir al-Qur'an Juz Amma, 118
Ta'if, 102, 119
Taiwan, 64, 68
Tak Bai, 284, 288
Taksin, King, 41, 215
Tadhkirât al-Mawḏû'ât, 98
Tafsir, 116
Taliban, 279
Talok Manok, 206
Tambralinga, 60, 263

Tamil, 133
Tarikh Fatani, xxv, 203, 257–8, 260, 264
Tarjamah Bidâyat al-Hidâyah, 105
tariqa, 91, 94, 98
    Sammâniyyah, 98
    Shaṭṭâriyyah, 102, 140
taṣawwuf, 101, 103–7, 116, 222–3
tawhid, 126
temporary marriage, 17
Tengku Abdul Jalal (Adul Na Saiburi),
    237–8
Tengku 'Abdul Jalal Bin al-Marhum
    Tengku Abdul-Muttalib, 191
Tengku Abdul Kadir Kamaruddin, 221,
    231, 236–7, 256, 275
Tengku Bira Kotanila, 239
Tengku Lamidin, 166, 269, 271, 275
Tengku Mahmud Mahyuddin, *see*
    Muhyiddin, Prince
Tengku Ramli Bin Tengku 'Abdullah,
    213
Teochew, 7
Ternate, 15
Thaksin, 282
Theravada Buddhism, 19–20, 24
Timor, 17, 29, 82
tin, xxiii, 9, 166
Tok Guru Wae Muso, 144
Tok Kenali (Che Muhammad Yusuf),
    108, 143
Tok Senggora, 127
Tok Wan Zainab, 115
Tokugawa, 4
Tonkin, 75, 211
Tôsen Fusetsu-gaki, 69, 83
Toungoo, 64, 264
Trang, 5
Trengganu, 73–4, 96, 114, 157, 201,
    213, 267
tribute missions, 8
Tuan Loh Teh (ruler of Raman), 166–7
Tuan Sulong, 221
Tuḥfat al-Muḥtâj, 104
Tunku 'Abdul Qadir Qamarud-Din, *see*
    Tengku Abdul Kadir Kamaruddin

Tunku Abdul Jalil, 121
Tu-shu-bian [An Illustrated
    Compendium], 64

Ummat Islam Patani, 202
United Malays National Organization
    (UMNO), 191
Ustaz Karim Hassan, 239
usûl al-dîn, 107

van Neck, Jacob, xx, 11, 14–7, 19–20,
    22–30
velvet, 16, 29
Vietnam, 130

Wa, 4
Wahhabis, 120, 126, 145, 205, 206,
    224
wali sanga, 99, 131
Wan Husayn, 206
Wan Kadir Che Man, xvii, xxviii
Wan Mohd Shaghir Abdullah, 98

War on Terror, xxvii
wax, 29
Westphalia system, 3
Wu-bei-zhi, 63
Wyatt, David, 4

Xiamen, 26n65, 71, 78

Yala, xxv, 31, 63, 220, 228, 231
Yala Technical College, 220
Yarang, 5, 56, 63
Yaring, 228
Yue-hai-guan-zhi [Account of the
    Canton Customs], 75
Yûsuf al-Makassâri, 90

Zabaj, 83
Zakariyyâ al-Anṣârî, 101, 104
Zheng He, 61, 76
Zionism, 206, 218, 295
Zomia, 4
Zhu-fan-zhi, 60–1